PRINCIPLES
OF LIFE AND HEALTH
INSURANCE

Gene A. Morton, FLMI

Edited by
Dani L. Long, FLMI

FLMI Insurance Education Program
Life Management Institute LOMA
100 Colony Square, Atlanta, Georgia 30361

The Life Office Management Association is a research and educational association of life insurance companies operating in the United States, Canada, and a number of other countries. Among its activities is the sponsorship of an educational program intended primarily for home office and branch office employees of these companies.

The FLMI Insurance Education Program is comprised of two courses – Course I, "Fundamentals of Life Insurance," and Course II, "Advanced Life Insurance." Upon the completion of Course I, the student is awarded a Certificate. Upon the completion of both courses, the student is designated a Fellow of the Life Management Institute (FLMI) and is awarded a Diploma.

ISBN 0-915322-58-7

First printing, April 1984
Second printing, October 1984

Library of Congress Catalog Card Number: 83-83153

Printed in the United States of America

Preface

This text is designed to give the reader a full understanding of the basic principles underlying the life and health insurance industry and to describe the insurance industry's most widely marketed products. Although the book has been written for students taking the introductory course in LOMA's FLMI Insurance Education Program, it is well suited for any learning situation in which there is a need for a base of knowledge in the fundamentals of life and health insurance. A student guide and an instructor's manual have been developed to accompany the book.

Because this book will serve as an introduction to the subject of insurance for many of its readers, jargon and technical language have been kept to a minimum. Each important term (indicated in boldface type) is defined and/or explained in nontechnical language when it is introduced; further, the text contains a comprehensive glossary of insurance terms. For the reader who does not have access to insurance forms, the appendix contains a sample life insurance policy and application blank, and examples of other insurance forms are included within the text.

Industry statistics are cited throughout the text primarily to give the reader a "feel" for the size and the economic impact of the insurance industry in the United States and Canada, as well as to indicate evolving patterns and trends within the industry. Unless otherwise noted, those statistics which are given in the text and accompanying figures have been taken from the 1983 *Life Insurance Fact Book* (a publication of the American Council of Life Insurance) and the 1983 edition of *Canadian Life Insurance Facts* (a publication of the Canadian Life and Health Insurance Association).

In developing *Principles of Life and Health Insurance,* I have drawn on the knowledge and experience of many people. I am especially indebted to the following members of the Life Management Institute's Curriculum

Committee, who reviewed and shaped the text in each of its stages, from outline to finished manuscript:

Eric C. Bacon, FLMI, Corporate Vice President, Claims and Policy Service, New York Life Insurance Company – Canadian Head Office

Muriel L. Crawford, J.D., FLMI, CLU, Assistant General Counsel, Washington National Insurance Company

George C. Erickson, FLMI, Manager, Human Resources Department, Iowa Farm Bureau Life Insurance Company

Donald E. Joslin, FLMI, President and CEO, Monitor Life Insurance Company of New York

Gerald B. O'Connell, FLMI, Second Vice President, Human Resources, Time Insurance Company

Robert A. Powers, FLMI, CLU, Senior Claim Consultant, Prudential Insurance Company of America

Jacques Turmel, FLMI, Manager, Life Underwriting, Les Coopérants Société Mutuelle d'Assurance-Vie

L. Neal Williams, FLMI, Assistant Secretary, Policyowner Service, Liberty Life Insurance Company

In addition, I would like to thank Christina Marshall, FLMI, Manufacturers Life Insurance Company, Robert A. Marshall, Ph.D., CLU, Florida State University, and Marilyn A. Pageau, FLMI, Sun Life Assurance Company of Canada, for their careful reviews of the final draft of the manuscript.

I would also like to express my sincere appreciation to the following organizations and individuals whose knowledge and skills added substantially to the quality and technical accuracy of selected chapters and other aspects of the text which had their attention: Leonard E. Barnes, Life Insurers Conference; J. Martin Dickler, FSA, MAAA, Health Insurance Association of America; Charles R. Griffith, Provident Life and Accident Insurance Company; Dave Johnson, CLU, Bankers Life of Iowa; Lester L. Long, Jr., CLU, New York Life Insurance Company; William C. Reid, CLU, New York Life Insurance Company; Joel C. Shannon, New York Life Insurance Company; Nancy E. Strickler, FLMI, Travelers Insurance Company; George J. Trapp, New York Life Insurance Company; and William G. Williams, CLU, Provident Mutual Life Insurance Company.

Members of the LOMA staff provided a great deal of editorial help and encouragement. In particular, Katherine C. Milligan, FLMI, Coordinator of the Curriculum Department, spent a considerable amount of time and energy ensuring that the manuscript would become a textbook of high quality suitable for use in the FLMI Program. Kenneth R. Huggins, FLMI, Brian K. McGreevy, J.D., FLMI, John R. Crane, FLMI, and Lana Ann Sprinkle, FLMI, of the Institute devoted their considerable talents as reviewers and provided assistance during the editing process. Alexa M. Selph was also of great help in ensuring that the text contained as few typos and unclear references as possible. Julius Taré Donovant, of LOMA's graphics department, deserves special thanks for the design of all figures used in this text. Dennis W. Goodwin, FLMI, Coordinator of the Curriculum Department, Ernest L. Martin, Ph.D., FLMI, Manager of the Examinations Department, and William H. Rabel, Ph.D., FLMI, CLU, Vice President and Director of the Life Management Institute, also deserve thanks for their help, guidance, and support.

Finally, my heartfelt thanks go to Dani L. Long, FLMI, who ably directed the work of the reviewers and who, through her editorial and technical knowledge, made an outstanding contribution to the book.

Gene A. Morton

Contents

1

Insurance and the Insurance Industry

In terms of its age, the modern life insurance business is an infant when compared to many other industries. In terms of its size, however, the industry is among the world's largest. Life insurance products were not widely offered until the 1800s, and health insurance products were not available generally until the early part of this century. Yet, through time, the amount of life insurance in force in the United States and Canada has grown to over $5 trillion, and health insurance products cover most of the people in both countries.

The primary reason for this tremendous growth lies in the nature and purpose of insurance products. All insurance provides protection against some of the economic consequences of loss. Thus, insurance responds to the need of all persons for security. The insurance industry designs, revises, alters, and updates its insurance policies constantly to meet this need. However, despite these changes, the underlying purpose of these policies remains the same: providing economic protection against financial loss.

Essentially, an insurance policy is a contract—a legally enforceable agreement—under which the insurance company agrees to pay a certain amount of money, called the policy benefit, when specific losses occur, provided the insurer receives a specified amount of money, called the premium. In this way, the risk, or chance, of economic loss is transferred to the insurance company. This text will be concerned primarily with the kinds of insurance which provide protection from the economic losses resulting from death, disability (because of accident or sickness), and old age. These kinds of insurance are, respectively, life insurance, health insurance, and annuities, and they may be designed to cover individuals or members of groups. Figure 1-1 illustrates the percentage of life insurance companies' business attributable to each of these kinds of insurance.

FIGURE 1-1
Distribution of premium income of United States life insurance companies

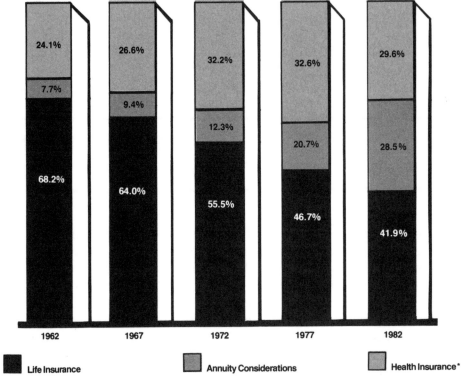

*Includes some premiums for Workers' Compensation and some premiums for auto and other liability insurance.

Life insurance provides a specified sum of money if the person who is insured dies while the policy is in effect. *Health insurance* pays specified benefits if the person who is insured becomes sick or has an accident. Health insurance can take two forms, medical expense coverage and disability income coverage. Medical expense coverage provides for payment of hospital, surgical, and doctor bills and related medical expenses to the extent specified in the policy. Disability income coverage provides for payment of a specified income benefit while the person who is insured is unable to work because of disability. An *annuity* provides a series of benefit payments for either a specified period or for the lifetime of the person receiving the benefit.

Although this text will concentrate on life insurance, health insurance, and annuities, these are not the only kinds of insurance available. Property and liability insurance are two other major kinds of insurance. *Property insurance* provides a benefit should covered property be damaged or lost because of fire, theft, accident, or other cause described in the policy. **Liability insurance** provides a benefit payable on behalf of a covered party who is held legally responsible (liable) for harming others or their property. Both property and liability policies place limits on the amount of the benefit that the company will pay.

Automobile insurance policies often include both property and liability coverage. Suppose, for example, that you are driving a car which is covered by an automobile policy and you accidentally crash through your neighbor's front door. The damage to your neighbor's home will be paid by your policy's liability coverage; the money to repair your car will come from your policy's property coverage. This example, of course, does not cover all the types of property and liability insurance on the market today, but it provides instead an indication of the nature of such coverage.

LOSS AND THE BASIC PRINCIPLES OF INSURANCE

All insurance products are designed according to certain basic principles which apply to the concept of economic loss. In order for a potential loss situation to be considered insurable, it must have certain characteristics:

1. The loss must occur by *chance*.
2. The loss must be *definite*.
3. The loss must be *significant*.
4. The *rate* of loss must be *predictable*.
5. The loss must *not* be *catastrophic* to the insurer.

These five basic principles form the foundation for the business of insurance, much as the rules of physics form the foundation for airplane design. A *potential* loss which does not have these characteristics generally is not considered an *insurable* loss unless the lack of one or more characteristics can be compensated for in some way.

The Loss Must Occur by Chance

In order for any potential loss to be insurable, the element of chance must be present. The loss should be caused by either an unexpected event or by an event which is not intentionally caused by the person covered by the insurance. For example, people cannot generally control whether they will become disabled and unable to work because of accident or sickness; hence, insurance companies can offer disability income policies to provide economic protection against financial losses caused by such chance events. When this principle of loss is applied in its strictest sense to life insurance, an apparent problem arises: death is *certain* to occur. However, the *timing* of an individual's death is normally out of the control of the individual.

Therefore, although the event being insured – death – is a certain event rather than a chance event, the timing of that event usually does occur by chance.

The Loss Must Be Definite

An insurable loss must be definite in terms of *time* and *amount*. An insurer must be able to determine *when* to pay a benefit and *how much* the benefit should be. Death, disability, and old age are generally identifiable conditions. The amount of economic loss resulting from these conditions can, however, be subject to interpretation.

Insurers use two types of contracts to define the amount of the benefit that will be due – *valued contracts* and *contracts of indemnity*. A **valued contract** is one in which the amount of the benefit is set in advance. In life insurance, the amount of the death benefit is specified in the policy. For example, if a woman buys a $50,000 insurance policy on her life, the $50,000 death benefit is listed in the policy. The amount of this stated benefit is called the **face amount** or **face value** of the policy because this amount is generally listed on the face, or first, page of a life insurance policy.

A **contract of indemnity** is one in which the amount of the benefit is based on the actual amount of financial loss as determined at the time of loss. The contract states that the amount of the benefit is equal to the amount of the financial loss or the maximum amount stated in the policy, whichever is *less*. Hence, the policyowner cannot submit a **claim** – that is, a request for payment under the terms of the policy – for an amount which is higher than the actual amount of the financial loss.

Many hospital expense policies pay a benefit based on the actual cost of an individual's hospitalization and, as such, are contracts of indemnity. For example, if a man buys a hospital expense policy, the policy will state the maximum amount payable to cover his expenses while he is hospitalized. If his actual expenses while he is hospitalized are less than that maximum amount, the insurance company will not pay him the stated maximum; instead, the insurance company will pay him a sum based on the actual amount of his hospital bill.

The Loss Must Be Significant

People lose things with frustrating regularity. Pens, umbrellas, and sunglasses are all too often not where we know we left them. Such losses are not apt to be very significant financially. Replacing a pen does not cause financial hardship to most people. These types of losses are *not* normally insured; the administrative expense of paying benefits when such a small loss occurs would drive the cost for such insurance protection so high in relation to the amount of the potential loss that most people would find the protection uneconomical.

On the other hand, some types of losses would cause financial hardship to most people. For example, if an employed person were to be injured in an accident which resulted in that person's being unable to work for a year, the resulting income loss would be significant. Hence, this type of loss is insurable.

The Rate of Loss Must Be Predictable

To provide a benefit in case of a specific loss, an insurer must be able to predict the probable rate of loss, or loss rate. The **loss rate** is the number and timing of losses that will occur in a given group of insureds while the coverage is in force. An insurer must be able to predict this loss rate in order to determine the proper premium amount to charge each policyowner to ensure that adequate funds are on hand to pay claims as they become due.

However, from an individual's viewpoint, losses which may be suffered are not predictable; through the ages, people have tried crystal balls, tarot cards, and tea leaves in an attempt to predict an individual's future. Neither an individual nor an insurance company can determine in advance when a *specific person* will die, become disabled, or need hospitalization. However, it is possible to predict with a high degree of accuracy the number of people in a *given large group* who will die or become disabled or need hospitalization during a given period of time.

These predictions of future losses are based on the concept that events which *seem* to occur at random *actually* follow a pattern. When the pattern is identified through observation of the past, the likelihood that a given event will occur, called the **probability** of the event, can be determined.

An important concept in determining this probability is the **law of large numbers**. According to the law of large numbers, the larger the number of observations made of a particular event, the more likely it will be that the observed results produce an estimate of the "true" probability of the event's occurring. For example, if you toss an ordinary coin, there is a 50-50 probability that it will land with the heads side up; this is a calculable probability. Two or even a dozen tosses might not give the result of an equal number of heads and tails. If you tossed the coin 1,000 times, though, you could expect a count of approximately 500 heads and 500 tails to occur. The more often you toss the coin, the closer you will come to observing an equal number of heads and tails, and the closer your findings will be to the "true" probability.

The law of large numbers is applied to insurance company predictions of probable future losses. An insurance company collects specific information about a large number of people so that the insurance company can identify the pattern of past losses experienced by those people. Using this information, the insurance company can predict fairly accurately the number of future losses which will occur in a similar group of people – that is, the insurer can predict the number of people in a given group who will die or become disabled or need hospitalization. For many years, for example, life insurance companies have recorded how many of their insureds have died and how old they were when they died. Insurance companies then compared this information with the general population records of the United States and Canada, noting what age people in the general population had attained when they died. By using these statistical records, insurance companies have been able to develop charts which indicate with great accuracy the number of people in a large group (of 100,000 or more) who are likely to die at each age. These charts are called **mortality tables** and display the **rate of mortality**, or incidence of death, by age, among given groups of people. Insurance companies have developed similar charts, called **morbidity tables**, which display the **rate of morbidity**, or incidence of sicknesses and accidents occurring among given groups of people categorized by age.

By using accurate mortality and morbidity tables, insurance companies can predict the probable loss rate, establish adequate premium rates, and be prepared to pay claims. The manner in which insurance companies use these statistics to establish premium rates will be discussed more fully in chapter 2, "Pricing Life Insurance."

The Loss Must Not Be Catastrophic

A potential loss is not considered insurable if a single occurrence – either of the loss insured or of an outside event – is likely to cause or contribute to catastrophic financial damage to the insurer. Such a loss is not insurable because the insurer could not responsibly promise to pay benefits for the loss. To prevent the possibility of catastrophic loss and ensure that losses occur independently of each other, an insurer might **spread the risks** it chooses to insure – that is, issue policies over a wide territory. For example, a property insurer would be unwise to issue policies covering all the homes within a 50-mile radius of an active volcano, since one eruption of the volcano could result in more claims occurring at one time than the insurer could pay. Instead, the property insurer would also issue policies covering homes in areas not threatened by the volcano. An insurer offering life insurance may refuse to sell a disproportionate amount of coverage on a single life in order to avoid one death's producing catastrophic financial results for the company.

Alternatively, an insurer could reduce the possibility of catastrophic losses by **transferring risks** to another insurer – that is, another insurer would accept responsibility for paying all or part of the claims in exchange for all or part of the premium. Transferring a potential loss in this manner to another insurer is called **reinsuring** the risk, and the company which reinsures the risk is called the **reinsurer**. Through reinsurance, each insurance company's exposure to the possibility of catastrophic loss is reduced or eliminated.

INSURABLE INTEREST AND ANTISELECTION

An insurance company considers the five basic principles of insurance as it designs an insurance product so that the insurer can properly provide protection against the financial losses resulting from specified risks. Then the insurance company must consider *insurable interest* and *antiselection* before selling one of these products to a specific individual.

Insurable Interest

Insurance companies must evaluate each application for an insurance policy in order to make sure that the person applying for the policy and the person who is to receive the policy benefit have an **insurable interest** in the potential loss – that is, that such persons would suffer a genuine loss should the event insured against occur. For example, a property insurance company would not sell a fire insurance policy on a particular building to a person who does not own the building, since such a person would not suffer an economic loss if the building were to be destroyed by fire. In property insurance, ownership of property is one way in which an insurable interest is established in property.

Before discussing how insurable interest is established for a life insurance policy, it is important for you to be able to distinguish between an *applicant*, a *policyowner*, an *insured*, and a *beneficiary*. The **applicant** is the person who applies for the insurance policy. After the application for the policy is approved by the insurer, the insurer issues a policy. Once the applicant accepts the policy and pays the first premium, he or she becomes the **policyowner**. The **insured** is the person whose life is insured under the policy.* The policyowner and the insured may be and often are the same person. If, for example, you apply for and are issued an insurance policy on your life, then you are both the policyowner and the insured. If, however, your mother applies for and is issued the policy on your life, then she is the policyowner and you are the insured. When the insured dies during the term of a life insurance policy, the insurer pays the policy benefit, or

---

*The revised Uniform Life Insurance Act, which has been adopted by most provinces in Canada, legally defines the insured as the person who applies for the policy. However, this text, in keeping with general usage in Canada and the United States, will use the term *insured* to mean the person whose life is insured under the policy.

proceeds. The **beneficiary** is the person, persons, or other party designated by the policyowner to receive the proceeds.

Before approving an application for life insurance, the insurer examines the relationships between the applicant, the designated beneficiary, and the proposed insured to make sure that through these relationships an insurable interest exists in the life of the proposed insured. The presence of an insurable interest for life insurance can usually be found by applying the following general rule: If there is adequate reason to show that the applicant and the designated beneficiary have more to gain if the proposed insured continues to live than if the proposed insured dies, an insurable interest is considered to be present. The presence of insurable interest must be established for every life insurance policy so that the insurance contract will not be formed as an illegal "wagering contract." Wagering on a human life – betting that a person will die – is considered to be against the public good and is illegal in the United States and Canada.

It is legally established that all persons have an insurable interest in their own lives. A person is always considered to have more to gain by living than by dying. Hence, an insurable interest between the applicant and the proposed insured is presumed when the applicant and the proposed insured are the same person. Such an applicant-proposed insured also has the legal right to designate as beneficiary any person or party desired. However, the insurer may decline to issue a life insurance policy to an applicant-proposed insured if the insurer questions the appropriateness of the beneficiary designation.

Certain family relationships create an insurable interest between an applicant or designated beneficiary and a proposed insured. The natural bonds of affection and financial dependence between these people make this a reasonable assumption. In general, the proposed insured's husband, wife, parent, child, grandparent, grandchild, brother, and sister have an insurable interest in the life of the proposed insured.

However, an insurable interest is *not* presumed when the applicant or designated beneficiary is more distantly related to the proposed insured than the relatives described above or when the applicant or designated beneficiary is not related by blood or marriage to the proposed insured. In these cases, a financial interest in the continued life of the proposed insured must be demonstrated in order to satisfy the insurable interest requirement. For instance, if Mary Mulhouse gets a $50,000 mortgage loan from the Lone Star Bank of Vermont, the bank would have a financial, and hence insurable, interest in Ms. Mulhouse's life. If Ms. Mulhouse should die before the loan were repaid, the bank could lose some or all of the money it lent her. Similar examples of financial interest can be found in other business relationships.

The insurable interest requirement must be met before the life insurance policy will be issued. As we shall see in chapter 6, "The Policy Contract

Is Issued," after the life insurance policy is in force, the presence or absence of insurable interest is no longer relevant. Therefore, a beneficiary need not provide evidence of insurable interest to receive the proceeds of a life insurance policy.

For health insurance purposes, the insurable interest requirement is met if the applicant can demonstrate a genuine risk of economic loss should the proposed insured require medical care or become disabled.

Antiselection

The second factor an insurer must consider when a person applies for a life or health insurance policy is the possibility of antiselection. *Antiselection*, which is also called *adverse selection* or *selection against the insurer*, refers to the tendency of people who have a greater-than-average likelihood of loss to apply for or continue insurance protection to a greater extent than those who have an average or less-than-average likelihood of the same loss.

For example, there is a tendency for people who have some reason to expect a shorter-than-average life span to seek to purchase life insurance. These may be persons who are in poor health or who are engaged in hazardous occupations. If an insurer does not consider the possibility of antiselection when reviewing applications, the insurer may end up insuring a relatively large number of such persons. The insurer would then experience more losses – pay more death benefits – than were expected when the insurance company decided how much to charge for the coverage.

To diminish the effects of antiselection, an insurer must screen each application in order to identify and classify the potential degree of risk, or the probability of loss, for each proposed insured. This process of identifying and classifying the potential degree of risk represented by a proposed insured is called *underwriting*, or *selection of risks*, and those persons who are responsible for evaluating the potential degree of risk are called *underwriters*. Those people who have an average or less-than-average likelihood of loss are called *standard risks*, and the premium rates they are charged are called standard premium rates. Those people who have a greater-than-average likelihood of loss are called *substandard risks* or *special class risks* and they are charged a higher premium rate, called a substandard or special class rate. If the likelihood of loss is too great, the person may be declined for the coverage by the insurer, but only a very small percentage of life insurance applications are actually declined.

Today's insurance industry is able to design financially sound products by adhering to the basic principles of insurance, and insurers are able to offer those products to individuals by considering the insurable interest and antiselection factors just discussed. The insurance industry, however, did not spring into being simply because someone discovered these principles. The concept of insurance protection has existed for centuries, though early versions of insurance bear only slight resemblance to many of the insurance products offered today.

HOW THE INSURANCE INDUSTRY BEGAN

Property insurance, the first form of insurance of which we have any record, apparently existed over 2,000 years ago in the Mediterranean area, but no comprehensive records of its use were kept until the late Middle Ages. Most experts believe the earliest type of property insurance was maritime insurance – insurance on ships and their cargoes. Shipping was at best a hazardous venture, especially when long distances were involved, and the likelihood of loss acted as a deterrent to trade. The fact that cargoes and ships could be insured encouraged people to risk their money in overseas trade, and the resulting investments helped the shipping industry to flourish.

Early Underwriters

The first insurers were individuals who were willing to assume someone else's risk of economic loss in return for a mutually agreed-upon price or premium. The seller usually issued a contract or policy which was signed at the bottom to show that the risk had been accepted. This signature under the terms of the contract is the origin of the insurance term *underwriter*. The insurance issuer had "underwritten," or accepted, the risk by placing a signature on the contract, normally at the end, under the terms and conditions. These insurers were known as individual underwriters.

Issuing insurance was actually a speculative business venture in those early days. An essential principle of insurance – the ability to accurately predict losses through the law of large numbers – was absent. Very little information regarding the numbers and values of losses had been collected. Therefore, it was not possible to determine accurately the likelihood of loss. As underwriters gained experience and accumulated more statistics on past losses, they were better able to predict the likelihood of loss in a particular situation and could charge premium rates which more accurately reflected the risk of loss the underwriter assumed.

Early Life Insurance

Life insurance was developed after property insurance. There are records which indicate that a form of life insurance existed in the ancient world and in sixteenth century England. Until the middle of the eighteenth century, however, those few life insurance contracts that existed were issued by individual underwriters who operated in the same fashion as the early individual property underwriters. As in the case with property insurance, a primary problem with early life insurance was that the available information was not sufficient to enable the underwriters to predict accurately the probable rate of loss. Policies usually were issued for a specified period, and the underwriters had to guess at the likelihood that death would occur during that term. Therefore, the price charged for the insurance – the premium – was set arbitrarily.

This problem was alleviated by the accumulation of statistics which were used in setting more accurate premiums for life insurance. Statistical information gathered from birth and death records and census figures was used to calculate average life spans and develop early mortality tables. Although these early statistics would be considered incomplete and misleading by today's standards, they did help underwriters estimate more confidently how long potential insureds would be likely to live.

A second problem in the early days of property insurance and life insurance was that the individual underwriter's obligation to a person who purchased insurance could not be enforced if the underwriter died. It was hard for those purchasing the insurance to feel confidence in their insurance protection when they might outlive the person issuing the insurance! This second problem was solved by the establishment of companies to issue life insurance policies. Because such companies could continue to operate even after the deaths of their founders, these organizations provided the permanence and stability which individual underwriters lacked and, therefore, made it practical for long-term insurance contracts to be issued.

First Life Insurance Companies

In 1759, the "Corporation for Relief of Poor and Distressed Presbyterian Ministers and of the Poor and Distressed Widows and Children of Presbyterian Ministers" established a plan to provide life insurance benefits. This North American corporation was originally established some years before as a charitable organization, and the life insurance benefits provided by the organization were available only for people in the Presbyterian church. In 1762, "The Society for Equitable Assurance on Lives and Survivorships" was established in England and sold life insurance contracts to the general public in that country.

During the late 1700s, a few companies were also organized in North America with the power to issue life insurance policies to the general public. However, only one actually did so, and, after issuing a few policies, this company ceased its life insurance operations altogether. In 1812, the "Pennsylvania Company for Insurance on Lives and Granting Annuities" was chartered to sell life insurance, thus becoming the first company in North

America which was organized specifically for the purpose of issuing life insurance to the general public *and* which sold a substantial number of life insurance policies.

During the nineteenth and early twentieth centuries, the life insurance industry in North America developed the operating principles which, although altered over the years to meet changing conditions, still form the basis for present-day life insurance company operations. With these principles, insurance companies could offer financially sound products to the general public.

The first insurance companies waited for persons to approach them to request insurance. As more companies entered the insurance business, insurance companies employed agents to actively seek prospects for the sale of life insurance. Promoting life insurance products as well as taking these products to the people became the agent's role. The "agency system," as it came to be called, has been one of the most important factors in the rapid growth of the life insurance industry. Figure 1–2 shows the growth

FIGURE 1-2

Growth in the number of United States life insurance companies from 1760-1980*

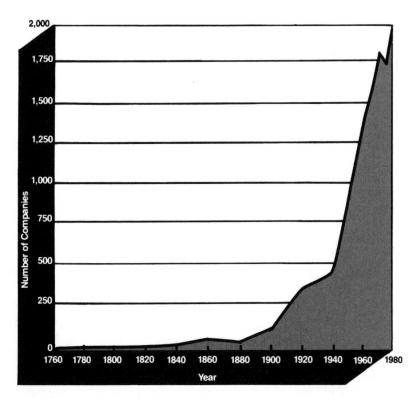

*Does not include figures for fraternal benefit societies.

in the number of life insurance companies actively doing business in the United States.

Early Health Insurance

Health insurance coverage was first available in the mid-1800s. This coverage was in the form of accident policies, which were issued by travel companies to cover passengers on specific journeys. Early accident policies provided for both a death benefit if the traveler died as the result of an accident and an income benefit amount if the traveler incurred specified injuries as the result of traveling on a particular train ride or boat trip. The success of these travel accident policies led insurers to issue accident policies which provided such coverage against accidental death or injury but which were not related to travel-related risks. Many life insurance policies issued during this period provided for the payment of income benefits during periods of disability, and accident insurers used this idea as the basis for the development of policies which paid income benefits during the period of disability which resulted from an accident.

Insurance against losses caused by sickness, rather than by accidents, was not sold in the early days of health insurance. However, around 1900, some accident insurers made sickness insurance available to customers who already had purchased accident policies. Most of these early sickness policies provided for only a disability income benefit, although a limited number of such policies included some medical expense coverage.

It was not until the 1930s that insurance companies seriously promoted the sale of medical expense health insurance. At this time, the first major group health insurance plans were introduced, and several hospitals began offering hospital services to people in exchange for a regular monthly payment. The concept of health insurance was quickly accepted by the public, and the period during World War II witnessed rapid growth in the sale of health insurance. While much of this growth was in the area of group health insurance, the sale of individual health insurance policies also increased rapidly.

MODERN LIFE AND HEALTH INSURANCE COMPANIES

Although some life and health insurance is provided by government bodies, fraternal organizations, and, in some areas of the United States, savings banks and other financial institutions, the majority of life and health insurance products are sold by insurance companies. Because this text discusses the insurance products sold by life and health insurance companies, we will take a brief look at the way these insurance companies are organized and regulated.

Organization

Most life and health insurance companies are organized to do business as either stock companies or mutual companies.

Stock companies

Most life and health insurance companies were initially established and organized as *stock companies*. Such companies were formed as corporations, and the funds necessary to begin operations came from individuals who bought stock – ownership shares – in the corporation. Stock companies are therefore owned by the individuals who own the stock, and operating profits are distributed to these stockholders.

Mutual companies

Life and health insurance companies may, however, also be organized as *mutual companies*. Before a mutual company may be formed, a certain number of policies must be "sold" in advance to provide the funds needed to begin operations. Since, however, people are reluctant to buy something from a company that does not yet exist, most mutuals started as stock companies and converted to mutuals at a later date. A mutual insurance company is owned by the people who own insurance policies issued by the company, and operating profits are distributed to these policyowners.

Although there are far more stock insurance companies than mutual insurance companies in North America, mutual companies account for about half of the life insurance in force – primarily because most of the largest life insurance corporations operate as mutual companies.

Regulation

The life insurance industry involves the public trust; insurance products promise economic protection in the event of loss, and policyowners rely on their policies for financial security. To make sure that life insurance companies can meet obligations to their policyowners, government bodies in the United States and Canada closely regulate the life insurance industry. Each state in the United States and each province in Canada enacts laws and enforces regulations which the insurance industry must follow. These laws and regulations relate to the financial stability of the insurance companies, the products an insurance company can offer, and the manner in which each insurance company sells and administers these products.

The financial soundness of insurance companies is of primary importance, and insurance companies are closely regulated to make sure that they remain **solvent**, that is, able to pay expenses and obligations. Thus, both the adequacy of premium rates and the amount of funds the insurance company must have available to meet its obligations are closely scrutinized. The premiums which policyowners pay for their insurance policies are invested by the insurance company until the funds are needed to pay claims. The manner in which insurance companies may invest these premiums is also closely regulated to assure that the investments are prudent. Figure 1–3 illustrates the percentage of life insurance company assets which are invested in each of several types of investments.

Each policy an insurance company develops must also meet government standards before that policy may be offered to the public. These standards govern the benefits provided by the policy, the wording of the policy, and the reasons a company may use to deny a claim for the policy's benefits. Further, insurance companies are regulated to make sure they provide for fair and equitable treatment of their policyowners.

FIGURE 1-3
Distribution of Canadian and United States life insurance company assets in 1982

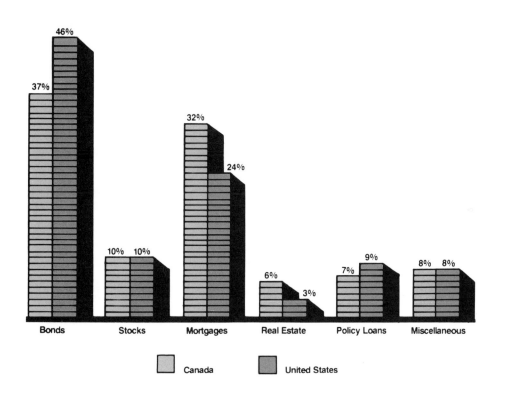

ECONOMIC AND SOCIAL IMPORTANCE OF THE INDUSTRY

The insurance industry is an important part of the economy of many countries, including the United States and Canada. The benefits paid help individuals and households to remain self-supporting despite the economic losses caused by sickness, disability, death, and old age. The funds insurance companies invest enable businesses to get started and expand, creating new jobs in the process. Thus, insurance companies and their investments have enormous economic importance both to individuals and to businesses.

In recent years, some insurance companies which have traditionally concentrated on selling life and health insurance products have begun to provide their customers with the opportunity to purchase such products as property and liability insurance as well as securities and other investment products. This trend toward broadened financial services is having a continuous impact on every facet of the life insurance industry.

From its earliest days, the insurance industry has had to change with the times. Changes in lifestyles, incomes, educational levels, and the economic climate alter the shape of the industry and its products. The insurance industry's ability to respond to changing conditions, while preserving its primary objective of providing economic protection, is the most important factor in the insurance industry's growth and is the reason the insurance industry has become an important force in today's society.

2

Pricing Life Insurance

When an insurance company sells life insurance, it is selling protection – protection against financial loss caused by the death of the person whose life is insured under the life insurance policy. The insurer agrees to pay a certain amount of money, the death benefit, when the insured dies, provided that premiums have been paid as specified in the policy. Many other benefits may be provided through life insurance policies, but this chapter will concentrate on the death benefit.

The *premium* is the payment, or one of a series of payments, required by the insurer to put the life insurance policy in force and to keep it in force. In order for the insurer to have enough money available to pay death benefits when they become due, the insurer determines the premium the company must charge for the specific insurance coverage provided. Calculating premium rates is one of the functions of an actuary; insurance companies employ actuaries to develop the mathematical bases and calculations for insurance products. In this chapter we will discuss the factors that currently are used to determine the amounts of premiums and the methods that have evolved over the years for determining premiums.

EARLY METHODS OF FUNDING LIFE INSURANCE

The earliest life insurers, the individual underwriters, did not use businesslike methods to solve the problem of pricing. As we noted in chapter 1, their operations resembled gambling ventures. If an underwriter underestimated the cost on too many insurance ventures, the money to pay the claims would have to be taken from the underwriter's personal funds, possibly causing the underwriter to become bankrupt. When organizations began to issue life insurance, they first experimented with two funding systems: the mutual benefit method and the assessment method.

Mutual Benefit Method

An early method of obtaining money to pay death claims was developed by groups which were known as mutual benefit societies. These organizations attempted to solve the funding problem by collecting money after the death of the person who was insured. This funding method became known as the **mutual benefit method** or the **post-death assessment method**. Each member of the society agreed to pay an equal, specific amount of money when any other member died. For example, to provide a $5,000 death benefit, a society with approximately 500 members might require a $10 payment from each surviving participant when one member died. Usually, the person or persons doing the administrative work for the society would receive a fee, often a small percentage of the money collected, and the rest would be paid to the insured's beneficiary.

There were three principal problems with the mutual benefit method. First was the problem of collecting money to pay the death benefit. There was no way that members could be forced to pay their shares. As a result, the amount of the death benefit could not be guaranteed. Nonpaying members could, of course, be dropped from the society, but this action did nothing to help those beneficiaries who received smaller death benefits than they should have.

Second, unless new members were continually recruited, the size of the group would become smaller and smaller because of deaths and resignations. As membership declined, either the amount of the death benefit would decrease or the amount each survivor was asked to pay would increase.

The third problem with the mutual benefit method was the aging of the membership. As the members of the original group grew older, the number of deaths which occurred each year increased. Even a steady influx of young members into a group did not offset the increasing number of deaths which occurred as the original group aged. As the number of deaths occurring each year in a particular mutual benefit society increased, the number of death benefits paid also increased and, hence, it became more expensive to be a member of a particular society. Since the cost of society membership increased, attracting new members became even more difficult, and membership decreased further. Finally, faced with high contributions, all but those in the poorest health dropped out of the mutual benefit society, and the contributions required of each member soared.

In an attempt to cope with these problems, a new form of funding, the pre-death assessment method, commonly referred to as simply the assessment method, was developed.

Assessment Method

Under the **assessment method**, the organization running the insurance system estimated its operating costs for a selected period, usually one year. These operating costs took into account administrative expenses as well as anticipated death claims. The total amount of money needed was divided by the number of participants in the plan, and each participant was then charged, or assessed, an equal amount. If the total actual cost of operations during the period was less than expected, then each participant received a refund; if the cost was higher, then the organization levied an additional charge or assessment on each member.

Although the prepayment of assessments solved the major collection problem which the mutual benefit societies had faced, collecting any additional levies which had to be charged was still difficult. In addition, the assessment method did not solve the problem of aging for a group of insureds. As time passed, the number of deaths occurring in the group increased, and the size of each assessment had to be increased. This higher cost acted as a deterrent to new membership, and the price of assessment insurance often became so high that it was no longer affordable. In an attempt to make an assessment plan more attractive to younger people, some organizations did charge somewhat higher assessments for older members. This, however, succeeded only in discouraging the healthier older participants from continuing in the insurance program, and many dropped out.

The first organizations to use the assessment method of funding life insurance were fraternal orders, often called lodges. Fraternal orders are organized groups of people of the same occupation or interest. Many of these groups used the assessment method to provide benefits for their members. However, the assessment method was also used by many commercial establishments which operated on a profit-making basis. Fraternal orders had an automatic influx of new members which permitted them to conduct their assessment life insurance operations on a sound basis for a longer period of time than could the commercial assessment associations. Eventually, however, even the fraternals found it necessary to look for a different way to fund their life insurance operations.

THE FUNDING OF MODERN LIFE INSURANCE

The modern pricing system for life insurance evolved from these early funding methods. It is called the **legal reserve system** and is based on several premises:

- The amount of the death benefit should be predetermined; that is, a person should purchase a specified amount of insurance per premium dollar.

- The money needed to pay death benefits should be collected in advance, so that the organization running the insurance program will have funds available to pay claims and expenses as they occur.
- The price of the insurance should be accurately determined; that is, the premium should be based on correct and complete information, and each individual should pay a premium which is proportionately related to the amount of risk which the system assumes for that person.

Life insurance cannot be provided on a financially sound basis unless the following factors are included in the calculation of life insurance premium rates:

- *Rate of mortality*–This is the rate at which the people whose lives are insured may be expected to die.
- *Interest*–This is the money which is earned when an insurance company invests premium dollars paid for the policies.
- *Expenses*–These are all the costs involved in operating an insurance company.

We will devote a large portion of this chapter to discussing these factors and how they are used to determine premium rates.

Rate of Mortality

One of the greatest concerns of life insurers is that they have enough money to pay death claims. As noted in chapter 1, in order to determine how much money will be needed to pay future claims, an insurer must be able to accurately estimate the number and timing of claims. In life insurance, this means predicting the number of deaths which will occur each year among a given group of insureds of the same risk classification. Note that the insurance company is concerned with predicting the number of deaths occurring in a given group, called a **block of insureds**, not with predicting which individual insureds will die. Therefore, when a single life insurance policy is mentioned, you can assume that all calculations relating to that policy are based on calculations for a *block of policies* just like the individual policy.

In the early days of the industry, very few statistics were available for insurers to use to predict mortality rates. The information which was gathered included figures for the entire population, even people who were in such poor health that they would have been considered uninsurable. Once companies started issuing policies and accumulating claims experience, it was possible to collect data regarding insured lives. These figures were more accurate for the purpose of developing insurance mortality statistics, since they related only to people who had been considered by an insurer to be acceptable risks.

Mortality tables and how they are used

All companies issuing life insurance accumulate and share information so that figures on overall industry mortality experience may be developed for all companies to use. This information has been organized into mortality tables showing the mortality rates which are expected to occur at each age. The term **expected mortality** is used in life insurance to mean the number of deaths which should occur according to the mortality table. This is also called **tabular mortality**. The actual number of deaths which do occur is referred to as **mortality experience**.

Mortality tables, therefore, show the death rates an insurer may reasonably anticipate among a particular group of insured lives at certain ages—how many people in each specific age group may be expected to die in a particular year. While the rates of mortality actually experienced may fluctuate from group to group, the fluctuations will tend to offset one another, being higher than expected for one group and lower than expected for another.

An example of a mortality table is shown in Figure 2-1. It is based on the 1958 Commissioners Standard Ordinary (CSO) Mortality Table, which is widely used by insurance department regulators to monitor the adequacy of life insurance premium rates. The table has four columns which give the following information:

- Column 1 shows the age of all people in the group.
- Column 2 shows the number of people still alive at each age at the beginning of the year.
- Column 3 shows the number of people expected to die at each age during the year.
- Column 4 shows how many people out of each thousand are expected to die at each age during the year.

This table begins with a group of 10 million people. By using extensive statistics about the rate of mortality, insurance companies have been able to calculate that 70,800 of the original 10 million people may be expected to die before they reach their first birthday. This indicates that 7.08 out of every 1,000 people will die between birth and age 1.

If you go down to the next row of numbers to age 1, you will see that out of the original 10 million people, there are now 9,929,200 left. The latter number is found by subtracting the 70,800 deaths from the original 10 million people (10,000,000 − 70,800 = 9,929,200). Of the number of people living at age 1, 17,475 are expected to die before reaching age 2, indicating that 1.76 out of every 1,000 people who have reached age 1 will die before they are 2 years old. Thus, you can follow the progression of the mortality table from age 0 to age 99, at which age the last people in the original group of 10 million can be expected to die. Life insurers realize that some people live beyond the age of 99, but the number of people living beyond that age is so statistically insignificant that it is easier to conclude the table at a very high age, such as age 99. Although this table concludes at age 99, others may conclude at a lower or higher age.

For a more graphic representation of the rate of mortality, look at Figure 2-2. If you follow the line showing the mortality curve, you will see that infant mortality tends to be high. After age 1, the mortality rate *decreases* until a low is reached somewhere around age 10, after which the rate of mortality *increases* at a growing rate. Finally, the mortality rate for persons age 65 or over accelerates sharply—so sharply, in fact, that Figure 2-2 must stop at age 70. To go to age 99, Figure 2-2 would have to be nearly 20 times as tall as it is now.

Using the 1958 CSO Mortality Table, or others like it, life insurers can take their first step in determining the price of blocks of insurance policies— that is, the price of all policies issued to specific blocks of insureds. The higher the mortality rate is for a group, the higher the premium rate will be for the block of policies issued to that group. If a life insurer based premium rates on the mortality rate shown in Figure 2-1, the insurer would charge a lower premium rate for policies issued to people age 25 than it would charge for comparable policies issued to people age 35. Similarly, the insurer would charge premium rates for policies issued to people age 35 that would be much lower than premium rates for comparable policies issued to people age 60. In most cases, the premium rate the insurer sets is based on a $1,000 life insurance coverage amount. Consequently, the premium rate is often expressed as the "rate per thousand."

The mortality table which we have used as an example shows the expected mortality rate for the insured population as a whole. The mortality rates of some groups of people, however, do not follow this standard mortality rate and are not represented in that table. For example, factors such as being overweight or underweight, engaging in certain occupations, and having various illnesses have all been studied, and results have been compiled to show how such factors affect the death rate. When these results indicate that a particular factor increases the mortality rate, an insurer may choose to charge a higher premium rate for people who possess such a risk factor based on this higher mortality rate. As noted in chapter 1, people who must pay a higher rate than standard because they possess such risk factors are called substandard risks, and the premium rate charged to these people is called a substandard premium rate.

Mortality tables also show that, on the average, women live longer than men. Recognizing this difference in expected life spans, most insurers price equivalent life insurance policies at a lower rate for women than for men of the same age. However, some companies charge men and women the same rate based on newly constructed unisex mortality tables. Further-

FIGURE 2-1

The 1958 Commissioners Standard Ordinary (CSO) Mortality Table

Age	Number Living	Number Dying	Deaths per 1,000	Age	Number Living	Number Dying	Deaths per 1,000
0	10,000,000	70,800	7.08	50	8,762,306	72,902	8.32
1	9,929,200	17,475	1.76	51	8,689,404	79,160	9.11
2	9,911,725	15,066	1.52	52	8,610,244	85,758	9.96
3	9,896,659	14,449	1.46	53	8,524,486	92,832	10.89
4	9,882,210	13,835	1.40	54	8,431,654	100,337	11.90
5	9,868,375	13,322	1.35	55	8,331,317	108,307	13.00
6	9,855,053	12,812	1.30	56	8,223,010	116,849	14.21
7	9,842,241	12,401	1.26	57	8,106,161	125,970	15.54
8	9,829,840	12,091	1.23	58	7,980,191	135,663	17.00
9	9,817,749	11,879	1.21	59	7,844,528	145,830	18.59
10	9,805,870	11,865	1.21	60	7,698,698	156,592	20.34
11	9,794,005	12,047	1.23	61	7,542,106	167,736	22.24
12	9,781,958	12,325	1.26	62	7,374,370	179,271	24.31
13	9,769,633	12,896	1.32	63	7,195,099	191,174	26.57
14	9,756,737	13,562	1.39	64	7,003,925	203,394	29.04
15	9,743,175	14,225	1.46	65	6,800,531	215,917	31.75
16	9,728,950	14,983	1.54	66	6,584,614	228,749	34.74
17	9,713,967	15,737	1.62	67	6,355,865	241,777	38.04
18	9,698,230	16,390	1.69	68	6,114,088	254,835	41.68
19	9,681,840	16,846	1.74	69	5,859,253	267,241	45.61
20	9,664,994	17,300	1.79	70	5,592,012	278,426	49.79
21	9,647,694	17,655	1.83	71	5,313,586	287,731	54.15
22	9,630,039	17,912	1.86	72	5,025,855	294,766	58.65
23	9,612,127	18,167	1.89	73	4,731,089	299,289	63.26
24	9,593,960	18,324	1.91	74	4,431,800	301,894	68.12
25	9,575,636	18,481	1.93	75	4,129,906	303,011	73.37
26	9,557,155	18,732	1.96	76	3,826,895	303,014	79.18
27	9,538,423	18,981	1.99	77	3,523,881	301,997	85.70
28	9,519,442	19,324	2.03	78	3,221,884	299,829	93.06
29	9,500,118	19,760	2.08	79	2,922,055	295,683	101.19
30	9,480,358	20,193	2.13	80	2,626,372	288,848	109.98
31	9,460,165	20,718	2.19	81	2,337,524	278,983	119.35
32	9,439,447	21,239	2.25	82	2,058,541	265,902	129.17
33	9,418,208	21,850	2.32	83	1,792,639	249,858	139.38
34	9,396,358	22,551	2.40	84	1,542,781	231,433	150.01
35	9,373,807	23,528	2.51	85	1,311,348	211,311	161.14
36	9,350,279	24,685	2.64	86	1,100,037	190,108	172.82
37	9,325,594	26,112	2.80	87	909,929	168,455	185.13
38	9,299,482	27,991	3.01	88	741,474	146,997	198.25
39	9,271,491	30,132	3.25	89	594,477	126,303	212.46
40	9,241,359	32,622	3.53	90	468,174	106,809	228.14
41	9,208,737	35,362	3.84	91	361,365	88,813	245.77
42	9,173,375	38,253	4.17	92	272,552	72,480	265.93
43	9,135,122	41,382	4.53	93	200,072	57,881	289.30
44	9,093,740	44,741	4.92	94	142,191	45,026	316.66
45	9,048,999	48,412	5.35	95	97,165	34,128	351.24
46	9,000,587	52,473	5.83	96	63,037	25,250	400.56
47	8,948,114	56,910	6.36	97	37,787	18,456	488.42
48	8,891,204	61,794	6.95	98	19,331	12,916	668.15
49	8,829,410	67,104	7.60	99	6,415	6,415	1000.00

more, the use of sex-based premium rates is being examined by the courts and legislative bodies in the United States and may become illegal because of alleged social inequities caused by recognizing sex-based characteristics.

The Interest Factor

Premiums are the primary source of the funds used to pay life insurance claims. However, since all policies will not immediately result in claims, premium dollars can be invested by the insurer. Insurance companies invest in government and industrial bonds, in real estate, in mortgages, and in corporate stock. In fact, companies place money in any secure investment which is not prohibited by government regulation and which promises good earnings. The earnings from these investments provide additional funds which make it possible for insurance companies to charge lower premium rates. The proportion of insurance company income which is derived from investment earnings is shown in Figure 2–3.

FIGURE 2-2
The mortality curve, based on the 1958 CSO Mortality Table

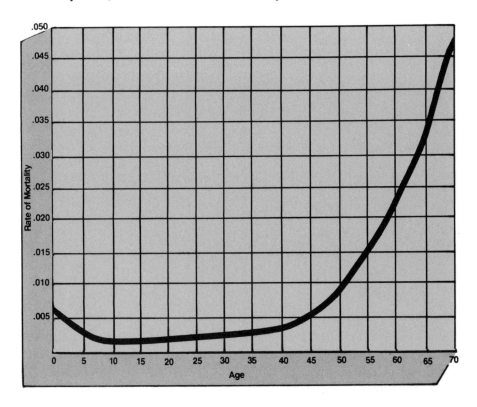

FIGURE 2-3

Portion of each dollar of insurance company income derived from investment earnings

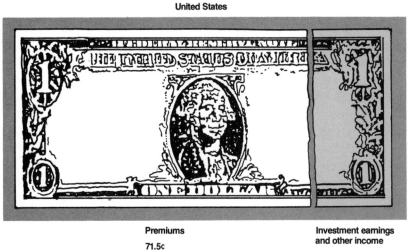

United States

Premiums
71.5¢

Investment earnings
and other income
28.5¢

Canada

Premiums
61.8¢

Net earnings from investments
38.2¢

How interest is earned

Interest is basically money that is paid for the use of money. For example, if you were to lend your brother $100 for one year at an annual in-
terest rate of 10 percent, he would owe you $110 at the end of the year—
the $100 you loaned plus $10 for letting him use your $100 for one year.
Interest paid on an original loan is known as ***simple interest***. When an

insurance company lends money to a business firm, the insurance company is letting that firm use the money. In return for this use, the firm pays the insurance company interest on that money.

Since many life insurance policies are long-term contracts, insurers are concerned with the effect of interest over a long period of time. When interest has been *earned* on money, but not *paid*, interest can accumulate on that unpaid interest. For example, if you permitted your brother to retain the $100 loan for an additional year without paying you the $10 of interest for the previous year, you would actually be making a loan of $110 (the amount due you at the end of one year) for the second year. This amount at 10 percent interest for one additional year would earn $11 interest, and at the end of the second year, $121 ($100 + $10 + $11) would be due you. Paying interest on interest is called **compounding**, and the interest paid on loans made under these conditions is known as **compound interest**. In the example cited, the interest was compounded annually. However, interest can be compounded at the end of any selected period – a half-year, a month, or more often.

The power of compound interest is very great over a long period. For example, if you were to save $1,000 per year for 25 years at no interest, you would have $25,000. However, if you saved the same $1,000 per year at an interest rate of 8 percent, compounded annually, you would have over $73,000 at the end of the 25 years! Figure 2–4 illustrates this example.

How interest affects pricing

The effect of interest on insurance companies and their policyowners becomes especially important in premium rate calculation, because the interest that an insurance company can earn on premiums enables the company to charge lower premium rates than would be possible considering only the rate of mortality.

For example, assume that 1,000 people age 35 are being insured by an insurance company for $10,000 each for 25 years. The company uses a mortality table to find the number of people in this group who can be expected to die each year during the next 25 years and the number of people who will be left alive to pay premiums each year. Using a mortality table like the 1958 CSO Mortality Table, the insurance company will find that approximately 183 of the insured people will die during the next 25 years. Therefore, it will need a total of $1,830,000 just to provide enough money to pay for all expected claims. Then, based on calculations which take into account the number of people who are expected to die each year and the number who are expected to stay alive, the insurer can determine that if each person purchasing a policy will pay a premium of approximately $80 each year, then the insurer will have enough money to pay benefits as the insureds die.

FIGURE 2-4

Comparison of savings with compound interest and with no interest

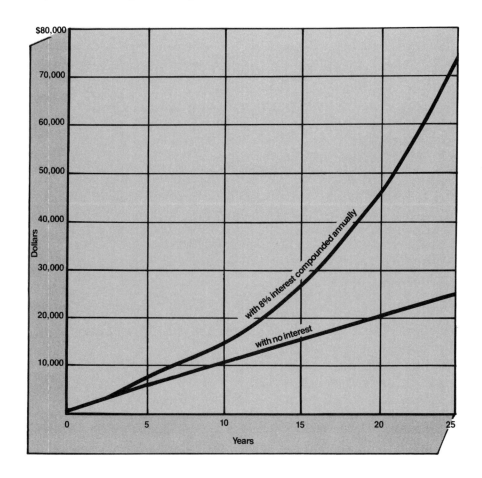

In calculating this premium, however, we have assumed that the life insurance company will take the money paid as premiums and put it in a vault or some other safe place; each year the insurance company will add the new premium money to the pile of money in the vault and take out as much money as is needed to pay claims, but will do nothing else with the money.

However, insurance companies invest the premiums that are paid to them. Therefore, if our insurance company in the example above finds that the money paid as premiums can be invested as it comes in to earn 3 percent interest compounded each year for 25 years, the company can reduce the premium charged each policyowner to $67.93. This means that compound interest is responsible for approximately a 15 percent reduction in the premium the insurer will charge for this policy. If the insurance company knew that it could earn more interest, then the insurance company could reduce the premium amount even further.

Expenses

Premium rates which are based only on mortality rates and interest are called **net premiums**. Net premiums are sufficient to provide the money to pay death claims. However, insurance companies must also consider operating costs, such as sales and commission costs, personnel salaries, and the cost of establishing and maintaining a home office and sales offices. In addition, recordkeeping costs, including operating both manual and computer systems, are a major expense for insurance companies. The insurance company must add an amount to the net premium to cover these operating expenses. Further, an insurer must be prepared for unexpected losses and other unanticipated costs. The insurer must collect a certain sum to cover all such contingencies and to produce profits for its owners. Figure 2–5 shows the proportion of insurance company expenditures which is attributable to expenses.

The total amount which is added to the net premium in consideration of all of the insurer's costs of doing business is called the **loading**. The net premium with the loading added is called the **gross premium** and is the amount the policyowner actually pays.

We have now looked at three factors which must be considered in calculating the premium rate for a life insurance policy. The first is mortality and the second is interest; these two factors comprise the net premium. Finally, a factor is added to cover the expenses of insurance operations, margins for contingencies, and contributions for profit. This expense factor is called loading and, when added to the net premium, produces the gross premium.

The Level Premium System

We have seen how mortality rates affect the price of life insurance; as mortality rates rise with age, the price of life insurance must follow suit. In order to provide life insurance coverage for periods of more than one year at a premium rate which does *not* increase each year with the insured's age, the life insurance industry has developed a pricing method known as the **level premium system**.

With the level premium system, the purchaser pays the same premium rate each year. If the insurance is for the whole of life, equal premiums are payable each year until death occurs or, in some cases, until the end of the premium-payment period specified in the policy. If the insurance policy is issued to cover only a specified number of years, equal premiums are generally payable for the duration of the policy.

The leveling of premiums is possible because premium rates charged under level premium policies are higher than needed to pay claims and expenses that occur during the early years of the policy. In the early years, the premium dollars not needed to pay claims and expenses are invested to accumulate at interest. As the group of persons insured under level premium policies ages, the company can anticipate an increasing number of death claims from that group each year. Under the level premium system, these claims can be paid in large part with the funds which have accumulated

FIGURE 2-5
Portion of each dollar of insurance company expenditures attributable to expenses

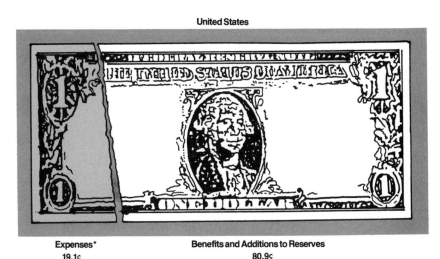

United States

Expenses*
19.1¢

Benefits and Additions to Reserves
80.9¢

Canada

Expenses*
14.4¢

Benefits and Additions to Reserves
85.6¢

*Includes taxes and dividends.

at interest. Thus, the premium on the policy can remain level throughout the duration of the policy.

To demonstrate the relationship between the premium rate for a level premium policy and the premium rates for a series of one-year policies, we can return to a previous example. Just a few pages back, we described how 1,000 persons age 35 could buy $10,000 life insurance policies for which each person would pay the same premium – $67.93 – each year for 25 years. If the same 1,000 persons age 35 each bought a $10,000 life insurance policy which provided coverage for one year, instead of 25 years, the premium that each person would pay that year would be $24.37. This price is much lower than the $67.93 charged for the level premium policy, because the price is based only on the mortality rate of a group of 35-year-olds for one year. If the policyowner repurchased the $10,000 policy each succeeding year, the one-year policy would cost $51.94 by the insured's age 45. This is still less than the premium for the level premium policy, but the price has more than doubled since the insureds were age 35 because of the higher mortality rate of a group of 45-year-olds. By the time the insureds had reached age 55, each would pay a premium for the one-year policy which would have increased to $126.21, almost double the premium for the level premium policy, and by the time the insureds reached age 60, the premium would reach $197.49. The difference between the level premium amount and the premium amounts for the one-year policies is shown in Figure 2–6.

One-year insurance policies are less expensive than similar level premium, long-term policies; hence, one-year policies can provide cheap, short-term protection if that is needed. However, as mortality rates rise, so do the premium rates of one-year policies. The premium rate for a level premium policy, on the other hand, does not increase after the policy has been purchased. Thus, the level premium system allows people to buy long-term life insurance policies which protect them at a steady, reasonable cost even while their risk of death is increasing over the duration of the policy.

Reserves

The level premium system also introduces policy reserves into the life insurance business. Every business maintains an accounting system to show what is happening to it financially, and "reserves" are kinds of accounts. Different kinds of reserves are handled in different ways, depending on how business in general has agreed to treat them. **Policy reserves** account for the money which the insurance company must pay in future claims. Hence, policy reserves are treated as **liabilities**, or amounts that the company must pay out at some time, and the insurance company must maintain financial resources, or **assets**, to offset the amount of the policy reserve liabilities. If the company has invested the excess premiums it has received under the level premium system – that is, those premium amounts which

FIGURE 2-6

Cost of one-year policies issued at various ages compared with the cost of a level premium policy

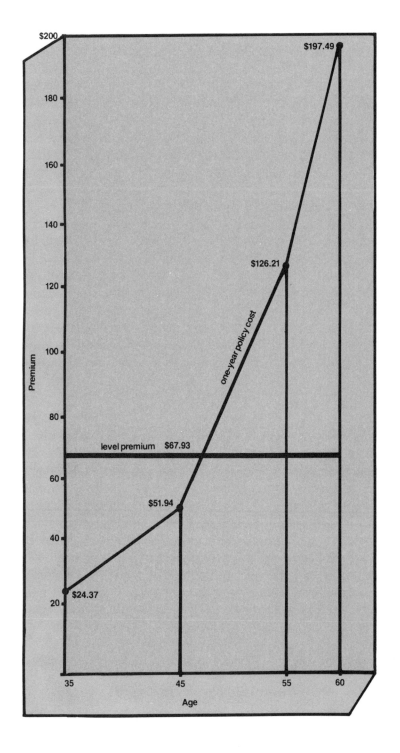

are not needed to meet current claims and expenses – and if the insurer has earned exactly the amount of interest it expected, then it will have assets that equal the amount of the policy reserve liability.

Because the overwhelming majority of companies have always had assets that exceeded the policy reserve liability, it has become common practice to refer to the assets that offset the amount of the policy reserve liability as if these assets were policy reserves themselves. This book will follow that practice. However, the reader should be aware that some authorities still maintain that the term "reserves" or "policy reserves" should not be used to refer to "assets offsetting policy reserves."

Since policy reserves have been accumulated for the purpose of paying future claims on the policies issued by the company, it is clear that the company may not simply do as it pleases with such reserves. The money is not extra money. It is the money which is required by law to be kept available to pay claims which the insurance company has promised to pay. Therefore, policy reserves are also known as **legal reserves**.

Since the primary purpose of these policy reserves is to pay claims when they become due, it is important that policy reserves be adequate and that the funds be safely invested. Much of the regulation of the life insurance industry by governmental bodies has to do with these policy reserves. Government rules require that a certain minimum reserve level be maintained and that the funds be placed in secure investments. This type of regulation is designed to protect the interest of the policyowners and beneficiaries who rely on the long-term solvency of the life insurance companies.

Net amount at risk

The difference between the face amount of a policy – the amount which will be paid as a death benefit – and the policy's reserve at the end of a policy year is known as the insurance company's **net amount at risk** for that policy. For example, if a $10,000 policy with a reserve of $3,000 should become payable, $3,000 of the death benefit would be covered by the reserve on that particular policy, and $7,000, the net amount at risk, would have to be paid from a charge assessed against all other policies. If you look at Figure 2–7, you can see how a reserve can build up while a policy is in force. As the reserve *increases*, the net amount at risk *decreases*. In the early years of a policy, the net amount at risk is very great, but by the policy's final years the reserve can grow large enough to pay for all or almost all of the death benefit.

Contingency reserves

Insurance companies must be sure that they can pay death claims even if conditions occur which are less favorable than those expected when the

FIGURE 2-7

Relationship between the net amount at risk and the reserve*

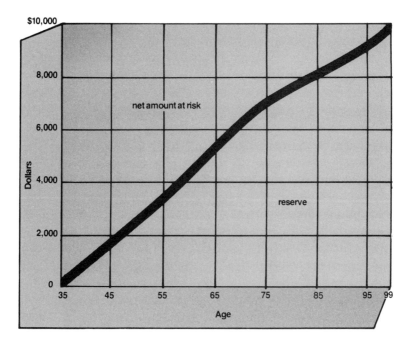

* Based on a $10,000 policy issued for the whole of life to a 35-year-old.

premium rates were calculated. While mortality statistics show the overall rate of mortality which may be expected, it is possible for fluctuations to occur in special instances – for example, in the case of an influenza epidemic. Such unexpected occurrences could have an effect on the mortality rate experienced by individual insurance companies. Insurers also have limited control over the interest rates they earn on their investments, and a company may not be able to earn the rate of investment return anticipated. Additionally, operating expenses may rise faster than an insurer expected.

As mentioned earlier, insurers add a small amount to the net premium as part of the loading to cover such contingencies. Companies use these funds to set up **contingency reserves**, which are reserves against unusual conditions that may occur. Contingency reserves provide a safety margin in case actual experience in any area – mortality, interest, and/or expense – is worse than expected.

Dividends

Life insurance policies can be issued on either a participating or non-participating basis. A **participating policy** is one under which the policyowner shares in the insurance company's surplus. **Surplus** is the accumulation of earnings that result from a company's profitable operations. The amount of this surplus which is available for distribution to policyowners is called the **divisible surplus**, and a policyowner's share of this divisible surplus is called a **policy dividend**.

The most important concern of insurers is to assure that enough money will be available to pay anticipated claims and expenses, as well as any additional, unexpected claims and expenses. However, insurers are generally very cautious when making assumptions about mortality, interest, expenses, and contingencies. Actual experience in these areas is often not as bad as anticipated. By issuing participating policies, insurance companies can return money to policyowners in the form of dividends when conditions are favorable, while still being prepared for adverse conditions.

Each cost element involved in setting premium rates is a potential source of surplus. If a company earns a higher rate of return on investments than anticipated, there will be more interest income than needed to maintain the reserves at the required levels. If the people insured by a company experience a more favorable mortality rate than the company expected, fewer claims will be paid. And, in addition, if a company spends less money on administrative expense than was planned, additional funds will be available from the loading. A portion of an insurer's surplus funds is available for distribution to the owners of participating policies in the form of policy dividends.

A **nonparticipating policy** is one in which the policyowner does not share in any surplus. Generally, the premium rates for nonparticipating policies are lower than the premium rates for equivalent participating policies, because insurers issuing nonparticipating policies often use less conservative assumptions regarding mortality, interest, expenses, and contingencies. It is difficult to determine in advance, though, which type of policy – participating or nonparticipating – will be the least expensive, because dividends received by the owner of a participating policy serve to reduce the amount of a participating policy's actual cost, but the amount of this dividend, if any, is not known in advance, nor is it guaranteed.

In the United States, there is no legal requirement that dividends be declared. However, policies must state whether they are participating or nonparticipating policies, and participating policies must indicate that when dividends are declared, they will be paid yearly on the policy anniversary date. In Canada, a specific percentage of divisible surplus must be returned to the owner of a participating policy each year.

The dividend provision included in a participating policy also gives the policyowner several choices in the way dividends can be used. These choices are known as dividend options, which will be discussed in a later chapter.

In chapter 1, we mentioned that an organization which sells life insurance may be set up as a stock insurance company or as a mutual insurance company. Generally, stock companies issue their policies on a non-participating basis, and mutual companies issue policies on a participating basis. However, some stock companies do offer some participating policies as a part of their product line and, in very rare instances, some mutuals have sold nonparticipating policies in addition to participating policies.

3

Basic Types
of Life Insurance

While the need for life insurance protection is shared by most people, no single type of life insurance policy fits the insurance needs of everyone. Consequently, the insurance industry has developed a variety of policies to meet the specific needs of the public. This chapter defines the major classifications of life insurance policies and describes the basic types of life insurance coverage.

LINES AND PLANS OF LIFE INSURANCE

Traditionally, life insurance has been classified according to *line* and *plan*. The term **line of insurance** refers to any one of three different approaches to providing insurance coverage. The three major lines of life insurance are *ordinary, industrial,* and *group* insurance. It is important to note, however, that no approach is totally distinct from the others; all three have certain features in common.

The term **plan of insurance** refers to the basic policy type. There are three basic plans of insurance: *term, whole life,* and *endowment.* All three basic plans are sold as ordinary insurance and will be discussed in this chapter in this context; however, these plans are not restricted to the ordinary insurance line.

This book will use the terms *line* and *plan* as explained above. The reader should be aware, however, that the two terms are not used in the same way by all people in the industry, and that other authors may use the terms somewhat differently.

Three Lines of Life Insurance

As we have noted, there are three major lines of life insurance sold

37

FIGURE 3-1

Life insurance purchases in the United States (by line of insurance)

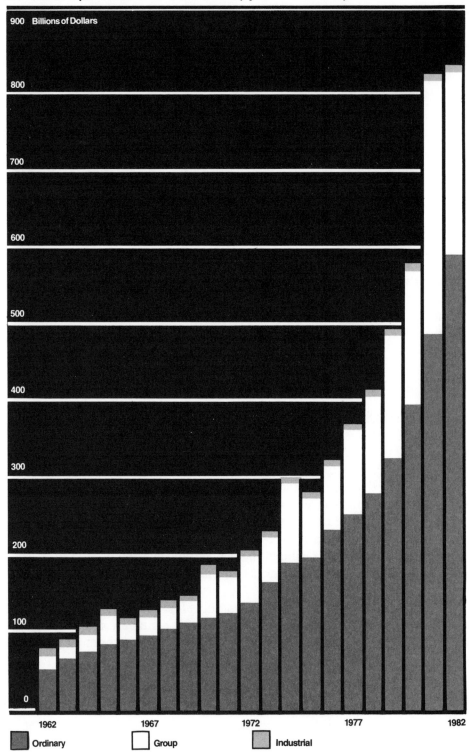

today – ordinary, industrial, and group. Figure 3–1 illustrates the proportion of life insurance purchased in each of these three lines of insurance.

Ordinary life insurance is available to individuals in relatively unrestricted maximum amounts, and the face amount must be at least a stated minimum. The minimum face amount may be as low as $1,000 but usually is $5,000 or more. The premium for an ordinary life insurance policy may be paid in a lump sum, or premium payments may be made annually, semi-annually, quarterly, or monthly.

As is the case with ordinary insurance, *industrial insurance* is sold to individuals, but in relatively smaller maximum amounts. The minimum face amount for an industrial policy may be less than $1,000 but usually ranges from $1,000 to $3,000. Industrial insurance, which is also sometimes called *debit insurance*, was originally developed to provide some insurance coverage, particularly to pay for burial expenses, for low-income laborers in industrial cities. Industrial insurance premiums are usually collected weekly or monthly by an insurance agent who goes to the policyowner's home. This premium collection method is one aspect of the *home service system*, which is used to market industrial insurance in addition to ordinary and group insurance.

Group insurance provides coverage for a group of people under one contract. The group itself must exist for some purpose other than to obtain insurance protection. The most common eligible group consists of the employees of a business firm. The group insurance contract is sold to the employer for the benefit of the employees. Thus, there is one master contract covering many individual lives. Both life and health insurance may be provided in this fashion.

In this chapter we will focus on the ordinary line of life insurance, which accounts for the greatest part of the insurance sold to individuals. Group insurance, as well as industrial insurance and the home service system, will be discussed in later chapters.

Three Plans of Ordinary Life Insurance

The three basic plans of ordinary life insurance are term, whole life, and endowment insurance. Figure 3–2 illustrates the proportion of ordinary life insurance purchased from 1955 to 1980 in each of these three plans.

Insurance issued to provide coverage for a specified period or term is called *term insurance*. If the insured dies during the period that the term insurance is in force, the policy benefit becomes payable. At the end of the period – unless the policy is renewed – the insurance is no longer in effect.

Whole life insurance is permanent; it provides insurance coverage during the insured's entire lifetime. Unlike term plans, there is no fixed expiration date for coverage. The amount of the premium for a whole life policy does not increase along with the insured's age but generally remains

FIGURE 3-2

Ordinary life insurance purchases in the United States (by plan of insurance)

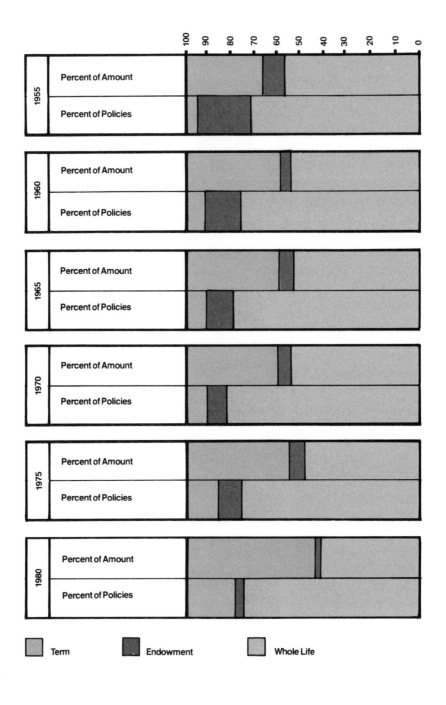

fixed during the premium paying period, which may be either a limited number of years or the entire lifetime of the insured.

Endowment insurance is similar to term insurance in that the endowment policy is effective for only a limited period of time. However, endowment insurance provides a benefit equivalent to the face amount of the policy regardless of whether the insured lives to the end of the period selected *or* dies during the period.

The remainder of this chapter will be devoted to a complete description of the features and characteristics of each of these three plans.

TERM LIFE INSURANCE

Although term insurance is life insurance that is effective for a specified period of time – the term – the length of the term for which such a policy is issued may vary considerably. The term may be as short as the time it takes to complete a trip or as long as 30, 40, or more years. In practice, term insurance is usually not sold to cover a period of less than 1 year. The term may be described as a specified number of years – 1 year, 5 years, 10 years, 20 years – or it may be defined by specifying the age of the insured at the end of the term. For example, a term insurance plan that covers a person until the person reaches age 65 is referred to as "term to age 65," and the policy's coverage expires on the *policy anniversary* nearest the insured person's 65th birthday. The **policy anniversary** is the anniversary of the date on which the policy was issued. For example, if a company issues a policy on December 2 of a given year, then every succeeding December 2 is the policy anniversary.

Term life insurance protection, or coverage, is usually provided by a policy, but it can also be provided by a *rider* attached to a policy. A policy **rider**, which is also called an **endorsement**, is an addition to a policy that becomes a part of the contract and is as legally effective as any other part of the policy. Riders are commonly used to provide some type of supplementary benefit or to increase the amount of the death benefit provided in a policy, although riders may also be used to limit or modify a policy's coverage.

Types of Term Insurance Coverage

The coverage provided by a term life insurance policy or rider usually is an amount that remains the same, or *level*, throughout the term. However, term life insurance may be purchased to provide a benefit that *decreases* over the term, or a benefit that *increases* over the term.

Level term life insurance

In level term life insurance, the death benefit remains the same over the period specified. For example, a five-year level term policy providing $10,000 of coverage specifies that the insurer will pay $10,000 if the insured dies at any time during the five-year period that the policy is in force. Level term insurance policies are issued in amounts of $5,000 and up, even to several million dollars. Premiums for level term insurance policies usually remain the same throughout each term of coverage.

Decreasing term life insurance

In decreasing term life insurance, the death benefit starts as a set face amount and then the face amount *decreases* over the term of coverage in some specified manner. For example, the benefit during the first year of coverage of a five-year decreasing term policy or rider may be $10,000 and then may decrease by $2,000 on each policy anniversary; the coverage would be $8,000 during the second year, $6,000 in the third year, $4,000 in the fourth, and $2,000 in the last year. At the end of the fifth year the coverage would expire. The premium for decreasing term insurance usually remains level during the period of coverage.

Increasing term life insurance

The amount of the death benefit in an increasing term life insurance policy starts at one level and *increases* at stated intervals by some specified amount or percentage. For example, an insurance company may offer a policy which has a face amount that starts at $10,000 and then increases by 5 percent on each policy anniversary date throughout the term of the policy. The premium either remains level or increases with the coverage. It is usually possible for a policyowner to freeze the amount of coverage provided by an increasing term life insurance policy at any time. This coverage may be sold as a single policy or, more commonly, as a rider to an existing policy.

Increasing term coverage was not often sold in the past, but recently it has enjoyed more popularity. In anticipation of the rising cost of living or increasing family responsibilities, more policyowners are buying increasing term insurance coverage to make sure a policy's benefit does not become inadequate to meet future needs.

Renewable and Convertible Term Insurance

By definition, term life insurance provides only temporary protection. At the end of the specified period, the policy is no longer in force. There are times, however, when the policyowner may wish to continue the coverage beyond the term specified. To deal with these situations, many insurers offer *renewable term insurance policies*, which give the policyowner the option to renew the term policy at the end of the term, and *convertible term insurance policies*, which give the policyowner the right to convert the term policy to a whole life plan of insurance.

Renewable term insurance

Renewable term insurance policies include a *renewal provision*, which gives the policyowner the right to renew the insurance coverage at the end of the specified term without submitting *evidence of insurability* – evidence that the insured person continues to be an insurable risk. Even though the insured may be suffering from some health problem that has developed since the renewable term policy was issued, the insurance company must renew the coverage at the policyowner's request and cannot charge a new premium rate based on the insured's higher rate of risk. Normally, however, the insurer will charge a new premium rate based on the current age of the insured. The renewal feature can lead to some antiselection; insureds in poor health will be more likely to renew their policies, since they may not be able to obtain other life insurance. Because of this risk, the premium for a renewable term insurance policy is usually slightly higher than the premium for a similar nonrenewable policy.

Nearly all renewable term policies are renewable for the same term and amount as originally issued. For example, a 10-year $20,000 renewable term policy can usually be renewed for another 10-year period for $20,000 in coverage. Most companies will also allow a policyowner to renew the policy for a *smaller* amount and/or for a *shorter* period than provided by the original contract, but not for a larger amount and/or longer period.

In many cases the renewal provision in the policy will specify that the right to renew will be limited, either by the age of the insured or by the maximum number of renewals permitted. For example, the renewal provision of a policy may specify that the coverage is not renewable after the person insured has reached the age of 65. Another policy may specify that it is renewable no more than three times. Such restrictions exist in order to minimize antiselection.

The premium rate will normally *increase* when the term insurance policy is renewed. This increase takes place because renewal premium rates are based on the insured person's *attained age* – the age the person has reached (attained) on the renewal date. Since premium rates increase with the insured's age, the higher premium rate is to be expected, because the insured person will be older. The premiums will then usually be level throughout the new term, though they will be higher than during the previous term.

One-year term policies and riders are usually renewable. This coverage is called yearly renewable term (YRT) or annually renewable term (ART) insurance. The right to renew a YRT policy is usually limited either by the age of the insured or by the maximum number of renewals permitted. The premium rates for such coverage are generally low, but they will increase each year at renewal.

Convertible term insurance policies

A convertible term policy contains a **conversion privilege**, which allows the policyowner to change (convert) the term insurance plan to a whole life plan. Even if the health of the person insured by a convertible term policy has deteriorated to the point that he or she would otherwise be uninsurable, the policyowner can obtain lifetime insurance coverage on that person because evidence of insurability is not required at the time of conversion. The premium the policyowner is charged for the whole life policy cannot be based on any increase in the insured's degree of risk, except with regard to an increase in the insured's age. In order to cover the costs of providing the conversion privilege, insurers usually charge higher premium rates for convertible term policies than for nonconvertible term policies. When a policyowner converts a term policy to a whole life plan of insurance, he or she usually will receive a new policy and will pay a premium rate appropriate for the whole life coverage.

To help prevent antiselection, the insurer will usually limit the conversion privilege in some way. For instance, some policies do not permit conversion after the insured has attained a specific age, such as 55 or 65. In addition, conversion may be limited to a period which is less than the full term of the original policy or to an amount which is only a percentage of the original face amount. For example, a 10-year term policy may permit conversion only during the first seven or eight years of the term. Another 10-year term policy may permit conversion of 100 percent of the face amount only within the first five years of the term, and a smaller percentage, such as 50 percent or 75 percent of the face amount, if the policy is converted in the last five years. Insurers may permit conversions after these specified time periods have passed, but in such cases the insurer may require evidence of insurability before permitting the conversion.

The premium rate for a whole life insurance policy is higher than the premium rate for a term insurance policy of the same amount of coverage. Hence, when a term insurance policy is converted to a whole life insurance policy, the new premium rate is higher. In addition, this new rate is usually based on the age of the insured at the time of conversion and is called an **attained age conversion**. For example, suppose John Matthews is 35 when he buys a five-year convertible term policy on his life. If one year before the policy term is over he converts the term insurance policy to a whole life policy, the new whole life premium rate will be the rate for insureds at age 39, his *attained* age at conversion time.

In some cases, a policyowner may be permitted to convert the term policy based on the insured's age at the time the original policy was purchased. This is called an ***original age conversion***. The new whole life premium rate will be lower if the conversion is an original age conversion rather than an attained age conversion, since the insured was younger at the time the original policy was purchased. Therefore, if in the example above, Mr. Matthews chose an original age conversion, the premium rate for the whole life insurance paid thereafter would be the whole life premium rate for a 35-year-old, even though he was 39 at the time of conversion. In many cases, an insurance company will not allow original age conversions if more than a specified number of years—such as more than five years—have elapsed since the original policy was purchased.

If a policy is converted on an original age basis, the insurance company will need to establish for the new policy a reserve equal to the reserve which would have accumulated under the policy had it actually been issued at the original age as a whole life policy. In order to provide the insurer with the funds to establish this reserve, the policyowner will have to pay some part of or the entire difference between the premiums already paid for term insurance and the premiums which would have been payable for the whole life policy. This payment will often represent a sizeable initial outlay of money upon conversion, so it is no wonder that only about 5 percent of term conversions are made on an original age basis.

Some term policies automatically convert to whole life insurance either at the end of a specified period—often three or five years—or at the time the insured reaches a specific age. Of course, even though conversion is automatic on these policies, the policyowner can always refuse the new whole life policy. While such automatic actions are binding on the insurer, they are not binding on the policyowner. After all, if the policyowner does not pay the premium, the insurance will not be in force.

The privileges of renewal and conversion are of obvious potential value to the policyowner, but they are also of value to the insurance company. Most policyowners renew or convert their term policies not because they are in poor health but because they want to continue their insurance protection. Therefore, insurance companies are able to keep this insurance in force without the expense of initiating new sales. It should also be noted that relatively few term insurance policies result in a death claim, because term insurance is normally purchased to cover periods when the mortality rate for insureds is low. Usually, a term policy will (1) expire before the insured dies, (2) be converted to whole life insurance, or (3) terminate because renewal premiums have not been paid.

WHOLE LIFE INSURANCE

Whole life insurance differs from term insurance in three primary characteristics:
- ***Whole life insurance is permanent***. Whereas term life insurance provides protection for a certain period of time and pays no benefits

after that period ends, whole life insurance provides protection for the entire life of the insured, if premiums are paid as specified in the policy.

- **Whole life premiums generally remain level throughout the premium-payment period**. Whereas term life insurance premium rates increase at every policy renewal, whole life insurance premium rates generally remain level throughout the premium-payment period and will not increase based on any increase in the age of the person insured.
- **Whole life combines insurance and savings**. Whereas term life insurance almost always provides for insurance protection only, whole life insurance allows policyowners to accumulate savings funds.

The Savings Element of Whole Life Insurance

Whole life insurance premium rates are calculated based on the level premium system described in chapter 2. For this reason, premium rates themselves do not increase with the age of the person once he or she is insured. As noted in chapter 2, the level premium system depends on the accumulation of *policy reserves*, and insurers must charge policyowners more than the actual cost of claims and expenses in the early years of a level premium policy because in later years the level premium amount is less than the amount needed to pay claims and expenses. Thus, the premium rate for a one-year term insurance policy is lower than the premium rate for a whole life policy for the same face amount. However, the premium rate for the term insurance policy will increase at each renewal because of the insured's increasing age, while the premium rate for the whole life policy will not increase according to the insured's age. Figure 3–3 illustrates the relationship between term insurance premium rates and a whole life insurance policy's premium rate.

The policy reserves that build under the level premium system are also responsible for the savings element of whole life policies. Policyowners possess an interest in the funds accumulated in the policy reserves. Therefore, insurance companies provide a cash value for each whole life policy. This **cash value** is the amount of money which the policyowner will receive as a refund if the policyowner cancels the coverage and surrenders the policy to the company. For this reason, the cash value is sometimes referred to as the **surrender value**. The cash value is not necessarily equal to the actual reserve held for a policy, but the amount of the cash value is roughly related to, although somewhat lower than, the amount of the reserve.

The size of a policy's cash value depends on both the face amount of the policy and the length of time the policy has been in force. The reserve and the cash value of a whole life policy will increase throughout the life of the policy and will eventually equal the face amount of the policy. However,

FIGURE 3-3

Comparison of term insurance premium rates* and a whole life insurance premium rate for policies issued to a male classified as a standard risk

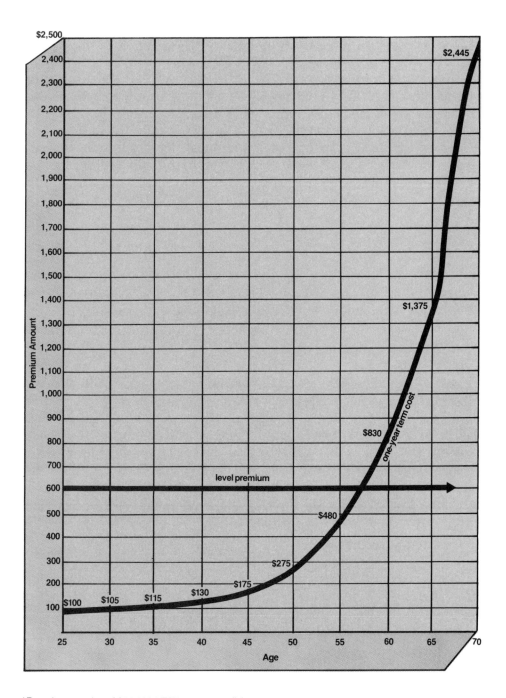

*Based on a series of $50,000 YRT insurance policies

the cash value does not equal the face amount until the time the insured reaches the age at the end of the mortality table used to calculate premiums for that policy. At that point, it is customary for the insurance company to pay the face amount of the policy to the policyowner. A term policy will also build up some reserve and, if the term is long enough, some temporary cash value. However, the cash value for a term policy will diminish along with the reserve, reaching zero at the end of the term of the policy.

Any whole life insurance policy which has accumulated a cash value may be used as security for a loan. The policyowner may request a loan, known as a **policy loan**, from the insurance company itself, or the policyowner may use the cash value of the policy as collateral for a loan from another financial institution. However, if the insured dies before a policy loan is repaid, then the unpaid amount of the loan plus any interest outstanding is subtracted from the policy benefit. Policy loans will be discussed in more detail in chapter 7, "The Policy Contract."

Premium Payment Periods

Whole life policies are classified on the basis of their premium payment schedules. The most common whole life policies are (1) *continuous-premium policies* and (2) *limited-payment policies*.

Continuous-premium policies

Under **continuous-premium policies,** which are usually called **straight life** insurance policies, premiums are payable until the death of the insured. Since continuous-premium, or straight life, policies anticipate that premiums will be paid for an insured's entire lifetime, the amount of the annual premium will be lower than the amount of the annual premium for a limited payment whole life policy with the same face amount. We can say, therefore, that continuous-premium policies offer the greatest amount of whole life insurance protection for the lowest annual premium.

Limited-payment policies

Unlike continuous-premium whole life policies, **limited-payment whole life policies** do not require premium payments over the entire lifetime of the person insured. Some limited-payment policies – for example, 20-payment whole life or 30-payment whole life – specify the number of years during which premiums are payable. Other policies specify an age after which premiums are no longer payable – for example, life-paid-up at age 65. The latter policy provides that premiums are payable until the insured reaches the policy anniversary nearest his or her 65th birthday, at which time the payments cease but the coverage continues. If the person insured dies before the end of the specified premium payment period, the benefit is paid, and no further premium payments are due.

The use of these limited-payment policies is based on the concept that, after a certain period of time or after the insured reaches a certain age, the policyowner may find it difficult to maintain premium payments. For example, after retirement the policyowner's income may drop considerably, and, while protection may still be needed, the payment of premiums might be burdensome.

Under all limited-payment policies, the premium amounts are established so that, at the end of the premium payment period, the policies are *paid up* – the policyowner has paid enough in premiums to keep the policy in force for the rest of the insured's lifetime. Since fewer premium payments are expected to be made under a limited-payment policy than under a continuous-premium policy, each of the premium payments for the limited-payment policy must be larger than each premium payment for an equivalent continuous-premium policy.

Both continuous-premium and limited-payment life insurance policies steadily build up guaranteed cash values. Cash values do not accumulate as rapidly under continuous-premium policies as they do under limited-payment policies, and such cash values are not usually available under continuous-premium policies until the end of the third policy year.

Single-premium whole life policies are an extreme type of a limited-payment policy, requiring only one premium payment. Under the single-premium life insurance policy, a large part of the premium is used to set up the policy's reserve. Single-premium life insurance requires a relatively large initial outlay of money – one so high in relation to the face amount of the policy that such policies are usually purchased only for special purposes. However, since the cash value available on any policy is related to the reserve – although the cash value is usually somewhat lower than the reserve – there will be a sizeable cash value available immediately on any single-premium policy purchased.

Figure 3–4 shows the impact of the number of premium payment periods on the reserve for a whole life policy. The shorter the premium payment period, the more quickly the reserve builds. Note that the reserve on all whole life policies eventually equals the face amount of the contract. Since Figure 3–4 is based on the use of a mortality table which ends at age 100, the reserve equals the face amount at age 100.

Modified Whole Life Policies

Many insurers also offer modified whole life policies. There are two types of modified whole life insurance policies that are commonly issued today. The first of these involves modifying the premium, that is, altering

FIGURE 3-4

Comparison of reserve accumulation under whole life policies with different premium-payment periods*

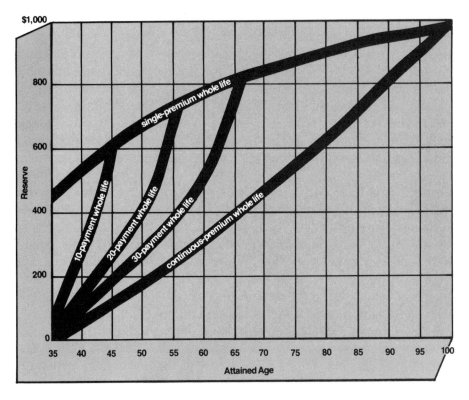

*Based on 1958 CSO Mortality Table, assuming 2½ percent interest, and a $1,000 face amount.

the amount of the premium. The second manner of modifying a whole life insurance contract involves altering the amount payable as a death benefit.

Modified premiums

A **modified-premium whole life policy** usually provides that the policyowner will pay a lower premium for a specified period, such as five years, than the policyowner would normally pay for a similar whole life policy which was not issued on a modified-premium plan. After the specified period, the premium increases to an amount somewhat higher than the usual (non-modified) premium would have been. This new increased premium is then payable for the rest of the life of the policy. The amount of the benefit, however, remains level during the entire period. For example, a $50,000 continuous-premium whole life policy issued on the life of a 25-year-old man might call for a premium of $600 per year. The premium for a modified-premium whole life policy for the same amount could be $400 per year for the first 10 years, with the premium increasing to $1,100 per year thereafter for the rest of the life of the policy. Figure 3–5 illustrates this example.

We saw earlier that a whole life policy could be purchased with a single premium, a series of level premiums for a specified number of years, or a series of level premiums over the lifetime of the insured. The modified-premium plan is simply another way of paying premiums – one which can be either advantageous or disadvantageous, depending on the needs of the policyowner.

The chief advantage to the policyowner of buying the modified-premium whole life policy is that the policyowner may purchase a higher amount of whole life insurance than would otherwise be affordable based upon the policyowner's current income level. The assumption is that improvement in future income will enable the policyowner to continue the policy after the period of lower premiums. For example, a young person starting a family may be able to purchase a larger policy on a modified plan than on a regular

FIGURE 3-5

Comparison of premium amounts required for a continuous-premium whole life policy and a modified-premium whole life policy of the same face amount

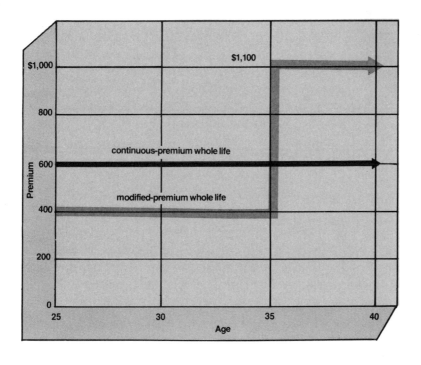

whole life plan, with the expectation that by the time the premium increases, he or she will have a larger income from which to pay premiums. On the other hand, the cash value for a modified-premium policy will build more slowly. However, for many policyowners the advantage of a lower initial premium outweighs any other considerations.

Some companies issue policies in which premium payments are modified even more frequently. Generally known as **graded-premium policies**, these policies call for three or more levels of premium payment amounts, increasing at specified points in time – such as every three years – until the amount to be paid as a level premium for the rest of the life of the contract is reached. As in all modified-premium plans, the face amount of insurance remains level throughout the contract.

Modified amount of coverage

Another type of modified whole life insurance offered by life insurance companies is based on the assumption that the need for large amounts of life insurance is likely to diminish as the insured person grows older. As a policyowner's children leave home, and as the policyowner accumulates other financial reserves, the need for economic protection may become less important. A policy with modified coverage provides that the amount of insurance will decrease by specific percentages or amounts at certain stated ages. For example, a $100,000 policy may decrease to $75,000 at age 60, to $50,000 at age 70, and then remain level in face amount for the rest of the insured's lifetime.

In anticipation of such reduced coverage at the older ages, an insurer will be able, from the time of policy issue, to provide the $100,000 modified whole life policy for a lower premium than it could if it were liable for the full $100,000 of coverage throughout the entire expected lifetime of the insured. Note also that during the period of greatest risk of death, the period when the person insured is at an advanced age, the face amount of the policy will be at its lowest level. In many cases, however, this will be the period when the need for life insurance is lowest.

ENDOWMENT INSURANCE

Another type of ordinary insurance that is provided by life insurance companies is endowment insurance. In general terms, an **endowment** is money or property that is bestowed upon a person or an institution. The meaning of endowment in the insurance business is more specific. It refers to a sum of money which a person receives from an insurer when an endowment insurance policy **matures**, that is, when it reaches the end of its term and becomes payable. An endowment insurance policy can be considered a combination of level term insurance and what is known in the insurance industry as a "pure endowment." Although pure endowment contracts are not sold today, knowing how the pure endowment portion of endowment insurance operates is helpful in order to gain an understanding of endowment insurance.

Pure Endowment

A **pure endowment contract** is one which pays a benefit *only* to those persons who survive a certain period of time; those who do not survive that period of time receive nothing. In this way, the pure endowment contract is the opposite of a term insurance policy, which pays a benefit only if the person insured does not survive a certain period of time. To calculate the amount of money required to provide pure endowment benefits, an insurer uses mortality statistics to predict the number of persons who will survive to receive the benefits. The amount of money required to provide the pure endowment benefit then reflects the fact that not all those who purchase such a contract will survive and receive the benefit.

For example, suppose you want to have $20,000 paid to you at the end of 10 years. Because of the interest you could earn while saving the money, it would take you about 10 yearly payments of approximately $1,500 to accumulate the $20,000. However, if you could purchase a pure endowment, you would pay less than $1,500 each year because you would agree to forfeit the right to any money should you die before the end of the 10 years. If you do not live the 10 years, the payments you made for the pure endowment, plus the interest earned, would be used to pay benefits to others in the pure endowment plan who did survive for the entire period.

Endowment Insurance

Today, endowment insurance pays a fixed benefit either if the insured survives to the maturity date of the policy or if the insured dies before that maturity date. It contains both a level term insurance element and a pure endowment element. The *term insurance* element provides the death benefit if the insured *dies* during the term of the policy. The *pure endowment* element provides the benefit if the insured *survives* to the end of the term.

Since an endowment insurance policy guarantees payment of a benefit, it has been used as a savings instrument when a person anticipates a need for a large sum on a specific date. Matured endowment benefits are examples of what are often called the **living benefits** of life insurance, since they are paid while the insured is alive.

Premiums are level during the term of an endowment policy. Endowment insurance is sold either for a stated term—such as 20 years—or to a selected age – such as age 65. Since the pure endowment portion of the contract is essentially a savings feature, these policies also have guaranteed cash values.

The three basic plans of insurance were all developed to serve special purposes and meet different needs. Term insurance provides the most insurance protection for the lowest initial premium, but the coverage is temporary. Whole life insurance is designed to provide permanent protection; if coverage is needed for life, a whole life policy can provide it. Through its cash value accumulation, a whole life policy provides a policyowner flexibility to meet changing needs. Endowment insurance provides the least amount of insurance protection for a given premium dollar but assures that a specific sum of money will be available whether the insured lives or dies during a given period.

4

Specialized Policies and Supplementary Benefit Riders

When deciding what kind of life insurance coverage to purchase, a person must consider a wide variety of factors, including the length of time the coverage is needed and the length of the premium payment period desired. Before purchasing a policy, an individual consumer should also weigh other factors and answer specific questions about his or her needs. For example, a consumer might consider:

- *the resources available*
  How much can I afford to pay for an insurance program?
- *the rising cost of living*
  Will the policy's benefit keep pace with inflation?
- *the family situation*
  Do my spouse and I both need coverage? Can we afford enough insurance on both of our lives?

These and other consumer concerns have led insurers to design policies which are special combinations and variations of the basic plans of insurance. These specialized policies are not new plans of insurance; rather, they are adaptations or combinations of basic plans tailored to meet changing conditions and needs. Insurers also offer certain supplementary benefit riders which may be added to life insurance policies to provide additional benefits.

SPECIALIZED POLICIES

The number of specialized policies available to consumers has been increasing rapidly. Every week, it seems, another "new product" is introduced. This text cannot and will not attempt to provide a complete description of each product variation. Instead, some of the most common and representative examples of these specialized policies will be explained in terms of their uses and distinguishing characteristics. Once you are familiar with the uses and characteristics of these specialized policies, you should be able to understand the way that most other specialty policies are constructed.

Universal Life

Universal life insurance policies are a fairly recent entry into the insurance marketplace. Designed to provide a great deal of flexibility and to reflect current conditions in financial markets, these policies include two separate components: a **protection element** (term insurance) and a **savings element** (cash value).

A universal life policy is considered an "unbundled" policy because the mortality, interest, and expense factors used to calculate premium rates and cash values are expressed separately in the policy. In traditional life insurance policies, these pricing factors are used to calculate premium rates and to determine cash values, but they are not listed separately in the policy.

For example, if Douglas Brown purchases a $100,000 whole life policy, he is informed by the insurance company of the premium amount required for that policy, and he is guaranteed that the cash value in his policy will accumulate in a specified manner while the policy is in force. On the other hand, if Mr. Brown purchases a universal life policy, the insurance company will inform him of (1) the amount of money needed to cover the policy costs based on expected mortality rates and expense charges and (2) the interest rate which he will earn on any premium amounts paid in excess of the amount needed to cover these policy costs. Mr. Brown will then decide the actual premium amount he will pay for the policy, subject to certain limits. The amount of the cash value in the universal life policy, which is referred to as the policy's *savings element*, would then be based on the premium amount Mr. Brown chooses to pay.

In this way, a universal life policy allows a policyowner to choose, within certain limits, the amount of premium which he or she wishes to pay each year, depending on (1) the amount of insurance protection needed and (2) the amount of money the policyowner wishes to place in the policy's savings element. Most insurers, though, do not permit the amount of money in the policy's savings element to exceed a defined percentage of the policy's face amount.

The cost of the protection element of a universal life insurance policy is usually referred to as the policy's **mortality charge**. This mortality charge is based on the net amount at risk under the policy, the insured's risk classification at the time the policy was originally purchased, and the insured's *current* age. Like YRT insurance premium rates, then, the mortality charge per thousand dollars of insurance coverage increases each year with the insured's age. However, under the form of universal life policy most commonly sold, the amount of money in the policy's savings element decreases the net amount at risk; hence, the actual amount of the mortality charge does not necessarily increase each year. Figure 4–1 illustrates the effect of a varying savings element on the net amount at risk under a universal life policy.

FIGURE 4-1

Example of the effect a varying savings element can have on the net amount at risk under a universal life policy

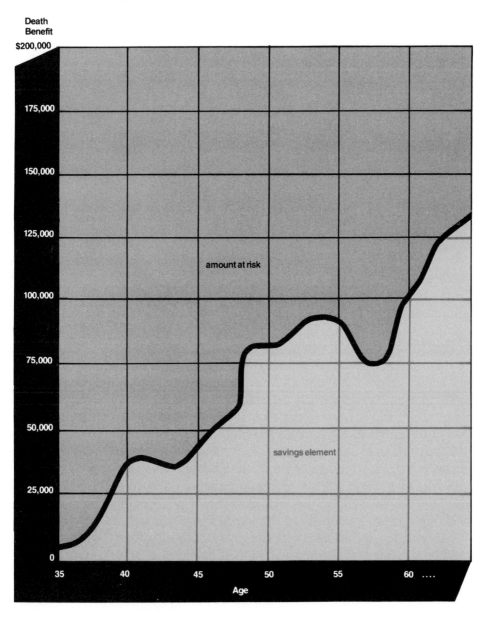

For example, if the face amount of a universal life policy is $150,000 and the amount in the policy's savings element is $20,000, then the mortality charge would be based on the cost of $130,000 of coverage – the net amount at risk under the policy. If the amount in the policy's savings element is later increased to $30,000, then the mortality charge would be based on the cost of $120,000 of coverage, the new net amount at risk under the policy. A maximum mortality charge per thousand dollars of coverage at each age is guaranteed in the policy; however, if an insurer's mortality experience is better than expected, the insurer can reduce this charge.

The initial, or first, annual premium a policyowner pays for a universal life policy is usually a matter of individual choice, as long as that initial amount chosen meets or exceeds the minimum amount specified by the insurance company. Note that the minimum annual premium amount specified by the insurer applies only to the *initial* premium payment. The policyowner chooses the amount of premium he or she pays each succeeding year. The more a policyowner pays in premium above the amount needed to pay the policy's costs, the more money is credited to the policy's savings element.

Suppose, for example, the ABC Insurance Company has established a $1,200 minimum initial annual premium for its universal life policies. Colleen and Jennifer MacRay are twin sisters and are both considered standard risks. Each woman purchases from ABC a $100,000 universal life policy on her own life. Colleen decides to pay a $3,000 initial annual premium, while Jennifer chooses to pay a $2,000 initial annual premium. Colleen will then have more money credited to her policy's savings element in the first year than Jennifer will have credited. In the second policy year, Jennifer increases her premium to $3,000, so that more money will be added to her policy's savings element. Colleen, on the other hand, decides to pay a $1,000 annual premium in the second year, resulting in a smaller amount being credited to her universal life insurance policy's savings element. Thus, while both sisters have $100,000 of life insurance protection, each is allowed to pay a different premium amount for her policy. Further, although both sisters are of the same age and risk classification, the amount of the mortality charge will not be the same for each sister's policy because the net amount at risk under the two policies is not the same.

Most universal life policies guarantee a minimum interest rate of 4 or 4½ percent on the money in the policy's savings element; that is, the insurance company guarantees that the money in this savings element will increase by at least 4 or 4½ percent each year. The interest rate actually paid, though, depends on the company's earnings. Normally, companies state that the interest rate paid on the savings element will reflect current interest rates in the economy. Some policies specify that the interest rate paid on this savings element will be tied to the rate paid on a standard investment, such as United States Government Treasury Bills. Often, only a portion of the money in the savings element – for example, only the amount over $1,000 – is credited with these higher interest rates, and amounts less than the minimum are credited with only the minimum rate guaranteed. In all cases, the interest rate paid will not fall below the rate guaranteed in the policy.

The money in a universal life insurance policy's savings element may be used as collateral for a policy loan in much the same way that the cash value of a whole life policy may be used. Alternatively, the money in the policy's savings element may also be withdrawn, rather than used as collateral for a policy loan. Any portion of a universal life policy's savings element which has been used as security for a policy loan will earn only the minimum rate of interest guaranteed in the policy.

A policyowner may increase or decrease the face amount of a universal life policy. Thus, as illustrated in Figure 4–2, a universal life policy's face amount need not remain constant. The insurer may, however, require evidence of the insured's continued good health before the policyowner can

FIGURE 4-2

The death benefit of a universal life policy may be changed by a policyowner

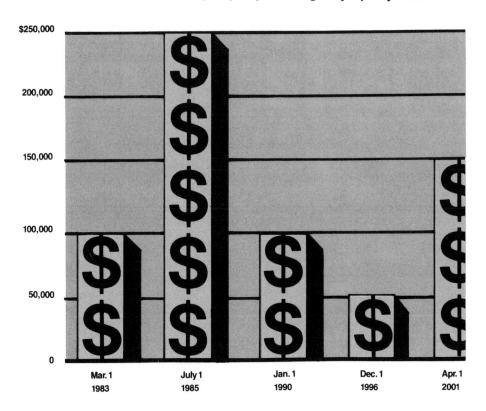

increase the policy's face amount. Such an increase will, of course, raise the net amount at risk under the policy and, hence, the mortality charge.

Insurance companies charge universal life policyowners various fees to cover the expenses involved in administering their policies. These expense charges are listed separately in each policy. Generally, these charges take three different forms:

1. a flat charge in the first policy year to cover sales and issue costs
2. a percentage of each premium payment, generally 7 to 10 percent
3. specific service charges for policy surrenders, cash withdrawals, and coverage changes

The nature and amount of these charges vary from company to company. At times, instead of a flat first-year charge, an insurer will impose penalties for policy cancellation. These penalties are generally highest in the early years of the policy and decrease steadily over time.

A policyowner can increase, decrease, or stop paying premiums on a universal life policy. Any increase in premium may be directed toward increasing the savings element, covering the cost of increased protection, or both. If a policyowner stops paying premiums or does not pay enough in premiums in a given period to cover the full mortality charges and expense costs associated with his or her policy, these costs will be deducted from the policy's savings element. If the savings element becomes depleted and no further premiums are paid, the policy will terminate. For example, suppose Colleen MacRay further decreased her annual premium payment to $200, and suppose that her policy's combined current mortality charge and expense costs are $900. The insurance company will use the money in her policy's savings element to pay the $700 difference. If the amount in her policy's savings element is less than $700 and Colleen does not pay an additional premium amount, her policy will terminate.

Since so many aspects of a universal life policy change over the course of a year, insurers send each policyowner an annual report giving the policy's current values and benefits. A sample universal life insurance policy annual report is shown in Figure 4–3. Generally, this report includes information about the

- current face amount of the policy
- current savings element in the policy
- cash surrender value of the policy
- interest earned on the savings element
- current protection (mortality) charges
- expense charges
- premiums paid for the policy
- loans outstanding
- savings element withdrawals
- projected savings and cash surrender values

FIGURE 4-3

A sample annual report for a universal life policy

ABC Life Insurance Company

Universal Life Policy
Summary of Policy Activity for Year Ending: October 11, 1983
Policy Number: 000-000-00   **Name of Insured:** Mary Doe

Mary Doe   Benefits: Shown Below
200 Spring Street
Anytown, Anystate 10000

Reserve As Of   October 11, 1982:   2,743.96

Month Ending	Premiums Received	Cost* of Protection	Other Charges	Amount Needed To Repay Loan	Interest Credited	Month End Savings Element	Basic Death Benefit
11/11/82	100.00	25.51	37.50	.00	19.70	2,800.65	75,000
12/11/82	.00	25.50	30.00	.00	20.24	2,765.39	75,000
01/11/83	200.00	25.50	45.00	1,005.62	14.87	2,909.76	75,000
02/11/83	100.00	25.48	37.50	1,012.66	15.39	2,962.17	75,000
03/11/83	100.00	25.47	37.50	2,025.70	10.68	3,009.88	75,000
04/11/83	100.00	25.46	37.50	2,039.67	10.86	3,057.78	75,000
05/11/83	100.00	25.45	37.50	2,053.64	11.03	3,105.86	75,000
06/11/83	.00	25.44	30.00	2,067.61	11.21	3,061.63	75,000
07/11/83	200.00	25.45	45.00	2,081.58	11.44	3,202.62	75,000
08/11/83	100.00	25.42	37.50	2,095.55	11.83	3,251.53	75,000
09/11/83	.00	25.97	.00	2,110.73	12.44	3,238.00	75,000
10/11/83	200.00	25.97	15.00	2,125.92	13.01	3,410.04	75,000
	1,200.00	306.62	390.00		162.70		

The first $1,000 of the Savings Element was credited with 4.50% guaranteed interest rate. The amount loaned was credited with 4.50%. The remaining amount of the savings element was credited with the current interest rate shown at the end of this statement.

*Includes mortality charge for base policy, and any rider or benefit shown above.

Please remember that the values illustrated in the above table would be reduced by the amount of your outstanding loan in the event of a claim.

In the event you surrender this policy during the current year, a surrender fee of $371.25 will be deducted, as provided by the policy.

Summary of Current Interest Rates for Year Ending   October 11, 1983

Month Ending	Effective Annual Current Interest Rate
11/11/82	12.00%
12/11/82	12.00%
01/11/83	12.00%
02/11/83	12.00%
03/11/83	12.00%
04/11/83	12.00%
05/11/83	11.50%
06/11/83	11.50%
07/11/83	11.50%
08/11/83	11.00%
09/11/83	11.00%
10/11/83	11.00%

Initially, universal life policies were offered only in large amounts, usually over $100,000, and minimum initial premium payments were often required to be as high as $1,000. However, many innovations have developed in the relatively short period these policies have been on the market, and further changes in their design and administration are expected.

Mortgage Redemption Insurance

A *mortgage redemption policy* is a form of decreasing term insurance which covers the life of a person who takes out a mortgage. As shown in Figure 4-4, the amount of the benefit decreases as the amount owed on the mortgage declines. The term of the policy depends on the length of the mortgage, usually 20 or 30 years, and premiums are generally level throughout the term. This type of insurance may be issued as a policy or as a rider to an existing policy.

FIGURE 4-4

The declining benefit amount of a mortgage redemption policy

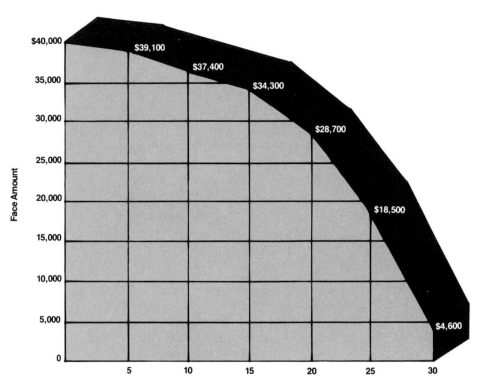

Years of Policy Duration (Term of Mortgage)

In most instances, the policy is independent of the mortgage– that is, the institution granting the mortgage is not a party to the insurance agreement–and the beneficiary is not required to use the proceeds of the policy to repay the mortgage. For example, suppose Bill Marley buys a mortgage redemption policy and names his wife, Allyson, as beneficiary. At Bill's death, Allyson may choose to return to school and use the policy proceeds to pay her college tuition costs, rather than the balance due on the mortgage. However, some institutions granting mortgages may require that the borrower obtain mortgage redemption insurance and require that the policyowner instruct the insurance company to pay the proceeds directly to the lending institution.

Credit Life Insurance

Credit life insurance, like mortgage redemption insurance, is a type of decreasing term insurance designed to pay the balance due on a loan should the borrower die. Unlike mortgage redemption insurance, the policy benefit is always paid directly to the creditor if the insured borrower dies during the policy's term. Generally, the loan must be of a type that is repaid in 10 years or less. Most financial institutions provide this type of coverage for their customers through a life insurance company. While credit life insurance is available on an individual insurance basis, most credit life insurance is sold to lending institutions as group insurance to cover the lives of the borrowers of that lender. Group credit life will be discussed more fully in chapter 13, "Group Life Insurance."

Credit life insurance is available for automobile loans, furniture loans, and other personal loans. In addition, many credit card holders are covered by credit life insurance for the amount they have charged. Credit life insurance guarantees the lender repayment of these outstanding debts if the insured borrower dies before the loan is repaid. Credit life insurance also protects the insured's estate from having to pay these outstanding debts.

The amount of the policy's benefit is usually equal to the amount of the debt. Premiums may be level over the duration of the loan or, in cases where the amount of the loan varies, may increase or decrease with the loan and corresponding benefit amount. These premiums may be paid by the lender, by the insured borrower, or by both.

Joint Life Insurance

Today a majority of households depend on more than one person's income for support. Also, businesses often depend on the continued services of more than one person. In recognition of these and other instances of shared financial responsibilities, life insurance companies issue policies which insure more than one person. The cost of purchasing a joint life insurance policy is less than the cost of purchasing two individual policies, partly because it is less expensive for an insurance company to administer one joint life insurance policy than two individual policies. The most common types of such policies are *joint whole life insurance, joint mortgage redemption insurance*, and *last survivor life insurance*.

Joint whole life insurance

A *joint whole life* policy has the same features and benefits as an individual whole life policy, except that it insures two lives under the same contract. Upon the death of the first person insured, the policy benefit is paid. The surviving insured is generally given the option to purchase an individual whole life policy for the same face amount within 60 to 90 days after the death of the first insured; the surviving insured does not have to provide evidence of insurability to make such a purchase. Often, the joint whole life policy provides temporary term insurance coverage for the surviving insured during the period when this option may be exercised. This type of contract is available for business as well as for personal uses.

Joint mortgage redemption insurance

A *joint mortgage redemption* policy provides the same benefit as an individual mortgage redemption policy except that it insures two people. This type of protection is appropriate when the income of two people is needed to meet mortgage payments. As under the joint whole life plan, the policy's benefit is paid when the first insured person dies. Unlike the joint whole life plan, however, the survivor is generally not given the option to purchase an individual policy of the same type, because the mortgage has, in theory, been repaid with the policy benefit and such coverage is no longer needed.

Last survivor life insurance

The *last survivor life* insurance policy is a type of joint whole life insurance designed primarily for married couples. In the United States, estate taxes* do not have to be paid on property left to a spouse. However, when the surviving spouse (second insured) dies, the estate taxes due can be quite high. If, for example, Bill Jones dies and his wife Bertha inherits his portion of their farm, Bertha would not be required to pay estate taxes. But when Bertha dies, her estate may have to pay considerable estate taxes before the farm may be passed to her heirs.

---

*Estate taxes are taxes on the money and property left by someone who has died.

The last survivor life insurance policy was designed to provide funds to pay these estate taxes. The policy insures both the husband and wife. Premiums are payable until the first insured dies. At that time, the policy benefit is *not* paid, but no more premium payments are due. The face amount of the policy is paid when the surviving spouse dies. In this way, funds are available when the estate tax bill becomes due.

Family Insurance

A ***family insurance*** policy covers all the members of a family under one contract. The usual family policy provides whole life insurance on the life of the family's primary breadwinner, and the premium rate for the family policy is based on that person's age and risk classification. The policy also provides insurance on the life of the primary insured's spouse and on the life of each child. The spouse's coverage may be whole life insurance, term insurance, or a combination of both; the children's insurance is nearly always term insurance.

The amount of insurance on the spouse and the children is a fraction, generally 1/4 or 1/5, of the amount of insurance on the life of the primary insured. For example, a family with three children might purchase a policy which would provide $50,000 of whole life insurance on the life of the primary insured, $12,500 of either term or whole life insurance on the life of the spouse, and $10,000 of term insurance on the life of each child. Thus, a total of $92,500 of life insurance would be provided by one family policy.

One premium rate is charged for coverage of the entire family under a family policy. For the purpose of premium calculation, the insurer assumes that the number and ages of children in families insured under such contracts will be a predictable average. Therefore, the same premium is charged for a family with one child as is charged for a family with six children. For this reason, it is not necessary to revise the premium for a family policy if additional children are born or adopted into the family after the policy is purchased. They are included automatically under the policy at no extra premium charge. The term insurance coverage on the life of each child generally expires when the child reaches an age specified in the contract but may be converted to an individual policy on the life of the child.

There are several additional benefits which are sometimes included in family policies. These include:

- the privilege to convert the term part of the contract to permanent insurance
- a feature which provides that the insurance on the dependents will become paid-up when the primary insured dies
- a decrease in the premium and/or an automatic increase in the amount of insurance on the primary insured if his or her spouse dies first

Juvenile Insurance

An individual insurance policy can be issued on the life of a child, even when the child is too young to purchase a life insurance policy. Life insurance companies issue insurance on such children when the application is made by the person who is legally responsible for the child, such as the child's parent or grandparent. These insurance policies, often referred to as *juvenile insurance policies*, usually include a provision which states that when the child reaches a certain age, he or she will be granted ownership and control of the policy.

While juvenile insurance may be issued on any plan offered by the insurer, the most commonly selected plans are limited-payment whole life policies, such as life-paid-up at age 65, or endowment insurance policies maturing at ages 16 to 18 (when the child may need the money for educational purposes). Term insurance is rarely made available for purchase on the life of a child. For many years the amount of insurance available on juveniles was limited to relatively small amounts, such as amounts less than $1,000. Today, however, if there are no legal limitations to the contrary, most companies will issue juvenile policies for larger amounts.

Some juvenile policies include a "waiver of premium for payor" benefit. To "waive" means to voluntarily give up a right. This feature provides that the insurer will waive payment of the policy's premiums if the adult policyowner, not the insured child, dies or becomes disabled. Additionally, many juvenile insurance policies include an automatically increasing policy benefit and/or a guaranteed insurability rider. (The guaranteed insurability rider will be described in detail later in this chapter.) These features are valuable because insurance is purchased on a child's life more often to establish an insurance program for the child at low rates than to provide a death benefit for the family in the event of the child's death.

Family Income Policies

The *family income policy* provides an income benefit which helps support a family after the death of a breadwinner for a specified period of time. The benefit period is determined when the policy is purchased and generally is scheduled to last either until the family's income needs are assumed to decline or until additional sources of support are found. This coverage is provided by combining decreasing term coverage, such as 10- or 20-year decreasing term, with a permanent policy.

The death benefit from the decreasing term insurance portion of the policy is paid in monthly income installments. However, the monthly benefit paid when an insured dies during the term of the policy continues only until the date that was specified when the policy was purchased. For example, if Arnold Aceelo buys a 15-year family income policy and dies 2 years later, the monthly income benefit would be paid for 13 years. If he dies 10 years after buying the policy, the monthly income benefit would be paid for 5 years. If he dies 20 years after purchasing the policy, no income benefit would be paid because the decreasing term insurance portion of the policy would have expired.

The death benefit from the permanent insurance portion of the policy is usually paid in a lump sum when the insured dies, although some family income policies state that the company will pay these proceeds to the beneficiary at the end of the installment period. Interest on these proceeds may either be added to the installment amount or paid with the proceeds at the end of the installment period.

Adjustable Life Insurance

Adjustable life insurance policies are designed to allow policyowners to vary their coverage as their needs change. The applicant usually specifies the face amount of the adjustable life policy *and* the premium amount he or she wishes to pay for the coverage. The insurance company then calculates the specific plan of insurance which can be provided based on the requested face amount and premium. This plan of insurance can range from a term insurance policy of short duration to a limited-payment whole life policy. Alternatively, the applicant may specify the face amount and plan of insurance desired, and the insurance company would then calculate the premium required.

As the policyowner's needs change, the policy's face amount and premium amount may be changed within specified limits. Any *increase in premium* or *decrease in face amount* will change the plan of insurance to either lengthen the term of the policy or shorten the premium payment period. Conversely, any *decrease in premium* or *increase in face amount* will either shorten the term of the policy or lengthen the premium payment period. Any adjustments, however, must result in a plan, premium, and face amount which fall within the minimums and maximums specified in the adjustable life policy. Increases in face amount must usually be accompanied by evidence of insurability, but changes in premium or plan do not require such evidence.

For example, assume a policyowner chooses an amount of premium and face amount that result in an adjustable life policy that functions as a 20-payment whole life policy. If, after the first policy year, the policyowner chooses to reduce the premium amount but still desires the same face amount of coverage, the policy would no longer function as a 20-payment whole life policy. Instead, it could resemble any of several other plans, depending on the new premium amount. For example, with a slight premium reduction, the policy could still function as a whole life policy, but it would have a premium payment period that was longer than 20 years. A more significant premium reduction might change the plan to one that resembles a term policy.

The adjustable life policy usually includes a provision that gives the policyowner the right to periodically increase the face amount of the adjustable life policy according to any increase in the Consumer Price Index (CPI). These face amount increases are subject to a stated maximum and do not require the insured to provide evidence of insurability.

Changes in an adjustable life policy do not require the insurer to issue a new policy, and the policyowner is not charged a separate service charge when such a change is requested. Hence, it is usually less expensive for a policyowner to change coverage under an adjustable life policy than to purchase a new policy to meet new needs. However, because of the high expenses an insurer incurs administering an adjustable life policy, the initial price of an adjustable life policy may be higher than the price of a comparable policy which does not have the flexibility of the adjustable life policy.

Non-guaranteed Premium Life Insurance

A **non-guaranteed premium life insurance policy**—also sometimes called a **flexible-** or **variable-premium policy**—is a whole life policy which specifies two premium rates. When the policy is purchased, the insurer guarantees that the premium rate will never exceed a stated maximum; generally this maximum premium rate is slightly higher than the rate for an equivalent nonparticipating whole life policy. A lower premium rate is actually paid when the contract is purchased. This lower premium rate is guaranteed for only a specified period of time, such as two or ten years from the date the policy was purchased. After that period, a new premium rate is set based on the insurer's projected experience. This new premium rate may be higher or lower than the premium the policyowner was charged when the policy was purchased, but in no case will the premium exceed the maximum rate guaranteed in the policy.

In all other respects, the non-guaranteed premium policy functions in the same manner as a nonparticipating whole life policy. It is designed to enable those companies issuing nonparticipating policies to be more flexible in their pricing, because these companies may change the premium rate to reflect changes in the mortality rate experienced, interest earned, and expenses incurred.

Indexed Life Insurance

An **indexed life insurance policy** is essentially an increasing-benefit whole life plan. The face amount of the policy and, correspondingly, the premium rate automatically increase every year based on an increase in the Consumer Price Index (CPI). For example, if the CPI rises 5 percent during a year, then the face amount of a $20,000 indexed life insurance policy would increase by 5 percent to $21,000. If the CPI decreases during a year, the policy benefit generally remains level. Such policies will often specify that the death benefit may be increased only to a stated maximum amount based on these increases in the CPI.

Using an indexed life insurance policy, a policyowner can rest assured that the life insurance coverage will not fall behind the inflation rate and fail to cover the needs it was purchased to meet. Since increases in coverage are accomplished by adjusting the policy benefit rather than by issuing a new policy, fewer expenses are incurred by the insurance company. Therefore, the premium rate charged for the increased coverage is lower than the premium rate that would be charged if a new policy were purchased.

Variable Life Insurance

A **variable life insurance policy** is similar to a whole life policy. A variable life policy remains in force during the insured's entire life, provided premium payments are made, and premiums for most forms of variable life policies sold in North America remain level throughout the lifetime of the insured.

The major difference between a variable life policy and a whole life policy is that the face amount and the cash value of a variable life policy depend on the investment performance of a special fund, often referred to as a "separate account." Most variable life policies guarantee that the face amount will not fall below a specified minimum. A minimum cash value is rarely guaranteed. Assets representing policy reserves of regular whole life policies are considered part of the company's *general account* and are placed in a varied line of secure investments; an insurer can then anticipate a steady rate of return on these assets. Assets representing the reserves for *variable* life insurance policies are placed in a *separate* investment account. The money in this **separate account** is placed in investments such as common stocks, and the values of the separate accounts increase or decrease, depending on the returns from the separate investments. Therefore, the face amount of insurance and the cash value of variable life insurance policies will depend on how well these special investments do. In some cases, the policyowner can select from among several separate accounts which have different investment strategies.

Purchasing this type of insurance, despite its minimum face amount guarantees, is riskier than purchasing a whole life policy. For example, if the stock market fails to perform well, the variable life insurance policy may not provide as high a face amount for a given premium as a whole life policy will provide. However, there is a potential for substantial gain when a variable life insurance policy is purchased, and there is some evidence to support the idea that over long periods of time the face amount of a variable life policy will keep pace with inflation.

When purchasing any life insurance product, a person should keep his or her needs and resources firmly in mind. The same life insurance policy may be an appropriate purchase for one individual and a sorely inadequate purchase for another. That is why it is important to plan an insurance program carefully. There must be enough insurance, at an affordable price, which will continue in force for as long as needed.

SUPPLEMENTARY BENEFIT RIDERS

The coverage under most life insurance policies may be expanded by adding supplementary benefit riders to them. In chapter 3 we mentioned that term insurance coverage may be provided either by a term insurance policy or by adding a term insurance rider to an existing policy. Policy riders benefit both the policyowner and the insurer because new contracts need not be drawn up to provide additional coverages – existing contracts can be adapted to the special needs of the policyowner. There are many additional benefits which, for an additional premium amount, can be provided by riders. We will not attempt to present all of the many riders that different companies include in life insurance policies. However, in addition to term insurance riders, there are three important benefit riders which are widely used throughout the life insurance industry: *guaranteed insurability*, *waiver of premium for disability*, and *accidental death benefit*.

Guaranteed Insurability Rider

The **guaranteed insurability** (GI) rider gives the policyowner the right to purchase additional insurance of the same type as the original policy on specified dates for specified amounts without supplying additional evidence of insurability. Normally, the rider states that the amount of coverage the policyowner may purchase on an option date is limited to the face amount provided under the original policy *or* an amount specified in the rider, whichever is smaller. For example, a guaranteed insurability rider may state either that the owner of a $10,000 whole life policy has the right to purchase additional $10,000 whole life insurance policies when the insured is 30, 35, and 40 years old, or the rider may permit such purchases on the third, sixth, and ninth policy anniversaries. It may also permit the purchase of additional insurance when certain events occur, such as marriage or the birth of a child.

The rider guarantees that the policyowner will be able to obtain increased coverage even though the insured may no longer be in good health. Also, many insurers provide a premium discount for insurance purchased on any of the option dates specified in the guaranteed insurability rider. The guaranteed insurability rider usually is available only with whole life and endowment policies.

While the right to purchase the extra insurance is automatic, the actual purchase is not; the policyowner who desires the extra insurance must take positive action to purchase the new coverage. If the policyowner does not exercise the option on one of the specified dates, that option is lost forever, though the policyowner can still exercise the next option when it comes due. Suppose, for example, that Barney Higgins purchased a whole life policy with a guaranteed insurability rider when he was 28 years old. The rider specified that he could purchase additional whole life policies for the same face amounts as his original policy when he is 30, 33, 35, and 40 years old. When Mr. Higgins is 30 years old, he decides not to purchase an additional policy, and, hence, that option is forfeited. However, when he is 33 years old, another option to purchase an additional policy is granted under his rider, and he may purchase a policy at that time.

Some guaranteed insurability riders provide automatic temporary term insurance coverage for the period during which the option to purchase can be exercised. This term insurance coverage usually lasts 60 to 90 days and is designed to protect the beneficiary in cases in which the policyowner is delayed in taking the necessary action.

Waiver of Premium for Disability

One of the most common riders available in nearly all types of life insurance contracts is the *waiver of premium for disability* (WP) benefit. For a very small additional premium, the insurance company will agree to waive a policy's premium payments for as long as the insured is totally disabled according to the definition of disability in the particular rider. These "waived" premiums are actually paid by the insurance company; hence, if the policy is one that builds cash values, these cash values will continue to increase just as if the premiums were paid by the policyowner.

There are some limitations to the use of this benefit. First, there is usually a waiting period between the time the disability begins and the commencement of the time during which premium payments will be waived. Thus, if the rider calls for a six-month waiting period, the policyowner must continue to pay any premiums due during the first six months of the insured's disability. Some, but not all, waiver of premium riders provide that if the insured is still disabled when the waiting period ends, then the waiver will be retroactive to the beginning of the disability and that the premiums paid during the waiting period will be refunded.

A second limitation is that the benefit is available only to cover disabilities which occur within a specified age span, for example, between the ages of 15 and 65. Since the WP rider is designed to pay premiums when the insured is unable to work, it is appropriate for the benefit to be in effect only during an insured's normal working years.

A third limitation included in most WP riders is that once the disability begins, the interval at which premium payments are due cannot be changed. This limitation prevents a policyowner from changing from an annual premium payment schedule to more frequent premium payments so that, should the disability last less than a year, some of the premiums would be waived.

Finally, some risks are excluded from coverage under the WP rider. For example, disabilities resulting from intentionally self-inflicted injuries or from any act of war while the insured is in military service are often excluded from coverage.

The policyowner must notify the company in writing of a claim for the waiver of premium benefit and must provide proof of disability in order to receive the benefit. The company reserves the right to require periodic submission of proof of continued disability.

The waiver of premium rider may be added to nearly all life insurance policies, including renewable and convertible term insurance policies. If a renewable term policy's premium is being waived on a renewal date, the policy generally is renewed automatically. Then the new, and higher, premium will continue to be waived until the person has recovered or until the date at which the policy is no longer renewable. Convertible term policies with premiums that are being waived at the end of the term can still be converted to a permanent plan of insurance, in accordance with the policy provision, but the waiver may or may not be included in the new policy. Some WP riders provide for automatic conversion of a convertible term insurance policy to some permanent plan and specify that the company will continue to waive premiums until the recovery or death of the person who is insured.

At times, the waiver of premium rider may be included in a policy which also includes the guaranteed insurability rider. If the insured is disabled according to the terms of the WP rider when an option to purchase additional insurance goes into effect, then the company will automatically issue the additional policy and waive premiums both for that new policy and for all other policies covered by the WP rider.

In all cases, the rider specifies that premiums will not be waived after the insured ceases to be disabled as defined in the policy.

Accidental Death Benefit

The ***accidental death benefit*** (ADB) rider provides an additional death benefit amount when the insured dies as the result of an accident. This additional sum is often equal to the policy's face amount. When the benefit is for an amount equal to the face amount of the policy, the benefit is often referred to as **double indemnity**. The additional sum may also be a multiple of the policy's face amount, such as three times the face amount, or it may be an amount unrelated to the policy's face amount.

In order for the additional benefit to be paid, the insured's death must be "accidental" as described in the rider. However, the term "death by accident" is not always as clear-cut as it appears. For example, if an insured with a history of heart problems dies in an auto accident, his or her death may have been caused by the accident itself. On the other hand, it is also possible that the insured may have died from a heart attack and then had the accident. Generally, in order for the accidental death benefit to be payable, the insured person's death must have been caused, directly and independently of all other causes, by an accidental bodily injury.

The accidental death benefit rider will often contain several exclusions and restrictions. The exclusions state that if the insured's death results from certain specified types of accidents, the company will not be required to pay the extra benefit. Commonly excluded accidents include the following:

- accidents caused by self-inflicted injuries – suicide
- war-related accidents
- accidents resulting from aviation activities if, during the flight, the insured acted in any capacity other than as a passenger
- accidents resulting from illegal activities

In addition, certain accidents resulting from causes which are related to possible health problems – such as the use of narcotics – are often excluded. In some jurisdictions, however, insurers are not permitted to include some of these exclusions in their accidental death benefit riders.

Another restriction included in many accidental death benefit riders concerns the time span between the death of the insured and the accident which caused that death. The time span specified in the ADB rider is usually stated as 90, 180, or 365 days. The insured's death must occur within that specified number of days after the accident in order for the additional benefit to be payable. In cases where the reason for death was obviously an accident, many companies will disregard the time limit they set, especially since in an increasing number of cases medical science has been able to prolong life functions almost indefinitely.

Keep in mind that these exclusions and limitations relate only to the additional benefits from the accidental death benefit rider. The basic benefit under the policy is not generally affected by the cause of an insured's death.

Most accidental death benefit riders expire when the insured is age 60 or 65, although some companies use age 70 as the cutoff point. The additional coverage ceases at this prestated age, and the premium for the policy is reduced by the amount required for the rider.

Dismemberment benefits

An accidental death benefit rider may also provide for additional benefits for dismemberment, in which case the rider is called an **accidental death and dismemberment** (AD&D) rider. These riders generally specify that the accidental death benefit amount will also be paid if the insured loses any two limbs or the sight in both eyes. In many cases, the rider specifies that a smaller amount, such as half the accidental death benefit amount, will be payable if the insured loses one limb or the use of one eye. The loss of a limb may be defined as the actual physical loss of the limb or as the loss of the use of the limb.

An AD&D rider specifies that the insurer will not pay both accidental death benefits and dismemberment benefits for injuries suffered in the same accident. While dismemberment benefits are often included in life insurance policies, this form of protection is not strictly life insurance. Consequently, many companies offer accidental death benefits without providing coverage for dismemberment.

The plan variations and supplementary benefits insurers have developed are numerous. As economic conditions and lifestyles change, insurers will develop new special policies and benefits to meet these changing needs. All such products will continue to have the same purpose – meeting the needs people have for economic protection in case of loss.

Meeting Needs
for Life Insurance

Life insurance is one means of meeting the need most people have for financial security. Although the basic need for financial security is common to most people, specific needs of individuals are different, and, for most people, needs change over time. This chapter will examine the most common personal and business needs for life insurance, as well as the principal marketing methods that insurers have developed to help people identify and satisfy these needs.

NEEDS MET BY LIFE INSURANCE

Term, endowment, and whole life insurance plans – and all variations and combinations of these plans – provide a monetary benefit if the insured person dies. In addition, some policies provide cash benefits while the insured is still alive. The needs for these benefits are as numerous as the needs for any other sum of money. We will discuss the needs met by life insurance products with respect to both *personal* and *business needs*.

Personal Needs

Personal needs met by life insurance encompass a very wide range. Some of the most common are the needs for funds to provide for final expenses, dependents' support, educational funds, and retirement income.

Final expenses

When any person dies, there are certain bills which may become due immediately. These bills include debts, such as personal loans, charge accounts, car loans, etc. In addition, there are the expenses related to the death itself, such as doctors' and hospital bills, funeral expenses, and, in some cases, estate taxes. Many of these bills would exist whether or not the deceased worked and/or had any dependents. A lump-sum life insurance death benefit designed to pay outstanding debts and final expenses is often called a *clean-up fund*.

Dependents' support

One of the major selling points for life insurance is that people have a need to provide for their dependents. The first organization to offer life insurance in North America issued policies for the relief of widows and children of Presbyterian ministers. The situation is similar today—the principal need for life insurance is to provide financial support for dependents when a breadwinner dies. Depending on individual circumstances, this financial support may be needed for a short or long period of time.

Short-term income needs. If the person who died supported or helped to support a family, the family may face serious problems in the months immediately following the person's death. Household expenses go on. Rent or mortgage payments must still be made, utility bills paid, food and clothing purchased—all while family members try to cope with the emotional effects of the death. Relatively few people have sufficient funds to pay their usual expenses for several months if the family income ceases or is substantially reduced. Even if another member of the family is able to go to work, it may take time for that person to find suitable employment or to get the training needed to begin a career. Insurance can provide funds to support the family until new methods of household support are obtained or until the family members adjust to a lower standard of living.

Long-term income needs. Dependents of the deceased insured will require a continuing source of income. In some cases, a spouse or other dependent may be able to assume the role of sole breadwinner and provide adequate support for the family. In most households today, however, both spouses are already employed and both incomes are needed to pay the usual family bills. The loss of either income often results in a substantial reduction in the family's standard of living. The proceeds of a life insurance policy may be used to supplement the family's income. In a family in which surviving dependents are not able to work outside the home, it may be necessary to provide a continuing income from sources other than employment. The proceeds of a life insurance policy may be needed to provide such an income.

Educational funds

One of the prime objectives of many parents is to be financially able to send their children to a university or college. Because the death of a working father or mother could mean that college tuition would be beyond the family's reduced resources, parents often purchase life insurance to help assure that educational funds will be available.

Parents can also use an insurance policy to provide educational funds, even if the parents are alive during the child's college years. At one time, endowment insurance policies were used to accumulate these funds. Today, little endowment insurance is sold at all, and policyowners are more likely to use the cash values in other life insurance policies to pay the cost of their children's tuition.

Retirement income

A policyowner who is approaching retirement and whose need for life insurance has diminished can use the funds which have accumulated in a cash value life insurance policy to purchase an annuity. Many life insurance policies which accumulate cash values include this option and list guaranteed annuity benefits in the contract. For such a policyowner, the policy will have served the original purpose of providing insurance protection when it was needed, and it is now able to provide another benefit – retirement income. An annuity will guarantee a series of payments – usually on a monthly or annual basis – either for a limited period of time or for life.

Some people purchase endowment policies and use the matured endowment benefit to purchase an annuity, which provides retirement income. The right of the policyowner to use the matured endowment benefits to purchase an annuity is often stated in the endowment policy. Of course, the accumulated cash value of the endowment or matured endowment benefits may also be used by the policyowner to meet other retirement needs, such as paying off a mortgage or buying a retirement residence.

Other personal uses for policy proceeds

The proceeds of a life insurance policy may also be donated to a church, a charity, or an educational institution. For example, a person may designate an animal shelter as the beneficiary of his or her policy, or the proceeds may be left to a college with instructions to begin a scholarship fund. Some people even list a local educational television station as a beneficiary.

Life insurance policies that accumulate cash values can also be used as a savings or investment medium. While the interest earnings on a policy's cash value may be lower than earnings available through other investments, there are advantages to investing in cash value life insurance. A person cannot lose his or her initial investment; money placed in an insurance policy is safe. Also, the rate of interest earned on a policy's cash accumulation usually is guaranteed. Finally, there are tax advantages to the policyowner concerning the interest earned on money placed in an insurance policy. These tax advantages serve to increase the actual earnings on these funds, since such earnings are not reduced by taxation in most cases.

Business Needs

Business needs for individual life insurance policies may exist almost anytime there is a business relationship. Such relationships may be as simple as those between an employer and employee. The relationship may also be complicated – for example, the relationship between members of a partnership in which each member makes an essential contribution to the firm. A firm may purchase life insurance products which will help protect against financial loss if the death of an interested party should occur. A business firm may also purchase life insurance as an employee benefit.

Insurance on key persons

Many businesses, both large and small, are dependent on the continued participation of certain valuable associates or employees. An organization has an insurable interest in the lives of these key persons, since the organization stands to lose financially if one of them dies prematurely. The loss of such a person's expertise and services may seriously affect the firm's earnings. For example, a great scientist, a top salesperson, or a person with important business contacts may be responsible for a large portion of a firm's earnings. In addition to the potential loss of such a person's services, a firm must also consider the cost of training or finding a replacement for that person if he or she dies. Hence, firms may purchase life insurance policies on the lives of these key persons both to cover the firm's loss of earnings and to provide funds to find a replacement for the deceased associate. Such insurance policies are often referred to as "key-person" or "key-man" policies.

Insurance on business owners

Businesses organized as sole proprietorships – those businesses which are owned and run by one person – or as partnerships – those businesses which are owned and run by two or more people – also need life insurance protection for their owners.

When the sole proprietor of a business dies, the heirs of the proprietor who depended on the business for their income may lack the maturity, inclination, or expertise to continue operation of the business. Insurance on the life of the owner may provide funds to carry on business operations or to provide time for the heirs to dispose of the business in an orderly fashion, avoiding a distress sale.

Life insurance may also be used to help solve the financial problems that can result when a member of a partnership dies. The death of a partner legally dissolves a partnership, and the deceased partner's heirs are entitled to receive that partner's share of the firm's assets. The remaining partners in the firm may be forced to sell some of the firm's assets to pay the heirs of the deceased their share, if funds have not been specifically provided for this purpose. To avoid this potential problem, the firm can purchase insurance on the life of each partner so that the death benefit will provide enough funds for surviving partners to buy from the heirs the deceased partner's interest in the firm. Members of a partnership often form agreements, called **buy-sell agreements**, which stipulate that the partners must purchase a deceased partner's interest in the firm and that the partners' heirs must accept a preset sum from the surviving partners as compensation for the deceased partner's interest in the business.

Employee benefits

Individual life insurance can be used to provide a form of employee benefit for selected classes of employees. One such employee benefit provided through individual life insurance is a **deferred compensation plan** in which an employer establishes a plan to provide benefits to the employee at a later date, such as after the employee's retirement. Establishment of a deferred compensation plan can provide tax advantages for the employer and/or the employee.

Insurance products are often used by business firms to provide benefits for all employees of the firm. Group insurance, both life and health, is the principal line of insurance which is used in this manner; we will discuss group insurance in detail later in the text.

MARKETING THE PRODUCT

There are many personal and business needs for life insurance in addition to the ones just discussed, and the need for insurance products is not limited to any single age group or sex (see Figure 5-1). When a person buys a life insurance policy, he or she is essentially buying a source of funds to meet future financial needs. Most people recognize that these needs are important, but they are reluctant to seek life insurance products to meet these needs. For this reason, the insurance industry has developed several approaches for marketing insurance products to the public.

In its broadest sense, **marketing** refers to the complete function of determining consumer needs, designing products and services to meet those

FIGURE 5-1
Analysis of ordinary life insurance purchases

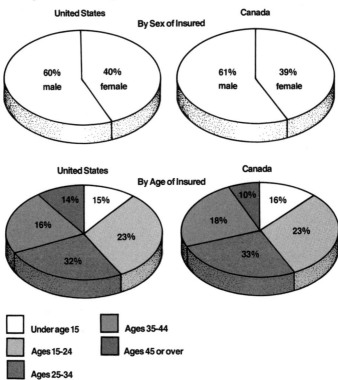

needs, and establishing methods of promoting and distributing those products and services to the public. Since we have already discussed the needs met by life insurance as well as the products insurance companies have developed to meet those needs, we will concentrate in this section on the promotion and distribution aspects of marketing insurance products.

Promotion of Life Insurance

Generally, life insurance must be actively promoted. People will go to a bank to deposit money, a grocery store to buy food, a department store to buy clothes; but they will not often contact an insurer to buy life insurance.

There are many reasons for a person's reluctance to seek life insurance. One reason lies in the nature of the risk to be insured. Most people find the thought of death – especially their own – disturbing. Such feelings can cause a psychological block to discussions regarding the purchase of life insurance. Furthermore, most healthy people do not believe that they will die in the immediate future; hence, the need for financial protection does not appear so immediately pressing to them as does the need to satisfy a desire to purchase a new car, a stereo system, or a vacation trip. It often seems convenient to these people to defer the purchase of financial protection when there are so many other needs and wants competing for their attention and dollars. Finally, life insurance is an intangible product, and this lack of physical substance can contribute to some consumers' reluctance to seek life insurance.

Insurance companies must overcome this problem of consumer reluctance in order to sell life insurance products. For this reason, insurance companies actively promote life insurance and have done so through advertising and public education as well as through the agency system.

Advertising and public education

To counter consumers' reluctance to purchase insurance, the insurance industry uses advertisements and public education programs to alert the public to the need for insurance products. Advertisements are primarily intended to promote a specific company or one of its products. Company logos and/or slogans are featured prominently in these ads. The ads also serve to remind the public of its need to prepare financially for retirement and death.

The insurance industry has also developed numerous public education programs over the years. Earlier programs consisted of what is often called *institutional advertising*—advertising which promotes an "institution," in this case life insurance, without attempting to promote the immediate sale of a specific product. Some of this advertising was done by individual life insurance companies and some by organizations comprised of many insurers. One such institutional advertising campaign was conducted by a single company and consisted of a series of informational essays about various illnesses and their effects on mortality. (See Figure 5-2.) This series, which ran from the 1920s through the 1940s, was lauded both for its service to the public and for its daring to speak publicly about certain health subjects that are not usually discussed. It also gave great impetus to that insurance company's sales, an impetus which spilled over to other insurers.

Today, public education, including institutional advertising, is conducted through all communications media. Films and video tapes which tell the public about life insurance and the life insurance industry are available. Information about new products and about the insurers which sell them appears frequently in newspapers and magazines. Brochures and leaflets which explain the products of the industry in simple terms are available from insurance companies and allied insurance organizations. Finally, an enormous quantity of text material has made it possible for life insurance and its allied subjects to be studied at all educational levels.

FIGURE 5-2
Early Institutional Advertising

The Anemia Mystery

It may be the beginning of one of Nature's mysteries which can be solved only by the painstaking investigation of a physician.

When, without apparent reason, someone you care for — young or old — complains of feeling tired or exhausted and begins to lose color, becoming paler and weaker as the days go by, you may have good cause to suspect some form of anemia.

The anemic person lacks good red blood.

Sometimes anemia is a symptom of a condition which is unknown or neglected by the sufferer and which may be either slight or serious. A frequent, though small, loss of blood, a wasting disease, or infections in the body may produce anemia. If, however, the cause is diligently searched for — and can be removed or corrected — the anemia will usually disappear under proper treatment.

Anemia may also be caused by a lack in the diet of certain food elements necessary for normal blood formation — especially when there are associated functional defects (often symptomless) of the stomach and intestines. A correct diet alone sometimes conquers such anemia. But proper treatment with an appropriate quantity and quality of iron is often of fundamental importance in producing a sufficient amount of blood coloring matter.

People may also become anemic because they are unable to utilize from an adequate diet the food material necessary to make red corpuscles. This may be dependent upon a deficiency in the function of the digestive organs. The most common type of such anemia is called by doctors Pernicious Anemia. Until recently it was always fatal. In 1926, however, an incredibly simple remedy was found — liver.

Pernicious Anemia can now be kept under control by the regular use of liver or an effective substitute PROVIDED A PROPER AMOUNT IS PRESCRIBED FROM TIME TO TIME FOR EACH INDIVIDUAL CASE. But — liver or potent substitutes are not a panacea for all forms of anemia. Although they save lives in cases of pernicious and allied anemia, they are frequently ineffective in treating ordinary forms of the condition.

If there is an anemia mystery in your family, don't guess about it. Ask your doctor to find the solution.

ABC Life Insurance Company

Life Insurance Distribution Systems

Agents

Since the early 1900s, life insurance companies have used sales agents to promote and distribute life insurance. Stories and jokes about early life insurance agents abound, and in some cases, unfortunately, these stories are not without foundation. Early life insurance agents were strictly sellers, and the order of the day was often "sell by any means." However outmoded these methods may seem today, they did produce results: life insurance was bought, companies developed, and families were protected.

The agency system has changed dramatically over the years, and the stereotypical "foot-in-the-door" agent is no longer representative of the life insurance sales force. Today's agents must be professionals, capable of providing a complex array of financial services to a demanding clientele. Life insurance agents must be well educated in taxation, economics, law, and other business subjects. To prepare agents to deal competently and professionally with their clients, both the industry as a whole and individual companies provide educational and training courses in these business areas, as well as courses in the techniques of selling. Several agents' organizations also provide education and establish professional standards for their members. With such a background, agents can advise their clients on the life insurance products and other financial products available to meet their specific needs.

The sales process. The first step in the life insurance sales procedure is the identification of potential customers for life insurance. This step is called ***prospecting***. A good prospect is a person who has a need for insurance, is able to pay, is insurable, and is approachable. The second step is for the agent to make contact with the prospect, generally either by letter or by telephone, or both. If the prospect agrees to a meeting, the agent makes a sales call, often at the home or office of the prospect.

An agent often will sit down with the prospect and do some form of ***needs analysis***. This needs analysis determines how much money a person would require to take care of the person's financial obligations should he or she die. The agent will then help the person determine how much of that money is already available through social security benefits, group life insurance, and personal assets. The difference between the amount of money needed and the amount which will be available when the person dies is then calculated. The agent and the prospect can then determine the best methods of providing the difference between the resources available and the amount needed.

In addition, the agent and the client may discuss the client's "living needs" and decide whether a life insurance policy which accumulates cash value would meet those needs.

Agency relationship. The life insurance sales agent may either work directly for an insurance company or be employed by a sales agency authorized to do business for an insurance company. The agent may be called a *sales agent*, a *life* or *field underwriter*, a *sales representative*, a *soliciting agent*, or an *insurance agent*.

The right of the sales representative to transact business for the insurer means that legally an *agency relationship* has been established. In law, *agency* is a relationship between two parties by which one party, usually called an *agent*, is authorized to perform certain acts for the other party, usually called the *principal*. Because of this authorization, the actions and knowledge of the agent have the same force in law as though they were the actions and knowledge of the principal. With respect to a sales representative in the life insurance business, the sales representative is the agent, and the insurance company is the principal.

The agency relationship gives the life insurance agent the legal right to act for the insurer for such purposes as are specified in the agent's contract with the insurance company. The usual powers granted are the right to act for the principal in soliciting applications for life insurance and the right to accept the initial premium, but not renewal premiums, for a life insurance policy. (Home service agents are granted the additional power to accept renewal premiums.) Unlike agents for property and liability insurance companies, life insurance agents seldom have the right to legally bind the company to an insurance contract.

If an agent acts within the scope of granted authority:

- The agent's actions are legally considered to be the actions of the insurance company, and
- The agent's knowledge relating to information about an applicant or application is considered to be the knowledge of the company.

Therefore, if an agent were to act in a way which was not in the best interest of the principal, problems could arise. For example, if an agent instructed an applicant to fill out the application incorrectly, such action could be considered as "permission" granted by the insurance company. Legally, then, the company could not contest, or dispute, a claim on the basis of the incorrect application, unless it could prove there was an improper agreement between the agent and the applicant to defraud the company. Furthermore, if the applicant were to give the agent information, a court might hold that such information had been communicated to the company, even if the agent withheld such information from the company. From the two examples given above, it should be apparent that many legal problems can arise out of an improper use of this agency relationship.

Licensing life insurance agents. Governmental authorities are also concerned that agents be able to do their jobs properly. Therefore, all states and provinces require that life insurance agents be licensed. To obtain a license other than a temporary license, agents must usually pass an examination on life insurance. This license authorizes the agent to sell insurance in a particular jurisdiction. In addition, many jurisdictions require that agents continue to study life insurance and allied subjects, such as finance, in order to keep their licenses in force.

Alternative distribution systems

The great majority of individual life insurance policies are sold through the agency system. However, life insurance is also promoted and delivered in other ways. Some companies solicit and sell life insurance by mail, or through newspaper or television advertisements. This approach to sales is called **direct response marketing**, and policies sold through this method are usually for small or moderate amounts of insurance which do not require the detailed evidence of insurability generally needed for larger policies. Some policies sold through direct response marketing limit the death benefit payable if death occurs in the first few policy years. These restrictions protect the insurer from antiselection. Generally, such policies do not have as many optional coverages as policies sold through an agent. Policies marketed through direct response marketing must, however, comply with all the legal requirements of the jurisdictions where they are sold.

In three states – New York, Massachusetts, and Connecticut – life insurance policies may be purchased directly from savings banks, and these policies are referred to as **savings bank life insurance** (SBLI). The amount of SBLI that may be purchased by any one person is strictly limited by law to relatively low amounts, and only people who live or work in one of these three states are eligible to purchase savings bank life insurance. In addition, SBLI is available on only a few plans of insurance.

Some life insurance companies work through various organizations, such as clubs and associations, to sell insurance to the members of these organizations. This approach is called the **third-party endorsement** method. Sometimes the organization is the owner of a group insurance policy, and the individual members pay the premiums. In other cases, the insurer sells individual policies to the members who want the coverage.

Additionally, life insurance may be purchased in some department stores, at airports, in shopping malls, and, recently, from certain grocery stores. In these instances, consumers initiate the contact with the life insurance company in much the same way they would buy any other consumer item. While most individual life insurance is still purchased through the agency system, these alternate methods of marketing are accounting for an increasing number of sales.

6

The Policy Contract Is Issued

In the last chapter, we discussed the needs people have which can be met with life insurance and the methods used by the life insurance industry to match consumers with the appropriate insurance coverage. However, before a consumer and an insurer may enter into an agreement concerning this coverage, each must meet certain requirements.

A life insurance policy is a legal contract. As such, a life insurance policy is subject to the principles of contract law, although in many instances contract law has been substantially modified with regard to life insurance contracts. This chapter will identify various types of contracts and discuss how the general principles of contract law have been applied to life insurance policies.

In addition, we will examine both the requirements set by an insurance company which must be met before the insurer will issue a policy to a specific applicant and the process by which people become insured. We will describe the process that takes place from the time the initial application is completed, signed, and sent to the insurance company, to the time that the policy is delivered to the policyowner.

CONTRACTS

A *contract* is a legally binding agreement between two or more parties. The agreement involves a promise or a set of promises to perform one or more acts; the promise or promises may be made by only one of the parties to the contract, or by all the parties involved.

Types of Contracts

In chapter 1, we described valued contracts and contracts of indemnity and noted that the life insurance contract is a valued contract. Contracts may be described in several other ways, depending on the actual form of the contract, the types of promises made in the contract, and the nature of the relationship between the parties to the contract. In order to understand how a life insurance policy functions as a contract, we will discuss each of the following pairs of terms which are used to categorize and describe contracts:

- formal contracts – informal contracts
- bilateral contracts – unilateral contracts
- commutative contracts – aleatory contracts
- bargaining contracts – contracts of adhesion

We will determine which descriptive term in each pair applies to a life insurance contract and why that term is appropriate.

Formal contracts and informal contracts

Contracts are either formal or informal. A contract is called **formal** if it is legally binding because of its form. Formal contracts must meet special requirements, such as having been written and/or endorsed in a specific way, or issued with a legal seal attached. Certain bonds and property deeds are examples of formal contracts. A life insurance contract is *not* a formal contract.

A life insurance contract (policy) is an informal contract. A contract is called **informal** if its enforceability does not depend on the form in which it is written, but rather on whether it meets certain prerequisites which give rise to an enforceable contract. These prerequisites relate to the nature of the contract and the qualifications of the parties to the contract and will be discussed fully in the next section of this chapter.

An informal contract may be expressed in either an oral or a written fashion. Writing down an agreement is merely evidence of the contract and is not always necessary; an oral agreement or contract may be legally binding under certain circumstances. For example, suppose you were to agree to pay Kate Chastain $5 to mow your lawn on Saturday. When she finishes mowing on Saturday, you become legally obligated to pay her the $5. This would be true whether or not you wrote down the agreement. If the agreement was not in writing, you would have made an oral contract.

In theory, as an informal contract, a life insurance contract could be made in either written or oral form. However, a life insurance contract must be in written form for several practical reasons. While the laws of most jurisdictions do not specifically require that the life insurance policy be in writing, the laws of most jurisdictions do refer to such topics as the size and color of the print used in life insurance policies, as well as other topics which imply that the policy is a written document. A second reason that the policy must be in writing is that a policy must contain a large number of provisions. These provisions set forth the conditions of the contract and enable the company to carry out the wishes of the policyowner. If the contract is not in writing, legal problems may arise as a result of disputes among the parties as to the terms of the agreement. A third reason the life insurance contract should be in writing is that a life insurance policy is often in effect for many decades. It would be difficult, if not impossible, to rely on someone's memory of oral promises made 50 or more years in the past. Thus, a life insurance contract is always in written form.

Bilateral and unilateral contracts

A contract between two parties may be either unilateral or bilateral. Stated more simply, the contracts may be called either one-sided or two-sided. If both parties can be compelled, under law, to perform what they have promised in a contract, the contract is **bilateral**; if only one of the parties can be compelled by law to perform, the contract is **unilateral**.

Suppose, for example, you contracted with the Jim Juniper Construction Company to have the company erect a building for a mutually agreed-upon fair price. The builder has promised to complete the construction for that price, and you have promised to pay that amount. This contract is bilateral—both you and the construction company have made legally enforceable promises.

A life insurance policy is, however, a unilateral contract. The insurer promises to provide insurance in return for a price or premium. The policyowner, on the other hand, does *not* promise to pay the premiums and cannot be compelled by law to pay premiums. A policyowner may at any time cease premium payments. If the premium is not paid, the insurer will no longer be bound to its promises. However, if the premium is paid, the insurer is legally bound by its promises. Hence, since only the insurer can be legally held to its promises, the life insurance contract is unilateral.

Commutative and aleatory contracts

Contracts may also be classified as either commutative or aleatory. A **commutative** contract is an agreement under which each party specifies in advance the values which will be exchanged; thus, each party generally exchanges items of equal value. The contract with the builder which was just discussed is an example of a commutative contract. When the contract was made, both parties specified the service or item to be exchanged, and each party received items judged by them to be of similar value under the terms of the contract. Most contracts fall into this "like for like" category and are classified as commutative.

In an **aleatory** contract, one party provides something of value to another party in exchange for a promise that the other party will perform a stated act *if* a specified, uncertain event occurs. If the event occurs, then the promise must be performed; if the event does not occur, the promise will not be performed. Thus, under an aleatory contract, if the event occurs, then one party may receive something of greater value than that party gave.

A life insurance policy is an aleatory contract, since the performance of the insurer's promise to pay the policy proceeds is contingent on an uncertain event, the death of the insured. No one can say with certainty when the person whose life is insured will die. In fact, if a policy is allowed to terminate prior to the death of the insured, the promise will never be performed, even if a number of premiums have been paid. Conversely, death may occur soon after a life insurance policy is issued, and the face value then becomes payable. The beneficiary would, in such a case, receive substantially more than had been paid in premiums.

FIGURE 6-1
The life insurance contract

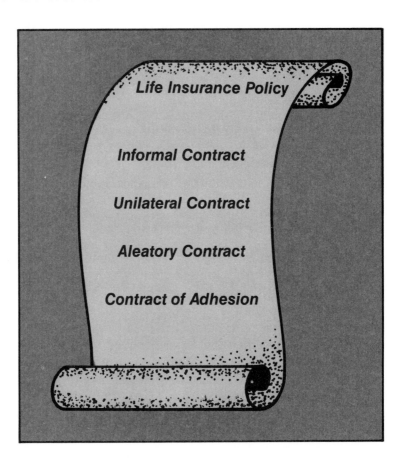

Bargaining contracts and contracts of adhesion

Contracts may be further classified as either bargaining contracts or contracts of adhesion. Suppose that when you made your contract with Jim Juniper, the builder, you had several discussions about the contents of the contract. You asked him to specify his time schedule, the materials he would use, and the way the actual construction would be accomplished. In turn, he quoted a price for each of your requirements. Suppose you then bargained with one another until you arrived at a contract agreeable to both of you. This is an example of a **bargaining contract**, one in which both parties, as equals, set the terms and conditions of the contract.

Life insurance policies are not bargaining contracts. Rather, a life insurance policy is a **contract of adhesion** – a contract which is prepared by one party and must be accepted or rejected as a whole by the other party. While the applicant has choices as to some of the contract provisions, generally the contract must be accepted or rejected as written by the life insurance company. Because a life insurance policy is a contract of adhesion and the policyowner is not permitted to participate in the setting of the terms and the writing of the contract, any portions of the policy which are not clear in intent are usually interpreted by the courts in whatever manner would be most favorable to the policyowner or beneficiary.

General Requirements for a Contract

The principles of contract law determine the legal status of a contract; that is, they dictate whether an agreement is a contract which is both legally binding on the parties involved and enforceable in the courts. In describing the legal status of a contract, the words *valid, void,* and *voidable* are often used. Each of these terms is explained below:

- **Valid** – A valid contract is one which is enforceable at law.
- **Void** – The term "void" is used in law to describe something which never had validity. The usual term used is *void ab initio* which means "void from the start." A void contract is one which never was enforceable at law.
- **Voidable** – At times, there may be legal grounds for one of the parties to an otherwise enforceable contract to reject, or *avoid*, it. Such a contract is said to be voidable.

Four general requirements must be present for an informal contract to be binding on all parties. These requirements are as follows:

1. There must be a manifestation of **mutual assent** to the terms of the contract by each of the parties to the contract.
2. The parties to the contract must have the **legal capacity** to make a contract.

3. The parties to the contract must exchange **legal consideration**.
4. The contract must be for a **lawful purpose**.

These requirements must be met in the case of a life insurance policy, since it is an informal contract.

Mutual assent

Whether a contract is made by several parties signing a formal printed agreement or two parties shaking hands, the parties involved have agreed to something. This is the basis of the legal requirement of mutual assent. Mutual assent presumes that one party has made an offer and that the other party has accepted that offer. If there is not a manifestation of mutual assent by the parties to the promises and terms of the agreement, no legally enforceable contract can exist. **Manifestation of assent** means that it would appear to any reasonable person that there was agreement between the parties involved.

In the case of life insurance policies, as well as other contracts, the requirement of mutual assent is met by the existence of the process of **offer and acceptance**. However, in life insurance there are several variables which must be considered in determining who is the **offeror** – the one who has actually made the offer – and who is the **offeree** – the one to whom the offer has been made. This question of offer and acceptance in the making of a life insurance contract will be considered later in this chapter when we discuss the application which is filled out by a person who wishes to purchase life insurance.

Legal capacity

In order for a contract to be binding on all parties, the parties must have the legal capacity to make a contract. This requirement, when applied to insurance contracts, means that the insurance company must have the legal capacity to issue the policy and that the applicant must have the legal capacity to purchase the policy.

An insurer acquires its legal capacity to make a contract by being licensed or authorized to do business by the proper regulating authorities. A company which is not licensed or authorized as an insurance company does not have the legal capacity to make an insurance contract. Should an unauthorized insurer issue a policy to a person who is unaware of the insurer's lack of legal capacity, the policy is enforceable to protect the person who owns the policy. Thus, such a policy is voidable only by the policyowner.

Any individual usually has the legal capacity to enter into a contract as long as he or she is *of legal age* and *mentally competent*. Any person who has not attained legal age or who does not possess mental competence may not enter into any contract *except* a contract which provides for funds to cover the reasonable cost of necessaries. **Necessaries** are items needed to sustain well-being, such as food, housing, and clothing. A contract for necessaries is valid even if one of the parties does not have the legal capacity to contract. Life insurance policies have not been considered necessaries by the courts.

Legal age to contract. Except for contracts for necessaries and unless there are laws to the contrary, contracts made by a minor are voidable only at the option of the minor. A **minor** is a person who has not attained the legal age to make a contract. The legal age to make a contract is called the **age of majority**. While the age of majority is 18 in most states in the United States, the age of majority for the purpose of making life insurance contracts has been modified by law in most jurisdictions. Statutes in a number of states enable minors at ages 16, 15, or even 14 to purchase life insurance and to exercise some of the policy's ownership rights. The laws of these states generally require that the beneficiary of such a policy be a member of the minor's immediate family. The revised Uniform Life Insurance Act, which applies to all Canadian provinces except Quebec, modifies the age of majority, which is 19 in those provinces, so that minors who have attained the age of 16 have the right to enter into life insurance contracts as adults. Quebec laws do not vary the age of majority, which is 18, for the purpose of making life insurance contracts.

Laws altering the age of majority for the purpose of entering into life insurance contracts protect insurance companies from the possibility that minors will later use their lack of legal capacity to avoid the contract. If a life insurance company were to sell an insurance policy to a person who legally *is* considered a minor, the company would have to uphold its end of the contract. However, the minor could sue to avoid the policy, and the insurance company would have to return the premiums paid on that policy, although it had provided insurance protection for the period during which the policy was in force.

Mental competence. If a contract is made by a person who was mentally incompetent at the time of contracting, but who either (1) had not been declared legally incompetent by a court, *or* (2) had been legally declared incompetent by a court but had no court-appointed guardian at the time of contracting, then the contract is *voidable* by that person. If the person later regains mental competence in the eyes of the courts, he or she may either reject the contract *or* require that it be carried out. The other party to the contract does not have the right to reject the contract and must carry out its terms if required to do so. However, if a contract is made by a person who (1) has been declared legally incompetent *and* (2) has a court-appointed legal guardian, then the contract is void from the start.

Consideration

The parties to an informal contract legally must exchange consideration; that is, each must give or promise something which will be of value to the other party.

The application and the initial premium are given by the policyowner as legal consideration for the life insurance contract. This consideration is in return for the promise on the part of the insurer to pay the benefit if the insured should die while the policy is in force. If the initial premium is not paid, then a valid contract has not been formed between the applicant and the insurance company, because the applicant would not have provided the required consideration. **Renewal premiums**, which are premiums payable after the initial premium, are a condition for continuance of the policy contract and are *not* consideration for the policy.

Lawful purpose

No contract can be made for a purpose which is illegal or against the public interest – a contract must be made for a lawful purpose. The courts will not enforce an agreement in which one person promises to perform an illegal act. For example, unless there are statutes to the contrary, gambling "contracts" will not be enforceable at law. Also, one person could not make a legally enforceable contract which required another person to do something which was in conflict with an existing law; for example, a "contract" which required one person to kill another would not be legally enforceable.

The requirement of "lawful purpose" in the making of a life insurance contract is fulfilled by the presence of insurable interest. The primary purpose of all insurance is to protect against financial loss rather than to provide a means of possible financial gain. In chapter 1, we discussed insurable interest and its importance in insurance. The requirement that insurable interest be present at the time of application provides assurance that a life insurance contract is being made for a lawful purpose, protection against financial loss due to death, rather than an unlawful purpose, such as gambling or speculating on a life. The lawful purpose requirement must be met as a condition for the *formation* of a contract. Once the contract has been formed, proof of continued insurable interest is not required. Thus, the beneficiary need not provide proof of insurable interest in order to receive life insurance policy proceeds, nor must the policyowner's insurable interest continue in order for the contract to remain valid.

COMPANY REQUIREMENTS

An insurance company must decide whether it wishes to enter into a contract with an applicant. In order to make this decision, the insurer must gather information about the applicant and, if they are not the same person, the proposed insured as well. Based on this information, the insurance company will decide whether to accept the risk. The company must also collect the initial premium, as well as issue and deliver the approved policy.

The Application

Though each company's application form is different, in general the application form for an individual life insurance policy has two sections. The first section, called Part I by many companies, contains basic information concerning the applicant and the proposed insured and describes the specific insurance coverage requested. The second section, often called Part II, concerns the health of the proposed insured. The entire application is used by the insurer's home office underwriters when deciding whether or not to accept the risk and issue the policy. When the policy is issued, the application becomes a part of the insurance contract.

Part I

The first section of Part I identifies the name and address of the applicant and the proposed insured. If the proposed insured is not the applicant, the applicant will have to describe his or her relationship to the proposed insured in order to prove that an insurable interest exists. Further information found in Part I concerning the proposed insured includes occupation, date of birth, and, in some cases, marital status. A sample Part I application is included in the appendix.

The first section also describes the requested coverage: the amount of insurance (face value of the policy), the plan of insurance, the frequency with which premiums are to be paid (annually, semiannually, etc.) and the way the dividends, if any, are to be used. The applicant also selects the beneficiary or beneficiaries of the policy, the manner in which the proceeds will be paid (in a lump sum or under one of the settlement options) and, at times, the nonforfeiture option desired, if applicable. (Settlement options and nonforfeiture options will be explained in later chapters.)

Part I of the application also asks for other information which might affect the company's decision as to whether or not it should accept the risk. This information might include such items as the proposed insured's hobbies, pastimes, aviation activities, and plans for future residence in foreign lands. Other questions concern the amount of insurance currently in force on the life of the proposed insured, the names of companies carrying that insurance, and any refusals by an insurer to issue life insurance to the proposed insured.

The laws in most jurisdictions also require that the application include a question concerning whether or not the policy requested is being purchased as a replacement policy. An applicant who purchases a replacement policy does so with the intent to cancel some or all of his or her current insurance coverage and to use the new policy as a substitute or replacement for that coverage. If the policy is intended to be a replacement policy, then several disclosure forms may be required of the insurance company by the regulators to verify that the applicant was informed of all relevant information before making the change.

Part II

The second part of the application, often called Part II, includes questions about the health of the proposed insured. Ordinary individual insurance applications are taken on either a medical or a nonmedical basis. The type of application the insurer requires depends primarily on the type and amount of insurance being requested as well as the age of the proposed insured.

Medical applications. If the insurer requires a medical application, the proposed insured will have to undergo a medical examination. This medical examination usually is conducted by a physician who is located in the insured's area and who has been appointed by the insurance company to perform these examinations. The physician completes the part of the application that describes the person's state of health. In addition to recording the results of a physical examination, the physician also asks the proposed insured about his or her medical history and writes the answers on the form. At times, the physical examination includes special blood, urine, and other tests, as well as X-rays. This information is used by home office underwriters to make a judgment about the person's insurability. A sample physician's report portion of a Part II Medical Application is shown in Figure 6–2.

The examining physician has a special relationship with the insurance company. The examining physician is an agent of the insurance company, and the same laws of agency apply in the relationship between the examining physician and the insurer as in that between the sales agent and the insurer. Anything the proposed insured tells the physician will be presumed to be the knowledge of the company; if the proposed insured were to inform the physician of a health problem which was pertinent to the risk, and the physician did not communicate this information to the company, the courts might not permit the company to use this "lack" of knowledge to deny a claim.

Traditionally, medical examinations have been conducted by a physician, but in recent decades, life insurance companies have begun using paramedical examinations. These examinations do not require the services of a medical doctor; instead, the proposed insured undergoes several office and laboratory tests performed by a medical technician, a physician's assistant (P.A.), or a nurse. These tests and the health history of the proposed insured generally provide the underwriters with the information they need to make a judgment about the person's insurability.

The amount of insurance applied for is the most important factor in determining how extensive the physical examination of the proposed insured should be. An examination by a medical doctor is generally more extensive and more expensive than an examination by a paramedical service. Each insurance company sets its own standards for determining how extensive the physical examination will be and which tests it needs. As a rule, the insurance company pays for the physical examination.

FIGURE 6-2

Sample Part II medical application questions

```
——————— PHYSICIAN'S REPORT—NOT PART OF THE APPLICATION ———————
        This examination should be made in private—if third person present, give details.
```

1. a. Person examined _____
   b. Male ☐ Female ☐   c. Occupation? _____
2. a. Field Underwriter _____
   b. General Office _____
3. Are you related to the person examined? (If "Yes," give details) . . . . Yes ☐ No ☐
4. Has the person examined ever consulted you for any reason other than insurance
   examination(s)? . . . . Yes ☐ No ☐
   If "Yes," please give details for any consultation that is not described in full in the medical history.

```
       FOR EACH "YES" ANSWER IN QUESTIONS 7 THROUGH 11, GIVE FULL DETAILS
```

5. Measurements *(in normal heel shoes, clothed)*
   a. Height? _____ Ft. _____ In.   Did you measure? _____ Yes ☐ No ☐
   b. Weight? _____ Lbs.   Did you weigh? _____ Yes ☐ No ☐

6. Blood Pressure. *Take a second reading at the end of the examination. Report all observations. (Do not complete if examinee is less than 12 years old.)*

	1st Reading	2nd Reading
a. Systolic:	_____ mm.	_____ mm.
b. Diastolic:	_____ mm.	_____ mm.

7. Pulse. *(Do not complete if examinee is less than 12 years old.)*

	At Rest	After Exercise	5 Min. Later
a. Pulse rate?			
b. Any extra-systoles? Yes ☐ No ☐			
c. Any other arrhythmia? Yes ☐ No ☐			

8. Is there evidence of past or present disease or disorder of

	Yes	No
a. Brain or Nervous System? *(Please test major reflexes.)*	☐	☐ a
b. Lungs or other parts of the Respiratory System?	☐	☐ b
c. Gastrointestinal Tract including Hernia?	☐	☐ c
d. Genito-Urinary System (males only)	☐	☐ d
e. Ears, Eyes, Nose, Throat, Neck or Glands? *(If there is marked impairment of vision, include corrected acuity.)*	☐	☐ e
f. Bones, Joints, Arteries, Veins or Skin?	☐	☐ f
g. Any other part of body excluding Cardiovascular System?	☐	☐ g

9. Is there any paralysis, deformity, lameness or loss of limb? . . . . ☐ ☐

10. Cardiovascular Examination. *Examine heart before and after exercise in upright and recumbent positions. Do not exercise if contraindicated.*

	Yes	No
a. Is there any evidence of cardiac hypertrophy, failure or other cardiovascular disease excluding murmur?	☐	☐ a
b. Is a murmur present? *(If "Yes," complete this section.)*	☐	☐ b

Timing: ☐ Systolic   ☐ Presytolic   ☐ Diastolic
Location: ☐ Apex   ☐ Aortic   ☐ Pulmonic
            ☐ Other _____
Transmission: ☐ Axilla   ☐ Neck   ☐ Precordium
                ☐ None   ☐ Other _____
Intensity: ☐ Soft (Gr.-1-2)   ☐ Mod (Gr. 3-4)   ☐ Loud (Gr. 5-6)
After   ☐ Increased   ☐ Decreased
Exercise: ☐ Unchanged   ☐ Absent
Impression: _____

11. In your opinion, is there anything about the person's health, habits, character or mode of life   Yes   No
    which might unfavorably affect insurability? . . . .   ☐   ☐

12. Urinalysis. *(Do not complete if examinee is less than 12 years old).*
    Albumin _____   Sugar _____   Occult Blood _____
    Do not send *a portion of original specimen to the Home Office* **unless** *there is a positive urinary finding. Check if urine specimen forwarded to H.O.* ☐

Nonmedical applications. An insurer must balance the cost of a medical examination and the subsequent underwriting procedure against the amount of potential loss the policy represents. Obviously, the potential of loss on a $1,000,000 policy would logically require an insurance company to take considerable care before assuming such a risk.

Most insurance applications do not involve such a large sum of money and so do not justify expensive and complicated medical examination procedures. For this reason, most insurers accept applications on a nonmedical basis. A nonmedical application is one which does not automatically require that the proposed insured be examined by a physician or a paramedical service employee. Instead, the company uses a "nonmedical" application form which contains a large number of questions which the proposed insured must answer about the past and present condition of his or her health. Some of the questions commonly included in a Part II Nonmedical Application are shown in Figure 6–3. The insurance company underwriters use this information to evaluate the risk and decide whether to accept or reject the application. The insurance company will, however, always reserve the right to require a medical examination if the information in the nonmedical application indicates that there may be a health problem.

An insurance company usually sets a limit on the amount of insurance it will issue on a "nonmedical" basis. This amount varies according to the age of the proposed insured. For example, a company may issue, using a nonmedical application, amounts of insurance up to $50,000 to proposed insureds who have not reached the age of 40, or up to $100,000 to proposed insureds who are under age 30. The trend is toward extending the age limits at which larger amounts of insurance can be issued on a nonmedical basis. A growing proportion of life insurance is now issued using nonmedical applications.

Agent's statement

Companies usually include a group of questions on the application which must be answered by the sales agent. These questions relate to the agent's personal observations and knowledge of the applicant, and give the agent a chance to communicate any information which may be relevant to the company's decision to issue the policy. Some companies also use this part of the application to obtain marketing information for company studies. This portion of the application is *not*, however, included with the other parts of the application when the completed application is attached to and made a part of the policy contract.

Statements in the application

Because the insurance company's evaluation of the risk and its deci-

FIGURE 6-3

Typical Part II nonmedical application questions

1.	a. PROPOSED INSURED?_____ Height?___ ft.___ in.; Weight?____ lbs.
	b. SPOUSE, if proposed for coverage?_____ Height?___ ft.___ in.; Weight?____ lbs.
	c. CHILDREN, if proposed for coverage (give full names)?_____
	_____

2. Personal physicians (give consultation details)   Name?   Address?   Date last consulted?
   a.   For Proposed Insured_____
   b.   For Spouse named in Ques. 1_____

Give the following information, so far as known, for all persons listed in Ques. 1. If "Yes" to any question, give full details.

3. During the past 10 years has any such person consulted a physician or practitioner for, or been treated for, or had   Yes No
   a. elevated blood pressure, rheumatic fever, heart murmur, chest pain, angina, heart trouble, stroke or irregular pulse? . . . .   ☐ ☐ a
   b. diabetes, anemia, thyroid or other gland or blood disorder? . . . .   ☐ ☐ b
   c. asthma, bronchitis, emphysema, tuberculosis, coughing of blood, or nose, throat, lung or other respiratory disorder? . . . .   ☐ ☐ c
   d. ulcer, gall bladder disease, colitis, pancreatitis, internal bleeding, hernia or other digestive or intestinal trouble? . . . .   ☐ ☐ d
   e. hepatitis, cirrhosis or other liver troubles? . . . .   ☐ ☐ e
   f. kidney or urinary tract stone, infection, or other disorder; sugar, albumin, blood or pus in urine? . . . .   ☐ ☐ f
   g. psychiatric, emotional or mental health condition requiring medication or hospitalization? . . . .   ☐ ☐ g
   h. epilepsy, convulsions, dizziness, loss of consciousness, frequent headaches or other nervous system disorder? . . . .   ☐ ☐ h
   i. cancer, tumor, cyst; allergy; eye, ear or skin disorder? . . . .   ☐ ☐ i
   j. hemorrhoids, varicose veins, phlebitis, circulatory disorder? . . . .   ☐ ☐ j
   k. arthritis, rheumatism, sciatica, gout or other disorder of muscles, bones, joints, back or spine? . . . .   ☐ ☐ k
   l. (males only) disorder of prostate or reproductive organs? . . . .   ☐ ☐ l
   m. (females only) disorder of pelvic organs, breasts, menses or pregnancy, or is she now pregnant? . . . .   ☐ ☐ m

4. During the past 10 years has any such person been counselled, treated, or hospitalized for the use of alcohol or drugs? . . . .   ☐ ☐

5. Has any such person, for physical or mental health reasons, ever
   a. received disability benefits, compensation or pension? . . . .   ☐ ☐ a
   b. been rejected for, or discharged from, military service? . . . .   ☐ ☐ b

6. Is any such person disabled, deformed, paralyzed, blind, deaf, physically or mentally handicapped, or an amputee? . . . .   ☐ ☐

7. Other than as stated, has any such person within past 5 years
   a. been treated or had surgery in a hospital or other facility? . . . .   ☐ ☐ a
   b. had an electrocardiogram, x-ray or other diagnostic test? . . . .   ☐ ☐ b
   c. been advised to have any treatment, surgery or diagnostic test which was not completed? . . . .   ☐ ☐ c

8. Other than as stated, has any such person within past 2 years had any illness or consulted any physician or practictioner for any reason, including routine or checkup examination?   ☐ ☐

9. Any history of hypertension or heart trouble before age 60 among natural parents, brothers or sisters of Prop. Insured? . . . .   ☐ ☐
   If "Yes," give relationship, age at onset and subsequent history.

10. Answer if any child named above has not reached first birthday
    a. Is there any abnormality? . . . .   ☐ ☐ a
    b. Was birth weight under 5 lbs.? (If "Yes," wt. now_____lbs.)   ☐ ☐ b

11. GIVE FULL DETAILS FOR LAST CONSULTATION WITH PERSONAL PHYSICIAN WITHIN PAST 2 YEARS, AND FOR EACH "YES" ANSWER TO QUESTIONS 3-10.

sion whether or not to insure the life of a particular person are based on statements made in the application, it is important that the insurance company be able to rely on the truth of these statements. In fact, the life insurance contract is considered a **good faith contract** because the contract requires that both parties to the contract deal fairly and truthfully with each other. The applicant must be able to rely on the insurance company's promises and agreements, and the insurance company must be able to rely on the applicant's honest answers to questions in the application.

However, not every statement made by the applicant must be *literally* true. If this were so, any little mistake made by the applicant would cause the insurance contract to be void. Neither the policyowner nor the insurance company would favor this situation. After all, many misstatements would not affect the insurer's decision about whether to accept the risk and issue the policy. For example, a statement that the proposed insured had visited a doctor on July 10 when the actual date of the visit was July 9 would not affect the insurer's decision, nor would a statement that one's mother had died at age 68 when her actual age at death was 67.

In law, statements that must be literally true are called **warranties**. If a situation is not literally true as stated, a contract based on these warranties is void. Statements made in applications for life insurance are *not* warranties: they are considered, legally, to be representations. A **representation** is a statement by an applicant that is substantially true. Thus, if the applicant states that a visit to the doctor two years ago was for an infected toe on the left foot and it was really for an infected toe on the right foot, the misstatement of fact will not affect the validity of the life insurance contract because the statement is a representation, not a warranty. However, if the applicant says that the doctor's visit was for treatment of an infected toe and it was really for treatment of heart disease, then the misstatement might well have an effect on the insurer's decision about issuing the policy. A misrepresentation which is relevant to the company's acceptance of the risk is called a **material misrepresentation**. A misstatement is material when, if the truth had been known, the insurance company would not have issued the policy or would have issued the policy only on a different basis, such as for a higher premium or for a lower face amount. If the insurer discovers a material misrepresentation on an application within a specified period, called the contestable period, the insurer may decide to reject or avoid the contract. (The contestable period will be described in more detail in chapter 7, "The Life Insurance Policy.")

Third party applications

As mentioned in chapter 1, the person who applies for the insurance and becomes the policyowner is not always the same person as the proposed insured. There are situations in which one person can apply for insurance on the life of another. A business owner applying for a policy on the life of a key employee and a creditor applying for coverage on the life of a debtor are examples. If the applicant and the proposed insured are not the same person, the application is called a *third party application*.

The question of insurable interest is a crucial one in third party applications. To take out insurance on the life of another, the applicant must show that he or she has an insurable interest in the proposed insured's life. In third party applications, the proposed insured usually must sign the application. The primary reason that this signature is required is to prevent anyone from illegally speculating on the life of another by obtaining insurance without that person's knowledge. The one common exception to this rule is a parent applying for insurance on the life of a young child, as a young child cannot be expected to sign the application. Some states also allow one spouse to insure the other without a signature.

Once the policy is issued, the applicant becomes the owner of the policy unless another party is designated to become the policyowner. The person whose life is insured cannot exercise any ownership rights under the policy; only the policyowner can.

The Initial Premium

As part of the sales process, the agent will inform the applicant of the amount of the premium required for the face amount and plan of insurance being purchased. In completing the application, the prospective policyowner chooses the frequency with which premiums are to be paid—annually, semi-annually, quarterly, or monthly. The frequency with which premiums are to be paid is referred to as the *mode* of premium payment. With this information, the agent will be able to tell the applicant the amount of the first premium due.

The sales agent is authorized by the company to accept payment of this initial premium and to forward it, along with the completed application, to the insurer's home office. The applicant has the right to defer payment of the initial premium until the policy is issued and actually delivered. The contract is not in effect, however, until this initial premium is paid, since the entire consideration required will not have been provided by the applicant.

Usually, the initial premium is submitted along with the application. There are advantages to this approach from the standpoint of the agent, the insurer, and the applicant. The advantage to the agent and the insurer is that the applicant is less likely to have a change of mind before the policy is delivered. If the applicant refuses to accept the policy, the agent will not earn the commission on the sale and the company will have lost the applicant's business. Of course, most insurance policies grant the applicant the right to refuse an issued policy and obtain a refund of the initial premium. However, statistics show that a policy is far more likely to be accepted by the applicant when the application is accompanied by the initial premium. The advantage to the applicant of paying the premium at the same time the application is submitted is that, under certain circumstances, the insurance coverage will be put in force before the policy itself is actually delivered.

The effective date of the insurance coverage depends upon the contract requirements of offer and acceptance (which were mentioned earlier in this chapter), as well as upon the wording of the receipt, if there is one, for the initial premium.

The question of which party to a contract is making the offer and which party is accepting the offer is important because the answer determines when the contract becomes effective. Let us examine how offer and acceptance work with respect to an application for life insurance and the payment of the initial premium.

If the applicant does not pay the initial premium at the time of application, then the applicant is not making an offer. The company "makes the offer" if and when it approves the application and delivers the policy. In other words, the company is offering the applicant the policy and asking the applicant to accept the offer by paying the initial premium. The applicant "accepts" the company's offer by accepting the policy and paying the initial premium. Only when an offer is made and accepted will the policy contract become effective.

When the initial premium is sent to the company along with the application, the legal position of the applicant depends on (1) whether or not a receipt is issued by the sales agent, and (2) if a receipt is issued, what type of receipt it is.

No premium receipt issued

Infrequently, an agent will accept an application for life insurance along with the initial premium but will not give the applicant a receipt for the money. In this situation, the insurance contract does not take effect until the policy is issued by the company and delivered to the applicant. With regard to offer and acceptance, the applicant is making the offer, and the insurer accepts the offer by issuing and delivering the policy. Life insurance companies actively discourage agents from neglecting to give receipts for the initial premium.

Binding premium receipt issued

If you have ever purchased an automobile insurance policy or some other property or liability insurance, you probably were given a receipt for your initial premium and told that as of a certain time on a certain date your insurance was effective. This meant that you were insured even though no policy had been issued. The receipt you got was a "binding" receipt— one which bound the company to a temporary contract of insurance.

When a **binding receipt** is given, the applicant is fully insured, but only for a short, stated period of time, not permanently. The insurance coverage begins immediately and remains in effect until the company either rejects the application or approves it and issues a policy.

A binding receipt given for any type of insurance benefits the applicant, since there is interim coverage even if the applicant should prove to be uninsurable. When a binding receipt is given for the initial premium for life insurance, the amount of coverage is usually the face amount requested on the application, although most companies specify in the receipt a limit on the amount of coverage in force during this period—perhaps $100,000 or $150,000. The rest of the coverage, if any, does not go into effect unless and until the application is approved and a policy is issued.

When binding receipts are used, the question of offer and acceptance depends on the actual wording in the particular receipt. Usually the wording is such that the insurer is considered to be the offeror of temporary coverage. The applicant then accepts the temporary coverage offer by paying the premium with the application.

Traditionally, binding receipts have not been used frequently by life insurance companies. However, in certain states, courts have ruled that, in effect, any receipt is binding regardless of the wording. In these jurisdictions, then, some companies may issue only binding receipts for premiums collected with applications.

Conditional premium receipts

In many sales situations, the applicant pays the initial premium and the agent issues a conditional receipt. According to the terms of a **conditional receipt**, the insurance will become effective and a policy will be issued if the proposed insured is found to be insurable. Conditional receipts, then, require that a condition be met before the insurance becomes effective.

When a conditional premium receipt is issued, the applicant is considered to be making an offer to the insurance company. In other words, the applicant is offering the company the application and initial premium in exchange for a life insurance policy, and the applicant is asking the company to accept the offer. The company "accepts" the offer by approving the application and issuing the policy exactly as applied for.

The date the insurance takes effect depends on the wording of the receipt. While there are many variations among the companies, basically these conditional receipts are either of the *insurability type* or of the *approval type.*

Insurability type receipt. The more commonly used type of conditional receipt is the insurability receipt. Under the conditions of this receipt, if the proposed insured would be granted the requested coverage, the coverage would be effective even if the proposed insured should die before the underwriting procedure is completed. The date the coverage provided by this receipt takes effect is usually specified as the later of (1) the date the application was signed, or (2) the date the medical examination, if required, was given. Under a few conditional receipts–those used in Quebec, for example–coverage begins on the date the application was signed, rather than the date of the medical examination. Therefore, according to the terms of a conditional receipt, even if the proposed insured should become uninsurable or even die in the interim between the date of the application–or medical examination if required–and the date the application is actually approved by the company, the coverage would still be granted retroactively.

However, if the underwriter determines that the proposed insured was *not* insurable on the date the application was signed or on the date the medical examination, if required, was taken, then no coverage will be in effect under this receipt, and the initial premium will be refunded.

Suppose, for example, David Black applies for a life insurance policy on his own life, pays his initial premium, and receives a conditional receipt of the insurability type on May 25. He undergoes the medical examination on May 29. If Mr. Black dies in an automobile accident on May 30, the home office underwriters will still evaluate his application and medical examination. If, according to the standards of the company, Mr. Black would have been considered insurable for the policy as applied for, Mr. Black's coverage usually will be considered to have been in effect as of May 29, the date he underwent the medical examination. His beneficiary will receive the full policy proceeds.

Approval type receipt. Under the approval type of conditional receipt, the proposed insured will be covered only if the application is approved by the company, and coverage will be retroactive to the date specified in the receipt, usually either the date of the application or the date of the medical examination. However, the point to note is that the coverage becomes effective *only if* the company has actually gone through the process of approval. Even if the proposed insured is insurable and would have been approved for the insurance requested, there is no coverage if the company has not completed the entire approval process. As you might expect, there could be a claim problem if such a proposed insured died before the policy was approved. Despite the actual wording of the approval type of receipt, courts have often ruled against the insurer when such cases went to trial. As a consequence, the approval type of conditional receipt is not widely used today.

Selection of Risks

In the discussion of the application, frequent references have been made to the fact that the home office of the insurance company makes the decision as to whether or not to accept a particular risk – that is, whether to issue insurance on the life of a particular person. This decision-making process is called underwriting, or the selection of risks, and is a major function of life insurance company administration. For the purposes of this discussion of risk selection, we will assume that the applicant and the proposed insured are the same person.

Theory of risk selection

The risk appraisal procedure in a life insurance company is intended to determine the proper risk classification in which to place a particular applicant. About 92 percent of all applicants for life insurance are considered standard risks.

A proposed insured who does not meet the requirements to be classified as a standard risk may still be able to obtain life insurance; he or she instead might be classified as a substandard risk, or special class risk. Over the years, the industry has developed statistics which can be used to predict the adverse effect that various factors, such as health problems or certain occupations, hobbies, and pastimes, are likely to have on mortality. People who have these health problems, work in these occupations, or engage in these hobbies and pastimes present a greater risk for the insurer. About 6 percent of insurance applicants possess one or more of these factors and fall into the substandard risk category.

As you will remember, mortality is a major factor in the calculation of the cost of life insurance. In order to insure these substandard risks, the insurance company will have to charge higher premium rates (called substandard rates) for the same amounts and plans of insurance coverage than would be charged to applicants who were standard risks. For this reason, policies issued to substandard risks are often called *rated policies*. Each company sets its own criteria or underwriting requirements to determine whether or not a particular applicant is a standard risk. It is possible, therefore, that someone who is regarded as a substandard risk in one company might be considered a standard risk in another company. There are even some companies that specialize in marketing insurance coverage to persons who are generally considered substandard risks.

There are instances, however, when an applicant may be uninsurable. These people fall into the third and by far the smallest category (2 percent) of applicants – the uninsurable. The primary reason why this group cannot be insured lies in the pricing of life insurance policies. It is very difficult to set a proper premium for someone who is in extremely poor health, who has undergone some form of experimental health treatment, or who engages in an extremely dangerous occupation or hobby. In addition, the premium is likely to be very high. For example, the premium for someone who is diagnosed as having only a few months to live would be close to the face value of the policy!

Figure 6–4 summarizes the three major categories of applicants: (1) those insurable at standard premium rates – the standard risks, by far the largest group; (2) those insurable at somewhat higher premium rates – the substandard risks, a small group; and (3) those who cannot be insured – the uninsurables, a very small percentage of all applicants for life insurance.

Some companies have also developed criteria for a fourth group – a preferred risk, or superstandard, group. This is a group of individuals whose physical conditions, health histories, occupations, and lifestyles indicate the probability of a lower-than-usual mortality rate. For instance, such individuals might be nonsmokers who are regularly involved in physical fitness programs. These people may be offered insurance at lower-than-usual premium rates. However, if such a group of good risks is removed from the standard risk group, then the mortality rate for standard risks will increase and hence standard premium rates will also have to be increased.

FIGURE 6-4
Percentage of ordinary life insurance applicants in the United States in each major underwriting category

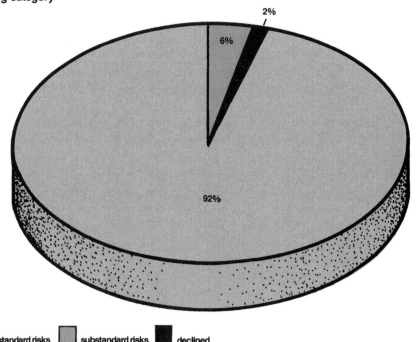

Sources of underwriting information

The home office underwriter uses several sources of information to decide whether or not a risk is acceptable according to the company's criteria. As we have seen, the completed application, including the agent's statement and the report from the medical examination or the nonmedical questionnaire, contains a great deal of data about the proposed insured. In most instances, these documents will provide enough information for the underwriter to reach a decision about whether to issue a policy and in what underwriting classification. However, when the policy is for an exceptionally large amount or when some of the data suggest a problem, companies may seek further information. The underwriter may request a physical examination for a proposed insured whose application is on a nonmedical basis, or the underwriter may ask a proposed insured whose application was on a medical basis to undergo a more detailed physical examination. The underwriter may also request that a doctor who has treated the proposed insured for an illness or injury complete a form called an *Attending Physician's Statement* (APS), to give details of the diagnosis and treatment.

If the underwriter is questioning something other than the health of the proposed insured, the underwriter may ask for an inspection report. An *inspection report* provides the results of an investigation of such factors as the applicant's lifestyle, activities, occupation, and economic standing. For example, the underwriter may request an inspection report if there is some evidence that the proposed insured may be engaged in a dangerous pastime, such as skydiving. The investigation is usually done by an outside organization which specializes in such investigations. However, such additional data-seeking is expensive, and this practice is not applied unless there is good and sufficient reason. Further, the insurer must obtain the applicant's written permission before requesting information from any outside source.

Once the underwriter has classified the risk involved and approved the application, the application is forwarded to the department of the company which actually issues the policy.

Policy Issue

A life insurance policy is a printed contract, worded in relatively straightforward terms that conform to the requirements of the jurisdiction or jurisdictions where it will be issued or delivered. The policy generally contains blank areas where the company fills in the specific information which makes this particular policy form into a contract with a named policyowner. A sample policy is included as an appendix to this text.

Before the insurer issues the policy, it must be included in the insurance company's master records. Each policy must have its own policy record or file which will be updated over the years so that the company will have an accurate history of that policy. This policy record will indicate the payment of premiums, the designated beneficiary, the options chosen, current addresses, and any other information which is necessary to provide effective service to the owner of the policy and/or the beneficiary.

Depending on the company, some or much of this information is now stored in computerized master files. Some records, though, such as the application and underwriting papers, are still kept in original paper form in a physical file stored at the company. The company usually sets up computerized records for premium billing and reserve valuation when it issues the policy.

Delivery

Several times during this chapter we have mentioned delivery of the policy. Legally, delivery can take more than one form. **Actual delivery**, or **manual delivery**, occurs when the policy is actually handed to the applicant—now the policyowner—by the soliciting agent. However, in law, there is a process which is known as *constructive delivery*. Under certain circumstances, a policy can be considered as being "delivered" even if the new policyowner does not actually take possession of the policy. **Constructive delivery** of a policy takes place when a company gives up control of the policy by mailing it to the policyowner or the agent of the policyowner if nothing remains to be done but to see that the policyowner receives the policy. In such a case, constructive delivery will have been accomplished in the legal sense even if the policyowner never receives the policy. In other words, if the insurer places the policy unconditionally in the control of someone acting for the policyowner—such as the post office, a delivery service, the policyowner's spouse, or the policyowner's secretary—then delivery is deemed to have taken effect.

Policy inspection

There are times when an applicant may have possession of a policy, but delivery in a legal sense has not taken place and the coverage is not in effect. Such is the case when a policy is given to the applicant for a period of examination. The applicant will usually have to sign an inspection receipt stating that the policy has not been "delivered." During this inspection period, the applicant has the right to accept or reject the policy; the inspection receipt states that coverage is not in effect during the inspection period.

This situation can pose legal problems should the insured die during the inspection period. If such a case goes to trial, the judgment of the court will be influenced by (1) the wording of the inspection receipt and (2) whether the initial premium had been paid. Thus, there is a possibility that the court will hold the company liable for the claim, even though the applicant signed the inspection receipt.

Free examination period

A policyowner may also examine the policy after it is delivered using the "free examination period" provided by many companies in the United States and Canada. There is, however, a major difference between the free examination period provided by the policy and the policy inspection described above. In the case of the free examination, the insurance coverage is actually in effect throughout the specified period, or until the policyowner rejects the policy, if sooner. The specified period is usually 10 days; for this reason, this privilege is often referred to as a "10-day free look." A typical free examination period provision follows:

> **Ten-Day Free Examination Period.** Please examine your policy. Within 10 days after delivery, you can return it to the Company or to the agent through whom it was purchased, with a written request for a full refund of premium. Upon such a request, the policy will be void from the start.

Once the policyowner pays the initial premium and accepts the policy, he or she can take up to the time limit specified to make a final decision about keeping the policy. Before or at the end of the free examination period, the policyowner has the right to return the policy to the insurer for cancellation, and to receive a refund of the entire initial premium. If the policyowner exercises this right, he or she will have had the benefit of free insurance coverage for the period. Consumers like the free examination period because it gives them an opportunity to rethink the decision to purchase the policy. There is also no question about the insurer's liability during the period; the coverage is effective, and any valid claim arising from an insured's death during the period must be paid by the insurer.

Effective date of policy

The effective date of a life insurance policy depends on the factors just described. Thus, the policy's effective date may be the application date, the date the medical examination was taken, the date the risk was approved, the policy's issue date, the date the policy is delivered, or the date the initial premium is paid.

Sometimes, an applicant will request that the policy be issued with an effective date which is earlier than the date of the original application—

that is, the applicant will ask the insurer to "back-date" or "date back" the policy. In some situations, there is a financial advantage for the policyowner to an earlier policy issue date. For example, a whole life policy may be back-dated to a date when the age of the insured was lower. In this way, a lower premium rate based on the insured's lower age would be payable over the entire life of the policy. A disadvantage to back-dating a life insurance policy is that back premiums would have to be paid from the effective date of the policy. Hence, the policyowner would be required to pay back premiums for a period of time during which the coverage was not in force. Most jurisdictions specify that a policy may not be back-dated to a date which is more than six months earlier than the date of the original application.

Buyer's Guide and Policy Summary

In the United States, the majority of states require that a publication titled *Buyer's Guide* be given to applicants along with a policy summary either at delivery, if the policy includes a free examination period provision, or before the agent accepts the initial premium, if the free examination period provision is not provided.

The *Buyer's Guide* is a pamphlet designed to help the prospective purchaser of life insurance decide how much insurance coverage is needed and what types of policies are best suited to meet specified needs. The *Buyer's Guide* describes the basic plans of insurance in simple language. The policy summary is a document, often in the form of a computer printout, which contains certain legally required data regarding the specific policy being considered by the applicant. Such data includes premiums payable, benefits provided, cash values, and cost indexes. These figures and data enable the customer to compare the costs and benefits of similar policies issued by other insurers.

Companies selling life insurance in states where such disclosure is not required often follow the same procedures, both to provide a consumer service and to keep their own procedures uniform throughout their entire marketing area. Although Canadian regulations do not require insurers to provide a policy summary or the *Buyer's Guide,* most Canadian companies voluntarily provide very similar comparison statements.

7

The Life Insurance Policy

The life insurance policy is a written contract which contains the pertinent facts about the policyowner, the insurance coverage, the person whose life is insured, and the insurer. It also sets forth the legal rights and obligations of the insurer and the policyowner and contains all the information necessary to complete the contract. The policy also usually includes a copy of the application, which is considered part of the contract.

The contract with the builder we discussed in the last chapter was relatively simple. A life insurance contract, on the other hand, is not a simple document. In order to fully define all aspects of the transaction, the policy must include many provisions. A life insurance contract may also be of very long duration, spanning many decades. Further, a life insurance contract is technical – so much so that a person unfamiliar with insurance terminology might have difficulty understanding the full impact of the many provisions. For many years, these policies were written in legal language – language designed to hold up in a court of law. However, most jurisdictions require that policies issued today be written in "readable language" – language which the policyowner should be able to understand without a lawyer's or a court's assistance. But the life insurance policy is still a legal contract and, as such, must be phrased in language which will be upheld by the courts. Figure 7–1 illustrates differences in the policy language used in contracts issued before and after the "readable language" requirements were passed.

As you have seen, a life insurance policy is a contract of adhesion – one which is written by only one of the parties, the insurer, and which does not provide for bargaining on the part of the purchaser. Insurance companies cannot, however, write policies without regard for the rights of the other parties concerned. Government authorities in both the United States and Canada have taken action to assure that the rights of policyowners and

FIGURE 7-1

Policy provision used in contracts issued before and after "readable language" requirements

Before readability legislation	After readability legislation
Death of Beneficiary. If the last surviving beneficiary for any death benefit proceeds payable under this policy predeceases the Insured, the beneficial interest in such proceeds shall vest in the Owner. If any beneficiary dies simultaneously with the Insured or within fifteen days after the Insured but before due proof of the Insured's death has been received by the Company, the proceeds of the policy will be paid to the same payee or payees and in the same manner as though such beneficiary predeceased the Insured.	**Death of Beneficiary.** If no beneficiary for the life insurance proceeds, or for a stated share, survives the Insured, the right to these proceeds or this share will pass to you. If you are the Insured, this right will pass to your estate. If any beneficiary dies at the same time as the Insured, or within 15 days after the Insured but before we receive proof of the Insured's death, we will pay the proceeds as though that beneficiary died first.
Protection Against Creditors. To the extent allowed by law and subject to the terms and conditions of this policy, all benefits and money available or paid to any person and relating in any manner to this policy will be exempt and free from such person's debts, contracts and engagements, and from judicial process to levy upon or attach the same.	**Protection Against Creditors.** Except as stated in the Assignment provision, payments we make under this policy are, to the extent the law permits, exempt from the claims, attachments, or levies of any creditors.
Dividends. This is a participating contract and its share of divisible surplus will be determined annually by the Company. On each anniversary of this policy, any share of divisible surplus apportioned to it will be payable as a dividend if this policy is then in force and all premiums due have been paid to such anniversary. It is not expected that a dividend will be payable on this policy before its second anniversary.	**Annual Dividend.** While this policy is in force, except as extended insurance, it is eligible to share in our divisible surplus. Each year we determine the policy's share, if any. This share is payable as a dividend on the policy anniversary, if all premiums due before then have been paid. We do not expect a dividend to be payable before the second anniversary.

beneficiaries of life insurance policies are protected. Insurance departments have been established in each state and province and have been charged with regulating the insurance industry. In addition, the federal government in Canada also participates directly in supervising certain aspects of the insurance industry in that country.

REGULATION

In the United States, the heads of the various state insurance departments participate in an organization called the National Association of Insurance Commissioners (NAIC). This association was founded in 1871 to examine the need to regulate the insurance industry. Over the years the NAIC has been successful in promoting some uniformity in state insurance laws. One way the NAIC accomplishes this purpose is by developing "model bills" which each state is encouraged to pass. A *model bill* is a sample bill; states may adopt the model bill into law exactly as written or use the model bill as the basis for developing their own legislation. Because of these model bills, the laws concerning life insurance contracts are similar in all the states.

In Canada, the Association of Superintendents works to promote uniformity of insurance regulation. Except for the province of Quebec, life insurance contract law in each province follows the revised Uniform Life Insurance Act. This act was first introduced in 1924 and has been updated and revised several times over the years. The current revision was completed in 1962 and, while there are minor variations among the provinces, it forms the basis for life insurance regulation throughout most of Canada. The system of laws in the province of Quebec is derived from Roman law and belongs to the civil law system. The rest of the provinces have laws which are derived from the English common law system. Quebec has therefore enacted its own body of life insurance law. Despite the different sources of the basic systems, the laws regulating life insurance contracts in Quebec are similar to those regulating insurance contracts in other provinces of Canada.

Life insurance policies sold in the United States and Canada usually must be approved by the individual states and/or provinces in which they are issued. Since the ultimate purpose of regulation is the protection of the rights of policyowners and beneficiaries, the regulation of life insurance tends to be similar in all jurisdictions.

We shall now look at the provisions usually included in life insurance policies. In the United States, many provisions are required by law to be included in the policy contract. In Canada, the revised Uniform Life Insurance Act and Quebec insurance law specify the rights of policyowners and beneficiaries. Hence, Canadian insurance companies are not required by law to spell out these rights in policy provisions. In actual practice, however, Canadian companies issue policies which include the same basic provisions which are required by law in the United States. The major provisions described in this chapter will consequently be those which are included in ordinary life insurance policies issued in the United States and Canada. (The major provisions included in industrial and group insurance policies will be described in later chapters.) A sample life insurance policy is included in the appendix.

POLICY PROVISIONS

The major provisions which are typically included in life insurance contracts relate to the following aspects of an ordinary life insurance policy:

- the elements which constitute the *entire contract* between the policyowner and the company

- the *incontestability* of the contract after it has been in force for a specified period
- the *grace period* the company provides the policyowner for the payment of renewal premiums
- the *nonforfeiture benefits* available to the owner of a life insurance policy which has a cash value
- the *policy loan* privilege available to the owner of a policy which has a cash value
- the policyowner's *reinstatement* rights with respect to a lapsed policy
- the adjustment methods used to correct a *misstatement of age*
- the manner in which *dividends* may be used by the owner of a participating policy
- the *settlement options* the company offers for the payment of policy proceeds
- the requirements the policyowner must meet to effect a *change in type of insurance*

While the specific wording used in a life insurance policy varies from insurer to insurer, the content of these major provisions remains fairly constant. We will discuss each of the above topics separately.

Entire Contract

The entire contract provision states that the policy itself, along with the application for insurance, if attached, will constitute the entire contract. This provision assures that no other official documents, such as insurance company bylaws, or any oral statements can be used to modify the policy or to affect the benefits. This provision also usually states that only specified insurance company representatives, such as the president or secretary of the company, can change any of the policy's terms, and that any such changes must be agreed to in writing by the policyowner before those changes can be made. A typical entire contract provision follows:

> **Entire contract.** The entire contract consists of this policy and the attached copy of the application. Only our Chairman, President, Secretary, or one of our Vice Presidents can change the contract, and then only in writing. No change will be made in the contract unless you agree to it in writing.

As is the case regarding all policy provisions, the actual wording of the entire contract provision is up to each insurer; however, the wording must be approved by each jurisdiction in which the policy is to be sold.

There are two major reasons why the entire contract provision is important to both the insurer and the policyowner. The first reason is that many life insurance policies are long-term in nature. It would be virtually impossible to base a claim decision 30 or 40 years after the policy was issued on memory of what was said or orally promised at the time an application was completed. Moreover, it is not uncommon for the original policyowner to be deceased by the time the policy benefit becomes payable. Second, the entire contract provision guarantees the policyowner access to all of a policy's terms and conditions. For example, neither the policyowner nor the beneficiary would be likely to have a chance to see the insurance company's charter and bylaws or any modifications of these documents; hence, it would be unfair to let these documents have any influence on the operation of the contract.

The purpose of attaching a copy of the application to the policy is to forestall any controversy regarding the information contained in that document. As we have seen, the information contained in the application is important to the insurer in deciding whether or not to accept a particular risk.

Incontestability

Under general contract law, it is possible to *contest*–that is, to dispute–the validity of a contract if there has been misrepresentation of important facts or if fraud was involved when the contract was made. A contract for life insurance is also contestable. However, laws in the United States and in Canada require that policies include an incontestability provision, which provides a time limit on this right to contest. A typical incontestability provision included in policies issued in the United States follows:

> **Incontestability.** We will not contest this policy after it has been in force during the lifetime of the insured for two years from the date of issue.

The two-year period used in the above sample provision is the maximum period permitted by law. A shorter than two-year period is permitted since it would be more favorable to the policyowner, and some policies do specify shorter contestability periods. The phrase "during the lifetime of the insured" is very important, since, in effect, this phrase makes the policy *always* contestable if the person whose life is insured should die during the specified contestable period. If this phrase were not included and the insured's death occurred before the end of the contestable period, the beneficiary could delay making a death claim until after the period had expired. The insurer would then be prevented from contesting the policy and, hence, from refusing to pay the claim.

The purpose of the incontestability provision is to assure policyowners and beneficiaries that, after the contestable period has passed, the life insurance policy may not be cancelled on the basis that a material misstatement was made at the time the application for the policy was made. As mentioned in the last chapter, a fact is considered to be material if knowledge of that fact would have changed the decision of the company when it was considering whether to accept the risk. The effect of the incontestability clause is to *prevent* life insurance companies from cancelling a life insurance policy after a specified period, even if the application contained a *material* misrepresentation.

Suppose, for example, William McFinn stated in his application for insurance on his life that he had no history of heart ailments, although in fact he was being treated for a heart condition. If the insurer, relying on Mr. McFinn's statement, issued him a policy and Mr. McFinn died three years later of a heart attack, the company would not have the right to contest the policy and refuse to pay the claim; the contestability period would have expired. If William McFinn died a year after the policy was issued, and the standard two-year incontestability provision was included in the policy, the insurer would have the right to contest the claim based on the material misrepresentation in his application.

Canadian law differs from United States law in that Canadian law permits insurance companies to contest a contract at any time, even after the contestable period has expired, when statements in the application are fraudulent statements. A **fraudulent statement** is a misstatement made with the intent to deceive and do harm to another party. Companies in Canada seldom exercise the right to contest a policy based on fraud since it is usually difficult to obtain the evidence to prove intent to deceive and, hence, it is difficult to support such cases.

Grace Period

Life insurance policies are usually required to include a provision granting a grace period with regard to the payment of renewal premiums on a life insurance policy. Renewal premiums are those payable after the initial, or first, premium.

The **grace period** is a specified length of time, usually 30 or 31 days after a renewal premium is due, within which a premium may be paid without penalty. In most jurisdictions, the 30- or 31-day period is the minimum grace period allowed. A company can, and some companies do, provide a longer grace period. During this grace period, the policy remains in force, and, if the premium is paid during the grace period, the company will accept it as being paid "on time." If the insured dies during the grace period, the company pays the policy benefit, but usually deducts from the benefit amount due the amount of the unpaid premium. A typical grace period provision follows:

> **Grace period.** We allow 31 days from the due date for payment of a premium. All insurance continues during this grace period.

If a policy's premium is not paid during the grace period, the policy is said to **lapse**. It should be noted, however, that some insurers do not consider a policy as having "lapsed" if that policy has a cash value. However, this text, in keeping with general usage, will use the terms "lapse" or "lapsed" in connection with any policy on which premiums have not been paid by the end of the grace period.

Nonforfeiture Benefits

A life insurance company makes certain benefits, called *nonforfeiture benefits*, available to the owner of a policy which has a cash value when that policy lapses. At one time many companies simply retained the money backing reserves – the policyowner forfeited this money if the policy lapsed. In 1861, the state of Massachusetts required that this money be used to purchase some form of continued term insurance for the insured. This was the first legal requirement that some form of nonforfeiture benefit be provided, although some companies had felt it proper to return some of the reserve even though they were not required to do so. During the next decades many companies in the United States and Canada made provision for this continued term insurance and for some cash values in their policies.

In 1948, the National Association of Insurance Commissioners developed the Standard Nonforfeiture Law. This document was enacted in its original form or with slight variations in all states. In 1980, the NAIC adopted amendments to this law. In Canada, neither the revised Uniform Life Insurance Act nor Quebec insurance law requires that companies include provision for nonforfeiture benefits other than for automatic premium loans. However, laws require that if companies make such benefits available, then the benefits must be detailed in specific policy provisions. Most policies issued in Canada do include these nonforfeiture benefit provisions as a matter of course, for ethical and competitive reasons.

The Standard Nonforfeiture Law specifies that each policy which produces a reserve liability must provide for a cash surrender value and either reduced paid-up or extended term insurance. The cash surrender value is generally called, simply, the cash value. In all of Canada and in the state of Rhode Island, the automatic premium loan provision is regarded as a nonforfeiture benefit as well. We will look in some detail at each of these nonforfeiture benefits or nonforfeiture options, as they are sometimes called.

Cash value

The Standard Nonforfeiture Law requires that insurers provide cash values as soon as they are available according to the formula specified in that law. This formula takes into account the plan of insurance, the age of the policy, and the length of the policy's premium payment period. Therefore, some policies, such as endowment insurance policies, which have large premiums in relation to the amount of insurance, may have immediate cash values. Lower-premium policies, such as continuous premium whole life policies, will take longer to build up cash values. In most cases, if the policy is of the type that produces reserves, the Standard Nonforfeiture Law provides that a cash value must be provided after the policy has been in force for three years, although companies may provide cash values earlier.

The formula stated in the Standard Nonforfeiture Law is used to compute the minimum required cash value. Again, companies are permitted to provide higher cash values. Insurers often provide higher and earlier cash values as a means of competing in the sale of life insurance.

The policy must state the method used to compute all values and must list the cash value available at the end of each of the first 20 years the policy is in force. This listed cash value is the basic amount the policyowner will receive upon surrender of the policy.

The following table lists sample cash values for three types of policies issued on the life of a 35-year-old male.

Type of Policy	Cash Value per $1,000 of face amount at end of policy year				
	1	5	10	20	30
Whole Life	$ 0	$ 50	$145	$340	$ 530
Endowment at 65	10	110	250	600	1,000
Term to 65	0	20	55	95	0

The amount of cash value actually available to a policyowner may not be the exact amount listed in the policy. The amount the policyowner will actually receive is called the *net cash value*. Dividend additions, advance premium payments, policy loans, and interest due on policy loans will result in additions to and subtractions from the listed cash value.

As mentioned earlier in the text, participating life insurance policies will usually pay dividends to the policyowner. As we shall see in Chapter 10, one way in which these dividends can be used is to purchase additional paid-up insurance. These additional amounts of insurance purchased using dividends are called paid-up additions or dividend additions, and, since they represent paid-up insurance, they will have cash values. A sample calculation of a net cash value follows:

Cash Value Listed in Policy $5,000
Addition:
    Cash Value of Dividend Additions . . . . +150
Deductions:
    Policy Loan Outstanding $500
    Interest Due on Policy Loan 50
Total Deduction . . . . −550

Net Cash Value . . . . $5,000 + $150 − $550 = $4,600

Therefore, on this particular policy, the amount available to the policy-owner – the net cash value – is $4,600.

When a policyowner withdraws the *entire* cash value, the policy is terminated, and there is no longer any insurance coverage. In such a case, it is usual for the policyowner to surrender the policy, that is, return it to the insurer.

The Standard Nonforfeiture Law and Canadian laws allow an insurer to reserve the right to defer payment of any policy's cash value for a period of six months after the request for payment has been made. However, a few jurisdictions have shortened this period. The insurance company's right to defer payment is designed to relieve the pressure on the company's cash reserves should there be a sudden, unexpected rush of surrenders occurring over a short period.

There may be occasions when a policyowner is unable or unwilling to keep up the premium payments on a policy but still desires some form of insurance protection. Under the Standard Nonforfeiture Law, the cash value of the policy can be used to purchase continued coverage either as reduced paid-up insurance or as extended term insurance.

Reduced paid-up insurance

Under the reduced paid-up insurance nonforfeiture option, the net cash value of the policy is used as a net single premium to purchase paid-up life insurance of the same plan as the original policy. The premium charged for the paid-up insurance is based on the age the insured has attained when the option goes into effect. The amount of paid-up insurance which can be purchased under this option is smaller than the face value of the policy – hence the name "reduced paid-up insurance."

As required for the cash value, the policy must also contain a chart listing the amounts of reduced paid-up insurance which are available each year for the first 20 years the policy is in force. The actual amount of reduced paid-up insurance available might be higher or lower than the amount listed, depending on the size of the *net* cash value. The amount of reduced paid-up insurance listed for each year is based on the cash value listed in the policy for that year. If the net cash value is larger than the listed cash value amount, as might be the case if the policy includes dividend additions, then the amount of reduced paid-up insurance available would be higher than the reduced paid-up amount listed in the chart.

If there is a policy loan outstanding, the net cash value will be lower – the insurer will subtract the amount of the outstanding loan plus any interest due from the listed cash value – and, consequently, the amount of reduced paid-up insurance available will be less than the amount listed in the policy. However, the policyowner may request that the insurer use the actual cash value, without deducting the outstanding loan amount, to purchase the reduced paid-up insurance. This will mean that the insurer will continue to charge interest on the loan and that the loan either will have to be repaid at some future date or will be deducted from the amount payable when the insured dies. Continuing the loan, however, will mean that a greater amount of paid-up life insurance can be purchased.

The insurance purchased under the reduced paid-up insurance option will have the same duration as the original policy. Thus, if the original policy was a whole life policy, then the reduced paid-up coverage remains in force throughout the insured's entire lifetime. When an endowment insurance policy is continued on the reduced paid-up insurance option, both the life insurance benefit and the pure endowment benefit are reduced equally. The duration of the endowment policy is not changed when the coverage is continued under the reduced paid-up insurance option.

The premium amount charged by the insurer for this coverage is based on net premium rates; that is, the insurer does not add an amount to the premium to cover its expenses. Hence, buying insurance in this manner is less expensive than taking the policy's value in cash and purchasing another paid-up insurance policy at a later date. The new insurance issued under this option will continue to have and to build a cash value, and the policyowner will continue to have the rights available to the owner of any life insurance policy, including the right to surrender the policy for its cash value and the right to receive dividends if the original policy was on a participating basis. However, any supplemental benefits, such as accidental death benefits, which were available on the original policy are usually not available when the policy is continued as reduced paid-up insurance.

The following chart illustrates the amount of paid-up insurance which might be available to a male applicant 40 years of age under two whole life policies.

Type of Policy	Paid-up insurance per $1,000 of face amount at end of policy year		
	5	10	20
Continuous-Premium Whole Life Policy	$178	$368	$ 613
20-Payment Whole Life Policy	$283	$557	$1,000

Extended term insurance

The extended term insurance option allows the policyowner to use the net cash value of the policy to purchase term insurance for the amount of coverage available under the original policy. This term insurance, however, will be in effect for a length of time *less* than that provided by the original policy. The length of the term depends upon the amount of the coverage, the size of the net cash value, the sex of the insured, and the insured's attained age when the option is exercised. A policy with a high amount of available cash value may purchase extended term insurance that would cover many years. Most policies issued in the United States specify that, if no option is chosen by the policyowner, the extended term insurance option will automatically be considered the chosen option.

The amount of extended term insurance available under this option is equal to the amount of insurance that would have been payable under the original policy. Since the amount payable under the policy would be reduced by the amount of any indebtedness, such as a policy loan, and increased by the face amount of any dividend additions, such reductions and increases are also made by the insurer when calculating the amount of coverage available under the extended term insurance option. Otherwise, the insurer would, in effect, be granting a greater or lesser amount of actual coverage than that which was in effect before the nonforfeiture option was exercised.

Let us look at an example of how the amount of extended term insurance available would be calculated:

Face Value of Policy $10,000
    Addition: Face Value of Dividend Additions 200
    Deduction: Outstanding Policy Loan 1,000
Listed Cash Value 2,500
    Addition: Cash Value of Dividend Additions 50
    Deduction: Outstanding Policy Loan 1,000

Amount of Term Insurance
    Available .... $10,000 + $200 − $1,000 = $9,200

Net Cash Value .... $2,500 + $50 − $1,000 = $1,550

In this case, if the extended term insurance option were selected, the policyowner would receive $9,200 of term insurance for as long a term as the net cash value, $1,550, would provide.

When an endowment insurance policy is continued under the extended term insurance option, the net cash value is applied to purchase extended term insurance for the original face amount of the policy. If the net cash value is not large enough to continue the full face amount of coverage for the entire duration of the original policy, then the term extends for as long a period as the net cash value can purchase. When the amount of the net cash value exceeds the amount required to purchase extended term insurance for the entire duration of the original policy, as is often the case, then the remaining amount is used to provide an endowment benefit which will be paid on the original maturity date. The amount of this endowment benefit, though, will be lower than the amount of the endowment benefit which would have been provided had premium payments been continued.

Most policies specify that when the policy is continued on an extended-term basis, the policyowner cannot exercise the policy loan privilege or receive dividends. However, the policyowner may cancel the extended term insurance and surrender the policy for its remaining cash value. In addition, as with the reduced paid-up option, any supplementary benefits which were available under the original policy are usually not available when the policy is placed under the extended term insurance option.

As in the case of cash surrender values and reduced paid-up insurance, the life insurance policy must contain a chart showing the benefit available under the extended term option. The length of time the original face value of the policy will be continued in force under the extended term option must be shown for each of the first 20 policy years.

The sample table of guaranteed values for a whole life policy shown in Figure 7-2 includes the duration of extended term insurance available at the end of specified policy years.

Automatic premium loan

The automatic premium loan (APL) provision states that the insurer automatically will pay an overdue premium for the policyowner by making a loan against the policy's cash value. The use of the automatic premium loan keeps the original policy in force for the full amount of coverage, including all supplemental benefits. As previously noted, the automatic premium loan provision must be included in policies issued in Canada and in the state of Rhode Island because it is considered a nonforfeiture option in both jurisdictions. The provision is also widely used in policies issued in other jurisdictions, although other jurisdictions do not require the provision to be included. The laws in both Canada and Rhode Island specify that the automatic premium loan provision is the automatic nonforfeiture option. In other jurisdictions, the policyowner must request that the insurer apply the automatic premium loan provision in order for the insurer to act according to its terms.

Policy Loans

The policy loan provision gives the policyowner the right to borrow money from the insurance company using the cash value of the life insurance policy as security. The loan may be for any amount up to the net cash value of the policy minus one year's interest on the loan. Until recently, the rate of interest insurers would charge for this loan was specified and guaranteed in the policy. Currently, however, most states permit insurers to specify in

FIGURE 7-2

Sample table of guaranteed nonforfeiture values

| | | TABLE OF GUARANTEED VALUES (These values do not include dividend values nor reflect an unpaid loan) Plan: Whole Life Face Amount: $25,000 Age of Insured at Issue: 35 | | | | |

End of Policy Year	CASH VALUE	ALTERNATIVES TO CASH VALUE				End of Policy Year
		REDUCED PAID-UP INSURANCE	or	EXTENDED TERM INSURANCE		
				YEARS	DAYS	
1	.....	...		..	...	1
2	.....	...		..	...	2
3	$300.00	$1,150		3	13	3
4	625.00	2,325		5	211	4
5	975.00	3,475		7	264	5
6	1,325.00	4,550		9	135	6
7	1,675.00	5,550		10	233	7
8	2,050.00	6,575		11	268	8
9	2,425.00	7,500		12	211	9
10	2,825.00	8,450		13	117	10
11	3,225.00	9,325		13	323	11
12	3,625.00	10,150		14	108	12
13	4,050.00	10,975		14	242	13
14	4,450.00	11,675		14	309	14
15	4,900.00	12,450		15	29	15
16	5,325.00	13,100		15	58	16
17	5,775.00	13,775		15	84	17
18	6,225.00	14,400		15	85	18
19	6,675.00	14,975		15	65	19
20	7,125.00	15,525		15	26	20
AGE 60	9,400.00	17,825		14	41	AGE 60
AGE 65	11,725.00	19,625		12	319	AGE 65

policies now being issued that loan interest rates will vary – that is, the interest rate which will be charged may change from year to year based on the economic situation at the time the loan is requested. Most policies which include a varying loan interest rate specify that the rate charged will not exceed a certain maximum rate. In most of Canada, variable interest rates have been specified in life insurance policies since the mid-1960s.

It is in the area of repayment that a policy loan differs substantially from the usual commercial loan. The loan and/or interest may be repaid at any time, in whole or in part, but there is no set schedule of repayment. If the loan has not been repaid by the time a death claim is presented on the policy, then the amount of the loan plus any interest due on the loan will be deducted from the policy benefit payable.

The usual terms of a policy specify that the interest on a policy loan is charged annually. If this interest is not paid, the amount of the loan is increased by the interest amount. If the size of the loan increases to the point where there is not enough cash value remaining to pay the current interest due, the policy will terminate without further value and the contract will no longer be in force. The insurer will notify the policyowner when a policy is about to terminate.

The laws of Canada and most states permit companies to defer granting policy loans, except for loans made for the purpose of paying premiums, for a specified period, usually six months.

The policy loan option is very useful for a policyowner. Unless the loan is repaid, however, the amount of actual insurance coverage provided by the policy is reduced by the amount of the loan, plus interest, since that sum must be deducted from the face value when the policy becomes payable as a claim. For this reason, the policyowner should use discretion in exercising the policy loan privilege.

Reinstatement

A life insurance policy which has no cash value also has no nonforfeiture options; if premiums are not paid on such a policy, it lapses *and* there is no insurance coverage. The former owner of such a lapsed policy who again desires insurance may, of course, apply for and purchase a new insurance policy. However, under certain circumstances, it is possible to make the original policy again effective by means of reinstatement.

Reinstatement of a life insurance policy is the process by which a life insurance company puts back in force a policy which had terminated because of nonpayment of renewal premiums. In such a case, the original policy is again in effect; no new policy is issued. A policy provision allowing reinstatement is required in only about half the states but is required by law throughout Canada. Such a provision is, however, included as a matter of practice in almost all policies issued in Canada and the United States.

The Standard Nonforfeiture Law adopted by many states specifies a minimum period of three years during which the policyowner has the right to reinstate a lapsed policy, including policies which have been continued as extended term or reduced paid-up insurance. Canadian laws specify a minimum period of two years. Insurers are permitted to extend this period if they wish, and five-year time periods are not uncommon. In fact, a few companies set no time limit on the right to reinstate a policy.

As noted above, policies under which the insurance has been continued as extended term or reduced paid-up insurance are eligible for reinstatement. However, if a policy has been surrendered for its cash value, it is considered to have been cancelled and is ineligible for reinstatement.

Certain conditions must be met in order to reinstate a life insurance policy. The most significant condition for reinstatement is that the insured must supply satisfactory evidence of continued insurability to the insurance company. This condition is necessary to help prevent antiselection. If no evidence of insurability were required, those people who were unable to obtain insurance elsewhere because of poor health or other factors would be more likely to apply for reinstatement of their policies than would those who were in good health.

How much and what kind of evidence of insurability is necessary will depend upon the circumstances for each individual policy and upon the practices of each insurer. If a policy has been out of force for a very short time and there is no reason to suspect a problem, some companies will accept a simple statement from the insured certifying that he or she is in good health. In fact, if the reinstatement is requested and overdue premiums are paid only a month or so after the expiration of the grace period, many insurers require no evidence of insurability. However, if the grace period expired longer than a month before the reinstatement request and/or there is any reason to suspect that a health or other problem may be present, the company may require a medical examination and/or other evidence of insurability. A sample reinstatement application is shown in Figure 7–3.

The second condition which must be met in order to reinstate a policy is monetary. Upon reinstatement, the original policy will again be in force, and it must have a reserve which will be equal to the reserve for a similar policy which has been kept in force without a lapse in premium payments. Since premiums were not paid during the period the policy was not in force, the policyowner must, at the time of reinstatement, pay all back premiums, plus interest. Interest is charged at the rate specified in the policy for this type of transaction. In addition, some policies specify that any policy loan, plus interest, must be repaid before a policy will be reinstated.

Since a sizeable sum of money may be required to reinstate a life insurance policy, each policyowner must decide whether or not reinstatement of the original policy is more advantageous than applying for a new policy. One advantage to reinstating the original policy is that the premium rate for the original policy is based on the insured's age at the time that policy was purchased. A new policy will usually call for a higher premium rate because the new policy's premium rate will be based on the age the insured has attained, which is naturally higher than the age of the insured when the original policy was purchased. In addition, the original policy may contain certain provisions which are more liberal. For example, the interest rate for a policy loan on the original policy may be lower than the interest

FIGURE 7-3
Reinstatement Application

APPLICATION FOR REINSTATEMENT OF LIFE INSURANCE

ABC LIFE INSURANCE COMPANY
100 Ordinary Avenue, New York, New York 00000

Note: This form can be used only within the 6 months after the date in Section A.

SECTION A

The Insurer specified above is requested to reinstate Policy No. _____200 000 000_____
including any loan agreement. The first unpaid premium was due on _____April 1,_____,
19_83_ and the total sum required (including any interest) to reinstate is $____116.32____.
(Please enclose your check for this amount.)

SECTION B

1. INSURED? _____John_____Doe_____
                 First Name   Middle Initial   Last Name

2. DATE OF BIRTH?   Mo._7_ Day_1_ Yr._48_

3. Since the date in Section A, has the insured or any other person who was covered under the policy (in Section A):

                                                        Yes No

    (a) been in a hospital or other medical facility or been unable to be actively at work or to attend school?   ☐ ☒

    (b) consulted with, or intend to consult with, a physician for any illness or for symptoms of undiagnosed origin?   ☐ ☒
        (Do not include colds, minor virus infections, minor injuries, or normal pregnancy.)
        If "Yes" to either 3(a) or 3(b), this application may not be used. Contact your ABC agent or our local office for further assistance.

THOSE WHO SIGN THIS APPLICATION AGREE THAT:

1. Reinstatement will not take effect until (a) the Insurer approves the application, and (b) the sum required by the Insurer with respect to this application is paid during the lifetime of all persons to be covered under the reinstated policy.

2. All of the statements in this application are correctly recorded, and are complete and true to the best of the knowledge and belief of those who made them.

3. No agent has any right to accept risks, make or change contracts, or give up any of ABC's rights or requirements.

Dated at ____Any Town, Any State____
          (City or town, and state or province)

on _____July 1,_____, 19_83_

Countersigned by _____
       (Lic. resident agent, if required
        by statute or regulation)

Signature of
Insured ____John Doe____

Signature of Owner if other
than Insured _____

Spouse or Other Required
Signature, if any _____

rate which will be charged for policy loans under a new policy.

Another point which is important to the policyowner with respect to reinstatement is that, in most jurisdictions, a new contestable period begins on the date the policy is reinstated. During this new contestable period, the company may contest a reinstated policy *only* on the basis of statements which were made in the application for *reinstatement*. The insurer may not contest the policy based on statements made in the original application, unless the original contestable period has not yet expired.

Misstatement of Age

At times, an insurer or policyowner may discover that the age of the insured is incorrect as stated in the policy. If a clerical error causes the age to be misstated, and this error occurred *after* the policy was approved and the premium calculated, then the change required is simpler than the change required if the error occurred *before* the premium was set for the contract. If the error occurred before the premium was set, then the policyowner will probably be paying an incorrect premium for the amount of insurance purchased; if the age of the insured was overstated at the time of the application, it means that the policyowner has been paying premiums that are too high, and if the age was understated, the policyowner has been paying insufficient premiums.

Canadian laws and the laws in most states require that life insurance policies include a misstatement of age provision. This provision specifies that if the age of the insured is misstated and if this misstatement has resulted in an incorrect premium amount for the amount of insurance purchased, then the face amount of the policy will be adjusted to the amount the premium actually paid would have purchased had the insured's age been stated correctly. Therefore, according to the terms of this provision, if a person aged 30 had listed an age of 25 on the application, the size of the policy's face amount would be reduced; if a person aged 30 had listed an age of 35 on the application, the amount of insurance would be increased.

The procedure specified in the misstatement of age provision is always followed when the misstatement of age is discovered after the death of the insured. However, if the misstatement is discovered before the death of the insured, the insurer may grant the policyowner the option to (1) pay or receive any premium amount difference caused by the misstatement or (2) allow the policy's face amount to be adjusted to reflect the insured's correct age at the time the policy was issued.

Dividends

Earlier in this book, we discussed the dividends that are paid on participating policies. There are several options the policyowner may select as a way to use these dividends. A provision which describes dividend options in a participating policy is a standard provision required by law in most jurisdictions. The dividend options provisions will be discussed fully in chapter 10, "Additional Rights of Policy Ownership."

Settlement Options

Another provision included by insurers as a standard practice is a provision granting a policyowner and/or a beneficiary several choices in the way the policy proceeds are distributed. These options are detailed in the settlement options provision of the policy. This text will describe these options in chapter 9, "How the Proceeds Are Distributed."

Change in Type of Insurance Policy

When a life insurance policy is purchased, it is intended to meet specific needs. Very often these needs change; new occupations, larger families, and changing financial circumstances may make a previously purchased policy inappropriate. Many policies contain a provision which permits the policyowner to change an existing policy to one which better meets the needs of the policyowner as those needs change.

If the policyowner wishes to change to a type of policy which calls for a higher premium but which is for the same face amount, the insurance company usually requires only that the policyowner pay either (1) the difference in back premiums, with interest, or (2) an amount that will bring the reserve on the policy up to the amount of the reserve required on the new policy. Because the amount of the policy reserve under the new higher-premium policy is higher, the net amount at risk under the new policy will be lower than the net amount at risk under the original policy. Hence, evidence of insurability is not required when the policyowner changes from a lower-premium policy to a higher-premium policy.

However, if the change is to a policy which is for the same face amount but with lower premiums (for example, changing from a 20-payment whole life policy to a continuous-premium whole life policy), then the amount at risk will increase, because the amount of the reserve will decrease. In this situation, the company usually refunds the difference in cash values under the two policies. In addition, since there is a greater amount at risk for the insurer, it is usual to require evidence of insurability in such cases. Thus, this type of change can be made only with the insurer's consent.

Suppose Erica Burger was 25 years old when she bought a $50,000 endowment-at-age-65 policy on her own life from ABC Life Insurance Company. If she decides six years later to change that policy to a $50,000 10-payment whole life insurance policy which has higher premiums, she will have to pay the difference in back premiums, with interest, to ABC Life. If, on the other hand, Ms. Burger decides to change that policy to a $50,000 continuous-premium whole life insurance policy which has lower premiums than the endowment-at-age-65 policy, ABC Life will refund the difference in cash values between the two plans; however, Ms. Burger will need to submit evidence of insurability in order to make the change.

Optional Provisions

Life insurance policies may contain several provisions which are intended to limit the liability of the insurer under certain circumstances. The most common of these provisions are the Suicide Clause, the War Exclusion, and the Aviation Exclusion. These provisions are permitted, rather than required, by law to be included in policies.

Suicide clause

The earliest life insurance policies usually contained a statement to the effect that the proceeds of the policy would not be paid if the insured committed suicide. As a result, in such a situation, the beneficiary was denied the protection intended when the policy was purchased. As the life insurance industry developed, company attitudes changed and the general rule was established that, unless it could be proven that the insured had taken out a policy with the intention of committing suicide, the proceeds should be paid. Today, companies try to protect against the possibility of antiselection by excluding suicide as a covered risk for a specified period – usually two years. The general opinion is that this exclusion period is sufficient to protect against "planned" suicides. If an insured should commit suicide during the exclusion period, the beneficiary will usually receive the greater of either the policy's cash value or a refund of all premiums paid, with or without interest (depending on the terms of the policy). A sample suicide clause follows:

> **Suicide exclusion.** Suicide of the insured, while sane or insane, within two years of the date of issue, is not covered by this policy. In that event, this policy will end and the only amount payable will be the premiums paid to us, less any loan.

War exclusion

In past periods of war or threat of war, companies often included a provision which stated that the policy benefit would not be paid if the insured's death was connected with war. These clauses are seldom included in policies issued today, although many policies which are still in force contain a war exclusion. There are two types of war clauses which were generally used. One, called the *status* type, states that the insurer will not pay the death benefit if the insured dies while a member of the armed forces, no matter what the cause of death. The other type of war exclusion clause, the *result* type, states that the company will not pay the death benefit if the insured dies as the direct result of war or war-connected action. Therefore, someone in the armed forces who is killed in an accident while at home would be covered if the policy contained a result type exclusion, but not if the war exclusion clause was of the status type.

Aviation exclusion

In the early days of air travel, it was usual for life insurance policies to include a provision stating that the policy proceeds would not be paid if the insured's death resulted from aviation-related activities. However, today such exclusions are primarily applied to activities connected with military or experimental aircraft. Passengers on regularly scheduled or even nonscheduled flights are fully covered. Even commercial and private pilots are considered insurable, although they may have to pay slightly higher premium rates than those in less hazardous occupations or with safer pastimes.

8

Naming and Changing
the Beneficiary

Perhaps the most important right the policyowner has in a life insurance policy is the right to designate the beneficiary. After all, the primary benefit of a life insurance policy is the death benefit which will be paid when the insured dies. Both the policyowner and the insurance company have responsibilities with respect to making sure that the correct party receives this policy benefit. In this chapter we will discuss the laws and company practices pertaining to naming and changing the beneficiary.

NAMING THE BENEFICIARY

As noted previously, the proposed recipient of the proceeds of a life insurance policy is known as the beneficiary and is usually named in the policy. A typical beneficiary clause in a life insurance policy makes no mention of the beneficiary as a single human being. An applicant for insurance can name as beneficiary one person, more than one person, an estate, a trustee, a corporation, a charitable organization, or any other entity from which the company will be able to obtain a legal receipt for the proceeds. (See Figure 8–1 for a breakdown of the most common insured-to-beneficiary relationships.)

An applicant may also designate a group of persons as beneficiary of the policy proceeds. A beneficiary designation which identifies a certain group of persons, rather than naming each person, is called a ***class designation***. For example, the beneficiary designation "my children" is a class designation.

A beneficiary is named on the application for the policy, and the rules governing the naming of a beneficiary depend on the relationship between the applicant and the proposed insured. If the applicant is the proposed

FIGURE 8-1

Relationship of beneficiary to insured, based on claim payments made on individual life insurance policies

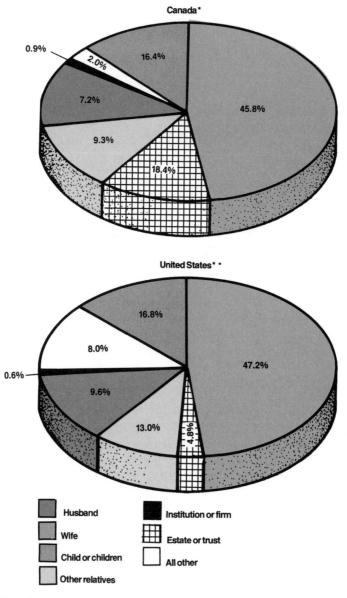

* Based on claim payments made in May 1980
**Based on claim payments made in April 1981

insured, then the applicant has the legal right to name anyone as beneficiary. The only restriction to this legal right is the contract requirement of "lawful purpose" which prevents a policy from being obtained for the purpose of speculation. An insurance company may, however, refuse to issue a policy to an applicant if the insurer questions the appropriateness of the beneficiary designated in the application.

If the applicant is not the person whose life is to be insured – in other words, if the applicant is a third party – the primary consideration in the naming of the beneficiary is the existence of an insurable interest. A person who purchases a policy on someone else's life is commonly referred to as the third party in the insurance transaction, and such a policy is called a ***third-party policy***. The proposed beneficiary must have an insurable interest in the life of the proposed insured or the insurer will refuse to issue such a third-party policy. The owner of a third-party policy may also be the beneficiary of the policy.

Primary and Contingent Beneficiaries

The ***primary*** or ***first beneficiary*** is the party or parties who will receive the proceeds of the policy when the proceeds become payable. If more than one party is named as primary beneficiary, the designation states how the proceeds are to be divided among the parties. The policyowner may also designate a ***contingent beneficiary*** – another party or parties who will receive the proceeds if the primary beneficiary should predecease the person whose life is insured. A contingent beneficiary, also sometimes called a ***secondary*** or ***successor beneficiary***, is entitled to the proceeds of a policy *if* the primary beneficiary has predeceased the insured.

An insurance company usually prefers that the policyowner name at least a primary and a contingent beneficiary, and most companies permit the designation of additional contingent beneficiaries. Naming contingent beneficiaries helps the policyowner to be certain that the proceeds will be paid to the desired party, and can be especially important in cases in which the primary beneficiary dies and the policyowner is unable to designate a new beneficiary before the policy becomes payable. If no beneficiary has been named or if the primary and all contingent beneficiaries are deceased at the time the policy becomes payable, then the proceeds are paid to the policyowner, if the policyowner is living, or to the policyowner's estate. There can be situations in which the policyowner prefers that the proceeds not be paid to his or her estate. The naming of several contingent beneficiaries is a safeguard against the occurrence of such a situation.

For example, suppose Danielle Dawson owns a $50,000 policy on her own life. If she names her husband, Victor, as primary beneficiary and names Marie and James, her children, as equal contingent beneficiaries of her policy, Victor will receive the entire $50,000 if he is still alive when she dies. If Victor dies before Danielle dies, then Marie and James will each receive half of the benefit. However, suppose Danielle instead names Marie and James as primary beneficiaries to share equally in the proceeds and names Victor as contingent beneficiary. If Marie should die before Danielle dies, then James, as the surviving primary beneficiary, would receive the entire $50,000 at Danielle's death. If neither her children nor her husband survive Danielle, and no other contingent beneficiary is named, then the $50,000 would be paid to her estate. Figure 8–2 provides a graphic illustration of the steps typically followed to determine the correct beneficiary of a policy.

Clarity of Designation

Making the beneficiary designation clear and distinct is of value to both the policyowner and the insurer. The policyowner wants to be sure that the proceeds are distributed in the desired manner. The goal of the life insurance company is to pay the proceeds in a simple and timely manner without any legal problems.

Problems occur when the way the designation was written leaves doubts as to how the policyowner wanted the proceeds to be distributed. For example, a designation such as "to my children: Charles and Tina" appears to be clear and uncomplicated. However, there might be a problem if Sally, a third child, were born four years after the designation was made and if she were never added to the designation. Should the company divide the proceeds between Charles and Tina, or should the company divide the proceeds among Charles, Tina, and Sally? Because the designation is unclear, the question would have to be settled before any proceeds could be paid.

It is important for a policyowner to update beneficiary designations when there are changes in family, marital, or financial situations. This step is necessary to be sure that the proceeds will be paid to the desired parties.

Preference Beneficiary Clause

Some policies contain a *preference* or *succession beneficiary clause* which states that, if no specific beneficiary is named, the company will pay the policy proceeds in a stated order of preference. For example, a preference beneficiary clause might list the following order: the spouse of the insured, then the children of the insured, then the parents of the insured, if living. If there were no living recipients available from that list, then the proceeds would be paid to the estate of the insured. The preference beneficiary clause is more often found in group and industrial insurance policies than in ordinary life insurance policies.

FIGURE 8-2
Primary steps in determining the correct beneficiary of life insurance policy proceeds after the claim has been approved for payment

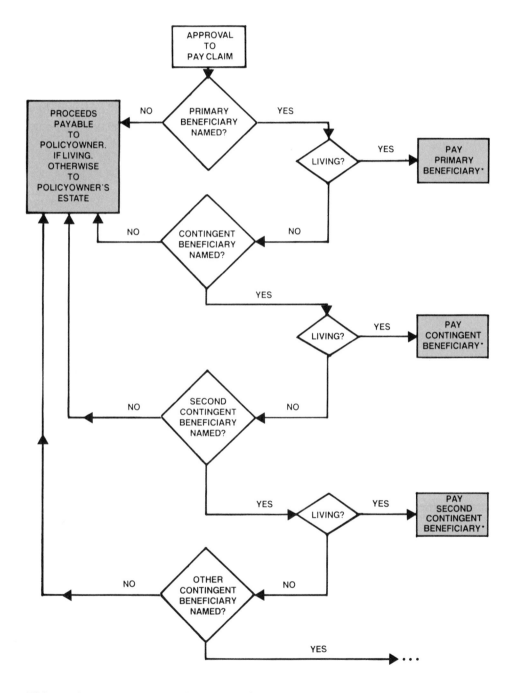

*Unless such party is ineligible to receive the proceeds.

The Beneficiary of an Endowment Policy

In an endowment insurance contract, the owner of the policy names (1) the person who will receive the benefit payable when the endowment matures and (2) the beneficiary who will receive the proceeds payable if the insured dies before the endowment matures. It is usual for the person whose life is insured to be named to receive the benefit payable when the endowment matures; if this person survives to the end of the endowment period, the proceeds will be payable to him or her. However, if the insured person dies before the endowment matures, the face amount of the policy will be payable to the named beneficiary in the same manner as under any other life insurance policy.

Naming a Minor as Beneficiary

A minor does not usually have the legal capacity to provide a valid receipt for the proceeds of a life insurance policy. If a company were to pay policy proceeds to a minor without obtaining a valid receipt, the minor, upon attaining the legal age of majority, has the legal right to demand payment of the proceeds a second time.

To avoid this problem, it is often necessary for the insurance company to ask a court to appoint a financial guardian for the minor. However, such a procedure is an expense to the minor-beneficiary, and the appointed guardian may make decisions of which the insured would not have approved.

Some jurisdictions permit the insurance company to make limited payments for the benefit of a minor-beneficiary when these payments are made to an adult who appears to be entitled to receive these payments, such as a relative who is supporting the minor. In some jurisdictions, it is legal for minors who have attained a certain age to give valid receipts for proceeds or a specified portion of those proceeds. For example, in New York, where the age of majority is 19, beneficiaries who are 18 years of age and who do not have legal guardians are permitted to give legally binding receipts for proceeds up to $3,000 per year.

If the insurance proceeds are not needed for the minor's immediate support, insurance companies may retain the proceeds at interest and make settlement of the proceeds and interest at a future date. This may be either the date when the minor reaches the age of majority or the date when a trustee or guardian is appointed who can give the insurer a valid receipt for the proceeds. A *trustee* is a person or an organization designated to control or manage another party's property.

Facility-of-Payment Clause

Certain types of policies may allow the insurance company to pay out some part of the proceeds to someone other than the named beneficiary. Group life, industrial life, and a few ordinary life insurance policies contain a *facility-of-payment clause*, which permits the insurance company to make payment of all or part of the proceeds to either a blood relative of the insured or anyone who has a valid claim to those proceeds. The amounts paid under this clause are usually small and are intended for funeral or final medical expenses incurred on behalf of the person whose life was insured. This clause can be very important in cases in which another party has assumed these expenses on behalf of the insured, but either the named beneficiary is a minor or the named beneficiary is dead and the policyowner's estate has become the beneficiary of the policy.

SPECIAL PROBLEMS: COMMON DISASTERS AND SHORT-TERM SURVIVORSHIP

Companies must occasionally deal with the special problems which result from two situations: (1) the apparent or actual simultaneous deaths of the insured and the primary beneficiary as the result of a common disaster, and (2) the death of the beneficiary soon after the death of the insured. Both specific legislation and policy wording are designed to help resolve these two problems.

Common Disasters

A problem arises when the insured and the primary beneficiary die in the same accident *and* when there is no proof that either party survived the other. Such situations are referred to as "common disasters" because the accident or disaster is common to more than one person. In such cases, companies might not be able to determine the proper recipient of the proceeds. On the one hand, if the beneficiary survived the insured, the proceeds would be payable to the beneficiary's estate. However, on the other hand, if the insured survived the beneficiary, the proceeds would be payable to the contingent beneficiary, if one had been named, or, if a contingent beneficiary had not been named, to the policyowner or to the policyowner's estate.

Legislation has been passed in the United States and Canada which specifically addresses the problem of determining survivorship in common disasters. Each of these pieces of legislation provides that, *if there is no evidence to the contrary*, it is presumed that the insured survived the beneficiary. Therefore, in such cases, the policy proceeds are distributed as if the insured had survived the beneficiary. Thus, in cases in which the insured is also the policyowner and no beneficiary is living, the proceeds would be payable to the policyowner-insured's estate.

Short-term Survivorship

These laws regarding simultaneous death do not, however, affect the way the policy proceeds are paid in those cases in which it is obvious that the beneficiary survived the insured but died soon afterward. In such a situation, the proceeds are payable to the estate of the beneficiary. This may not have been the desire of the policyowner; the policyowner may have intended to provide for the financial protection of the primary beneficiary but would have preferred that someone other than the heir of the primary beneficiary receive the benefit in such a situation.

To deal with this potential problem, many policies include a **common disaster clause**. This clause states that the primary beneficiary must survive the insured by a specified period, such as 15 or 60 days, in order to receive the policy proceeds. At the end of that period, the proceeds will be paid to the primary beneficiary if he or she is still living. Otherwise, the proceeds will be paid as though that beneficiary predeceased the insured. In this way, the policy proceeds are more likely to be distributed as the policyowner had intended.

A policyowner may also use the settlement options available in life insurance policies in order to avoid short-term survivorship problems. Settlement options will be described in the next chapter.

CHANGING THE BENEFICIARY

The laws in the United States regarding (1) the rights of the beneficiary and (2) the right of the policyowner to change the named beneficiary in a life insurance policy are different from those in Canada. In addition, these rights in the province of Quebec are determined by Quebec provincial law rather than by the revised Uniform Life Insurance Act, which has been enacted by other Canadian provinces. Therefore, for the purpose of discussing this subject, we shall address each area separately.

United States

Life insurance contracts issued in the United States usually give the policyowner the right to change the beneficiary designation as many times as desired over the life of the policy. This right to change the beneficiary designation is known as the right of revocation. A beneficiary designation is said to be a revocable beneficiary designation if there are no restrictions on the policyowner's right to change the designation. Most companies refer to beneficiaries so designated as **revocable beneficiaries**. If the policyowner waives the right to change the beneficiary designation, then the designation is known as an irrevocable beneficiary designation, and companies refer to any beneficiary so designated as an **irrevocable beneficiary**.

Revocable beneficiary

Unless the policyowner indicates to the contrary, the beneficiary is revocable. A revocable beneficiary generally has no legal interest in the proceeds or involvement with the policy until the instant the insured person dies. The exception to this rule arises in community property states, where the beneficiary-spouse may have certain rights to the proceeds. A community property state is one in which, by law, each spouse is entitled to an equal share of the income earned and, under some circumstances, property acquired by the other during the period of marriage. In the community property states (Arizona, California, Idaho, Louisiana, Nevada, New Mexico, Texas, and Washington), the consent of a beneficiary-spouse may be required if a beneficiary change would deprive the spouse of that part of the proceeds to which he or she otherwise would be entitled.

Irrevocable beneficiary

A policyowner may, however, at any time designate the beneficiary as an irrevocable beneficiary. The policyowner then gives up the right to change the beneficiary. The irrevocable beneficiary has a **vested interest** in the proceeds of the life insurance policy even during the lifetime of the insured. An interest is said to be **vested** if a person cannot be deprived of that interest without giving consent.

Because an irrevocable beneficiary has a vested interest in the policy proceeds, most insurers will not permit the policyowner who has designated an irrevocable beneficiary to exercise all the usual ownership rights under the contract without that irrevocable beneficiary's consent. For example, the policyowner cannot obtain a loan on the policy or surrender the policy for cash without the consent of the irrevocable beneficiary.

There are circumstances under which a policyowner may be able to name a new beneficiary, even if the original beneficiary designation is irrevocable. Commonly, if the policyowner wishes to make a change, the policyowner need only obtain the irrevocable beneficiary's written consent to the change of beneficiary. In addition, most life insurance policies contain a provision which states that the rights of any beneficiary, including an irrevocable beneficiary, will be surrendered if that beneficiary should die before the insured dies. This provision prevents the automatic payment of the proceeds to the heirs or estate of the irrevocable beneficiary and permits the policyowner to designate a new beneficiary.

Canada: Provinces other than Quebec

The provisions of the revised Uniform Life Insurance Act (1962) govern life insurance contracts issued for use in Canada since 1962, except those issued for use in the province of Quebec. As we noted earlier, this act sets forth the rights of policyowners; it also sets forth the rights of beneficiaries. Beneficiaries named in Canadian policies issued after 1962 are designated as revocable and irrevocable in the same manner as are beneficiaries in the United States.

Pre-1962 beneficiary designations

Canadian laws dealing with the rights of beneficiaries, however, date back to the earliest days of life insurance. Many policies issued prior to the revision of the laws in 1962 are still in force and are subject to the earlier legislation. The chief difference between the old and new laws with regard to the rights of beneficiaries is that the revised act discontinued two classes of beneficiaries provided for by earlier legislation: "preferred" beneficiaries and beneficiaries "for value."

Preferred beneficiaries. Early life insurance policies were almost always intended for the economic protection of the family, and the first legislation on beneficiary designations was primarily intended to protect the rights of the family. For this reason, the legislation established a class of beneficiaries consisting of the husband, wife, children, parents, and grand-children of the insured. Members of this group belonged to a "preferred" class and were known as *preferred beneficiaries*. As a class, these beneficiaries had vested rights to policy proceeds. The policyowner did have the right to change a preferred beneficiary, but only if the new beneficiary was also in the preferred class. If the preferred beneficiary consented, the policyowner could regain all rights of ownership, including the right to change the beneficiary to a person not included in the preferred class. In most cases, if the preferred beneficiary died before the insured died, all rights were returned to the policyowner.

Under the revised Uniform Life Insurance Act, there is no preferred class as such; protection for rights of close relatives can now be provided by naming them as irrevocable beneficiaries. However, the rules which were in effect previously with regard to preferred beneficiaries continue to ap-ply to those policies in which the beneficiary was a member of the preferred class as of June 30, 1962, unless the beneficiary had been changed to a beneficiary not in the preferred class. In such a case, future changes in the designation would then be governed by the new law.

Beneficiaries for value. Another type of beneficiary under the pre-1962 Uniform Act was a beneficiary for value. A *beneficiary for value* is one who was named as a beneficiary in return for providing consideration to the person whose life was insured. For example, if the insurance were ob-tained to protect a creditor who had granted the insured a loan, the creditor would be a beneficiary for value. Under such a designation, which could be noted in the original policy or in a declaration filed with the insurance company, the beneficiary for value had vested rights similar to the rights of a preferred beneficiary. The principal difference lay in the fact that the death of a beneficiary for value did *not* cancel the vested rights of the deceased beneficiary. Since consideration had been given, the vested interest passed on to the estate of the beneficiary for value.

The revised Uniform Life Insurance Act did away with this beneficiary designation, but, as in the case of the preferred beneficiary designation, those designations in effect on June 30, 1962, remain in effect today.

Quebec

In the province of Quebec, there has been a thorough revision of the laws governing the regulation of life insurance. For many years, the industry followed the directions of the Quebec Civil Code, and, particularly in the case of beneficiary designations, the Husbands' and Parents' Life Insurance Act. In 1976, the Civil Code of Quebec was revised, and policies issued since that time are subject to the revised legislation.

Under the 1976 revision of the Quebec Civil Code, unless otherwise stipulated, the designation of a beneficiary is revocable, and there is no special class of beneficiary. There is one exception to this rule: the policyowner's designation of a spouse as beneficiary is always irrevocable unless otherwise stated.

Pre-1976 beneficiary designations

Most life insurance policies issued before 1976 in Quebec are governed by the Husbands' and Parents' Life Insurance Act. This act created a special class of beneficiary consisting of the wife, children, wife's children, and any adopted children of the insured. This class was similar to the preferred class under the Uniform Life Insurance Act and had similar rights. Unlike the other provinces, Quebec had no beneficiary-for-value classification, and any other beneficiaries were revocable beneficiaries. One interesting feature of prior Quebec legislation was that a married woman could not insure her life and name her husband as beneficiary.

Policies issued prior to 1976 and still in force are released from the Husbands' and Parents' Life Insurance Act under certain circumstances, including (1) when a preferred type of beneficiary dies, and/or (2) when such a beneficiary consents to a change. In these situations, the policy returns to the control of the policyowner and becomes subject to the new legislation.

Change of Beneficiary Procedure

In the United States and all of Canada, if the policyowner has retained the power to change the beneficiary, the procedure to make such a change is straightforward and relatively simple. Each life insurance policy specifies the change of beneficiary procedure required.

The most important procedural point in a change of beneficiary is the written notification to the insurer of the change. Most insurance companies require only that the policyowner notify the company in writing of the change in beneficiary in order for the change to be effective. This method of changing the beneficiary is called the ***recording method***. Some insurers may also require that a change in beneficiary request be signed by disinterested witnesses or that the documents requesting the change be notarized.

A few insurance companies require a beneficiary change procedure known as the endorsement method. An endorsement is a document attached to a policy. Under the ***endorsement method***, the policy itself must be returned to the insurance company, and the name of the new beneficiary must be added to the policy in order for the change to be effective. The endorsement method is used rarely today, though it was a common procedure in the past.

The purpose of requiring written notification is to protect both the policyowner and the insurance company. The policyowner wants to be certain that policy proceeds will be distributed to the correct person. From the insurance company's standpoint, it is important that the proper beneficiary give a receipt for the proceeds. Otherwise, the company might be subject to a suit demanding payment of the proceeds for a second time to a "new" beneficiary.

Since it is the legal responsibility of the company to make payment to the proper party, it is legally permissible for the company to waive any of the policy's stated procedures for changing the beneficiary designation. This right to waive procedures can be especially important in cases in which the endorsement method is required and the policy has been lost or is not available to be sent to the company. A policy may be unavailable because the original revocable beneficiary has possession of the policy and refuses to release it so that the change can be made. For example, after an unfriendly divorce, a spouse who is the revocable beneficiary may have the policy and refuse to give it to the policyowner. In such a case, the insurer may waive the endorsement requirement and may accept the policyowner's written request for a change of beneficiary. The general rule is that a beneficiary change will be considered effective if the policyowner and the insurer have taken all reasonable steps to comply with the requirements of the policy.

In Canada, the revised Uniform Life Insurance Act and the Quebec Civil Code permit the policyowner to change a revocable beneficiary designation at any time either by using the endorsement method or by using a separate written form. This separate form must thoroughly identify the specific insurance policy involved in the beneficiary change.

Beneficiary Named in a Will

There are times when a policyowner may wish to use a will to indicate the way the proceeds of a life insurance policy should be distributed. This method of distributing policy proceeds is known as *testamentary disposition* of the proceeds.

In the United States, courts have not looked kindly on the use of wills to designate beneficiaries for life insurance contracts. In most states, beneficiary designations or changes in beneficiary designations by will have been held to be ineffective for most types of policies. However, United States Government Life Insurance policies and National Service Life Insurance policies issued to veterans and persons in the armed forces are allowed to specifically permit testamentary disposition of policy proceeds.

In all of Canada, including Quebec, wills can be used to designate the beneficiary of a life insurance policy. In Canada, a will can also be used to change the beneficiary of a policy. However, if a more recent change of beneficiary has been received by the insurance company, that change takes precedence over the designation in the will, even if the change is not noted in the will. It is important to recognize that in cases in which beneficiaries may legally be named or changed in a will, if the will should later be revoked, the designation or change of beneficiary is also revoked.

9
How the Proceeds
Are Distributed

The benefit of a life insurance policy is usually paid in a single lump sum when that policy matures or becomes a claim. In fact, early life insurers would pay benefits *only* in this manner. However, over the years, companies began making available to the beneficiary and the policyowner several alternatives to lump-sum payment of policy proceeds. These alternate methods of paying out the benefit of a life insurance policy or an endowment policy are called ***optional modes of settlement***. We will first describe lump-sum settlements and then discuss the optional modes of settlement.

LUMP-SUM SETTLEMENT

Some life insurance policies are purchased specifically because a single, large sum of money will be needed when the insured dies. Most policies which are purchased to meet business needs are intended to be paid in lump sums. The proceeds may be needed to pay debts, buy partnership shares, or be used in other ways for which a single sum of money is most appropriate. Additionally, a lump-sum distribution is best when money is needed to pay off a mortgage or to pay estate taxes.

Many people feel comfortable with the prospect of managing large sums of money. These people, as beneficiaries, wish to make their own decisions as to how they will invest or spend the proceeds of life insurance policies, and they prefer to receive lump-sum settlements. Figure 9-1 illustrates the percentage of policy benefits paid out to beneficiaries in lump-sum settlements.

On the other hand, some beneficiaries may not be capable of dealing satisfactorily with the sudden receipt of a large sum of money, either because of the emotional problems resulting from the death of a loved one or because

FIGURE 9-1
Methods of paying ordinary life insurance policy proceeds

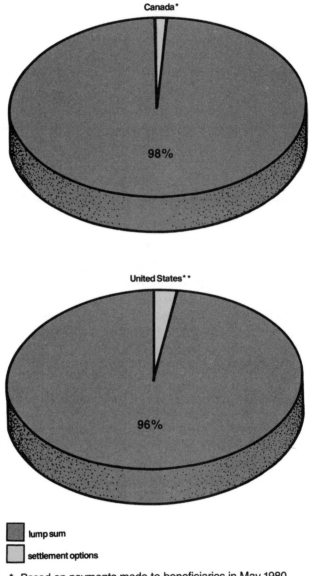

Canada*

98%

United States**

96%

■ lump sum

□ settlement options

* Based on payments made to beneficiaries in May 1980
**Based on payments made to beneficiaries in April 1981

the beneficiary is inexperienced in financial affairs.

Once a life insurance benefit has been paid to a beneficiary, the benefit is the sole property of the beneficiary. Both the insurance company and the policyowner lose control over the policy proceeds once those proceeds have been distributed. This loss of control can be a decided disadvantage to the policyowner. If, for example, the beneficiary dies shortly after receiving a lump-sum settlement, any remaining funds which the beneficiary has not spent are considered part of the beneficiary's estate and are distributed according to the beneficiary's will. The policyowner may have intended to provide for the financial security of the primary beneficiary but would prefer that someone other than the heir of the primary beneficiary receive any remaining benefits, if that primary beneficiary were not alive to use those benefits. By specifying an optional mode of settlement for the beneficiary and designating another person to receive any proceeds remaining when the primary beneficiary dies, the policyowner retains control over the distribution of the proceeds.

Additionally, if the benefit is paid in one sum, there is no way a policyowner can protect the proceeds against claims of creditors of the beneficiary. Such protection may be possible under some of the optional modes of settlement.

OPTIONAL MODES OF SETTLEMENT

Four optional modes of settlement are commonly offered: (1) the *interest option*, under which the proceeds are temporarily left on deposit with the company and the interest earned is paid out annually, semiannually, quarterly, or monthly; (2) the *fixed period option*, under which the company pays the proceeds and interest in a series of annual or more frequent installments for a preselected period; (3) the *fixed amount option*, under which the company uses the proceeds and interest to pay a preselected sum in a series of annual or more frequent installments for as long as the proceeds last; and (4) the *life income option*, under which the company uses the proceeds and interest to pay a series of annual or more frequent installments over the entire lifetime of the person designated to receive the policy benefit. With the exception of the interest option, each of these settlement options is actually a form of annuity. (Annuities will be discussed in detail in chapter 16.)

Choosing a Mode of Settlement

The needs of the policyowner and/or the beneficiary determine which method of settlement is best. The policyowner may select one of the optional modes of settlement at the time of application or at any time while the policy is in force during the lifetime of the insured. The policyowner also has the right to change to another settlement option at any time during the insured's lifetime. If the policyowner has not chosen a settlement mode at the time the policy proceeds become payable, then the beneficiary has the right to choose an optional mode of settlement rather than receiving a lump-sum payment of the policy benefit.

When a policy becomes payable, the terms of the policy contract are fulfilled, and the contract is terminated. If the proceeds are to be paid under one of the settlement options, a new contract, called a **supplementary contract**, is formed between the insurance company and the person or party designated to receive the policy benefit. This person or party is referred to as the **payee**.

When the policyowner elects an optional mode of settlement for the beneficiary, the policyowner may also designate the party who will receive any remaining benefits payable under the option when the primary beneficiary dies. When the beneficiary elects the optional mode of settlement, then the beneficiary designates the **contingent payee** or **successor payee**, the party who will receive any proceeds still payable at the time of the primary beneficiary's death.

When the policyowner selects the optional mode of settlement, the terms of the settlement are incorporated into a **settlement agreement**, which is considered part of the policy contract. The policyowner who selects an optional mode of settlement for the beneficiary may choose to make it irrevocable, in which case the beneficiary will be prevented from changing that option. If no statement indicating the irrevocability of the settlement mode is included in the settlement agreement, the mode is considered to be revocable, and the beneficiary has the right to specify another settlement mode at the time the policy benefit is payable. If the primary beneficiary dies before the insured dies, the contingent beneficiary will have the same right that was possessed by the primary beneficiary to select or change an optional mode of settlement. We will discuss each optional mode of settlement separately.

Interest Option

Under the interest option, the proceeds of a policy are held by the insurance company and earn interest. A minimum interest rate is usually guaranteed in the policy, but the insurer may pay a higher rate if the higher rate is consistent with the company's investment earnings. All interest earned on the proceeds is paid periodically to the beneficiary and cannot be left with the company to accumulate. If the beneficiary is a minor, however, companies will permit accumulation of interest until the minor reaches the age of majority.

Generally, the insurance company pays interest on the proceeds annually, unless the payee requests more frequent payments. A payee may request a more frequent payment schedule only if the amount of the proceeds being held is large enough to generate interest installments of at least a specified amount during each selected period. For example, a policy may state that a payee can request monthly installments only if the proceeds would earn at least $30 a month in interest. If the amount of each payment should fall below the specified minimium, then the insurance company's administrative costs of paying the proceeds would be too high. Therefore, the insurer would require the payee to change to a schedule of less frequent payments–annually or quarterly, for example.

The interest option is a temporary option, because companies will not hold the proceeds indefinitely. The maximum length of time the company will hold the proceeds at interest is usually the lifetime of the primary payee or 30 years, whichever is longer. Hence, if the primary payee lives for more than 30 years after the proceeds become payable, the total remaining proceeds must be paid out when that payee dies. However, if the primary payee survives the insured by less than 30 years, the contingent payee has the right to continue to have the insurance company hold the policy proceeds under the interest option until the 30-year period has expired.

If the policyowner chooses the interest option for the beneficiary, the policyowner may give the beneficiary the right to withdraw all or part of the funds. In other words, such a withdrawal privilege may be unrestricted, or the total amount that can be withdrawn may be limited to a specified sum. The policyowner usually gives the beneficiary the right to change from the interest option to any of the other settlement options. Often, the policyowner will specify the interest option as the mode of settlement so that the beneficiary will have the time to make a rational decision on which method of settlement, whether a lump sum or one of the options, will be most suitable. In such cases, an unrestricted withdrawal privilege is usually included in the option.

Fixed Period Option

Under the fixed period option, the company agrees to pay equal installments to the beneficiary for a fixed period of time. Each payment will consist partly of the policy proceeds being held by the company and partly of the interest earned on the proceeds. As with the interest option, the policy will cite a minimum interest rate which will be earned on the proceeds, with a provision that the rate may be higher if the company's investment returns are better than expected. The length of the payment period, however, remains fixed.

The size of each installment amount under the fixed period option depends primarily on the amount of the proceeds, the interest rate, and the length of the payment period chosen. These installments may be paid annually or more frequently–even monthly if each monthly installment amount is large enough to meet the company's minimum requirements. Policies usually contain a chart which shows, for selected payment periods, the amount of the monthly payment which will be made per thousand dollars of net policy proceeds.

For example, assume that Joel Shore, who owned a life insurance policy on his own life, specified a 10-year fixed period option and named his son Robert as sole beneficiary. At Joel's death, the policy proceeds amounted to $100,000. If the chart below were applicable, Robert would receive at least $972 ($9.72 × 100) per month for 10 years. This amount could be higher if the company experienced a more profitable rate of return than the rate guaranteed.

Fixed Period (years)	Monthly installment per $1,000 of proceeds
5	$18.07
10	9.72
20	5.56

Note that the total amount Robert would receive over the 10 years is $116,640 ($972 × 12 months × 10 years). This amount is greater than the $100,000 payable in a lump sum because the proceeds being held by the company are earning interest.

Since each payment reduces the amount of money the life insurance company is holding under this settlement option, the size of the fund is constantly decreasing. Therefore, at the end of the payment period, the fund is exhausted and no more money is due the payee. If the primary payee dies before the end of the payment period, any remaining funds are paid to the contingent payee.

The fixed period option is a good way to provide a temporary income for a specified period of time – for example, while children are dependent or while a spouse-payee is receiving education or training to become income-producing. It is also widely used to provide income until another anticipated income, such as a pension or social security, begins.

Under the fixed period option, the payee is usually not permitted to withdraw any part of the fund during the payment period. Such a partial withdrawal would reduce the size of the remaining fund and would require a recalculation of the entire schedule of benefit payments. However, many policies do permit the payee to cancel the option and collect all of the remaining proceeds and unpaid interest in a lump sum.

Fixed Amount Option

Under the mode of settlement known as the fixed amount option, the life insurance company pays the beneficiary equal installments of a set amount until the proceeds, plus the interest earned, are exhausted. With the fixed amount option, the person who chooses the option (either the policyowner or the beneficiary) specifies the *amount* of each installment but not the length of the installment period. In contrast, the person who chooses the fixed period option specifies the period over which installments are to be paid, but not the amount of each installment. One other difference between the fixed period and fixed amount options is in the effect of extra interest earnings. Under the fixed period option, extra interest earnings will increase the size of the installments; under the fixed amount option, extra interest earnings will lengthen the period over which the payments will be made. See Figure 9-2 for a graphic representation of the effect of extra interest earnings on the proceeds being paid under the fixed period and fixed amount settlement options.

The payee receiving the policy proceeds under the fixed amount settlement option generally is given the right to withdraw part or all of the remaining proceeds. Withdrawal of all the remaining policy proceeds will end the series of payments at that point. A partial withdrawal reduces the *number* of installments, not the size of each installment. In many cases, payees will have the additional privilege of increasing or decreasing the size of each installment. An increase in the size of each payment means that the proceeds will be exhausted more rapidly and fewer payments will be made. The reverse is the case if the size of each installment is reduced.

The policy may include a chart indicating the length of time for which various amounts would be payable under the fixed amount option. Here,

FIGURE 9-2

Effect of extra interest earnings on proceeds being paid under the fixed period and fixed amount settlement options

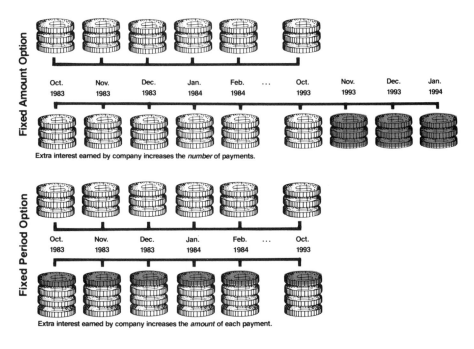

the number of payments listed is the guaranteed minimum. If the company is able to pay a higher-than-anticipated interest rate, the number of installments, rather than the amount of each payment, will be increased. The larger the amount of the proceeds, the longer the period for which a stated amount will be paid. If the primary payee dies before the proceeds are exhausted, the remaining proceeds are paid to the contingent payee.

The fixed amount option is useful when the policyowner or beneficiary wants to be sure that adequate income will be available, even if for only a short time. For instance, the beneficiary may have the capacity to earn an adequate income but may have reasons for delaying entry into gainful employment.

Life Income Option

When payments under the fixed amount or fixed period option cease, the policy benefits will have been paid and nothing more is due the beneficiary. Therefore, the policyowner or beneficiary choosing either of the fixed options must be sure that providing a temporary income is the best way to distribute the policy proceeds. When there is no prospect that other sources of income will be available in the future, the beneficiary may be better served by a permanent income provided through a life income option, even though this method of settlement may result in installment payments that are smaller in amount than payments under the fixed amount or fixed period options.

The life income option guarantees that payments will be made for as long as the beneficiary lives. As in the case of the two fixed options, the life insurance policy proceeds are retained by the insurance company and paid out in installments to the beneficiary. Each installment consists partly of the policy proceeds and partly of earned interest.

The major distinction between this option and the other options is that a *life contingency* is taken into account when the company calculates the amount of the installments payable; that is, the company considers the life expectancy of the recipient of the proceeds in addition to the amount of money payable under the policy. Since payments are guaranteed for life, a company expects to make more payments to a beneficiary who is age 50 when benefit payments begin than to one age 70 at the time payments start. Thus, if the amount of money originally available is the same, the size of the payments made to a payee age 50 will be lower than those made to a payee age 70.

Although the life income option may provide smaller installments per thousand dollars of proceeds than either of the fixed options, the installments are guaranteed to continue as long as the beneficiary lives. Because there are life contingencies involved in the life income options, life insurance companies are the primary financial institutions offering contracts of this type.

There are several varieties of the life income settlement option available. We will describe the straight life income, life income with period certain, refund life income, and the joint and survivorship life income option.

Straight life income option

Under the straight life income option, payments cease when the payee dies. No further payments are due, regardless of when that payee's death takes place. Therefore, if the payee dies after receiving only a few installments, then the total amount of all payments made to the payee may be considerably less than the amount of the original policy benefit.

The fact that only a small portion of the original proceeds would be paid if the payee dies soon after the payments begin is disturbing to many policyowners, and the straight life option is chosen less often than some of the other varieties of the life income option. However, the straight life income option provides a larger installment benefit per thousand dollars of proceeds than the other life income options. Hence, the straight life income option is advantageous to the beneficiary who has no dependents and who needs the lifetime protection and higher income this settlement option provides.

Life income with period certain option

The most commonly used settlement option is the life income with period certain option. Under this option, payments will be made by the company for *at least* a specified number of years, such as five, ten, or twenty years. If the payee is still alive at the end of this period, payments will continue until that person's death. If the payee dies before the end of the specified period, the contingent payee will receive either a lump-sum settlement of the remaining proceeds *or* installment payments until the specified period expires. For example, if Amos Baker chooses a ten-year period certain life income option and dies after installments have been paid for seven years, the company would either continue the payments for three more years to a contingent payee or pay the contingent payee the remaining funds in a lump sum. This guarantee of continued payments for the specified period, even if the payee dies during that period, distinguishes the life income with period certain from the straight life income option.

The life income with period certain option is often chosen in instances where there is a need to assure income to more than one person, such as a spouse and young children. The life income with period certain option could be used to assure that even if the spouse-beneficiary should die soon after payments began, there would still be a source of income for the children until they were able to support themselves.

Refund life income option

The refund life income option guarantees that the company will pay out at least the amount of the original policy proceeds. Under this option, payments are made for the lifetime of the payee. However, if the payee dies before the total amount the company has paid in installments equals the amount of the original policy proceeds payable, then the company would pay the difference to the contingent payee. This payment may be either in the form of continued installments or in a lump sum.

The refund life income option is useful in the same situations as the life income with period certain option and is primarily chosen when there is some reason to believe that the primary payee may not live long after payments start.

Joint and survivorship life income option

Another variation of the life income option is the joint and survivorship life income option. Under this option, the policyowner names two beneficiaries and the insurer makes payments until both beneficiaries have died. Since under the joint and survivorship option payments will continue even after one payee has died, the insurer must plan for the likelihood of more payments being made than if one person were receiving the life income option. Therefore, the amount available for each installment will be less than the amount that would have been payable if there were only one payee. Some companies also provide this option on either a period certain or a cash refund basis.

The policyowner and/or beneficiaries decide at the time this option is selected whether the size of each installment should either remain the same throughout the duration of the contract or be reduced upon the death of the first payee. The beneficiaries will receive higher initial installment payments if the amount of the installment is scheduled to be reduced after the death of the first beneficiary. Such a reduction would be chosen in the expectation that less income will be needed to support one person.

Charts in the policy list the minimum amounts guaranteed under the various life income options. These charts are more detailed than for the other settlement options since the amounts available must also take into account the age and sex of each payee. In addition, the charts show the amounts available for the guaranteed periods, for the installment refund, and for joint and survivorship variations. The policy usually also specifies that the beneficiary may receive a higher amount than the amount listed in the chart if, at the time the proceeds become payable, a higher amount is justified based on changes in the company's interest rate assumptions.

Figure 9-3 shows the monthly amounts which may be available per

$1,000 of proceeds under the various life income settlement options. Note the higher amounts available for male survivors. Since females as a group have a tendency to live longer than males, the insurer must be prepared to make more payments to females under these life income options. Some insurers have, however, begun using unisex tables to determine these amounts.

FIGURE 9-3
Sample monthly income amounts available per $1,000 of proceeds under life income options

Age	Straight Life Option	Period Certain Option		Installment Refund Option
		10 Yrs.	20 Yrs.	
Female				
55	$4.80	$4.78	$4.62	$4.65
65	6.10	5.95	5.22	5.68
70	7.18	6.80	5.60	6.44
Male				
55	5.30	5.20	4.90	5.00
65	6.90	6.50	5.50	6.15
70	8.25	7.36	5.70	7.01

Joint and Survivorship Option	
Male and Female the Same Age	Straight Life Income
55	$4.50
65	5.56
70	6.63

10

Additional Rights
of Policy Ownership

The owner of a life insurance policy has many rights under the contract. We have already discussed several of these rights, such as the owner's right to name the beneficiary, choose the settlement option, and receive a policy loan. This chapter will describe additional rights and choices available to the policyowner with respect to premium payments, dividends, and the ownership of the policy.

PREMIUM PAYMENTS

Mode of Premium Payment

Premiums on ordinary individual life insurance policies may be paid annually, semiannually, quarterly, or monthly. The frequency of premium payment is called the *mode* of payment and is selected by the policyowner in the application for insurance. After the policy is issued, the policyowner may change the mode of payment at any time.

The mode of premium payment affects the total amount of the gross premium which must be paid in a given year. Ordinary life insurance premium rates are expressed based on an annual mode of premium payment; that is, the insurer assumes that each year's premium is paid in full at the start of each policy year. The insurance company assumes, then, that the amount of the annual premium to be invested will be available at the beginning of each policy year. The earnings from these invested premiums reduce the amount of money the insurer needs to charge for the insurance coverage. If only a portion of the premium to be invested is received at the start of the year and if other installments are received and invested at a later date, then the amount of money the company earns by investing those premiums will be less, since portions of the money will have been invested for a shorter period. In addition, you may recall that when an insurance company computes a gross premium, it adds an amount—the loading factor—to the net premium to cover its projected expenses. These expenses include the billing, processing, and bookkeeping expenses the insurer will incur collecting annual premiums. The more frequently premiums are collected, the higher these expenses will be.

The insurer usually charges the policyowner who chooses a premium payment mode which is more frequent than annual an additional amount to cover losses resulting from reduced investment earnings and to cover the costs involved in processing the additional premium payments. Remember, when we speak of the amount of the premium paid by the policyowner, we are referring to the gross premium. The net premium remains the same. Therefore, the mode of premium payment does not affect the policy reserve or the total cash value of the policy.

The additional amount which the insurance company charges the policyowner for the privilege of paying premiums more frequently than annually is calculated by adding a prescribed percentage to the gross annual premium. Generally, the more frequent the payments, the higher the total additional charge which will be added to the premium. Usually, the additional percentage charge ranges from 2 percent to 6 percent of the gross annual premium. For example, a company might add a 2 percent charge for the privilege of paying premiums on a semiannual basis, a 4 percent charge for quarterly premium payments, and a 6 percent charge for monthly premium payments. Such a company's calculations for a quarterly premium payment on a policy which has a gross annual premium of $500 would be as follows:

Gross Annual Premium	$500
Additional 4% Charge	20
Total Gross Annual Premium	$520
Quarterly Payment Amount	$130
[Gross premium ($520) divided by number of payments per year (4)]	

Thus, the owner of the policy would make four payments of $130 during the course of the policy year.

Method of Premium Payment

Life insurance policies usually state that renewal premiums are payable at the home office and/or authorized branch office of the company. A policyowner does not, however, need to visit an insurance company office in order to pay each premium. Although renewal premiums for ordinary policies may be paid in person, it is more usual for the policyowner to pay premiums either by mail, by automatic payment techniques, or through payroll deduction. In most cases, renewal premiums for ordinary insurance policies are *not* paid to the agent of the insurance company, since these agents are only authorized to accept initial premiums. Figure 10–1 illustrates the most commonly selected methods of paying premiums.

Payment by mail

If a policyowner mails a renewal premium to the insurer, the insurer will generally accept the premium as having been paid on the date the envelope was postmarked.

A policyowner may pay the renewal premium in cash, by money order, or by check. A few insurers will also accept a charge against a policyowner's

FIGURE 10-1

Most commonly selected methods of premium payment*

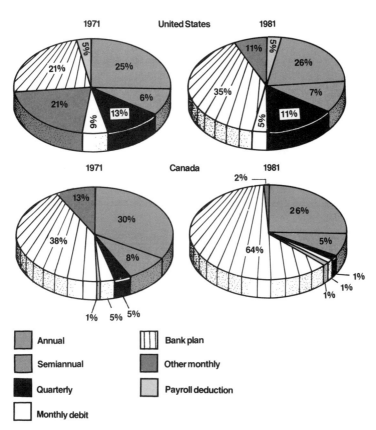

*Figures for annual, semiannual, quarterly, and "other monthly" reflect premium payment by mail. Most common mode of bank plan premium payment is monthly.

credit card as a means of paying the premium. If the payment is not made in cash, legal acceptance of the premium by the insurer is contingent on the actual collection of the money by the company.

Suppose, for example, a quarterly premium payment was due on Shelly Whitney's yearly renewable term (YRT) life insurance policy on April 8. She mailed a check to the ABC Life Insurance Company on May 5 for the full amount of the premium due. When the ABC Life Insurance Company received the check on May 10, the company deemed the premium was paid on May 5, which was the date the envelope was postmarked. Since May 5 is within the 31-day grace period provided by Ms. Whitney's policy, the policy would remain in force. However, if the check "bounces" because Ms. Whitney has insufficient funds in her account to cover the amount of the check when it is presented for payment, then ABC is considered to have never accepted the premium, and the policy is considered to have lapsed on the last day of the grace period.

Automatic payment techniques

An important trend in premium payment methods over recent years has been the development of automatic payment techniques. The most common of these techniques is the preauthorized check (PAC) system. Under this method of premium payment, the policyowner authorizes the insurance company to generate checks against the policyowner's account. The insurance company sends these checks directly to the policyowner's bank or savings institution for payment. The policyowner also authorizes the bank or savings institution to honor these checks and deduct the funds directly from the policyowner's account.

Policyowners can also authorize their banks to automatically pay premiums on the dates they are due using the electronic funds transfer (EFT) method. When this method is used, funds to pay premiums are automatically transferred by wire; no paper checks are generated, and notice of the transaction simply appears on the policyowner's bank statement.

Another automatic payment technique – the payroll deduction method – requires the cooperation of the policyowner's employer. Under the payroll deduction method, the employer will deduct life insurance premiums directly from an employee's paycheck. Generally, several employees must use the payroll deduction method and have policies with the same insurance company in order for the employer to institute the system. The employer usually sends the insurer a single check for the premiums due on all such policies.

These methods of automatic premium payment have produced two important results: reduced administrative expenses for the insurance companies on monthly and quarterly premium payment modes and fewer instances of a policyowner's forgetting to pay the premiums. Hence, most insurance companies forgo or reduce the extra charges which would otherwise be added for semiannual, quarterly, or monthly payment modes when the policyowner chooses one of these automatic payment methods.

POLICY DIVIDENDS

Earlier in this text, we discussed the dividends which may be paid to the owners of participating life insurance policies. Usually, the policy must be in force for two years before any dividends are payable. The amount which will be paid as a dividend is determined annually by the insurance company. The dividend amount reflects the insurance company's actual mortality, interest, and expense experience; the plan of insurance; the policy's premium amount; and the length of time the policy has been in force. Generally, dividend amounts increase substantially with the age of the policy and are payable on the policy's anniversary date.

Dividend Options

There are generally five **dividend options** available to policyowners; that is, policyowners may choose one of five methods for receiving or using dividends. The dividends may be (1) received in cash, (2) applied toward the payment of renewal premiums, (3) left with the company to accumulate at interest, (4) used to purchase paid-up additional insurance, or (5) used to purchase one-year term insurance. The policyowner selects one of these options at the time of application. The option chosen may be changed at any time, though a change to the one-year term insurance option is subject to certain restrictions. The policy specifies which option will apply in cases in which no option is chosen by the policyowner. In most policies, the dividend option that goes into effect automatically if an option is not specified by the policyowner is the paid-up additional insurance option. Figure 10-2 illustrates the percentage of dividends which are applied under each of these options.

Cash

The cash option is the simplest dividend option. According to its terms, the company will send the policyowner a check each year in the amount of the dividend (if any) which has been declared for that policy.

Payment of premiums

A dividend may be applied toward the payment of the policy's premium. A policy's annual dividend is rarely large enough to pay an entire annual premium. However, if a policyowner is paying the premium more often than

FIGURE 10-2

Percentage of dividends (life insurance and annuity) applied under each dividend option

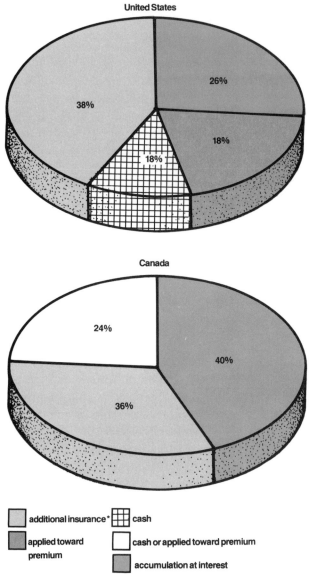

United States

26%

18%

18%

38%

Canada

24%

40%

36%

☐ additional insurance*   ⊞ cash

■ applied toward   ☐ cash or applied toward premium
  premium
                           ■ accumulation at interest

*Includes insurance purchased under both the paid-up additional insurance option and the one-year term insurance option.

annually, the dividend may cover one or more of the installments. If the premium is being paid annually, the policyowner receives notice of the amount of the dividend and pays the difference between the annual premium amount and the amount credited from the dividend.

Accumulation at interest

Under the accumulation at interest option, the dividends are left on deposit with the company. Interest is earned on dividend deposits, and both the interest and accumulated dividends are available for withdrawal at any time. The policy guarantees that at least a specified interest rate will be earned by these funds. The actual rate of interest which these funds will earn depends on the company's investment earnings and is usually greater than the rate guaranteed in the policy. If a policy is surrendered, or if the insured dies, accumulated dividends plus interest are paid as part of the policy's benefit amount.

A policyowner may also instruct the insurer to use money on deposit to pay an overdue premium if the policyowner misses a premium payment. In Canada, the insurer is required by law to apply accumulated dividends to pay any overdue premiums, unless the policyowner specifically requests that such action *not* be taken.

Paid-up additional insurance

The option to purchase additional insurance with each annual dividend is considered by many to be one of the most valuable rights available under a participating policy. An insured who might not otherwise be able to buy a new life insurance policy because of deterioration of health or a change to a dangerous occupation will still be able to obtain increased insurance coverage by using this dividend option. The insured has such a right under this option because no evidence of insurability is required by the company, either at the time the option is chosen or at the time the dividends are applied to purchase the additional coverage. This additional insurance coverage is *not* issued as a separate policy, but serves instead to increase the amount of insurance coverage provided by the existing policy.

The premium rate for insurance purchased under the paid-up additional insurance option is calculated without adding an amount to cover expenses. The insurance company automatically applies the annual dividend as a net single premium to purchase as much additional insurance on the same plan as the basic policy in whatever amount the dividend can provide at the insured's attained age. Thus, if the basic policy is a whole life policy, the additional insurance will be whole life; if the basic policy is an endowment, then the additional insurance will be endowment insurance. These additional amounts of insurance are generally called **paid-up additions**, or **dividend additions**, and these additions require no further premium payment.

Paid-up additions will have a cash value and may be surrendered for their cash value at any time. Although the face amount of the paid-up additions purchased each year under this option may be relatively small, over the life of a policy the total additional insurance available can be substantial. Suppose, for example, Wilbert White purchased a $100,000 participating whole life policy from XYZ Mutual Insurance Company when he was 40 years old and that he elected the paid-up addition option. His annual premium is $2,300. When Mr. White is 42 years old, XYZ declares a $90 dividend for his policy. The XYZ Company automatically applies this $90 dividend to purchase a paid-up whole life addition for $300, the amount of paid-up whole life insurance which the $90 net single premium would purchase at Mr. White's age. The death benefit which will be paid if Mr. White dies is increased to $100,300. (These figures are shown in the chart below.) The next year, XYZ again uses the policy's dividend–this time $160–to purchase another paid-up whole life addition–this time for $525–which would then increase the death benefit of Mr. White's policy to $100,825. When the policy is in its twentieth year and Mr. White is 60 years old, the policy's dividend may be as much as $2,000, and the total paid-up whole life additions purchased over the years using this dividend option would total over $50,000. Therefore, the death benefit which will be paid if Mr. White dies at age 60 would be over $150,000.

Insured's Age	Dividend Declared	Paid-up Dividend Additions Purchased to Date	Total Death Benefit
40	−0−	−0−	$100,000
42	$ 90	$ 300	100,300
43	160	825	100,825
•	•	•	•
•	•	•	•
•	•	•	•
60	$2,000	$50,000	$150,000

Additional term insurance

Under the additional term insurance dividend option, the annual dividend, if any, is applied as a net single premium to purchase one-year term insurance additions.

Since an insured who is in poor health would be more likely to apply dividends to purchase one-year term insurance than to purchase the more expensive paid-up additions, the question of antiselection arises. To protect against antiselection, insurance companies limit the amount of one-year term insurance which can be purchased under this dividend option. Usually, a company will specify that the amount of additional term insurance available in a given year may not exceed the original policy's cash value for that year. Also, if the additional term insurance option was not chosen at the time of application, companies usually will require evidence of insurability before a policyowner may change to this dividend option. Most companies allow a policyowner to change to the paid-up additional insurance option without providing evidence of insurability.

Dividends which are used to purchase one-year term insurance will initially provide a larger amount of additional insurance than can be obtained by the purchase of paid-up permanent additions. However, the term insurance purchased lasts for one year and one year only. At the end of the year, the additional term insurance coverage expires, and the face amount of the policy reverts to its original value. The following year's dividend is then applied to purchase additional term coverage for another year. If the annual dividend exceeds the premium required to purchase the amount of one-year term insurance permitted – generally the cash value of the policy – then the remaining dividend amount is applied under one of the other options.

Suppose, in our previous example, Wilbert White chose the one-year term insurance dividend option and that at the end of the policy's second year the policy's cash value was $3,800. As shown below, only $15 of the $90 dividend is needed to purchase the $3,800 additional term insurance permitted. The XYZ Company would then apply the remaining dividend amount, $75, under whichever dividend option Mr. White specified. If Mr. White specified that the company apply any remaining dividend amount to the paid-up additional insurance option, then the remaining $75 would be automatically applied by XYZ to purchase a paid-up whole life addition in the amount of $250. The one-year term insurance addition would expire at the end of the next year; the paid-up whole life addition would still be in effect. The following year, since the policy's cash value would have increased to $6,000 and Mr. White would be a year older, the amount of the dividend needed to purchase the one-year term insurance would be larger, $35. However, the dividend amount also increases to $160. Therefore, the amount which may be applied toward the purchase of a paid-up addition also increases.

Insured's Age	Dividend Declared	Amount of One-year Term Available (Cash Value of Policy)	Cost of One-year Term Insurance	Remaining Dividend	Total Amount of Paid-up Additions Purchased to Date	Total Death Benefit
40	–0–	–0–	–	–0–	–0–	$100,000
42	$ 90	$ 3,800	$ 15	$ 75	$ 250	$104,050
•	•	•	•	•	•	•
•	•	•	•	•	•	•
•	•	•	•	•	•	•
60	$2,000	$43,000	$735	$1,265	$37,000	$180,000

When the policy is in its twentieth year, $735 of the $2,000 dividend credited in that year will be used to purchase one-year term insurance coverage in the amount of $43,000 (the amount of the policy's cash value), and the remaining $1,265 will be used to purchase a paid-up addition. The total paid-up additions in force when Mr. White is 60 will be $37,000, and the death benefit which will be paid if he dies during that year will be $180,000 (the $100,000 original face amount, plus the $43,000 one-year term insurance, plus the $37,000 in paid-up whole life additions).

Policyowners often use the one-year term insurance dividend option when they have taken a loan against the policy's cash value. The amount of an outstanding policy loan plus interest is deducted from the face amount of the basic policy when the insured dies. The extra term insurance purchased through this option will permit the beneficiary to receive the full amount, or close to the full amount, of the original benefit even if the insured dies while the loan is outstanding.

Special Uses of Dividends

The cash value of paid-up additions and the dividends which have been left on deposit may be used by the policyowner in several ways. By using as a premium the cash value of the paid-up additions or the dividends which have been left on deposit along with the cash value of the policy, a policyowner may request that the insurance company pay up a whole life or endowment policy, shorten the term of an endowment, or even mature a whole life policy as an endowment policy. For example, if the net cash value of a whole life policy plus the net cash value of the paid-up additions equals or exceeds the *net* single premium for a whole life policy of the same face amount at the insured's attained age, then the policy can be endorsed by the company as a "paid-up policy," and no more premiums need to be paid for that policy. If an endowment policy becomes paid-up in this manner, then no further premiums are required for the endowment policy, and the policyowner will be entitled to the full endowment benefit on the original maturity date.

A whole life policy may be matured as an endowment policy if the net cash value of the basic policy plus the net cash value of the dividend additions is equal to the *face value* of the policy. In this case, the policy is matured as an endowment, and the policyowner receives the full face amount. Any accumulated dividends, plus interest, which have been left on deposit may be added to the cash value of the policy to achieve the same result.

Dividends may be used in many combinations, and each policyowner must determine which dividend option will serve his or her needs best. As circumstances change, the policyowner may change the dividend option to one that better meets current needs.

OWNERSHIP OF THE POLICY

Property such as an automobile or jewelry has value in and of itself. An automobile has value partially because it is useful; jewelry has value because it is considered desirable to own. An article which has inherent value is known as tangible property and is legally called a **chose in possession**.*

A life insurance policy is merely a claim to value; the policy itself is made of paper and has no inherent value. The actual value of a life insurance policy is the money the policy represents. Property which provides evidence of value or desirability is known as intangible property and is legally called a **chose in action**. Another example of a *chose in action* is a stock certificate, because it, too, represents rather than possesses value.

To use a life insurance policy in a financial transaction, the policyowner must transfer the ownership of either the value or part of the value represented by the policy; such a transfer is not accomplished simply by handing someone the actual policy. The two ways a policyowner may transfer ownership rights are by *assignment* and by *endorsement*.

Transfer of Ownership by Assignment

One way a policyowner may transfer some or all of the ownership rights of a life insurance policy is by assignment of the policy. Legally speaking, an **assignment** is the transfer of some or all of the ownership rights of a *chose in action*. The owner of the *chose in action* makes the assignment and is known as the **assignor**; the receiver of the property rights is known as the **assignee**.

A policyowner may negotiate a financial transaction by assigning some or all of the policy's ownership rights. In this way, the value represented by the policy is fully exchangeable. Often, a policyowner will assign a life insurance policy as collateral for a personal loan. In this case, the policyowner would be the assignor, and the lender the assignee. The terms of the assignment state whether the lender has complete ownership of the policy or has been granted only certain specified ownership rights, such as the right to surrender the policy for its cash value if the original policyowner defaults on the loan.

The right to assign any property, including a life insurance policy, is subject to some restrictions. An assignment of a life insurance policy must not be an infringement on the vested rights, if any, of a beneficiary. If the beneficiary of a policy has been named irrevocably, or is a member of the preferred class in Canada, then the policyowner cannot assign the policy without that beneficiary's permission. In these cases, the beneficiary has a vested right to the values represented by the policy and, unless the beneficiary consents, the policyowner cannot make an assignment which might cause the beneficiary to lose those rights.

In addition, the assignment cannot be made for illegal purposes, such as speculating on a life or committing fraud. For example, suppose David

---

*Legal language often makes use of Latin and French words; *chose* is a French word which means "thing."

Thorne owns a life insurance policy on the life of his wife. He assigns the policy to Mike Swann, who is gambling that Mrs. Thorne will die prematurely. Most courts would not uphold such an assignment because it was made for an illegal purpose, speculating on a life.

Assignment provision

Because the right to assign any *chose in action*, including a life insurance policy, is granted by law, there is no legal requirement that the policyowner be given notice of the right of assignment in the life insurance policy. Most policies do, however, include an assignment provision. This provision describes the respective roles of the insurer and the policyowner when a policy is assigned. The usual policy provision defines the required *notice of assignment*, details the *extent of the insurer's responsibility* with regard to the assignment, and grants the insurer first claim on the policy's values to satisfy any of the policyowner's *indebtedness to the insurer*.

Notice of assignment. The insurance company is not obligated to act in accordance with the terms of an assignment unless it has received written notice of the assignment. In order to protect his or her own interests, the assignee must, therefore, be sure that the insurance company has been informed of the assignment.

Extent of the insurer's responsibility. A policy assignment is an agreement between the assignee and the assignor. The insurance company is not a party to this agreement. Hence, the company states in its assignment provision that the company is not responsible for the validity of any assignment. If proper written notice of the assignment has been sent to the insurance company, then the assignment is presumed by the insurance company to be valid. The insurance company, however, has no control over the validity of the assignment and cannot be held liable for having acted in accordance with it should the assignment later be deemed invalid.

Indebtedness to the insurer. The assignment provision often specifies that the rights of the insurer take precedence over the rights of the assignee with regard to the proceeds of a policy. An assignee cannot receive an amount greater than the amount of the **net policy proceeds** – that is, the proceeds remaining after any overdue premiums and any outstanding policy loans and interest have been deducted.

Types of assignment

An assignment may take one of two forms: an **absolute** assignment, which transfers complete ownership of the policy permanently, or a **collateral** assignment, which transfers some of the ownership rights under the policy, generally for a temporary period.

Absolute assignment. When an absolute assignment is made, the assignee is granted all policy ownership rights; the assignor has no further rights under the contract. The assignment is total and permanent. If an absolute assignment is made without any payment to the assignor, it is considered to be a gift to the assignee. If financial compensation is involved, the absolute assignment is considered to be the equivalent of a sale of the policy. In most jurisdictions, the assignee need not have an insurable interest in the life of the insured as a prerequisite for an absolute assignment. Any assignment being made for an illegal purpose, however, is usually deemed invalid.

Collateral assignment. A collateral assignment is generally a temporary assignment of the values of a life insurance policy as collateral, or security, for a loan. For example, if a person takes out a personal loan from a bank, that person may assign a life insurance policy to the bank as security for the loan. A collateral assignment differs from an absolute assignment in that generally the collateral assignee's rights (1) are limited to those ownership rights which directly concern the monetary values of the policy; (2) are temporary–that is, these rights revert to the assignor when the loan is repaid; and (3) are limited to the amount of the loan.

The collateral assignee's rights to the policy's values are limited to the amount of the debt and any accumulated interest. Generally, the policyowner is still expected to pay all premiums due on the policy. Thus, if there are disability benefits under a policy, they are payable to the *assignor* even if there has been a collateral assignment. If the assignee should pay any of the policy's premiums, the amount of such premium payments is usually added to the amount of the assignor's debt. If the policy matures or the insured dies during the period the assignment is in effect, the assignee receives only the amount of the outstanding debt. Any remaining policy proceeds would be payable to the beneficiary named by the policyowner/assignor.

The policyowner is not permitted to receive a policy loan or to surrender the policy for its cash value while the collateral assignment is in effect without the consent of the assignee, since these actions would diminish the value of the policy. If the assignor repays the amount owed to the collateral assignee, the assignment is no longer in effect and all of the policy's ownership rights revert to the policyowner. The policyowner must send the insurance company a valid release from the assignee when the loan is repaid.

Assignment and the optional modes of settlement

One policy ownership right which is usually not granted to any assignee is the right to elect an optional mode of settlement as a means of receiving the policy proceeds. There is a provision in most policies stating that policy proceeds will be paid to an assignee only in a lump sum. The optional modes of settlement are designed primarily to provide for the needs of individuals or families who have suffered economic loss due to the death of the insured. Since assignments are usually made for business purposes, the use of settlement options by assignees generally is considered inappropriate.

Problems resulting from assignment

There are several problems which may arise when a life insurance policy is assigned. The most common problem occurs when the insurer is not notified of an assignment. An insurance company will pay the proceeds of a policy to the beneficiary or assignee noted in its records. If no notice of an assignment has been sent to the company, the company will pay the proceeds to the beneficiary. The assignee, unaware that no notice of assignment was sent to the insurer when the policy was assigned, might also attempt to collect the proceeds. The provision in the policy stating that the company must have written notification of an assignment, however, protects the insurer from being forced to pay the proceeds to the assignee after having already paid the proceeds to the beneficiary.

Other problems occur when a policyowner assigns a policy to two assignees or when an assignee and a beneficiary disagree as to which of them has first claim to the values of the policy. We will explore these two problems in more detail because the solution is not always found in the policy.

Assignment to two assignees. Consider a situation in which a policyowner uses a policy as collateral for two different loans taken out in quick succession from two different creditors. Assume that the total indebtedness of the policyowner for these two loans exceeds the policy's face value. If the policy were to become a death claim before the clerical work of both notifications had been completed, there could be a conflict between the two assignees regarding who has primary rights to the proceeds.

There are two general rules governing the payment of the benefit in this situation. The *American rule* is followed in most states in the United States. This rule grants the first assignee, according to the date of the assignment, primary rights to the values of the policy. The accepted rule in Canada is the *English rule*, which is also followed by some states in the United States. Under the English rule, the assignee who claims these proceeds first obtains primary rights.

In the United States, insurance companies sometimes deal with conflicting claims for policy proceeds, such as claims by two assignees, by using *interpleader*. The insurance company pays the policy proceeds to a court, stating that the company cannot determine the correct party to whom the proceeds should be paid. The insurance company asks the court to decide the proper recipient. The court examines the evidence, determines the proper party to receive the proceeds, and awards the money. By paying the proceeds to the court, the company has discharged its obligation under the policy and is not subject to any further claims by either assignee.

Conflict between assignee and beneficiary. Courts have generally held that, in a conflict with a beneficiary, an assignee has first claim to the proceeds of a life insurance policy. A revocable beneficiary has only an "expectation," not a vested right, to receive the policy proceeds. This expectation is not given preference over an assignment. Additionally, most insurance policies include a clause stating that the rights of any revocable beneficiary are secondary to the rights of an assignee.

If an irrevocable beneficiary has given consent to the assignment, then the irrevocable beneficiary has given up his or her vested rights, and the situation is legally identical to that described above; the assignee has first claim to the proceeds. In all cases, though, the collateral assignee's rights are limited to the amount of the outstanding debt, plus interest; any remaining proceeds are payable to the beneficiary.

American Bankers Association Assignment Form

In the United States, the banking industry and the life insurance industry worked together to develop a standard form for use in collateral assignments. This form, called the American Bankers Association (ABA) Assignment Form #10, is used by most creditors in the United States; it was designed to fully define the ownership rights being transferred under a collateral assignment and is intended to prevent many of the conflicting claim problems which have occurred in the past from recurring. While the ABA form is not used in Canada, most Canadian creditors use a form similar to it.

The ABA form contains the following information identifying the policy which is being assigned:

- the name of the insurance company
- the policy number
- the name of the policyowner
- the name of the insured
- the beneficiary of the proceeds

The form also specifies which ownership rights are being transferred to the assignee. Under certain circumstances, the assignee has the right to (1) collect the net policy proceeds, (2) surrender the policy for its cash value, (3) receive any policy dividends, (4) exercise the nonforfeiture rights, (5) receive a policy loan, or (6) use the policy as security for a loan from another lender or party.

Note that the ABA form grants the assignee the right to collect the *net policy proceeds* from the insurer, even if the amount of the net proceeds exceeds the amount of the policyowner's outstanding debt. The assigneee then has the legal responsibility to pay the beneficiary the amount of the proceeds which exceeds the amount to which the assignee is entitled.

According to the ABA form, the assignee's right to receive a policy loan or to surrender the policy for its cash value may be exercised in either of two situations: (1) if the assignor has not paid the premiums due on the policy or (2) if the assignor has defaulted in the loan payments. The assignee must give the assignor 20 days' written notice before surrendering or borrowing on the policy. During this period, the assignor has the opportunity to pay the overdue premiums or loan payments. The assignee also is granted the right to pay any premiums in default and to add the amount of such premium payments, plus interest, to the amount due from the assignor.

Under the ABA form, the assignor retains the right to change the beneficiary, select an optional mode of settlement, and collect any disability benefits. The assignor can exercise these rights because these actions will not decrease or jeopardize the value of the life insurance policy which has been assigned.

Transfer of Ownership by Endorsement

Most life insurance policies issued today specify a simple, direct method of transferring all the policy's rights of ownership. The policyowner must notify the insurer, in writing, of the intent to change the ownership of the policy, and the policy usually must be sent to the insurance company. The company then adds an endorsement to the policy which states the name of the new owner. This method is called the **endorsement method** and is a complete, permanent transfer of ownership. The endorsement method is commonly used when a policy is given as a gift. For example, a parent may give a child ownership of a policy on the child's life when the child reaches age 21.

The right to permanently change the policy's owner is generally specified in the policy. A typical change of ownership provision follows:

> **Change of ownership.** You can change the owner of this policy, from yourself to a new owner, in a notice you sign which gives us the facts that we need. When this change takes effect, all rights of ownership in this policy will pass to the new owner.
>
> When we record a change of owner or successor owner, these changes will take effect as of the date you signed the notice, subject to any payment we made or action we took before recording these changes. We may require that these changes be endorsed in the policy. Changing the owner or naming a new successor owner cancels any prior choice of successor owner, but does not change the beneficiary.

The effective date of the transfer of ownership is the date when the request for endorsement was made. However, the policy's transfer of ownership provision will usually state that the company is not responsible for any payments it made to the owner of record before the policy was endorsed. This provision protects the insurance company from the new owner's contesting the insurer's actions if a loan was granted or benefit payments were made between the date of the request and the date the endorsement was actually added.

The same problem with changing the beneficiary by using the endorsement method can also arise in changing the ownership of the policy by endorsement; there are cases in which the policy cannot be submitted to the company in order to complete the change in the ownership by the endorsement method. In such situations, the general law is that if all reasonable steps have been taken to submit the policy, and if the insurance company has received written notice to change the ownership of the policy, then the requested change of ownership will be effective.

11
The Proceeds Are Paid

We have discussed many of the ownership rights and benefits available in a life insurance policy. While these benefits are important, the primary reason most persons purchase an insurance policy is that the policy's death benefit will be needed when the insured person dies. To fulfill its responsibilities to its policyowners and beneficiaries, a life insurance company must take steps to ensure that this benefit is paid promptly to the correct party. Additionally, in order to protect the insurance industry and the general public from abuses of the insurance contract, companies must guard against paying fraudulent or improper claims.

This chapter will examine the procedures companies use to establish the validity of a death claim before paying the proceeds, and the methods companies use to contest an invalid claim. We will also discuss (1) the rights to policy proceeds possessed by creditors of the insured and creditors of the beneficiary, and (2) the taxation of policy proceeds.

CLAIM PROCEDURES

The claims department works closely with the company's legal and medical departments to establish standard claim examination procedures. These procedures are designed to strike a balance between the beneficiary's right to prompt settlement and the insurance company's need to examine each claim's validity.

The beneficiary has the right to promptly receive the policy proceeds to which he or she is entitled. The beneficiary may need these funds for immediate and pressing expenses connected with the insured's death. As we have mentioned, life insurance policies are often purchased to provide funds to meet these needs.

Not only does the beneficiary have the right to expect prompt settlement, but the laws of most jurisdictions require prompt settlement of claims. If an insurer delays payment of policy proceeds without good reason, the insurer can be sued by the beneficiary for the amount of the proceeds plus punitive damages.* Further, a company which develops slow or questionable claim practices will soon find that its reputation has been damaged and, subsequently, that its sales have suffered.

On the other hand, the beneficiary may have, intentionally or unintentionally, submitted an invalid claim for the policy proceeds. Each insurer must take reasonable precautions against paying such invalid claims. If the company does not take appropriate steps to safeguard itself, then the cost of insurance and, consequently, premium rates would rise dramatically. The insurance company must also be certain that it is paying the proceeds to the proper beneficiary, or else the insurer may be faced with a valid second claim.

Standard Claim Procedures

While specific claim examination guidelines differ among insurers, most follow certain standard procedures. The process begins when the claimant notifies the insurer of the claim and submits the proper documents to prove that the event insured against has occurred and that the claimant is entitled to the benefit.

Forms and documents

The claim form is, in effect, an application for payment of the policy proceeds. In most cases, the primary beneficiary of the policy is living at the time of the insured's death, and the beneficiary or his or her representative completes this claim form. In this text, we will assume that the primary beneficiary has submitted the claim form. The terms "claimant" and "beneficiary" will be used interchangeably.

In most states in the United States, the insurer must supply a claim form to the beneficiary within 15 days of a request for a claim form. If the company fails to do so, the law provides that the claimant will be presumed to have completed and submitted the form, and the insurer will be required to process the claim without this form. In Canada, there is no time requirement concerning the supplying of these forms. A sample claim form is shown in Figure 11-1.

The claim form is completed by the beneficiary, often with the aid of the insurance agent who is currently servicing the policy. This agent or

---

*Punitive damages are monetary awards above the amount in dispute. Generally speaking, a court of law awards punitive damages to punish a party which has wronged another.

FIGURE 11-1

Claim form for the proceeds of a life insurance policy

ABC LIFE INSURANCE COMPANY

100 Ordinary Avenue, New York, N. Y. 00000

Please see proof of death requirements on reverse side before completing this form.

Policies under which claim is made by the undersigned:

Numbers	Numbers	Numbers
_____	_____	_____
_____	_____	_____
_____	_____	_____

1. a. Deceased's name in full _____

   b. Residence _____

   c. Occupation _____

2. Date of birth_____ Place of birth_____

3. a. Date of death_____ Place of death_____

   b. Cause of death _____

   c. Duration of illness _____

4. Names & Addresses of Attending Physicians

Name	Address
_____	_____
_____	_____

5. a. What is your relationship to the deceased?_____

   b. Do you claim this insurance as beneficiary?_____

   c. If you are not the beneficiary, in what capacity are you making this claim?_____

NOTE: If you are a beneficiary designated to receive policy proceeds in a single sum and wish to have information regarding any optional methods of settlement which may be available to you, please consult your ABC agent or the Office through which you are submitting this statement.

Claimant's
Signature_____ Age_____

Address _____
          (Please print)   (Street)

_____
          (City)

Date_____ _____
          (State)

another company representative will also help the beneficiary obtain any other necessary documents.

Along with the claim form, the beneficiary must submit a notarized copy of the official death certificate of the insured. The insurer needs this certificate to establish that a loss has occurred. This document, which lists the cause of death and is signed by a physician, is issued by a local coroner or other government official, and usually has some type of government seal. As a rule, the death certificate is also needed by the funeral director, who usually will help the beneficiary or company agent obtain the necessary official copies.

In addition to the claim form and death certificate, an insurance company sometimes requests an Attending Physician's Statement (APS) from the physician who treated the insured prior to the insured's death. In some cases, the claimant is required to provide an autopsy report. An insurance company generally will ask for these additional documents only (1) when there are unusual circumstances surrounding the insured's death, so that there is reason to doubt the stated cause of death; (2) when the policy includes special additional death benefits, such as accidental death benefits; or (3) when the insured dies of natural causes during the contestable period.

After the beneficiary submits the required documents to the insurance company, the company continues the claim examination procedure.

Processing routine claims

The vast majority of claims are processed in a routine manner and the proceeds are paid promptly. Responsibility for conducting the claim examination is generally given to an insurance company employee with the title of *claims examiner, claims approver,* or *claims specialist.* In order to determine the validity of each claim, the claims examiner will (1) determine the status of the policy, (2) verify the identity of the insured, (3) identify the proper beneficiary, and (4) determine the settlement method that was chosen. We will examine each of these steps more closely.

Status of the policy. The claims examiner checks the status of the policy both to make sure the contract is still in force and to determine the amount of the company's liability under the contract. During this stage, the claims examiner must ask the following questions:

1. *Is the policy still in force?* The policy may have reached the end of its term and expired, or it may have lapsed because of nonpayment of premiums. If the policy is not in force, then the claim will be denied.
2. *Are the premiums paid to date?* If the policy is in force under the grace period provision, then the amount of the unpaid premium will be deducted from the face amount.
3. *Is there a policy loan outstanding?* If so, the amount of the loan and

any interest due will be deducted from the face amount of the policy.
4. *Have dividends been either left on deposit or used to purchase additional insurance?* If so, these amounts will be added to the face amount and paid to the beneficiary.
5. *Is the policy in force under the extended term or reduced paid-up insurance nonforfeiture option?* If the policy is in force as reduced paid-up insurance, what is the reduced face amount of the policy?

Based on this information regarding the policy's status, the claims examiner will either (1) approve payment of either the face amount of the policy or an amount adjusted to reflect transactions which occurred after the policy was issued, or (2) deny the claim.

Identification of the insured. The claim forms must be compared with the company's policy records to confirm that the person identified on the death certificate is the same person whose life was insured under the policy. This step is necessary to protect the insurance company from fraudulent claims and mistaken claims.

A fraudulent claim occurs when a claimant intentionally attempts to collect policy proceeds based on false information. For example, if the beneficiary submits an altered or forged death certificate in order to collect policy proceeds on the life of an insured person who is still living, then the beneficiary is committing fraud.

A mistaken claim occurs when a beneficiary makes an honest mistake in presenting a claim to the insurer. Such would be the case if the beneficiary believes that an insurance policy insures the life of one person when it really insures the life of another. For example, suppose Marvin Topaz, Jr., submits a claim to the ABC Insurance Company for the proceeds of a policy on his father's life. By checking the policy records, the claims examiner may find that Mr. Topaz is mistaken, and the policy actually insures the life of Mrs. Marvin Topaz, the beneficiary's mother.

It is the long-term nature of the life insurance contract which sometimes accounts for a misidentification of the insured. A policy may have been issued decades before the claim is submitted. As shown in Figure 11-2, the majority of life insurance policies are in force for at least 20 years before a claim is submitted. The original applicant, the sales agent, and others involved in the issue of the policy might have died, moved away, or become otherwise unavailable. The policy might have been issued prior to the birth of the beneficiary; beneficiary designations often are changed by the policyowner while the policy is in force. Hence, it is possible for a claimant to submit a claim for proceeds that are not yet payable.

The claims examiner also compares the insured's date of birth as shown on the policy's record to the date of birth or age at death given on the death certificate. If there is a discrepancy in age, the face amount of the policy will be adjusted to the amount that the premiums would have purchased at the insured's correct age at the time the policy was issued.

FIGURE 11-2
Duration of ordinary life insurance policy when a claim was presented

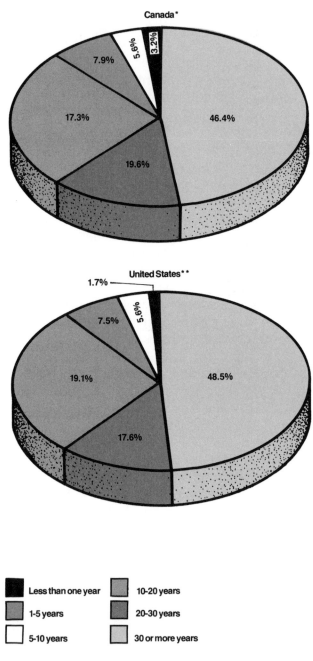

*Based on claim payments made in May 1980
**Based on claim payments made in April 1981

Proper beneficiary. Once the claim examination process shows that the claim is valid, the claims examiner identifies the proper payee, the party designated to receive the policy proceeds. As noted in chapter 7, the proceeds may be payable to a single beneficiary, or the proceeds may be payable to more than one beneficiary in the proportions noted in the designation. If the primary beneficiary (or beneficiaries) is deceased, then the insurer will identify the contingent beneficiary. The contingent beneficiary may be either the estate of the insured, the policyowner, or another person or party.

To determine the proper payee, the claims examiner also will check to see if the policy has been assigned. If a collateral assignment is in effect, the assignee(s) must be given priority in the payment of the proceeds.

Type of settlement. The proceeds of a policy will be paid to the beneficiary (or beneficiaries) either in a lump sum or under one of the optional modes of settlement. To ensure that the benefit is paid correctly, the claims examiner determines which method has been selected by the policyowner or beneficiary.

Special Claim Procedures

By following the steps outlined above, an insurance company can establish the validity of most claims and ensure that the proper amount is paid to the correct party. However, under certain circumstances, further investigation is needed before the proceeds are paid.

In general, special attention is given to a death claim in the following situations:

- The policy includes an accidental death benefit.
- The policy contains special exclusions.
- The insured dies during the contestable period.
- The insured disappears.
- The beneficiary in some manner caused the death of the insured.
- The insured and the beneficiary die as the result of a common disaster.

We will discuss the special claim procedures used in each of the above situations.

Accidental death benefits

If a policy includes an accidental death benefit, the cause of death will be examined carefully to determine whether the insured's death meets the policy's definition of "accidental." If it is found that the death was *not* accidental as defined in the policy, then the policy's face amount will be paid, but the additional benefit will be denied.

Some types of accidental deaths are specifically excluded from coverage. For example, accidental death benefits usually are not paid if the accident occurs while the insured is committing an illegal act. Hence, if the cause of death listed on the death certificate is "accidental drug overdose," the claims examiner will investigate further to determine whether the accidental death benefit should be paid. If the drugs involved were illegal substances, then the company may have grounds for denying the claim for accidental death benefits.

Special exclusions

In chapter 7, we mentioned that some insurance policies contain special exclusions. These exclusions limit the insurance company's liability if the insured dies due to specified causes. The causes include war or armed service involvement, certain aviation activities, and suicide within a stipulated period after the policy is issued. The claims examiner will consider the policy's exclusion provisions and the actual cause of death to determine the extent of the company's liability under the terms of the contract. If the cause of death is specifically excluded from coverage, then the company will not be liable for the full face amount, but usually is liable only for the premiums paid for the policy.

Contestable period

The claims examiner will also investigate the cause of death in those cases in which the insured dies during the contestable period. As noted earlier in this text, the incontestability provision limits the time period – generally to two years – during which an insurance company may contest a claim on the basis of statements made in the application. In Canada, a policy is always contestable on the basis of fraud; therefore, the time limit applies only to misstatements in the application which are not fraudulent. In both the United States and Canada, if the insured dies during the contestable period, the claims examiner will investigate to determine whether there is any reason to suspect material misrepresentation or fraud in any of the statements in the application.

For example, suppose Tara Svenson purchased a policy on her own life in June 1983 and died in March 1984. The claims examiner will pay close attention to the cause of death given on the death certificate. If Ms. Svenson died while a passenger on a plane that crashed, the cause of death is clear-cut and presents no reason for the claims examiner to suspect material misrepresentation in the application. On the other hand, if Ms. Svenson died of a heart attack and had indicated no history of heart problems on the application, then the claims examiner will need to investigate further to determine if Ms. Svenson had been treated for a heart problem before the policy was issued.

If the claims examiner determines that there was either material misrepresentation or fraud in the completion of the application and has sufficient evidence to substantiate the material misrepresentation or fraud, the insurance company will usually deny the claim and, if necessary, defend its position in court.

Disappearance of the insured

Sometimes a beneficiary files a claim for policy proceeds when the person insured has disappeared. A person who has disappeared without explanation may be legally presumed to be dead after a certain length of time has passed, depending on the circumstances of the individual case.

In most states in the United States, three conditions must be met in order for a person who has disappeared to be presumed dead. These conditions are as follows:

1. There must be an unexplained continuous absence of that person for a period of at least seven years.
2. A diligent but unsuccessful search for that person must have been conducted.
3. There must have been no contact or communication with the missing person during the seven-year period.

A beneficiary may ask a court to declare an insured person legally dead if each one of these conditions has been met. The proceeds of an insurance policy on that person's life may then be paid to the beneficiary.

However, if even one of these conditions is not met, then the missing person is not presumed to be dead. For example, suppose a bank employee disappeared with $1,000,000 in cash from the bank's vault. This disappearance would not be "unexplained," and the employee would not be presumed to be dead even after the usual seven-year period has passed. When there is any reason to suspect that the missing person may still be alive, it may be necessary to have the question of whether death has occurred settled in court.

In Canada, the beneficiary must also ask the courts to declare the missing person dead in order to receive the proceeds of a life insurance policy. The beneficiary may request this declaration after the insured has been missing and has not been heard from for seven years.

In both the United States and Canada, if the insured has been missing for less than seven years but evidence suggests that the person is dead, then the beneficiary may ask the courts to declare the insured dead. For example, the insured may have been last seen at a campsite in the mountains. If a forest fire consumes the area surrounding the campsite, and the insured person never returns, then there is reason to believe the insured may have died in the fire.

In both the United States and Canada, there is a legal presumption that the death occurred on the date the missing person was declared dead. Hence, the policyowner, the beneficiary, or other interested party must keep the policy in force until the end of the seven-year period. If the beneficiary is later able to prove that the missing person's death actually occurred earlier, then the premiums paid after the actual date of the insured's death will be refunded.

Beneficiary kills the insured

Another special situation which the claims examiner must occasionally face occurs when the beneficiary is believed to be responsible for the death of the insured. It would not be in the public interest to permit someone to benefit from a crime. Therefore, a beneficiary who is convicted of murdering the insured is prohibited by law in both the United States and Canada from receiving the proceeds of the policy.

The legal status of the policy in such cases depends on whether the policy was taken out by the beneficiary/policyowner with the intent to profit by the death of the insured. If such was the case, the contract usually is considered to have been void from the start, since there was no lawful purpose involved, and the insurer's only liability is a refund of the premiums paid.

If, as is usually the case, the intent to profit by the insured's death cannot be established, as would be the case if the insured purchased the policy, then the policy is a valid contract, and the company is liable for paying the entire policy proceeds. The guilty beneficiary may not, however, receive these proceeds. Laws differ among jurisdictions, but in the majority of such cases the proceeds are payable to the estate of the insured.

In the United States, the crime of manslaughter is treated differently from the crime of murder. The proceeds of a life insurance policy may be paid to a beneficiary who kills the insured but is convicted of manslaughter rather than murder. In Canada, however, a beneficiary convicted of manslaughter of the insured is *not* permitted to receive the policy proceeds. Special provisions in Quebec law provide further that (1) if the owner of a policy even attempts to kill the person whose life is insured, whether or not the attempt is successful, the policy is nullified and the surrender value paid, and (2) if a designated beneficiary attempts to kill the insured, then the policy remains in force, but that beneficiary is barred from ever receiving any benefits under the policy.

Common disaster

If the insured and the primary beneficiary die as the result of a common disaster, the claims examiner must evaluate carefully the circumstances surrounding the deaths and the times that the deaths occurred to determine the proper recipient for the proceeds. In chapter 7, we described both the common disaster clause which is often included in a life insurance policy and the laws regarding simultaneous death. It is the insurer's responsibility to determine the correct beneficiary according to the appropriate law and/or policy provision.

Contested Claims

Based on the claim examination, an insurance company may decide a claim is *not* valid as submitted, and, in such cases, the company will contest the claim. There are two basic positions a life insurance company may take when contesting a claim. The company may (1) deny *any* liability under the contract, or (2) dispute the *amount* of its liability under the contract.

Company denies any liability

The most common situation in which an insurance company will deny any liability under the contract is when the contract is found to be no longer in force. The policy may be a term insurance policy which expired, or a whole life policy for which premiums have not been paid for a number of years. Even if a whole life policy was continued under the extended term insurance nonforfeiture option, the term may have expired.

A beneficiary may have possession of a life insurance policy, assume it is still in force, and, upon the death of the insured, submit a claim. Often, a policy is found among a deceased person's papers. A beneficiary may innocently submit a claim for a policy that lapsed years before the insured's death. Usually, the beneficiary drops the claim when the insurer explains that the policy is no longer in force. However, at times the insurance company may have to defend itself in court in order to prove it is not liable for the proceeds.

An insurance company also may deny any liability under the contract in those cases in which the insured is believed to have died from a cause specifically excluded from coverage. If the beneficiary and the insurance company disagree over the cause of death, a court of law may be asked to decide the issue. For example, suppose the insured died six months after the policy was issued and the standard suicide exclusion was still in effect. The beneficiary may contend that the insured died of an accidental overdose of prescribed medications; the insurance company may believe, based on its investigation, that the overdose was intentional. If the *beneficiary* is correct, the insurance company will be liable for the full policy proceeds. If the *insurance company* is correct, the insurance company will be responsible only for a refund of the premiums paid. In this situation, the insurance company will have to prove in a court of law that the death was the result of suicide, before the company can deny liability for the policy proceeds.

Another situation in which an insurance company may deny liability is when the insured died during the contestable period, and an investigation shows there was material misrepresentation or fraud in the application. If the company has sufficient evidence of material misrepresentation or fraud, it may resist payment of the proceeds and, if necessary, contest the claim in court.

Amount in dispute

Most of the disagreements which occur between the insurance company and the beneficiary concern the amount of the benefit payable.

The net policy proceeds payable may be lower than the stated face amount for several reasons. As noted earlier in this chapter, the insurer adjusts the amount payable to reflect transactions which occurred after the policy was issued. During this stage, an outstanding policy loan may have been deducted from the face amount. If the policy were in force during the grace period, the premium due may have been deducted from the amount of the death benefit. The proceeds also may be less than expected in those cases in which the policy benefit was adjusted to reflect a misstatement of age or in those cases in which a policy has been kept in force under the reduced paid-up insurance nonforfeiture option.

In most such situations, when the insurer explains the reason for the reduction, the beneficiary accepts payment of the reduced amount. However, at times the dispute may not be resolved so easily, and the matter must be settled in court.

The accidental death benefit may be a subject of disagreement between the insurer and beneficiary. An insurer may believe that the cause of death does not meet the policy's definition of "accidental." The beneficiary may not agree with the company's findings and may demand payment of the additional accidental death benefit amount. If an agreement cannot be reached, it will be necessary to ask a court of law to rule on the case. The court will base its decision both on the cause of death and on the actual definition of "accidental" included in the life insurance policy.

Conflicting Beneficiaries

Despite the precautions an insurance company takes in establishing its beneficiary designation and beneficiary change procedures, occasionally situations occur in which the company cannot decide which of two or more claimants is the correct one.

The insurance company wants to be sure the proper beneficiary receives the proceeds so that the company will not be forced to pay the proceeds twice. For example, suppose two claimants, John Smith and Jack Jones, submit claims for the proceeds of a life insurance policy. The insurance company decides that Mr. Smith is the proper beneficiary and pays the proceeds to him. If Mr. Jones then brings suit for the proceeds and obtains a favorable court judgment, then the insurance company will have to pay the proceeds to Mr. Jones. The insurer will find it difficult, if not impossible, to obtain from Mr. Smith a refund of the policy proceeds it has already paid to him in error.

When an insurance company cannot determine the correct beneficiary for the policy proceeds, or fears that a court might disagree with its opinion as to the correct beneficiary, the company may use the remedy of interpleader. In chapter 10 we mentioned that an insurance company may use interpleader in those cases where it cannot choose between conflicting assignees. The use of interpleader in cases involving conflicting beneficiaries is similar to its use in cases involving conflicting assignees. The company pays the money to the court. The court then examines the evidence, determines the proper recipient, and pays the money to that recipient.

In these situations, the company is not denying or contesting the validity of the claim; rather, the insurer admits liability for the net proceeds of the policy but states that it is unable to determine the correct recipient. In paying the money to the court, the insurer has discharged its duties under the life insurance contract and is therefore protected from future claims under that contract.

As in the previous situations, the insurer first will try to bring about an agreement between the parties before resorting to court action. The time, expense, and ill will which often result from court proceedings generally make that step less attractive to both the insurer and the beneficiary.

RIGHTS OF CREDITORS

When the proceeds of a life insurance policy become payable, the creditors of the person insured under the policy or the creditors of the policy beneficiary may attempt to claim a share of these proceeds in order to satisfy outstanding debts. If a collateral assignment of the policy was in effect at the time of the insured's death, then the creditor to whom the policy was assigned has a valid claim to whatever amount was stipulated in the assignment form. If no assignment was in effect, then in certain situations the proceeds would be protected by law from seizure. The particular laws granting this protection vary among the states and provinces, but their effect is similar in most jurisdictions. Since these laws distinguish between creditors of the insured and creditors of the beneficiary, we will discuss these creditors separately.

Creditors of the Insured

When a beneficiary other than the estate of the insured is named in a life insurance policy, the proceeds of the policy are completely protected by law from seizure by creditors of the insured. When the insured dies, the proceeds become the property of the beneficiary. Hence, these proceeds may not be seized by the insured's creditors to satisfy the insured's debts. In Canada, this protection is granted by the revised Uniform Life Insurance Act and by the Quebec Civil Code. In the United States, the same protection is granted by various state laws. If the proceeds of a life insurance policy are payable to the estate of the insured, then the proceeds are considered to be a part of the insured's estate and can be used to satisfy the insured's debts.

Suppose, for example, that Marie Valenza owns a life insurance policy on her own life. If she names her church as beneficiary of her policy, then the church will receive the entire proceeds when she dies; her creditors cannot successfully claim these proceeds to satisfy Ms. Valenza's outstanding debts. If, on the other hand, Ms. Valenza uses a will to donate her estate to the church and names her estate as the beneficiary of her policy, then the situation is different. Her creditors' rights take first priority and must be satisfied before any of her estate – including the proceeds of her policy – can pass to the church.

Creditors of the Beneficiary

When the proceeds of a life insurance policy are paid to the beneficiary, the proceeds become the property of that beneficiary. As the property of the beneficiary, these proceeds generally are subject to seizure by the beneficiary's creditors, just as any other property owned by the beneficiary could be seized by creditors.

However, under certain conditions, the proceeds of a life insurance policy are protected from seizure by the beneficiary's creditors while these proceeds are still in the hands of the insurance company. Legislation in Canada and in some states in the United States provides this protection if both of the following two conditions are met:

1. The proceeds are payable in installments under one of the settlement options.
2. The settlement option was chosen by someone other than the beneficiary.

Under these circumstances, proceeds being held by the insurer cannot be taken directly from the insurer by the beneficiary's creditors. Of course, after each installment is paid to the beneficiary, the creditor may take legal action to seize these funds from the beneficiary.

Some insurance policies also include a "spendthrift trust" clause which, essentially, protects policy proceeds being held by the insurer from seizure by the beneficiary's creditors if the two conditions listed above are met. However, spendthrift trust clauses have been declared illegal in some states.

TAXATION OF INDIVIDUAL LIFE INSURANCE PROCEEDS

The proceeds of an individual life insurance policy are subject to income taxes and estate taxes in certain situations. These taxes are levied by the federal government, provincial government, or state government. While a detailed analysis of taxation is outside the scope of this text, it is important for you to have a basic understanding of the taxation of individual life insurance policy proceeds.

Income Taxes

In the United States and Canada, when the death benefit of a life insurance policy is paid in a lump sum to the beneficiary, the amount of the benefit is not usually considered taxable income to the beneficiary, whether the beneficiary is a person, the estate of the insured, a trustee, or an organization. The proceeds usually are nontaxable regardless of who owned the policy and paid the premiums.

Federal income taxes

The policy proceeds are excluded from federal income taxes, however, only if these proceeds are paid because of the death of the person insured. Thus, if a life insurance policy benefit becomes payable during the lifetime of the insured because the insured has reached the age specified in the mortality table, then the proceeds are not considered a death benefit and the income tax exclusion does not apply. Also, if an endowment policy matures as a living benefit, special income tax rules, which are discussed later in this section, will apply.

Notice also that the exemption from federal income taxes applies only when the death benefit is paid in a lump sum. Although the beneficiary does not pay taxes on the net amount of the proceeds, any interest earned while the insurance company retains all or part of the proceeds is subject to federal income taxes. For example, if the proceeds are being held under the interest option, then the interest earned under this option is subject to federal income tax. When one of the other optional modes of settlement is in effect, then the interest earnings portion of each installment is subject to taxation.

The federal tax laws provide a standard method of calculating the taxable portion of each payment. This method is based on the interest rate and mortality table used by the insurer to calculate the amount of the benefits and will not be discussed in this text.

Endowment policies. If an endowment insurance policy becomes payable as a *death claim*, then the proceeds are subject to the same federal income tax rules that apply to death benefits under life insurance policies. However, if the endowment policy matures as a living benefit, or if the policy is surrendered for its cash value, the tax laws treat the proceeds in a different manner.

When the proceeds of a matured endowment are paid in a lump sum, the taxable amount is the difference between the stated face amount and the total premiums paid. This tax generally is applied in the year the policy matured or was surrendered. For example, suppose that Jason Barker owns a $10,000 20-year endowment policy and he pays a $350 annual premium. When the endowment matures, Mr. Barker will receive the $10,000 face amount of the endowment. He will have paid $7,000 in premiums during the 20-year period. The difference between the amount he receives and the amount he has paid is $3,000. This $3,000 is taxable as income to him the year the endowment matures and he receives the benefit.

If the policyowner elects instead to receive the endowment proceeds under one of the settlement options, then the amount of the original gain may not be taxable as income in the year the endowment actually matures. Instead, the gain may be taxable when the proceeds are received. To qualify for this deferred taxation, the policyowner must (1) choose the interest option prior to the endowment's maturity date or choose one of the installment options *and* (2) give up the right to withdraw the proceeds or the right to change the settlement option. The interest earned on the proceeds being held by the company is considered taxable income to the policyowner.

Individual state and provincial income taxes

The laws regarding income taxation vary so much among the states and provinces that they will not be discussed here. However, as a general rule, the states and provinces that have an income tax system will tax life insurance policy proceeds according to rules similar to those used by the federal government.

Estate Taxes

Estate taxes are taxes which are levied on the money and property owned by a person when that person dies. Since 1972, the federal government in Canada has not levied estate taxes. In the United States, the federal government does levy an estate tax. When the proceeds of a life insurance policy are considered to be part of a person's estate, then these proceeds are subject to estate taxes in the same manner as any other valuable property. The proceeds will be considered part of the insured's estate if they are payable to the insured's estate *or* if the deceased insured was the owner of the policy.

In order for the proceeds of a life insurance policy to be excluded from the insured person's estate, and therefore *not* subject to these estate taxes, two conditions must be met:

1. The proceeds must be payable to a living beneficiary, *not* to the insured's estate.
2. Someone other than the insured must have sole and complete ownership of the policy; the insured must not have retained even one ownership right.

If both of the above conditions are not met, then the proceeds of the policy *are* considered to be part of the insured's estate and are therefore subject to federal estate taxes. Further, if the policy was sold or transferred from the policyowner-insured to the beneficiary within three years of the insured's death for an amount less than the policy's value, then the proceeds still will be considered part of the insured's taxable estate.

Estate taxes are also levied by individual states in the United States and by various provinces in Canada. In most provinces, the life insurance policy proceeds are granted a special exemption which reduces the amount of the estate tax. In all states in the United States, no special exemption is granted to the proceeds; if the proceeds are considered part of the insured's estate, then they are taxed accordingly.

12

Industrial Life Insurance and the Home Service System

In the late 1800s, insurance companies identified low income industrial workers as a market segment which had two distinct needs. These workers needed a small amount of insurance that would pay their burial and final expenses, and they needed to be able to purchase that insurance using a premium payment system which would not strain their budgets. The product which insurers developed to meet this need was industrial insurance, and the marketing method they chose to bring this product to the workers was the home service system.

In this chapter, we will discuss both the home service method of marketing insurance products and the industrial line of insurance. Since industrial life insurance policies have been undergoing numerous changes in their design and administration in recent years, we will describe both the traditional industrial policy and the industrial policy which is sold today. In addition, we will discuss several other life insurance products which are marketed through the home service system.

HOME SERVICE SYSTEM

The home service system is distinctive from other marketing methods because of the segment of the population served by the home service method of marketing and because of the role of the home service agent.

Home Service Market

The home service system was originally developed to meet the needs of industrial workers in metropolitan areas. Prior to the early 1900s, group life insurance did not exist, and the vast majority of industrial workers had no money to meet the expenses of their last illnesses and burials. The home service system was developed to sell policies with low face amounts and low premium amounts to these workers. Since these policies were sold primarily in areas of industrial concentration, they soon became known as industrial policies.

Industrial insurance was developed before the time of mass transit systems, and industrial workers and their families lived near the workplace in a relatively confined area. It was therefore possible and convenient for one agent to sell to and service a large group of policyowners and potential policyowners at their homes.

Most of these industrial workers were paid weekly, and the home service agent timed premium collection visits to coincide with this weekly paycheck; hence, a policyowner did not need to establish a savings plan to meet premium payments.

Today's home service market still consists primarily of low and lower-middle income families. These families may still rely on premium payment schedules which can be arranged to coincide with paydays. In addition, many persons with limited financial resources do not maintain checking accounts. Since the home service agent accepts cash, the policyowner need not establish a bank account or purchase money orders to pay policy premiums.

One of the needs for the insurance coverage marketed through the home service system remains the need for funds to pay for the insured's funeral and final expenses, and industrial policies are often purchased for this reason. But the income group targeted by home service companies today has more disposable income than in the past and, hence, is able to purchase a larger amount of coverage than a single industrial policy can provide. This increase in disposable income and the need for increased protection because of inflation accounts to a large extent for home service marketing's expansion into additional product lines.

Home Service Agent

Each home service agent is assigned a specific geographic territory, which may be as small as a dozen city blocks, and the agent generally is not permitted by the insurance company to sell home service products outside that area. In contrast, individual ordinary life insurance agents usually are not similarly restricted and may operate in any locations where they hold valid licenses. Insurance agents' licenses are issued by the states and provinces, and it is not unusual for an ordinary agent to be licensed to do business in several jurisdictions.

Within the assigned territory, the home service agent is responsible for all new sales of home service products and for policyowner service to all of the owners of the company's home service policies within the territory, whether or not that agent originally sold the policy. Policyowner service includes answering questions and solving specific problems. For example, when an insured person dies, the home service agent helps the beneficiary complete the claim form and delivers the check for the policy proceeds.

The home service agent also collects renewal premium payments for home service insurance products, sometimes as often as weekly, at the policyowner's home. (Ordinary insurance agents usually are *not* authorized to accept renewal premium payments.) The high visibility of the home service agent is a reminder to the policyowner of the importance of keeping the insurance coverage in force. A policyowner is less likely to discontinue premium payments if keeping the policy in force involves only the payment of a small weekly amount, with the added convenience of having the payment take place at home.

The frequent collection of these small amounts of money from many people requires that the insurance company use an accounting system which differs from the system used for ordinary life insurance policies. In the early days of home service, given the limited business equipment available at that time, maintaining detailed premium payment records at the home office for each policy would have been prohibitively expensive. Instead, insurance companies set up a bookkeeping *debit* against each agent's account for the total weekly premium amount due from all policyowners in that agent's territory. Under this system, the agent was considered to owe the company the amount of money which was supposed to be collected each week. The agent would turn in to the company the amount actually collected, and the company would credit this amount to the agent's account. Detailed premium payment records for each policy were kept by the agent, rather than by the home office.

Although the premium accounting system used today for home service policies has been automated by most companies, the responsibility for individual premium accounting still lies with the home service agent. However, premium payment records for individual policies are now usually kept in the insurance company's home office as well. The debit accounting system, which was first developed for agents who sold industrial insurance, led to each agent's territory's being termed the agent's *debit* and the agent's being called a *debit agent*. Although the term "debit agent" is still in use today, the term "home service agent" is more descriptive of the agent's role.

Many life insurance companies which offer home service products also offer regular ordinary insurance products and annuities, and the home service agent usually is authorized to sell these products as well. (Ordinary insurance plans and plan variations were described in chapters 3 and 4. Annuities will be discussed in chapter 16, "Annuities and Retirement Plans.")

PRODUCTS MARKETED THROUGH THE HOME SERVICE SYSTEM

Although an increasing percentage of the home service agent's sales (see Figure 12–1) comes from ordinary life insurance products, we will con-

FIGURE 12-1
Distribution of the home service agent's sales in the United States*

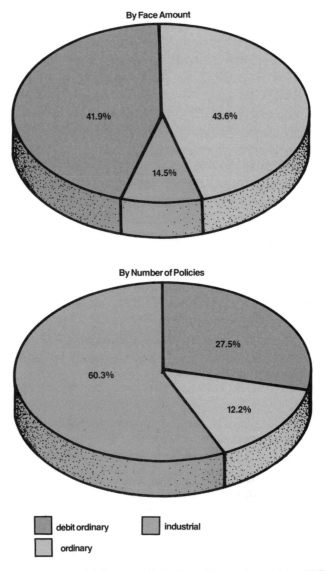

*Based on information furnished by the Life Insurance Marketing and Research Association (LIMRA) regarding sales in 1976.

centrate on the products marketed solely through the home service system. These products include industrial life insurance, weekly and monthly debit ordinary insurance, industrial health insurance, and monthly debit health insurance. We will examine each of these products, beginning with industrial life insurance.

Industrial Life Insurance

The industrial life insurance policy has two distinguishing characteristics: (1) the face amount of the policy is low, usually under $2,000; and (2) premiums are payable weekly or monthly. Further, industrial policies differ slightly from individual ordinary policies in such areas as plan availability, underwriting, and premium rate calculation. Insurance statutes also recognize industrial life insurance policies as a distinct line of insurance. Hence, industrial life insurance policy provisions have traditionally differed in certain respects from the provisions found in ordinary life insurance policies.

Plans available

Unlike individual ordinary insurance, which is available in three plans and many plan variations, industrial insurance is usually available only in a limited number of plans, and few variations are offered. Most industrial policies sold are limited-payment whole life insurance policies – such as whole life paid-up at age 65 or 70. Under such policies, premium payments stop when the policyowner retires and is living on a reduced income. Endowment plans are available, but term insurance plans are rarely offered.

Underwriting

The information needed by industrial life insurance underwriters to determine insurability is considerably less detailed than the information needed by ordinary insurance underwriters. Because of the small face amount of the industrial policy, an extensive and expensive underwriting process is unnecessary. The standard risk classification used by industrial insurance underwriters is also broader – to simplify the risk appraisal process – and fewer insureds are classified as substandard risks.

Premium rates

The premium *amount* charged for an industrial insurance policy is low because the amount of coverage provided by the policy is low. The premium *rate* per $1,000 of coverage, however, is higher than the premium rate per $1,000 of coverage charged for ordinary insurance policies. The higher mortality rate experienced under industrial insurance policies and the high expenses incurred in administering these policies account for the higher premium rate per $1,000 of coverage for industrial insurance.

Lower income groups have a traditionally higher rate of mortality than those earning average or above average incomes. Because persons insured under industrial policies are likely to have below average incomes and because underwriting requirements are less strict for industrial insurance, the mortality rate experienced among persons insured under industrial policies is higher than the mortality rate experienced by those persons insured under ordinary life insurance policies. Although this mortality rate difference is diminishing, the difference is still significant enough to cause most industrial insurers to use special mortality tables to calculate premium rates and policy reserves for industrial business. The use of these special mortality tables contributes to the higher premium rate.

Administering industrial policies is more expensive than administering ordinary policies. The most significant additional cost is the weekly or monthly premium collection. This extra service provided by the home service system creates an expense which must be included in the premium rate. Further, some policy administration expenses are the same for any policy, ordinary or industrial, regardless of its face amount. Since the face amount of an industrial policy is low, the proportion of the premium rate needed to cover these fixed expenses is higher in an industrial policy than the proportion needed to cover such fixed expenses in a policy with a large face amount.

In the early days of industrial insurance, a policy's face amount was determined largely by the premium amount an applicant could afford. For example, a man might decide he could afford 50¢ per week for an industrial insurance policy on his own life. The company would determine the face amount of coverage that 50¢ a week would purchase for a person of his age and would then issue the policy for that face amount. Today, industrial sales are usually based on the face amount requested, as are ordinary insurance sales.

Policy provisions

The standard policy provisions used in industrial insurance policies have traditionally differed significantly from those used in ordinary insurance policies. However, in 1982 the NAIC drafted an industrial insurance model bill which was designed to eliminate many of these differences. The model bill, however, even if passed into law in the various states, will not affect the contents of industrial life insurance policies which were in force before the law was passed. For this reason, we will describe industrial insurance policy provisions with respect to those policies currently in force, and we will note the industrial policy provisions which must be included in policies governed by the 1982 NAIC model bill.

Free examination period. The free examination period provision ("10-day free look") was at one time unique to industrial insurance policies, though it has now become a standard provision for nearly all life insurance policies. This provision grants the policyowner the right to examine a policy for a specified period of time, usually 10 days to two weeks after the policy has been delivered, with the option to either accept the coverage or surrender the policy. During that period, if the policy is rejected, the insurance company will refund the premium paid.

Grace period. A minor difference between weekly premium industrial policies and ordinary insurance policies has been the length of the grace period. The grace period for most weekly industrial policies has been four weeks – 28 days – while the grace period provided for most ordinary policies has been one month – 31 days. The 1982 model bill requires industrial policies to provide a 31-day grace period.

Change in mode of premium payment. Companies will usually permit an industrial insurance policyowner to change from weekly premium payments to monthly payments. If the policyowner is able to pay monthly premiums, then the insurer will reduce the premium rate since monthly collection is less expensive to administer than weekly collection. If the policyowner chooses a mode of premium payment which is even less frequent, such as an annual mode, then the insurer will provide a larger premium rate reduction.

Most insurers also provide a premium rate reduction if the policyowner sends the premium directly to the company's home office, rather than making payments to the home service agent. Usually, the policyowner must pay these premiums to the home office for a year before the company will grant a refund or reduction in the premium.

Incontestability. The incontestability provision that most insurers include in industrial policies generally limits an insurer's right to contest a policy on the grounds of material misrepresentation in the application to a period of one year from the policy's date of issue. Although industrial insurers are permitted by law to use a two-year period in the incontestability provision like the two-year period found in most ordinary insurance policies, few actually do so.

Reinstatement. Industrial insurance policies include a reinstatement provision which grants the policyowner the right to reinstate a policy. Generally, the reinstatement request must be made within three years of the date the policy terminates. Evidence of insurability and payment of past-due premiums are required, but only a few insurers charge interest on these past-due premiums. Some companies will permit reinstatement after periods of more than three years, but in such cases interest must usually be paid on the past-due premiums.

Suicide. A suicide exclusion provision is seldom included in industrial policies. The small face amounts of industrial policies make antiselection less likely, and therefore most insurers do not believe that it is necessary to include a suicide exclusion provision.

Nonforfeiture options. As in the case of other policies which accumulate reserves, industrial policies include nonforfeiture options. These nonforfeiture options – cash value, extended term insurance, and reduced paid-up insurance – function in the same way these options function in ordinary insurance contracts.

Policy loans. In the past, a policy loan privilege has not been granted to industrial insurance policyowners because such a privilege has been considered too costly to administer in relation to the cash value available. However, in recent years, several industrial insurers have begun including policy loan provisions in their industrial policies. The 1982 NAIC model bill requires the inclusion of a policy loan provision in industrial policies, although the insurer is permitted to refuse to grant policy loans for amounts less than $25.

Dividends. Although participating industrial policies provide dividends just as do participating ordinary policies, industrial policies specify the manner in which these dividends will be applied; the industrial policyowner is not given the right to choose a dividend option. Commonly, the industrial insurance contract states that dividends will be used to purchase paid-up additions, or the contract may state that these dividends will be used to prepay premiums. Dividends on industrial policies are usually payable on a calendar-year basis, rather than a policy-year basis.

Additional benefits. Most industrial life insurance policies automatically include an accidental death and dismemberment benefit and a waiver of premium for disability benefit. (These benefits were discussed in chapter 4.) In the past, the premium rate calculated for the industrial policy included the charge for these benefits; a separate premium amount for these benefits was not specified. However, the 1982 NAIC model industrial bill expressly requires insurers to state the charge for such benefits separately.

Assignment. In the past, industrial policies included a provision which specifically prohibited the assignment of the policy. In view of the low face amounts of these policies, an assignment privilege was considered to be of little value to the policyowner. In some instances, insurers have permitted owners of industrial policies to make collateral assignments of their policies to financial institutions despite the policy prohibition. The 1982 NAIC industrial model bill states that insurers may *not* include a provision which *restricts* a policyowner's right to assign the policy.

Facility-of-payment. The facility-of-payment clause mentioned in chapter 8 is always included in industrial insurance policies. This clause permits the company to distribute some or all of the policy proceeds to the person or party who appears to be equitably entitled to them, even if that person or party is not the named beneficiary. Because the primary purpose of most industrial insurance policies is to provide either clean-up or burial funds, it is important that the policy proceeds be available immediately to the person who incurred those costs on behalf of the insured. The facility-of-payment clause provides a legally acceptable method for the insurance company to release the policy proceeds to the party who incurred these expenses, and is often used when the beneficiary has not filed a claim for the proceeds within a certain period of time or when the beneficiary is a minor.

Settlement options. Most industrial policies do not offer any settlement options; the proceeds are payable only in a lump sum. However, some insurers do permit policyowners and beneficiaries to choose the interest option or, if a policy's face amount is large enough, an installment option.

Current status of industrial life insurance

While the amount of ordinary insurance in force has increased steadily during the past few decades, the amount of industrial insurance in force has remained fairly constant since 1955 (see Figure 12-2). Debit ordinary insurance, group life insurance, and the lump-sum death benefits paid by government programs are filling the financial security needs once met by industrial insurance policies. However, the coverage provided by the industrial policy still appeals to a special segment of the population.

Monthly Debit Ordinary

Since the face amount of an industrial insurance policy is often too small to meet the financial protection needs of today's workers, home service companies offer monthly debit ordinary (MDO) policies. These policies are marketed through the home service system but are available for larger face amounts than possible under an industrial policy.

The MDO policy is an individual ordinary insurance policy and contains the same provisions found in any other individual ordinary insurance policy. MDO policies include a policy loan provision and offer the standard nonforfeiture and dividend options, if applicable. The insurance company applies individual ordinary underwriting standards in determining insurability, and the policyowner may choose from a variety of plans, including term insurance. Although both an accidental death and dismemberment benefit and a waiver of premium for disability benefit may be added to an MDO policy for an additional premium, these benefits are not automatically included in MDO policies.

Premiums for an MDO policy are generally payable monthly; the home service agent collects premiums at the policyowner's home. Because of the expense of home collection, MDO premium rates are usually slightly higher than premium rates for other ordinary insurance. Some home service companies also offer weekly debit ordinary policies which function in the same manner as MDO policies, except that the premiums are payable weekly.

Sales of MDO policies are steadily increasing, and the amount of MDO coverage in force is greater than the amount of industrial insurance in force (see Figure 12–3). The advantages of the home service system – ease of purchase, home premium collection, and frequent service visits – coupled with the versatility of the ordinary insurance policy have made MDO the home service system's fastest-growing product.

FIGURE 12-2
Industrial life insurance in force with United States life insurance companies (000,000 omitted)

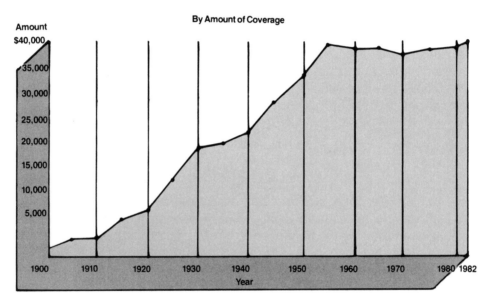

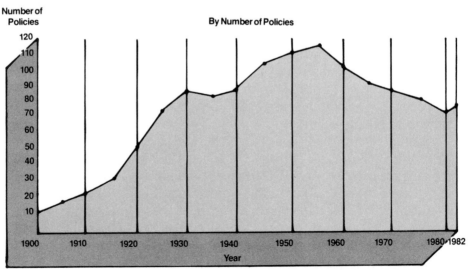

FIGURE 12-3

Comparison of amounts of monthly debit ordinary and industrial life insurance in force (000,000 omitted) with United States life insurance companies.

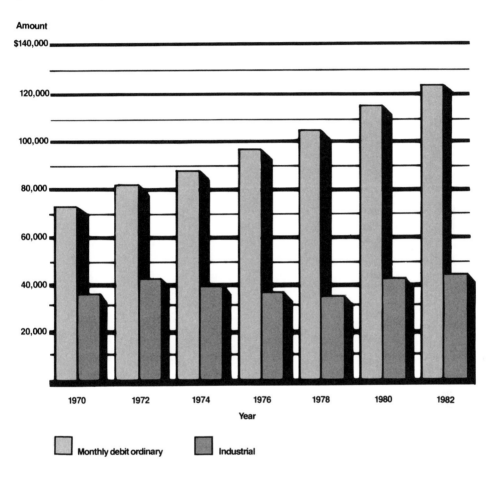

Home Service Health Insurance

The home service system is also used to market health insurance policies. These policies may be industrial health insurance policies, or they may be monthly debit health insurance policies. While we will not provide a detailed description of these plans and their provisions, we will note some of their features.

Industrial health insurance

The industrial health insurance policy is usually available only to persons already covered by an industrial life insurance policy. This limitation permits the agent to collect both premiums at the same time, thus making the collection function for each policy more cost-effective.

Generally, the coverage provided by an industrial health policy is limited, and the premium amounts charged for these policies reflect the limited coverage. Benefit amounts payable for covered losses are smaller than those typically payable under other health insurance policies. The policy lists the sums which will be paid for specific covered conditions. Since underwriting requirements are also liberal, such policies often exclude several risks from coverage.

MDO health insurance

The coverage provided by MDO health insurance policies is similar to the coverage provided by other individual health insurance policies. (Individual health insurance coverage will be described in chapter 14.) However, the home service agent collects premiums for MDO health insurance policies at the policyowner's home; the agent also usually helps the policyowner fill out claim forms. The policyowner need not own an MDO life insurance policy in order to be eligible to purchase an MDO health insurance policy.

13

Group Life Insurance

Group life insurance is the fastest growing line of life insurance in North America. In 1950, group life insurance accounted for about 20 percent of the total amount of life insurance coverage in force. During the decade of the 1970s alone, however, the amount of group life insurance in force in the United States tripled, and today the amount of group life insurance in force is nearly equal to the amount of individual life insurance in force; in Canada, the amount of group life insurance in force exceeds the amount of individual life insurance in force. Figure 13-1 illustrates the growth of group life insurance coverage in the United States and Canada.

A group life insurance policy insures a number of people under a single insurance contract, called a ***master contract***. The master group insurance contract is a contract between the insurance company and the group policyholder. The individuals insured under the group insurance policy are not parties to the contract, although these individual insureds do have certain rights.

Since the policy insures the group, in most cases the group itself — rather than the individual members of the group — must meet eligibility and insurability requirements. The objective of group underwriting is to determine whether a particular group of persons may be expected to produce loss experience that is predictable and acceptable to the insurer.

The groups most commonly covered by group life insurance are employer-employee groups. In this type of insured group, the employer is the group insurance policyholder and the employees are the insured members. Although 90 percent of the group life insurance policies in force are policies covering employer-employee groups, other types of groups are also eligible for coverage.

In this chapter, we will describe the regulation of group life insurance, define eligible groups, and discuss other aspects of group life insurance.

FIGURE 13-1

Group life insurance in force in the United States and Canada (000,000 omitted)

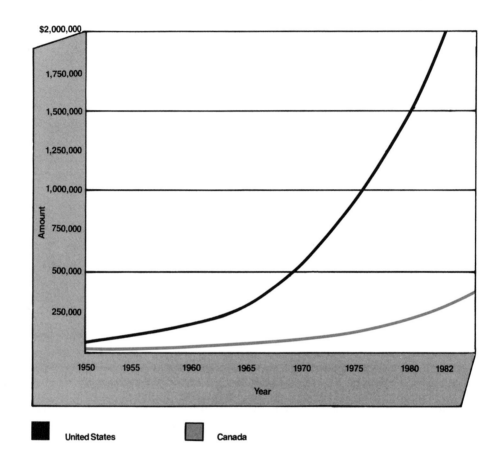

GROUP LIFE INSURANCE: REGULATION AND ELIGIBLE GROUPS

Regulation of Group Life Insurance

Although the concept of insuring a group of persons under one policy is commonly accepted today, this concept drew a great deal of criticism from some members of the insurance industry when it was first introduced in the early part of this century. These people believed that insurers would suffer financial instability as a result of poor mortality experience if a group as a whole, rather than the individual members of a group, were underwritten. Insurance industry concern was so great that the National Association of Insurance Commissioners (NAIC) established a committee to study the concept of group life insurance and recommend rules for the insurance industry to follow so that group life insurance would be administered on a financially sound basis.

The model bill recommended by the NAIC in 1917 did not bar insurers from using the group underwriting process. Rather, the model bill defined group life insurance and listed the standard policy provisions which should be included in group life insurance policies. This first model bill defined group life insurance, in part, as "that form of life insurance covering not less than 50 employees, with or without medical examination." The definition reflected the fact that the first group life policies were issued only to employer-employee groups.

The NAIC Group Life Insurance model bill has been revised and updated several times since 1917. The most recent version, which was adopted in 1980, forms the basis for much of the group life insurance legislation in the United States. Like other NAIC model bills, this model bill has served only as a guideline for states as they develop their own legislation. The 1980 Group Life Insurance model bill expands the definition of eligible groups to include a wide variety of groups and does not specify any minimum size requirements.

In Canada, the legislation governing group life insurance is not comprehensive. Instead, many aspects of group life insurance are governed by a document entitled "Rules Governing Group Life Insurance," which was issued by the Association of Superintendents of Insurance. Although this document does not have the power of law, life insurance companies in Canada abide by its rules as a matter of practice. These rules incorporate many of the features found in NAIC model legislation pertaining to group insurance.

Group Eligibility

In order for a group to be considered eligible for group life insurance coverage, the group must have a reason for existing that is unrelated to obtaining group life insurance. The likelihood of antiselection in a group formed solely to obtain group life insurance coverage would be very great, since persons believing they would not qualify for individual life insurance would naturally gravitate to such a group. For this reason, insurance company practices and the laws of most jurisdictions require that a group be organized and maintained for purposes other than obtaining group insurance in order to be eligible for coverage. We will describe (1) the types of groups legally eligible for group life insurance coverage and (2) common insurance company requirements relating to the nature of an eligible group.

Types of eligible groups

As noted earlier, the most common type of group associated with group insurance coverage consists of the employees of a single employer. Other types of groups also eligible for coverage according to the laws of most jurisdictions are described below.

Multiple-employer groups. These groups consist of the employees of two or more employers. Multiple-employer groups include:

- *Taft-Hartley groups*, which are formed by one or more employers in the same or related industries as the result of bargaining agreements with one or more unions.

- *Voluntary trade associations*, which are formed by several employers in the same industry who are members of a trade association. The trade association handles the group's funds and is the group policyholder.
- *Multiple Employer Trusts (METs)*, which are formed when several small employers band together and provide group insurance benefits for their employees; in most cases, these small employers belong to the same or a related industry.

Under both Taft-Hartley groups and METs, a trustee must be appointed to handle the group's funds. The trustee is the policyholder under both Taft-Hartley groups and METs.

Labor union groups. These groups consist of the members of a specific union; the union is the policyholder and the union members are the persons insured.

Professional and other association groups. These groups consist of the members of a specific organization. The organization is the policyholder and the members are the persons insured. Some examples of these groups are professional organizations, such as those consisting of doctors, accountants, lawyers, or teachers; college alumni associations; veterans groups; and fraternal groups.

Debtor-creditor groups. These groups consist primarily of persons who have borrowed funds from a lending institution, such as a bank. Coverage issued to this type of group is called "group creditor life" or "creditor group." This coverage differs in certain respects from other group life coverages. We will discuss group creditor life later in this chapter.

Nature of an eligible group

The fact that a group is legally eligible for group life insurance does not necessarily mean that an insurer will issue a policy covering that group. The group insurance underwriter must also consider additional factors about the nature of the group before accepting that group for coverage.

In particular, the insurance company is concerned with (1) the size of the group and (2) the flow of new members into the group. Each of these aspects of a group affects the likelihood that the group will experience a predictable average mortality rate.

Size of group. A group must be sufficiently large so that the overall combined mortality rate of the group will be reasonably close to the average mortality rate predicted for that group. In general, the larger the group, the more likely it is that the group will experience a mortality rate close to the average rate predicted. For employer-employee groups, the minimum group size necessary to obtain group insurance coverage varies by jurisdiction and ranges from two to ten employees, although a number of states follow the 1980 NAIC model bill, which does not include a minimum size requirement. (The relationship of group size to (1) the amount of group life insurance in force and (2) the number of group life insurance policies in force is depicted in Figure 13-2.)

In order to determine whether a small group, such as a group with fewer than 15 members, may be expected to experience an average mortality rate, an insurance company will often establish a requirement that each individual member of the small group submit satisfactory evidence of insurability. When calculating the anticipated mortality rate of a small group, such as a group with fewer than 100 members, insurers consider not only that particular group, but also the expected mortality experience among a "group of groups." Insurers which issue policies to a number of small groups will often pool the mortality experience of such small groups. Thus, the insurer can expect that one group's unfavorable mortality experience will be offset by a favorable mortality rate in one or more of the other small groups.

The insurance company must also be able to expect that the group will remain a group for a reasonable length of time and that the size of the group will remain stable. Hence, a group of seasonal or temporary workers generally would not be considered an insurable group.

Flow of new members into the group. Another important criterion for an eligible group is an expectation that there will be a sufficient number of young members entering the group. Young new members are needed both to replace those who leave the group and to keep the age distribution of the group stable. If a group did not add young new members for a number of years, then the increasing age of the group's original members would adversely affect the group's age distribution and, hence, the group's mortality rate would increase. But if young new members are continually joining the group, the age distribution of the group should remain more stable, as should the expected mortality rate.

Once an insurer has examined the nature of an eligible group to ensure that the group (1) was formed for a purpose other than obtaining group insurance, (2) is a type of group eligible for coverage, (3) meets the minimum size requirements, and (4) has a steady flow of new members, then the insurance company may issue a group life insurance policy to the group policyholder.

FIGURE 13-2
Percentage of United States group life insurance attributable to each group size

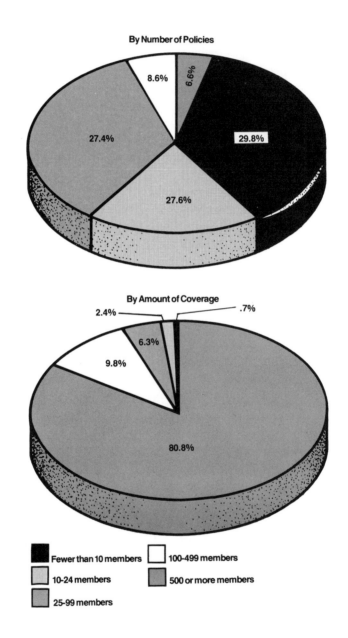

Group Membership Requirements

Eligibility of group members when plan is established

As a general rule, all members of an insured group are eligible for coverage when a group insurance plan is established. The percentage of a group which will participate depends primarily on whether the group insurance premium is paid entirely by the policyholder, or whether each covered member is required to contribute to the premium payment.

In an employer-employee group, the group life insurance premium may be paid entirely by the employer. In such a case, the plan is called **noncontributory**, because the employee is not expected to pay a portion of its cost. A group life insurance plan may also call for the individual insured to pay a portion of the premium. This type of plan is called a **contributory plan**. Most jurisdictions require that the employer in an employer-employee group pay at least a portion of the premium for the group life insurance coverage.

The laws of most jurisdictions require that, in a noncontributory plan, all eligible employees be covered; to do otherwise would be considered to be discriminatory. Therefore, 100 percent participation is expected in noncontributory plans. However, the employer-policyholder is permitted by law to define eligible employees as those employees in a specified class. These classes must be defined by requirements related to conditions of employment, such as salary, occupation, or length of employment. For example, many employers establish the requirement of full-time employment. Such employers would make group life insurance benefits available only to full-time employees, thereby excluding part-time workers from the class of eligible employees. However, an employer could not legally define a class of employees merely by listing those employees whom the employer wishes to include in the class; a list which is not based on some recognizable distinction among employees as to conditions of employment is not a valid description of a class.

In contrast to noncontributory plans, contributory group insurance plans need *not* cover all the eligible members of the group. Since contributory plans require each group member to pay a portion of the premium, it would be impossible to expect every individual in the group to agree to enroll in the plan. Therefore, although all eligible members of the group must be offered the group insurance coverage, 100 percent participation is not required. Most jurisdictions require only that 75 percent of the eligible employees in a contributory plan participate in the group insurance plan in order for the group to retain its eligibility for coverage. A higher percentage of employees may participate in the plan, but a percentage of participation lower than 75 percent could cause the group to lose its eligibility for coverage. Although the 1980 model bill does not include the 75 percent requirement, many jurisdictions have retained that requirement, and insurance companies often establish the 75 percent requirement in order to minimize antiselection.

Many group life insurance plans – contributory and noncontributory – also provide coverage for an insured member's dependents. Often, this coverage is available on an optional basis, and the group member must pay the premium required for the dependents' coverage. The amount of the coverage on each dependent is usually a specified flat amount and is less than the amount of coverage on the insured group member.

Employer-employee group life insurance plans (contributory and noncontributory) may contain an "actively at work" requirement, which states that an employee must be actively at work – rather than ill or on leave – on the day the plan takes effect in order for that employee to be eligible for coverage. If the employee is not actively at work on the day the plan takes effect, then the employee becomes eligible to enroll in the plan on the day he or she returns to work. In a contributory plan, an eligible employee who declines coverage at the time the plan is established or who drops out of the plan must usually submit evidence of insurability in order to be allowed to join the plan at a later date.

Eligibility of new group members

After a group life insurance plan has been established, new members joining the group must usually meet certain requirements before they are eligible for coverage.

Many employers establish a **probationary** or **waiting period**, which is a period of time which must pass after a new employee is hired before the new employee is eligible to enroll in the group plan. In most plans, the probationary period specified by the employer is from one to six months. If the plan is noncontributory, the new employee will be automatically enrolled at the end of the probationary period. If the group covered by a noncontributory plan is small, however, then the new employee may be required to submit evidence of insurability to the insurer in order for that employee's coverage to become effective.

In contributory plans, the probationary period is followed by an *eligibility period*. The **eligibility period**, which is usually 31 days, is the time during which a new employee may first apply for group insurance coverage. In a large group the new employee need only formally enroll in the plan and pay the appropriate portion of the premium due in order to join the plan during this period. The new employee in a *large* group usually will not be required to present evidence of insurability in order to join the plan during this period, but must submit evidence of insurability if he or she decides to enroll in the contributory plan after the eligibility period. New employees in a *small* group, such as a group with fewer than 15 members, usually will be required to submit evidence of insurability in order to enroll in the group plan, regardless of whether the eligibility period has expired.

GROUP LIFE INSURANCE CONTRACTS

Policy Provisions

A group life insurance contract, called a master policy, is a contract between the insurance company and the group policyholder. The term "policyholder," rather than "policyowner," is used to refer to the employer or other party that applies for the group insurance contract because the group policyholder does not have the same ownership rights under the contract that an individual life insurance policyowner enjoys. In a group insurance contract, the insured members of the group are granted certain of these ownership rights.

The NAIC Group Life Insurance model bill in the United States and the Superintendents' Rules Governing Group Life Insurance in Canada describe group life insurance policy provisions. Many of these provisions are very similar to the provisions found in individual policies. In this chapter, we will describe only those provisions of group life insurance policies which differ from those of individual life insurance policies. These provisions relate to (1) beneficiary designation, (2) individual certificates, (3) conversion, (4) participation requirements, (5) determination of benefit amounts, (6) grace period, (7) reinstatement, (8) misstatement of age, (9) incontestability, and (10) settlement options.

Beneficiary designation

In a group life insurance plan, each insured member of the group has the right to name a beneficiary to receive the policy proceeds payable at that member's death.* The insured member, rather than the group policyholder, must make this beneficiary designation. The insured also has the right to change the beneficiary designation. The beneficiary designation rules and restrictions applicable to ordinary individual beneficiary designations are also applicable to group insurance beneficiary designations. The only other restriction on the insured's right to name the beneficiary is that the group policyholder may *not* be named beneficiary.

The facility-of-payment clause and/or the preference beneficiary clause may be included in group life insurance policies. (These beneficiary clauses were discussed in the chapter on beneficiary designations.) However, ac-

---

*This right does not apply to group creditor life insurance plans.

cording to the 1980 model bill, only sums of up to $2,000 may be paid under the facility-of-payment clause; any remaining policy proceeds must be paid to the designated beneficiary or the estate of the insured. The preference beneficiary clause, often called the succession beneficiary clause in group life insurance policies, takes effect only if no named beneficiary survives the insured.

Group life insurance certificates

Individuals covered by a group life insurance policy are not parties to the contract and do not receive individual policies; instead, each participant usually is issued a certificate of insurance. Hence, an individual insured under a group plan is often referred to as a "certificate holder." The certificate of insurance must specify either the amount of coverage or the method of calculating the amount of coverage, the right to name the beneficiary, and the conversion provision. Some individual certificates also include a description of the master policy's major provisions. Many employer-policyholders describe the group life insurance coverage in a special employee benefit booklet. In such a situation, the benefit booklet contains the information which would be included in a certificate, and, hence, a certificate may not be given to the covered employees.

Conversion of group life insurance

The conversion clause contained in the group life insurance certificate gives an insured group member who is terminating group membership the right to convert the group insurance coverage in force to an individual permanent plan of insurance, without presenting evidence of insurability. Both the application for conversion and the payment of the first premium must be made within 31 days of termination of group membership; their acceptance by the insurer is contingent on the master policy's being in force on the date of conversion.

The individual life insurance policy purchased as a conversion may have a face value of any amount up to the amount of insurance the certificate holder had under the group plan, although some certificates now specify that this amount will be reduced by the amount of group life insurance coverage for which the terminating member becomes eligible within 31 days after leaving the original group. For example, if an employee leaves a group which has provided the employee with group life insurance coverage for a face amount of $30,000 and immediately joins another employer's group life insurance plan offering $20,000 in coverage, that employee would be eligible to purchase only $10,000 in individual coverage under the conversion provision. The $10,000 coverage amount is the difference between the coverage provided by the two plans.

Premium rates for these individual policies are based on the insurance company's ordinary individual premium rates for someone of the insured person's attained age. The conversion provision also states that if the certificate holder should die during the 31-day conversion period, the proceeds will be paid, whether or not the application for conversion has been made.

According to the 1980 model bill, each individual insured also must be granted the right to convert his or her group insurance coverage to individual coverage if the master policy terminates, provided that the insured group member has been covered under the plan for at least five years before the termination of the policy. In such a situation, each insured member of the group has the right to purchase, without submitting evidence of insurability, an individual policy for up to the lesser of either (1) $10,000 or (2) the amount of coverage in force under the group plan minus the amount of coverage for which the insured becomes entitled within 31 days of termination. Most jurisdictions require that an employer terminating a master group life insurance policy notify each participant of this conversion privilege and that the conversion privilege provision be included in the certificate of insurance.

Participation requirements

As noted earlier in this chapter, in order for a group to be insured under a group life insurance policy, usually a certain number or percentage of eligible members must participate in the group plan. A substantial drop in participation after the policy is issued may cause the group to become ineligible for coverage. The master policy usually states that if the number of insured members drops below a specified minimum, or if the percentage of participants in a contributory plan falls below 75 percent, then the insurer has the right to cancel the group policy.

Determination of benefit amounts

A unique feature of group life insurance is the method used to determine the amount of life insurance coverage available for each insured member. Insured members of the group are not permitted to select the amount of their life insurance coverage. Instead, the amount of insurance coverage for each member is determined automatically by one of two methods: (1) the amount of coverage is based on a preselected formula or (2) a flat amount is specified for each person in the group. For example, in an employer-employee group the amount of insurance for each eligible employee is often a specified multiple of that employee's salary. Alternatively, the amount of coverage may differ according to the employee's job classification, such as one amount for senior executives, another amount for managers, and a third amount for clerical staff.

Using an automatic method to determine the benefit for each member of the group is necessary to prevent antiselection. Otherwise, those members who are in poor health and unable to secure individual life insurance coverage would probably select a larger amount under the group plan than healthy members would select.

Grace period

A master group life insurance policy contains a 31-day grace period provision. As in the case of an individual life insurance policy, the insurance coverage provided by a group life insurance policy remains in force during the grace period. If the premium is not paid by the group policyholder within this period, the group policy will terminate. However, unlike the grace period provision in an individual life insurance policy, the grace period provision in a group insurance contract specifies that, if the policy terminates for nonpayment of premiums, the group policyholder *is* legally obligated to pay the premium for the coverage provided during the grace period.

Reinstatement

Neither the 1980 NAIC model bill nor any Canadian legislation requires group policies to contain a reinstatement provision. Hence, reinstatement procedures vary considerably; some insurers allow reinstatement of group policies, while others do not.

Misstatement of age

The misstatement of age provision in most group insurance contracts specifies that if the amount of the premium required for the plan is incorrect as the result of a misstatement of a group member's age, then the amount of the *premium* required for the plan will be adjusted to reflect the member's correct age. In all individual insurance contracts, the misstatement of age provision specifies that the amount of the *benefit* will be adjusted to reflect a misstatement of age. Since the amount of the benefit for group members is specified in the contract, this amount is not usually affected by a misstatement of age. Thus, most policies specify that the premium amount will be adjusted, although the laws of most jurisidictions permit an insurance company to adjust the benefit amount to the amount which would have been purchased for that member using the premium actually paid. The laws also specify that the misstatement of age method chosen must be described in the group life insurance master policy.

Incontestability

Like individual insurance policies, group life insurance policies must include an incontestability provision which limits the period during which an insurance company may use statements in the group insurance application to contest the policy's validity. Generally, the incontestability provision in a group master policy states that the group master policy is incontestable after two years from the date of issue.

The incontestability provision also allows an insurance company to contest an individual group member's coverage, without contesting the group policy itself, within two years of the date of that group member's application. For example, if a group member was required to fill out a medical questionnaire in order to be eligible for group coverage and made material misrepresentations in that questionnaire, the insurer could contest that member's coverage, but not the entire group contract, based on material misrepresentations made by the group member on that questionnaire. The period during which the coverage could be contested by the insurer, based on material misrepresentations, would be limited to two years from the date the group member applied for coverage under the plan.

Settlement options

The beneficiary of a group life insurance policy usually receives the proceeds of that policy in a lump sum. However, optional modes of settlement are also available. The policy may grant the right to choose a settlement option to the insured person and/or to the beneficiary. All of the usual modes of settlement are available as options to the insured person and/or beneficiary, but if the life income option is to be selected, then the amount of the benefit usually must be at least a stated minimum.

GROUP INSURANCE PLANS

Over 99 percent of all group life insurance policies are yearly renewable term (YRT) insurance plans. Group accidental death and dismemberment plans are also commonly issued, either as separate plans or in addition to other group life insurance coverage. Some permanent group life insurance plans are issued, but these plans are rare.

Group Term Insurance

The YRT insurance coverage under group life insurance policies is similar to YRT coverage under individual policies. Evidence of insurability is not required from the participants in the group plan each year when the coverage is renewed. These term policies do not build cash values, and the insurer has the right to increase premium rates each year.

In the United States, an employee can receive up to $50,000 of non-contributory group *term* coverage without paying income tax on the premiums the employer pays for the coverage.* The insured group member must pay taxes on premiums paid by the employer for amounts of term life insurance over $50,000. The employer usually may deduct from the company's taxable income the amount of premiums paid for up to $50,000 of group term insurance on each employee. In Canada, these same tax advantages apply to term coverage up to $25,000. Such tax benefits are considered by many to be the primary reason employer-employee group life insurance policies in both countries are generally written on a YRT plan.

Group Permanent Plans

Group plans providing permanent life insurance are less popular than term plans because the tax benefits these group permanent plans offer employees and employers are limited. However, group permanent life insurance plans are sometimes used by small companies that want to provide each of their employees with a paid-up insurance policy upon the employee's retirement. There are two types of permanent plans in use: the *group paid-up,* or *unit purchase, plan* and the *level premium plan.*

Group paid-up plans

Group life insurance purchased under a group paid-up plan combines paid-up whole life insurance and decreasing amounts of term insurance. These plans are contributory plans: the premium amount contributed by the employee each year is used as a single premium to purchase paid-up *whole life* insurance; the employer's premium contribution is used to purchase the amount of group *term* insurance required to bring the employee's total coverage up to a predetermined amount. The total amount of paid-up insurance on each employee will increase each year, and the amount of term insurance which must be purchased by the employer will decrease.

The premium paid by the employer for the *term* portion of the coverage is eligible for the same favorable tax treatment that group YRT premiums enjoy. Although the employee receives no tax benefits in connection with the premiums used to purchase permanent insurance, that insurance is in force for the employee's life and will stay in force after the employee retires or leaves the group.

---

*This exclusion from taxable income does not apply to certain employees as defined in the Tax Equity and Fiscal Responsibility Act (TEFRA) of 1982.

Level premium plans

Some insurance companies make level premium whole life insurance available on a group basis. Level premium plans are usually written on a limited-payment whole life plan, such as whole life paid-up at age 65. Because these policies build cash values, they may be used by employers to provide retirement income benefits for employees. If the group plan is noncontributory, then the employee's rights in the policy's values are not usually vested. If the group plan is contributory, then the employee's rights are vested up to the amount the employee contributed. A small portion of the employer's premium contribution may be tax deductible; the majority is not.

Accidental Death and Dismemberment Plans

Accidental death and dismemberment benefits may be included as part of a group life policy or may be issued under a separate group contract. The low cost of these benefits makes them an attractive addition to group plans, especially to plans covering employer-employee groups. When the accidental death benefit is added to a group term life insurance plan, the accidental death benefit amount is usually equal to the amount provided under the basic plan. In many plans, an additional "travel accident" benefit is provided which covers only accidents occurring while the employee is traveling for the company.

Accidental death and dismemberment policies are also often part of the group life insurance plans purchased by travel groups, automobile clubs, or transportation companies such as railroads and airlines.

GROUP CREDITOR LIFE

Under a group creditor life insurance plan, a creditor, such as a bank, is issued a master policy which covers the lives of its current and future debtors. Unlike other group life insurance plans, group creditor life plans designate the policyholder—the creditor—as the beneficiary. The amount of insurance on each group member is equal to the amount of the outstanding debt owed by that person to the policyholder-creditor. In several jurisdictions, the amount of insurance as well as the duration of a covered loan may be subject to maximum limits, regardless of the amount of the debt.

The premium for a group creditor life plan may be paid entirely by the debtor, paid entirely by the creditor, or shared by the creditor and debtor. Most jurisdictions set a maximum premium rate which a debtor may be charged for such coverage. This maximum is usually expressed in terms of a stated maximum premium amount per $1,000 of insurance coverage. If the debtor is required to pay a portion of the premium, the debtor must be given the right to refuse the group coverage; as a rule, the creditor is prohibited from requiring this group coverage as a condition of extending credit.

GROUP LIFE PREMIUMS

Premium rates for group life insurance are based primarily on mortality and expense factors. Since almost all group life plans are YRT plans and premiums are payable monthly, the interest factor important in ordinary life insurance premium calculation is of little consequence in group life insurance premium calculation.

Most insurers use a standard group mortality table to calculate initial premium rates for group insurance, much as insurers use a standard mortality table to establish life insurance premium rates for individual insurance. Renewal premium rates for group life insurance, however, are based on the mortality experience of each group or, if the group is small, on the mortality experience of that group and similar small groups.

Administrative expenses per $1,000 of group life insurance coverage tend to be lower than those per $1,000 of individual life insurance. Underwriting and policy issue costs are generally lower for group insurance because often the group as a whole is underwritten, rather than each individual member, and one master policy, rather than many individual policies, is issued. Expenses are also lower because the group master policyholder often handles many of the clerical duties which an insurer must perform for individual insurance. The premium rate per $1,000 of coverage under a group policy reflects these expense savings.

Premium Amounts

Once the initial group life insurance premium rates have been established by a particular insurer, the premium amount is then calculated for each new group. This premium amount is based on (1) the premium rate per $1,000 of coverage set by the insurance company, (2) the age and sex of each member of the group, and (3) the amount of insurance coverage on each member. This premium amount is then adjusted to reflect the size of the group – larger groups are granted volume discounts – and the group's risk classification.

A group is assigned a risk classification – standard, substandard, or declined – based on the group's normal activities. If the group's activities are *not* expected to contribute to a greater-than-average mortality rate among its members, then the group is classified as a standard risk. Most employer-employee and association groups qualify as standard risks.

A group whose activities may be expected to lead to a higher-than-average mortality rate among its members is classified as a substandard risk and charged a higher premium rate per $1,000 of coverage than a group classified as a standard risk would be charged. For example, a group consisting of coal miners may be classified as a substandard risk because of the hazards involved in mining. If the group's normal activities are extremely dangerous, some insurance companies will decline the group for coverage. For example, many insurers would decline for group life insurance coverage a group consisting entirely of race car drivers.

YRT group life insurance premium rates for each group are usually guaranteed for a policy year, and the premium is payable by the policyholder on a monthly basis. If the group plan is a contributory employer-employee plan, then the employer is responsible for collecting the employees' contributions – usually through payroll deductions – and submitting the entire monthly premium amount to the insurer. The monthly premium amount can be changed by the insurer only to reflect group membership and coverage changes. For example, if an employer hires several new employees one month, the premium *amount* the employer pays to the insurer will increase; the premium rate per $1,000 of coverage, though, does not change during the year.

Each year when the policy is renewed, the insurer calculates a new premium rate which reflects the changes in the group's age and sex distribution that occurred during the previous year. The insurer also considers the group's prior year's claims experience when calculating the group's renewal premium rate. This process of using the group's prior experience to establish premium rates is called *experience rating* and is most often fully applied only to employer-employee groups of at least several hundred employees. When calculating premium rates for smaller groups, an insurer will often consider that group's prior claims experience, but the insurer will not assign as great a degree of credibility to that past experience as the insurer will assign to the prior experience of larger groups.

Experience Refunds and Dividends

At the end of the policy year, a portion of the group life insurance premium may be refunded to the group policyholder. These refunds are called *dividends* or *experience refunds*. These group insurance premium refunds are similar to the policy dividends provided for participating individual life insurance policies and are usually called "dividends" by those companies which also issue individual participating policies. Companies which do not issue participating policies generally call these premium refunds "experience refunds."

The amount of this refund is based on the insurer's evaluation of the group's experience. If the group is large enough, the evaluation is based on that group's experience alone. If the group is small, the evaluation is based on the experience of that group and similar small groups. The refund is based primarily on the group's claims experience and the expenses the insurer incurred administering the plan. If the group incurred fewer claims or the insurer incurred lower administrative expenses than anticipated when the insurer established the group's premium rate, then the insurer will refund a portion of the premium paid for the coverage.

All premium refunds are payable to the group policyholder, even if the plan is contributory. If the amount of the refund to the policyholder of a contributory plan should exceed the portion of the group premium which was paid out of the policyholder's funds, then the excess must be used for the benefit of the individual participants in the plan. For example, an employer who receives a premium refund which exceeds the amount the employer paid out of the employer's own funds may apply the excess refund to pay a portion of the employees' contributions during the next year or to pay for additional benefits for the employees.

GROUP PLAN ADMINISTRATION

The administration of group life insurance plans is primarily a matter of recordkeeping. Some of the necessary records for a group plan include the name of each plan participant, the amount of insurance on each participant, and the name of each beneficiary. If the insurance company maintains these records, the plan is called *insurer-administered*. If the group policyholder keeps the records, the plan is called *self-administered*. In either case, information regarding the makeup of the group and any changes in the group is reported monthly to the insurer.

14

Individual Health Insurance

Most people cannot afford to pay the full costs of their medical treatment should they become seriously ill, nor can most people afford a loss of income when they are physically unable to work. In the United States and Canada, most people are covered by some form of health insurance to help them bear these financial losses.

Health insurance coverage is provided primarily through private insurance companies, government programs, Blue Cross/Blue Shield plans, and Health Maintenance Organizations (HMOs). The individual health insurance policies described in this chapter are sold by private insurance companies. The group health insurance coverage provided by private insurance companies, as well as the health insurance coverage provided by government health insurance programs and organizations other than private insurance companies, will be discussed in the next chapter, "Group Health Insurance and Alternative Sources of Health Insurance Coverage."

There are two distinct types of individual health insurance coverage: *medical expense* coverage, which provides benefits for the treatment of sickness or injury; and *disability income* coverage, which provides income benefits when the insured is unable to work because of sickness or injury. In this chapter, we will describe in detail these two types of coverage. In addition, we will discuss individual health insurance underwriting and explain the typical policy provisions found in individual health insurance policies of both types.

MEDICAL EXPENSE COVERAGE

Medical expense coverage is designed to provide benefits to help the insured pay for the costs of his or her medical treatment for a sickness

223

or injury. The specific benefits available depend on the type of medical expense coverage provided by the policy. In this chapter, we will examine the medical expense coverage provided by five types of medical expense policies: (1) hospital-surgical expense, (2) major medical, (3) social insurance supplement, (4) hospital confinement, and (5) limited coverage (dread disease). While these five types of individual health insurance policies are not the only types of medical expense policies marketed in the United States, the coverage provided by these policies is representative of the medical expense coverage usually available. In Canada, where all citizens are covered by government health insurance programs, social insurance supplement is the only type of medical expense coverage marketed by private insurance companies.

Hospital-Surgical Expense Policies

Hospital-surgical expense policies provide benefits related directly to hospitalization costs and associated medical expenses incurred by an insured for treatment of a sickness or injury. Hospital-surgical expense policies usually specify that the insured must be hospitalized before any benefits are payable, although some such policies provide benefits for certain specified outpatient charges. These policies also specify benefit amount limits for most covered expenses. The specific benefits available vary according to individual insurance company practices and according to certain limitations and exclusions. Generally, hospital-surgical expense policies cover:

- hospital charges for room, board, and hospital services
- surgeon's and physician's fees during an insured's hospital stay
- specified outpatient expenses
- extended care services, such as convalescent or nursing home costs
- limited maternity care costs

Any medical expenses incurred by an insured *other* than the expenses described in the policy are not "eligible expenses" and no policy benefits are payable for those expenses. The following description of these benefits, deductibles, and exclusions reflects the coverage typically provided by hospital-surgical expense policies. It should also be noted that some companies issue separate hospital expense and surgical expense policies, which provide only some of the benefits described.

Benefits

Hospital charges. The benefit payable for hospital room and board is limited to a maximum benefit amount per day. This maximum benefit amount is usually stated either in terms of a dollar limit or in terms of the customary charge for a semi-private room. Some hospital-surgical expense policies provide a higher maximum benefit amount per day for room and board charges when the insured must be confined in an intensive care or cardiac care unit, since these charges are considerably higher than the regular daily hospital room and board charge. In addition, most policies specify a maximum number of days for which the room and board benefit will be payable during each period of hospital confinement.

A separate hospital expense benefit is payable to cover miscellaneous hospital charges such as X-ray and laboratory fees, medicines, and the use of an operating room. Hospital-surgical expense policies usually specify a maximum benefit amount payable for all such hospital services. This amount is often set at a multiple of the maximum room and board benefit amount.

Specified outpatient expenses. Recently, some insurance companies have begun issuing hospital-surgical expense policies that include benefits for certain outpatient charges, such as charges for emergency room treatment of an accidental injury. Generally, the treatment must be administered within a specified period of time after the accident, usually 48 to 72 hours, in order for the benefit to be payable. Other outpatient charges often covered by hospital-surgical expense policies are those charges incurred for diagnostic tests performed in an adequately equipped doctor's office or clinic. These tests include X-rays and blood tests, among others. The policy states the maximum benefit amount which will be payable for these expenses.

Surgeon's and physician's fees. The amount of a surgeon's fee which the policy will cover is usually based on the policy's surgical schedule, which lists common surgical procedures and the maximum benefit amount the insurer will pay for each procedure. The insurer reserves the right to determine the maximum benefit payable for surgeon's fees for any operation not listed on the schedule. Some hospital-surgical expense policies do not include such a surgical schedule. Instead, these policies pay surgeon's benefits based on the "reasonable and customary" or "usual and customary" charge for the procedure performed – that is, the prevailing charge made by surgeons of similar expertise for a similar procedure in a particular geographic area. Fees for dental and obstetric surgery usually are not covered by hospital-surgical expense policies unless such surgery is necessary as the result of an accidental injury.

A separate benefit is payable to cover fees for services provided by an anesthesiologist during surgery. In addition, some policies cover physicians' fees for medical services that are not related to surgical procedures if these fees are incurred while the insured is hospitalized. The policy specifies the maximum benefit amount payable for each physician's visit in the hospital, as well as the maximum number of such visits which will be covered.

Extended-care services. The extended-care benefit of a hospital-surgical expense policy covers room and board charges, up to a specified maximum amount, when the insured is confined in an extended-care facility, such as a nursing or convalescent home. The benefit is designed to encourage the use of extended-care facilities by patients who need professional care while recovering from illnesses or surgery but who do not need the full services of a hospital. The insured's confinement in an extended-care facility must begin immediately after a hospital stay in order for the benefit to be payable. The policy specifies the maximum number of days and the maximum benefit for each day of confinement.

Maternity care costs. Individual hospital-surgical expense policies may provide limited benefits to cover normal maternity care costs; often maternity coverage is available only on an optional basis and requires an extra premium. Usually, the maternity benefit is described separately either in a special maternity benefits provision or, if it is an optional benefit, in a rider to the policy. This provision, or rider, typically requires that the insured's pregnancy must have begun after the policy became effective in order for any maternity benefit to be payable. The normal maternity benefit usually is limited to a flat amount, regardless of actual charges. Medical expenses caused by complications resulting from pregnancy, however, usually are *not* considered to be normal maternity care costs; these expenses *are* covered by a hospital-surgical expense policy on the same basis as any other illness or accident. Many states in the United States require that complications of pregnancy be covered on the same basis as any other illness or accident.

Deductible amounts

Some hospital-surgical expense policies specify that, before any benefits become payable under the policy, the insured must pay a portion of the eligible medical expenses which are incurred as the result of an illness or accident. The portion which the insured must pay before the insurance company will make any benefit payments is called the **deductible amount**, commonly shortened to the **deductible**. The deductible may be expressed either as a "per cause" deductible or as a "calendar year" deductible. A **per cause deductible** applies to all eligible medical expenses caused by a single illness or injury. A **calendar year deductible** applies to any eligible medical expenses incurred by the insured during any one calendar year. A calendar year is usually defined as beginning on January 1 and ending on December 31. An individual medical expense policy which covers all the members of a family will specify either (1) that the deductible will apply to each person on a "per cause" or "calendar year" basis, or (2) that once the deductible has been satisfied by any two or three family members, then the remaining family members will not be required to satisfy any deductible in that year.

For example, suppose Victoria Lang is insured under a hospital-surgical expense policy. She is hospitalized in January to have a gallstone removed and in April for an appendectomy. If her policy included a $100 "per cause" deductible, she would pay the first $100 of the eligible medical expenses she incurred for the gallstone operation and the first $100 of the eligible medical expenses she incurred for the appendectomy. If, on the other hand, her policy included a $100 per "calendar year" deductible, she would pay the first $100 of eligible medical expenses caused by the gallstone operation before any policy benefits would be payable, but she would *not* be required to pay another deductible when she was hospitalized again in April.

The inclusion of a deductible amount in health insurance policies enables an insurance company to charge lower premiums than would be possible if no deductible were included, since this relieves the insurer of processing and paying claims for the relatively minor medical expenses which would be less than the amount of the deductible. In general, the higher the deductible amount, the lower the premium will be for otherwise equivalent hospital-surgical expense policies.

Exclusions

Medical expenses which result from any of the following are usually *excluded* from coverage under individual hospital-surgical expense policies:

- cosmetic surgery, unless such corrective surgery is required due to accidental injury
- treatment for any injury or sickness which occurs while the insured is in military service or which is the result of an act of war
- treatment for injuries which are intentionally self-inflicted or which are the result of attempted suicide
- any hospital-surgical procedures for which expenses are paid by other organizations or which are provided free of charge in government facilities (For example, if the insured is receiving benefits for an occupational injury or illness from workers' compensation, the insured would not be permitted to collect duplicate benefits under an individual policy for treatment of the same occupational injury or sickness.)
- normal pregnancy or childbirth expenses, unless such coverage is selected on an optional basis

For many years, hospital-surgical expense policies excluded from coverage any costs incurred by the insured for the treatment of alcoholism, mental illness, drug addiction, or chemical dependency. However, an increasing number of jurisdictions now require that insurers provide some coverage for the treatment of these conditions.

Major Medical Policies

Although the benefit amounts available under hospital-surgical policies are high enough to cover the medical expenses caused by most illnesses and injuries, these benefit amounts may be insufficient to cover medical expenses which result from major illnesses or injuries requiring expensive or long-term care. To meet the need for economic protection in such cases, insurers developed major medical policies.

Coverage

Major medical policies generally provide broad coverage for both hospital expenses and outpatient expenses, and major medical policies include fewer limitations than hospital-surgical expense policies. Major medical policies include benefits for the same medical expenses that are covered by hospital-surgical expense policies. Major medical policies also provide coverage for expenses which may not be covered under basic hospital-surgical plans, including the costs incurred for (1) receiving outpatient treatment, (2) employing private-duty nurses, (3) renting or purchasing expensive treatment equipment and medical supplies, and (4) purchasing prescribed medicines.

Major medical policies generally provide a high maximum benefit amount, such as $100,000 or $1,000,000. The maximum benefit amount available under a major medical policy usually applies to each covered sickness or injury, rather than to each covered expense, although the policy may specify a maximum benefit amount per day for hospital room and board charges. Some major medical policies specify a lifetime maximum benefit amount, with the coverage expiring once the insured has received that amount in benefits.

Expense participation

Most insurers specify in their major medical policies that the insured must share in the payment of the medical expenses he or she incurs. Sharing in the cost of such medical expenses with the insurer is called *expense participation*. Expense participation encourages the insured to keep medical expenses to a minimum and, consequently, enables the insurer to keep premium rates to a lower level as well. The three expense participation methods most commonly used are discussed below.

Deductible amount. Many individual major medical policies specify an amount which the insured must pay before any policy benefits are payable. This deductible commonly is $500, $1,000, or even higher. As in the case of hospital-surgical expense policies, the major medical policy will specify whether the deductible will be a "per cause" deductible that applies to each illness or injury, or a "calendar year" deductible that applies to all eligible medical expenses incurred in a calendar year.

Corridor deductible. When a major medical policy is purchased to supplement a hospital-surgical expense policy, the major medical policy may include a ***corridor deductible***. The corridor deductible for a major medical plan is a flat amount which the insured must pay, such as $100 or $200, above the amount paid by the hospital-surgical expense policy before any benefits are payable under the major medical policy. For example, suppose Thomas Aster is covered both by a hospital-surgical expense policy which specifies a $2,000 maximum benefit amount per illness and by a major medical policy which includes a $200 corridor deductible. Once Mr. Aster receives $2,000 in benefit payments from his hospital-surgical expense policy for a single illness, he must pay the next $200 in expenses himself before any benefits will be paid under his major medical policy. In this example, no benefits are payable under the major medical policy until Mr. Aster's total eligible medical expenses exceed $2,200.

Coinsurance. Most major medical policies require that the insured pay a specified percentage of all the eligible medical expenses, in excess of the deductible, which he or she incurs as a result of a sickness or injury. This method of expense participation is called ***coinsurance*** or ***percentage participation***. A typical coinsurance provision requires that the insured pay a portion, such as 20 percent, of the eligible expenses incurred; the insurer will pay the remaining percentage, such as 80 percent, of the eligible expenses incurred, up to the maximum benefit amount. Often, a major medical policy will include both a coinsurance provision and a deductible amount.

For example, suppose Jane Clark is covered by a major medical policy which specifies a $500 deductible per cause and includes a 20 percent coinsurance provision. Ms. Clark is hospitalized for an injury and incurs $2,000 in eligible expenses. She must pay the first $500 of these expenses herself in order to satisfy the policy's deductible requirement. Additionally, she must pay the coinsurance factor of the remaining $1,500 in expenses – $300 (see calculations below). The total cost she must pay, then, is $800. The benefit amount the insurer will pay under the major medical policy will be $1,200.

$$
\begin{aligned}
\text{Expenses} &\quad \$2,000 \\
-\text{Deductible} &\quad -500 \\
\hline
\text{Remaining Expenses} &\quad \$1,500 \\
\times\text{Coinsurance Factor} &\quad \times.20 \\
\hline
&\quad \$300.00
\end{aligned}
$$

Ms. Clark's Total Payments: $500 + $300 = $800
Insurer's Payment: $2,000 – $800 = $1,200

Some individual health insurance policies, called **comprehensive health insurance policies**, combine the features and benefits of hospital-surgical expense policies and major medical policies. These policies, which generally provide the same benefits as major medical policies, often include an unlimited benefit amount. They do not specify as large a deductible as is generally found in major medical policies since comprehensive policies are designed to provide medical expense coverage for those persons with no other health insurance coverage.

These comprehensive policies also usually include a coinsurance feature. The amount of money the insured must pay under the coinsurance provision is limited, however, by a *stop-loss provision* that is also usually included in most comprehensive policies. The **stop-loss provision** specifies that the insurer will pay 100 percent of the insured's eligible medical expenses after the insured has incurred a specified amount of out-of-pocket expenses – such as $1,000 – under the coinsurance feature.

Some comprehensive policies are issued to cover only a short stated period of time, such as three or six months. These short-term comprehensive health insurance policies are a recent development and are designed for people who need strictly interim health insurance coverage. For example, a recent college graduate who is no longer covered under his or her parents' policy, but who is not yet covered by an employer's group health insurance policy, may purchase a short-term comprehensive policy.

Social Insurance Supplement Policies

Social insurance supplement policies are designed solely to complement specified government health insurance programs and are available exclusively to those persons eligible for benefits under such government programs. In the United States, the Old Age, Survivors, Disability, and Health Insurance program, popularly known as Social Security, includes a health insurance program called Medicare for those receiving Social Security benefits. In Canada, each province provides a health insurance program for its residents.

The benefits available under Medicare in the United States and under the provincial government programs in Canada will not cover all the medical expenses an insured may incur; therefore, private insurance companies have designed insurance products to supplement the coverage provided under these government programs. Social insurance supplement policies pay benefits for specified medical expenses not covered by government health insurance. For example, since Medicare benefits are usually subject to deductible amounts and coinsurance features, Medicare Supplement policies are designed to provide benefits to cover the deductible and coinsurance amounts. In Canada, since the hospital benefit provided by the provincial government programs is based on the cost of a bed in a ward, supplemental policies provide benefits to make up the difference in cost between a ward and a semiprivate room. (These government health insurance programs will be described in more detail in the next chapter.)

Hospital Confinement Policies

Hospital confinement policies, traditionally called hospital indemnity policies, provide a predetermined flat benefit amount for each day an insured is hospitalized. The amount of the daily benefit is specified in the policy and does not vary according to the amount of medical expenses the insured incurs.

The policyowner elects the amount of the policy's daily benefit, subject to the minimum and maximum amounts set by the insurer. The policyowner may also elect in some policies the maximum benefit period – the maximum number of days for which the benefit will be payable. The maximum benefit period allowed by insurers is commonly a set period between three months and one year in length. The policy also specifies whether the insurer will pay benefits beginning on the first day the insured is hospitalized, or whether the insurer will start to pay benefits only after the insured has been hospitalized for a specified period, such as three or five days.

Many hospital confinement policies vary the benefit amount according to the type of facility in which the insured is confined. Such policies typically provide a higher benefit amount – such as twice the normal daily benefit amount – when the insured is confined in an intensive care or cardiac care unit, and a smaller benefit amount – such as half the normal daily benefit amount – when the insured is confined in a convalescent or nursing care facility. For example, a hospital confinement policy may provide a $100 benefit for each day the insured is confined in a hospital, a $200 benefit for each day the insured is hospitalized in an intensive care unit, and a $50 benefit for each day the insured is confined in a nursing home.

Limited Coverage Policies

A limited coverage (dread disease) policy is a type of policy that is designed to cover only those medical expenses incurred by an insured who has contracted a specified disease, such as cancer, which is named in the policy. Such policies may be purchased to supplement basic hospital-surgical expense policies and can serve the same ultimate purpose as major medical policies if the insured should incur medical expenses as a result of contracting the disease named in the policy. However, if the insured incurs medical expenses for the treatment of any illness other than the one specified, no policy benefit will be payable.

DISABILITY INCOME POLICIES

A disability income policy provides a specified income benefit when the insured person becomes unable to work because of an illness or an accidental injury. These policies provide no medical expense coverage; they are intended to provide protection from the financial losses which result from a person's inability to work while disabled. The insured person's disability must meet the policy's definition of total disability in order for the insured to receive the income benefit.

Definition of Total Disability

At one time, total disability was defined in disability income insurance policies as a disability which prevented an insured from performing the duties of *any* occupation. Since a strict interpretation of this definition would prevent most people from ever qualifying for disability income benefits, most insurers have stopped using this definition.

Total disability: current definition

The usual definition of total disability included in disability income policies today is more liberal than the old definition just described, and the newer definition discusses disability in two stages. According to the current definition, at the start of disability, insureds are considered totally disabled if their disability prevents them from performing the essential duties of their *regular* occupations and they are not working in *any* occupation. However, at the end of a specified period after the disability has begun, usually two years, insureds are considered totally disabled only if their disabilities prevent them from working at *any* occupation for which they are reasonably fitted by education, training, or experience. This current definition of total disability usually specifies that whenever the insured is working in any gainful occupation, the insured is not considered to be totally disabled.

Suppose, for example, that Samuel Tyler, a surgeon, was insured under a disability income policy which contained the usual current definition of total disability. Dr. Tyler was involved in an accident and lost his right arm. Since Dr. Tyler is unable to perform surgery and is not working, he will receive the income benefit under his policy for up to two years. At the end of that time, Dr. Tyler may not be considered totally disabled because his education and training may qualify him for some other gainful occupation, such as teaching in a medical college, and the income benefit may cease.

Total disability: "own occupation"

Some companies have further liberalized the definition of total disability included in disability income policies which are issued to members of certain professional occupations. According to this definition, an insured is totally disabled if the insured is unable to perform the essential duties of his or her *own occupation*. In fact, policies using this "own occupation" definition specify that benefits will be paid even while the insured is gainfully employed in another occupation, as long as the insured is prevented by disability from engaging in his or her own *previous* occupation. Suppose, in the example given above, Dr. Tyler's disability income policy had contained this "own occupation" definition of total disability. After his accident, Dr. Tyler would continue to receive the full income benefit under the policy until the end of the policy's benefit period, even if he began teaching before the end of the policy's benefit period.

Presumptive disabilities

Most disability income policies also classify certain conditions as "presumptive disabilities." These presumptive disabilities include total and permanent blindness, loss of the use of any two limbs, and loss of speech or hearing. An insured who suffers any of these losses is automatically considered to be totally disabled.

Elimination Periods

Most disability income policies specify an **elimination** or **waiting period**—a specific period, beginning at the onset of the disability, which must pass before any policy benefits will be paid. The purpose of the elimination period is similar to the purpose of the deductible amount found in medical expense policies. By specifying an elimination period, the insurer may avoid the expense involved in processing and paying very small claims. This expense savings is reflected in the premium amount charged; the longer the elimination period, the lower the premium amount for otherwise equivalent disability income coverage. The length of the elimination period varies with the individual disability income policy and ranges from a month to a year or longer.

Disability Income Benefits

Benefit amount

The monthly benefit amount under a disability income policy is usually some flat amount stated in the policy. The maximum amount of the disability income benefit which a company will allow a particular applicant to purchase must bear a specified relationship to the income earned by that applicant. The purpose of limiting the amount of the disability income benefit available is to make sure that the benefit amount a person receives during a disability does not exceed the income earned by that person prior to the disability. Without restrictions on the income amounts available through disability income policies, an insured could receive as much or more income when disabled as he or she received when working; hence, an insured who becomes disabled would have little incentive to return to work and might manage to prolong the period of disability.

When determining the maximum amount of disability income available to an applicant, the insurer considers the applicant's

1. usual earned income, before taxes
2. unearned income, such as dividends and interest, which will continue during a disability
3. additional sources of income during a disability, such as group disability income coverage and government-sponsored disability income programs
4. current income tax bracket, because the applicant's usual earned income is reduced by taxes while disability income benefits from individual policies are not reduced by taxes

The specific amount of the disability income coverage which the insurance company will issue to a person, then, depends on the above factors. In general, the maximum amount of disability income available to an applicant equals 50 to 70 percent of the applicant's usual pre-tax earnings, thus approximating the amount of after-tax earned income actually received by the applicant when he or she was not disabled.

Since government disability income benefits are considered by the insurer when it determines the amount of the benefit which an applicant may purchase, many individual disability income policies specify that the benefit amount will be increased if the disabled person does not receive the anticipated disability income benefits from a government program.

Benefit periods

Disability income policies also prescribe a **maximum benefit period** – the maximum period over which income payments will be made during disability. In general, the longer the maximum benefit period, the higher the premium for otherwise equivalent disability income policies.

Short-term individual disability income policies are typically issued with maximum benefit periods ranging from one to five years in length. Individual long-term disability income policies specify maximum benefit periods of *at least* five or ten years. Many long-term disability income policies state that if the insured's disability is caused by an accident or sickness prior to the insured's attaining a specified age, such as 62, benefits will be paid to age 65 or, in some cases, for the insured's lifetime.

Residual disability benefit

Some disability income policies also provide benefits for periods when the insured experiences a residual disability. A **residual disability** usually is defined as a disability which prevents an insured either from engaging in some of the duties of his or her usual occupation or from engaging in his or her occupation on a full-time basis. In order for the residual disability benefit to be paid, the insured must also demonstrate that the disability resulted in a loss of at least a specified percentage of earnings, such as 20 or 25 percent. The amount of the residual benefit which will be paid is determined according to a formula specified in the policy. In some cases, the residual disability must immediately follow a period of total disability, as defined in the policy, in order for the benefits to be paid.

For example, suppose Cathy Snyder, the manager of the Snyder Shoe Store, is covered by an individual disability income policy which includes a residual disability benefit. She is involved in an accident. Her resulting disability completely prevents her from working at the store for eight months, and she receives the full disability income benefit under her policy. At the end of eight months, Ms. Snyder recovers enough to be able to return to work on a part-time basis. During this period, she will receive the residual disability benefit, which is a percentage of the full disability benefit.

Income Protection Policies

A new form of disability income insurance, called *income protection insurance*, was developed in the late 1970s and functions in a different manner from the disability income policies just described. These income protection policies, designed primarily for upper-income professionals, differ from traditional disability income policies primarily in their definition of disability. The definition of disability included in income protection policies specifies that an insured is disabled if that person suffers an *income loss* caused by the disability.

These income protection policies pay an income benefit both while the insured is totally disabled and unable to work *and* while the insured is able to work but, because of a disability, is earning less than he or she previously earned. Thus, income protection policies specify both a maximum benefit amount which will be paid when an insured is completely unable to work and a method for determining the amount of lost income when the disabled insured is working but earning less than he or she previously earned.

To illustrate, suppose that in our earlier example Samuel Tyler, the surgeon, was insured under an income protection policy. Because of his accident, Dr. Tyler was no longer able to perform surgery and therefore took a job teaching at a medical school. The salary he received as a professor was considerably less than his income as a surgeon. Under an income protection policy, he would be paid a policy benefit based on the difference between his salary as a professor and his income as a surgeon. The payments would continue until the end of the policy's maximum benefit period.

Income protection policies are a recent development in the insurance industry and are specifically designed to meet the needs of only a small segment of the public; hence, most disability income policies function as previously described.

Exclusions

Most individual disability income policies exclude from coverage disabilities which result from certain specified causes. The causes of disability which may be excluded from coverage include:

- injuries or sicknesses which result from military service or war
- self-inflicted injuries
- disabilities which result from pregnancy and childbirth
- occupation-related disabilities or sickness for which the insured is entitled to receive disability income benefits under some government program, such as workers' compensation

UNDERWRITING

Health insurance underwriting is necessary to determine the degree of risk an applicant for health insurance represents. Although each insurer sets its own underwriting guidelines, the primary factors which a health insurance underwriter usually considers are the applicant's (1) age, (2) current and past health, (3) sex, (4) occupation, (5) work history, (6)avocations, (7) income and financial status, and (8) habits and lifestyles. Each of these factors affects morbidity rates. *Morbidity rates* measure the incidence and severity of sickness and accidents which may be expected to occur in a predefined group of persons.

We will first examine the effect each of the factors has on morbidity rates and then discuss the various categories of risk which have been established to classify health insurance applicants on the basis of the probability that they will suffer an insured loss.

Underwriting Factors

Age

Like mortality rates, morbidity rates generally increase with the age of the population. Generally, as people grow older, they are more likely to become ill, and the average duration of their illnesses increases. The probability that a person will be accidentally injured also generally increases with age, as does the length of the period required to recuperate from any injury. Hence, premium rates for individual health insurance policies are higher for older people than for younger people.

Health

An applicant's health history and current health are both important underwriting factors in health insurance. Many illnesses have a tendency to recur. Morbidity statistics show the likely effect of past and current illnesses and injuries on a person's future health. The underwriter can thus predict the effect that the applicant's health will have on the likelihood that the person will suffer a loss in the future. Hence, the insurability of an applicant is closely related to the applicant's current health and health history.

While an applicant's health is also important to life insurance underwriters, the degree of risk represented by specific health problems is different for life and health insurance. For example, a history of back disorders is of more significance to the health insurance underwriter than to the life insurance underwriter because the recurrence of such a problem will more likely result in a health insurance claim than a life insurance claim.

Sex

The sex of a person has an effect on that person's probable morbidity rate. In general, females experience a *higher* morbidity rate than males. Hence, insurers usually charge higher premium rates to females than to males for equivalent health insurance coverage. (Note that this practice is the reverse of that followed in determining life insurance premium rates, which are lower for females than for males. Lower life insurance premium rates reflect the fact that females experience a *lower mortality rate* than males.) The use of sex-based health insurance premium rates is being examined by the courts and legislative bodies in the United States and may be declared illegal at some future date because of the alleged social inequity of recognizing sex-based characteristics in calculating premium rates, even though such recognition may be actuarially sound.

Occupation

Morbidity rates vary considerably according to a person's occupation. These rates reflect the hazards inherent in the occupation, the stability of the occupation, and the amount of recovery time usually needed by people in that occupation to resume their normal duties. To reflect these differences in morbidity, most insurance companies establish several occupational classes and rank these classes according to morbidity rate. Health insurance applicants in each class are charged a premium rate for health insurance that corresponds to the morbidity rate experienced by that class.

For example, an insurer might use the following occupational classes for health insurance:

Least hazardous	professional, executive, administrative and clerical employees; occupations with above average earning potential and employment stability
Mildly hazardous	skilled technicians, plumbers, electricians, and others whose occupation requires light physical labor or activity; occupations requiring education and training, but more skills-oriented than the above category
Most hazardous	truck drivers, coal miners, longshoremen, and others whose occupation requires heavy physical labor or involves dangerous situations; occupations requiring little technical training

Some occupations, such as experimental-aircraft testing, are considered by health insurers to be so risk-prone that applicants who work in these occupations are usually classified as uninsurable.

Avocations

The underwriter must consider an applicant's avocations when evaluating the potential health insurance risk which that applicant represents. Engaging in certain sports or hobbies may expose an applicant to a significant chance of injury or disease. For example, a mountain climber is more prone to accidental injury than a stamp collector. Hence, the manner in which a person spends leisure time may have a bearing on the person's exposure to health risks, and the premium rate for that person's health insurance coverage may be higher than the premium rate for a person who does not pursue that particular leisure activity.

Income and financial status

An insurer limits the amount of disability income coverage it will issue to any applicant to a specified percentage of the applicant's earned income. In many cases, an insurer will not issue any disability income coverage to people who earn less than a specified yearly salary or whose income is seasonal or cyclical in nature. Further, insurers usually will not issue disability income coverage to people whose total income consists of a high percentage of "unearned" income, such as interest income, because such income will continue during the insured's disability. For these reasons, health insurance underwriters need information relating to the sources and amount of an applicant's income.

Work history

Health insurance underwriters often require information concerning the work history of an applicant for a disability income policy. An applicant who has a number of gaps in his or her work record or who has a history of temporary jobs might be deemed to be a poor risk. Should such a person later become disabled, he or she might be more inclined to prolong the disability in order to continue receiving disability income benefits and avoid returning to work. Hence, information regarding an applicant's work history can be important to health insurance underwriters.

Habits and lifestyle

The habits and lifestyle of a person may expose that person to a high degree of risk of accidental injury or illness. The degree of risk inherent in various lifestyles is often difficult to identify precisely, and underwriters often must use their own judgment in these cases. However, while an applicant's habits and lifestyle are widely recognized as affecting the probable morbidity rate, the underwriter must keep anti-discrimination legislation in mind and must exercise caution in using habits and lifestyle as reasons to assign an applicant an additional premium charge.

Sources of Underwriting Information

The health insurance underwriter uses many of the same information-gathering tools that the life insurance underwriter uses. The health insurance underwriter's primary source of information about an applicant is the policy application, which often includes the results of a medical or paramedical examination. Questions on a typical application relate to such topics as the applicant's current physical condition, health history, earned income, occupation, and hobbies. Health insurance underwriters may require an attending physician's statement in addition to the application. An insurer also may employ an outside agency, such as a consumer investigation company, to prepare an inspection report on an applicant. These reports are requested primarily to verify information on such topics as an applicant's financial status or lifestyle. The insurer must obtain the health insurance applicant's written permission before requesting information from any outside source.

Risk Classifications

Each health insurer determines the underwriting criteria it will apply to its applicants for health insurance. Based on these predetermined criteria, the individual health insurance underwriter usually will place an applicant into one of three categories of risk: standard, substandard (or modified), or declined.

Standard risk

The standard risk classification in health insurance underwriting corresponds to the standard risk classification in life insurance underwriting. An applicant who is classified as a standard risk will be issued a policy at standard premium rates; the policy will not contain any special exclusions or reductions in benefits. Most applicants for both life and health insurance are classifed as standard risks.

Substandard risk

The substandard risk classification, also known as the modified risk classification, corresponds to the substandard risk classification in life insurance. Those applicants who may be expected to experience a higher-than-average morbidity rate are classified as substandard health insurance risks. Rather than decline such applicants for coverage, health insurers have developed several ways to modify health insurance policies for persons who fall into this category. Health insurers may compensate for a higher-than-average degree of risk by charging a higher premium rate to applicants who are substandard risks. Another alternative for the insurer may be to reduce or limit the benefits payable under a contract issued to an applicant who is a substandard risk. For example, the insurer may (1) include a longer elimination period in a policy issued to a substandard risk or (2) reduce either the maximum benefit amount payable under the policy or the maximum benefit period. Alternatively, health insurers who issue a policy to an applicant who presents a specific and definable extra degree of risk may issue such a policy with a rider which excludes a certain illness or type of accident from coverage under the policy.

Declined

While the great majority of applicants for health insurance are classified as standard or substandard risks, some applicants are considered to be uninsurable. These applicants may be uninsurable because they engage in extremely dangerous occupations or hobbies or because they have very poor health. Additionally, an insurer may decline a health insurance applicant for the reasons discussed in the section of this chapter called "Income and Financial Status." In recent years, many jurisdictions have issued regulations which prohibit insurers from declining coverage to physically disabled persons unless such action can be supported by morbidity statistics. When insuring disabled persons, insurers are allowed, however, to exclude benefits for the person's existing disability.

Premiums

In calculating individual health insurance premiums, an insurer must consider its expenses, its interest earnings, and morbidity – its expected exposure to loss. Health insurers must also establish reserves for contingencies such as epidemics and natural disasters. In addition, since most medical expense policies provide benefits based on the actual costs an insured incurs for treatment, insurers must estimate the probable future costs of this medical diagnosis and treatment. Since medical costs vary widely in different areas of the United States (see Figure 14–1), premium rates for medical expense policies often are calculated separately for different

FIGURE 14-1

Average surgical charges in 1982 for an appendectomy in selected metropolitan areas of the United States

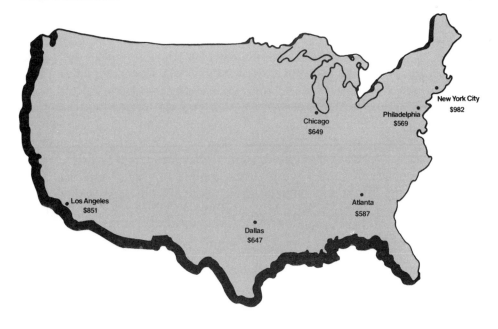

Source: *Source Book of Health Insurance Data: 1982-83* (Health Insurance Association of America).

geographic regions. Most individual health insurance policies provide that premium rates may be increased at the time of renewal, so that insurers are able to vary premium rates to reflect current costs.

INDIVIDUAL HEALTH INSURANCE CONTRACTS

An individual health insurance policy is a contract between the insurance company and the policyowner. It describes the type of coverage, the benefits payable under specified circumstances, and the premium amounts and their due dates. The application for coverage is attached to the policy. In individual health insurance policies, the policyowner and the insured are usually the same person, and benefit payments usually are made directly to this person.

Policy Provisions

Some of the policy provisions found in individual health insurance policies are identical to provisions found in individual life insurance policies. For example, the free examination period provision is identical in both life and health insurance policies. Other provisions in individual health insurance policies, such as the grace period provision, are similar but not identical to the corresponding provisions in individual life insurance policies. Still other provisions are found only in health insurance policies. In this section, we will describe those policy provisions in individual health insurance policies which differ in substance from provisions found in individual life insurance contracts.

The content of an individual health insurance policy is subject to regulation as is the content of an individual life insurance policy. In the United States, most states have enacted health insurance laws based on the NAIC Uniform Individual Accident and Sickness Policy Provisions model law. In all Canadian provinces except Quebec, the laws governing health insurance are based on the Canadian Uniform Accident and Sickness Act. In Quebec, health insurance contracts are regulated by the Quebec Insurance Act. Canadian health insurance laws, though, are substantially the same as United States health insurance laws, and, hence, individual health insurance policy provisions are similar in both countries. However, there are a few significant differences which we will note in the following descriptions of policy provisions; these differences are also summarized in Figure 14-2.

Renewal

The renewal provision in an individual health insurance policy describes the circumstances under which the insurance company may refuse

FIGURE 14-2

Comparison of United States and Canadian individual health insurance policy provisions

Although the Canadian laws regarding individual health insurance contracts are substantially the same as those enacted in the United States, there are some minor, but significant, differences in policy provisions. The following chart summarizes these differences.

PROVISION	UNITED STATES	CANADA (excluding Quebec)	QUEBEC
Misstatement of Age	Insurer adjusts benefits (same as under life insurance policies)	Insurer may adjust benefits or adjust the amount of premium	Insurer may adjust benefits or adjust the amount of premium
Grace Period	10 days for monthly premium policies; 31 days for less frequent premium payment schedules	No grace period required; insurer may cancel for nonpayment after notification (Grace period may be included at insurer's option)	30 day grace period required in all policies
Payment of Claims	Insurer must pay benefits immediately upon receipt of proof of loss	Insurer must pay benefits within 60 days of receipt of proof of loss for medical expense policies, and within 30 days of receipt of proof of loss for disability income policies	Insurer must pay benefits within 60 days of receipt of proof of loss for medical expense policies, and within 30 days of receipt of proof of loss for disability income insurance
Renewal	Renewal provisions specified in policy	All policies cancellable	Renewal provisions specified in policy
Change of Occupation	Adjustment of benefits or premium; not a required provision	Adjustment of benefits or premium; required provision	Adjustment of benefits or premium; required provision

to renew or may cancel the coverage. It also usually explains the insurance company's right to increase the policy's premium rate. Health insurance policies are distinguished from one another by their renewal provisions. In the United States and in the province of Quebec, health insurance policies fall into one of the following renewal categories: (1) cancellable, (2) optionally renewable, (3) conditionally renewable, (4) guaranteed renewable, or (5) noncancellable. In Canadian provinces other than Quebec, all health insurance policies are cancellable.

Cancellable. The renewal provision in a cancellable policy grants the insurer the right to terminate the individual policy at any time, for any reason, simply by notifying the insured that the policy is cancelled and by refunding any advance premium that the policyowner had paid. Some states in the United States have declared cancellable health insurance policies to be illegal.

Optionally renewable. The insurer has the right to refuse to renew an optionally renewable health policy on a date specified in the policy—usually either the policy anniversary date or, in some cases, a premium due date. The insurer also is permitted to add coverage limitations and/or to increase the premium rate for any *class* of optionally renewable individual health insurance policies. A ***class of policies*** consists of all policies of a particular type or all policies issued to a particular group of insureds. For example, a class of policies may be defined as all policies in force in a particular state, or all policies issued to insureds of a particular age or who fall into a specific risk category. Hence, an insurer may increase the premium rate for *all* optionally renewable health insurance policies in force in some particular state, such as California, but the insurer is not allowed to increase the premium rate for only one policy issued to a specific insured living in California. Some jurisdictions specify that any premium rate increase must be approved by the insurance department in that jurisdiction before the rate increase can take effect in that jurisdiction.

Conditionally renewable. A conditionally renewable health insurance policy grants an insurer a limited right to refuse to renew a health policy at the end of a premium payment period. Such a refusal to renew must be based on one or more specific reasons stated in the policy contract given to the insured. These reasons cannot be related to the insured's health. The age and employment status of the insured often are listed as reasons for possible nonrenewal. For example, a disability income policy may state that the insurer will renew the policy until the insured reaches a certain age *or* until the insured is no longer gainfully employed.

In addition, the insurer has the right to refuse to renew a conditionally renewable policy if the policy is of a type no longer issued by the insurer. For example, an insurer may refuse to renew a conditionally renewable major medical policy if the insurer no longer issues major medical policies. The insurer cannot, however, refuse to renew any policy simply because the insured is in poor health.

The insurer also has the right to increase the premium rate for any class of conditionally renewable policies, although such a premium rate increase may be subject to approval by any affected jurisdictions.

Guaranteed renewable. An insurer is required to renew a guaranteed renewable health insurance policy, as long as premium payments are made, until the insured reaches the age limit stated in the contract. These policies usually have age limits of 60 or 65, but some are renewable to age 70 or even for life. A company can increase the premium rate for a guaranteed renewable health insurance policy only if premium rates for that entire class of insureds are increased; a company is not permitted to increase the premium rate for only one individual in a class.

Noncancellable. An insurer does not have the right to increase premium rates for a noncancellable policy under any circumstances; these premium rates are specified and guaranteed in the policy. Noncancellable policies are also guaranteed to be renewable until the insured reaches the age limit specified in the contract.

Grace period

Most states in the United States require that an individual health insurance policy contain a grace period of at least 10 days for policies on which premiums are paid monthly and a grace period of at least 31 days for policies on which premiums are paid less frequently than monthly. Insurers may choose to specify a longer grace period. In Quebec, insurers are required to include a 30-day grace period in all policies. In other Canadian provinces, the grace period provision is not required to be included, although insurers may choose to include a grace period.

Reinstatement

The reinstatement provision states that the insurer will reinstate an individual health insurance policy if certain conditions are met. Usually, the insured must pay any overdue premiums, and the insured must complete a reinstatement application. The insurer has the right to evaluate the reinstatement application and to decline to reinstate the policy based on statements in that application. If the insurer does not complete the evaluation within 45 days after receiving the reinstatement application, or if the insurer accepts an overdue premium without a reinstatement application, then the policy is usually deemed to be automatically reinstated. Coverage under a reinstated policy is limited only to accidents which occur after the date of reinstatement and to sicknesses which begin more than 10 days after the date of reinstatement.

Time limit on certain defenses

Most health insurance policies contain a *time limit on certain defenses* provision, which is similar to the incontestability provision in a life insurance policy. The word "defenses" refers to any reasons which an insurer can use to deny liability under a contract; in this case, the term "defenses" refers specifically to any statements in the application which contain material misrepresentations. The time limit on certain defenses provision typically states that after a policy has been in force for a specified period of time, the insurer cannot use material misrepresentations in the application either to void the policy or to deny a claim *unless* the statements made by the applicant were fraudulent. A typical time limit on certain defenses provision follows:

> **Time limit on certain defenses.** After coverage on a covered person has been in force during the lifetime of that person for two years, only fraudulent misstatements in the application shall be used to void the coverage on that person.
>
> No claim for a covered charge which is incurred after those two years will be denied because of a pre-existing condition, unless that pre-existing condition was excluded from coverage, by name or specific description, on the date that charge was incurred.
>
> This provision does not have any effect on nor does it bar any other defenses under this policy.

Note that this provision differs from the incontestablity provision used in life insurance policies issued in the United States, under which even fraudulent statements in the application *cannot* be used to deny a claim after the expiration of the contestable period.

Although the NAIC model law permits insurers to specify a three-year period in the time limit on certain defenses provision, most states do not allow insurers to use any period longer than two years in such a provision. Some insurers use an incontestability provision, rather than a time limit on certain defenses provision, in their guaranteed renewable and non-cancellable health insurance policies.

Physical examination

The physical examination provision grants the insurer the right to have the insured examined by a doctor of the insurer's choice, at the insurer's expense. The purpose of such an examination is to gain information for the insurer's use in deciding whether a health insurance or disability claim made by the insured is valid. In disability income policies, this provision grants the insurer the right to require a disabled insured to undergo examinations at regular intervals so that the insurer can determine whether the insured is still disabled.

Pre-existing conditions

Most individual health insurance policies contain a pre-existing conditions provision which states that until the insured has been covered under the policy for a certain period, the insurer will not pay benefits for any health conditions which were present before the policy was issued. The pre-existing conditions provision is designed to prevent antiselection by those individuals who might seek to purchase an individual health insurance policy to provide benefits for a known health problem. A pre-existing condition usually is defined as an injury which occurred or a sickness which first appeared or manifested itself before the policy was issued and which was not disclosed on the application. Some policies specify that the insured person must have experienced symptoms of the condition during either a two- or five-year period before the policy was issued in order for the insurer to exclude that condition from coverage. A sample pre-existing conditions provision follows:

> **Pre-existing conditions.** Benefits for a charge that results from a covered person's pre-existing condition, as defined in this policy, will be provided only if that charge is a covered charge and is incurred by that person after coverage for that person has been in force for two years. However, if a condition is excluded from coverage by name or specific description, no benefits will be provided for any charges that result from that condition even after those two years.

In most states, the maximum period during which the insurer is permitted to exclude pre-existing conditions from coverage is two years. However, insurers are permitted to specify an exclusion period shorter than two years in these pre-existing conditions provisions.

Any condition which the insured disclosed on the application is *not* considered to be a pre-existing condition; insurance companies will pay benefits for the treatment of such disclosed conditions *unless* the policy specifically excludes such a condition from coverage. For example, suppose Mark York was treated for a back injury one year before he applied for a hospital surgical expense policy. If Mr. York disclosed the prior treatment for the injury on his application, then that condition would not be considered to be a pre-existing condition.

On the other hand, if Mr. York did *not* disclose the prior treatment for the back injury on his application, then that condition could be considered a pre-existing condition and thus excluded from coverage for two years. If within two years of the date of policy issue, Mr. York were to make a claim under his policy for expenses incurred in treating the back injury and if the insurer discovered that it was a pre-existing condition, no benefits would be payable.

Claims

The claims provision in an individual health insurance policy defines both the insurer's obligation to make prompt benefit payments to the claimant and the claimant's obligation to provide timely notification of loss to the insurer. In the United States, this provision states that insurers must make valid claim payments immediately upon receiving notification and proof that the insured has suffered a covered loss. In Canada, this provision states that the insurer must pay benefits within 60 days of receipt of proof of loss for a *medical expense* claim and within 30 days of receipt of proof of loss for a *disability income* claim.

The claims provision also states that if a claimant does not provide timely notification of a loss to an insurer, then in some cases the insurer has the right to deny benefits for the loss.

Legal actions

The legal actions provision limits the time period during which a claimant who is in disagreement with a settlement offered by an insurer may sue the insurance company to collect the amount the claimant believes is owed to him or her. This provision generally specifies that the suit must begin within three years after the claim was submitted. This provision further states that no claimant can bring suit on a particular claim against an insurance company until 60 days after the claim was submitted to the insurer.

Change of occupation

The premium rate for an applicant's health insurance policy bears a direct relationship to the hazards involved in that applicant's occupation. When a person insured under an individual health insurance policy changes occupation, the work required in the new occupation may be either more or less hazardous than that required in the person's previous occupation. Hence, many health insurance policies include a provision which permits the insurer to make an adjustment in the policy benefits and premium rate when the insured changes occupation. The change of occupation provision is an optional provision in the United States, but is a required provision in Canada.

According to the change of occupation provision, if the insured changes to a *more hazardous* occupation, the insurer has the right to reduce the amount of *benefits* payable under the policy; if the insured changes to a *less hazardous* occupation, the insurer has the right to reduce the *premium rate* charged. All benefit and premium rate changes take effect at the time the insured changes occupation.

For example, if a person were to stop teaching school and become a coal miner, then the insurer would reduce the health insurance benefits available under the person's policy to the amount of benefits the premium charged would have purchased for a coal miner; the policy's premium would not change. Alternatively, if a coal miner should change occupations and become a teacher, the policy's benefits would remain the same, but the insurer would reduce the premium rate to the premium rate charged to a teacher because the person changed to a safer occupation.

Overinsurance

An individual health insurance policy may contain an overinsurance provision which is intended to prevent an insured from profiting from his or her sickness or disability in those cases in which he or she is overinsured. A person is *overinsured* when he or she is either entitled to (1) receive medical expense benefits which would exceed the actual costs that are incurred for treatment because such benefits reflect duplicate coverage *or* (2) receive a greater income amount during disability than he or she earns while working.

An individual health insurance policy's overinsurance provision is designed to reduce benefits in cases in which the insured is overinsured either because of (1) duplicate coverage under several medical expense policies *or* (2) coverage under one or more disability income policies which is too high in relation to the insured's pre-disability earnings. The overinsurance provision takes effect in the above situations *only* if the insurer was *not* notified of the other coverage at the time of application.

In cases in which, because of overinsurance, the insurer reduces the amount of the benefits that would otherwise be payable under a policy, the insurer will refund any premium amount which has been paid by the policyowner for the excess coverage.

15

Group Health Insurance and Alternative Sources of Health Insurance Coverage

In the last chapter, we discussed the individual health insurance coverages which are available from private insurance companies. Health insurance coverage is also available through a wide variety of other sources. In this chapter, we will examine group health insurance coverage offered by private insurance companies and the health insurance coverage provided by Blue Cross and Blue Shield plans, health maintenance organizations, and government programs. These sources of health insurance coverage account for the majority of health insurance in force in the United States and Canada. In addition, we will look at some of the cost containment measures being taken by the insurance industry to curb the rising costs of health care.

GROUP HEALTH INSURANCE

More persons are covered under health insurance policies issued to cover members of groups than are covered under health insurance policies issued to individuals. Much of this group health insurance coverage is issued to employer-employee groups as an employee benefit.

Group health insurance coverage offers several advantages over individual health insurance coverage. A major advantage is that the premium rates for any type of group insurance – life or health – are usually lower than the premium rates for comparable individual coverage. Another important advantage of group health insurance coverage over individual health insurance coverage is that the benefits available under group health insurance policies are more varied and extensive than the benefits available under individual health insurance policies. As shown in Figure 15–1, in the United

FIGURE 15-1

Health insurance premium income of insurance companies in the United States (000,000 omitted)

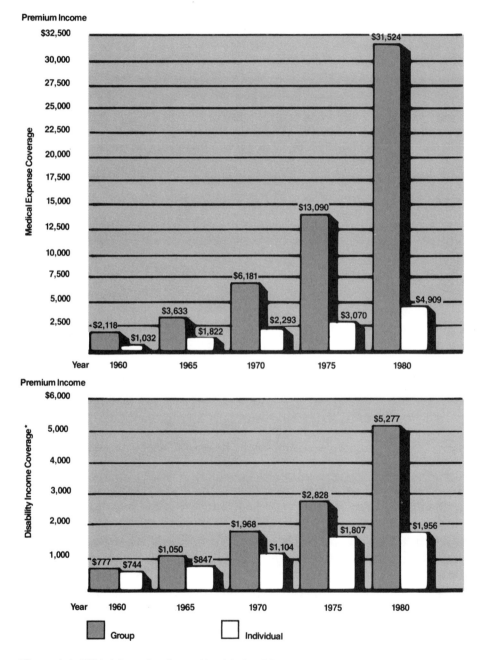

*Figures prior to 1972 include premiums from accidental death and dismemberment coverage.

Source: *Source Book of Health Insurance Data: 1982-83* (Health Insurance Association of America.)

States, the majority of the insurance industry's health insurance business is attributable to group insurance.

We will first discuss the administration of group health insurance. Since many characteristics of group insurance administration already were discussed in chapter 13, we will only summarize those administrative aspects which are the same for group health insurance and then discuss the administrative differences between group life and group health insurance. We will then examine the medical expense and disability income coverage provided by group health insurance policies. These coverages in many ways parallel the coverages provided under individual health insurance policies, though there are some important differences.

Administration of Group Health Insurance

Similarities between group life and group health administration

Many aspects of group health insurance are similar to those of group life insurance. Usually, the same types of groups are eligible for coverage under both group life and group health insurance policies, and most group health insurance policies are issued to employer-employee groups, as are most group life insurance policies.

A group health insurance policy is a contract between the insurance company and the master policyholder – the employer or other official representative of the group purchasing the group plan. The insured members of the group are not parties to this contract. Hence, group members are not given individual policies. Instead, each insured member is given a group health insurance certificate and/or a benefit booklet providing detailed health insurance coverage information.

When the insurer evaluates a group for group health insurance coverage, the insurer applies underwriting principles which are very similar to group life insurance underwriting principles. Usually the group as a whole – rather than the individual members of the group – must meet the insurer's underwriting requirements. However, the group *health* underwriter will classify the group as standard, substandard, or declined, based on the group's expected *morbidity* rate, rather than on the group's expected *mortality* rate, as is the case in group life insurance. This morbidity rate reflects the normal activities of the group as well as the age and sex distribution of the group. If the size of the group is small, the insurer may require the individual members of the group to submit evidence of insurability.

A group health insurance policy may be contributory or noncontributory. As is the case with noncontributory group life insurance plans, noncontributory group health insurance plans must cover all eligible members of the group. Further, contributory group health insurance plans, like contributory group life insurance plans, must in most cases cover at least 75 percent of the eligible members of the group.

Differences between group life and group health administration

Some marked differences exist between the administration of group life insurance plans and the administration of group health insurance plans. These differences concern: (1) dependents' coverage, (2) experience rating, and (3) conversion. We will examine each of these areas separately.

Dependents' coverage. The full coverage provided under group health insurance *medical expense* plans is usually available to the insured group member's family and dependents. This dependents' coverage is usually optional, and the group member usually must pay the premium amount required for this additional coverage if it is elected. Dependents' coverage is offered less commonly under group life insurance plans and, when offered, often is limited to an amount of coverage that is smaller than the amount provided on the insured group member. Group *disability income* plans *rarely* cover a group member's dependents.

Experience rating. Group health insurance premium rates are affected by experience rating to a greater extent than are group life insurance premium rates. Once a life insurance claim has been paid, the individual insured no longer presents a risk to the insurer. On the other hand, the same individual is likely to submit many separate health insurance claims over the period of coverage. Hence, group health insurance underwriters use experience rating when setting renewal premium rates for the group coverage. A group whose claims experience reflects higher-than-average claims costs will be charged a higher renewal premium rate than a group whose claims experience is average or less-than-average.

The group health underwriter also can assign a greater degree of credibility to the past claims experience of a group than can the group life underwriter. Health insurance coverage is characterized by more frequent claims per person than is life insurance coverage, and, hence, the same group generally has a larger volume of past health insurance claims experience than life insurance claims experience. This larger quantity of past experience increases the probability that the past experience accurately predicts the group's future experience – even if the group is relatively small.

Conversion. Both group life insurance certificates and group health insurance certificates issued in the United States include a conversion provision. In Canada, a group life insurance certificate must include a conversion provision, but this provision is not required to be included in group health insurance plans. The conversion provision of a group health insurance certificate states that an insured group member who is leaving the group has the right to purchase an individual health insurance policy from the group insurer without presenting proof of insurability. A group member who has exercised the right to convert from a group health insurance policy to an individual health insurance policy will find that the individual conversion policy differs in several respects from the group policy. Generally, the premium rate will be considerably higher *and* the benefits more restricted under the individual policy than under the group policy.

Requirements regarding the specific coverage which a conversion policy must provide vary from jurisdiction to jurisdiction. Generally, the benefits provided under the conversion policy will parallel the benefits available under similar individual health policies, rather than the benefits available under the group contract. However, the elimination period and the pre-existing conditions provision traditionally included in individual health insurance policies are not included in individual conversion policies; therefore, under an individual conversion policy, the insured is entitled to receive benefits immediately for eligible medical expenses and disabilities caused by an illness or injury, even if that illness or injury was a pre-existing condition at the time the application for conversion was made.

Coverage

A group health insurance policy may provide medical expense coverage similar to that provided under an individual hospital-surgical expense, major medical expense, social insurance supplement, or, in some cases, hospital confinement policy. Both short-term and long-term disability income coverage is also available through group health insurance policies, though the maximum benefit and elimination periods differ from those used in comparable individual disability income policies. However, group insurance policies seldom provide coverage similar to that provided under individual limited coverage (dread disease) policies.

In addition to providing types of coverage similar to those provided under individual health insurance policies, group health insurance policies can also provide certain types of coverage, such as dental, vision care, and prescription drug coverage, not generally offered on an individual basis.

Most group insurers will tailor group health insurance policies to meet the needs of each master policyholder, thus allowing the policyholder flexibility in choosing the specific benefits which will be included in the policy. The policyholder specifies the type of medical expense coverage (hospital-surgical, major medical, etc.), the benefit maximums (if any), the deductible amount, and the coinsurance features which will be included in the policy. For group policies which include disability income coverage, the policyholder specifies the benefit amount for specific classes of employees, the elimination period, and the maximum benefit period which will be included in the policy. The insurer then sets the premium rate for the policy, based on both the makeup of the particular group and the coverage specified by the master policyholder. The group insurer can provide all of a single group's coverage under one group health insurance policy, or it can issue separate master policies for each type of coverage provided. For example, the insurer can issue to one group both a group major medical policy and a group disability income policy.

Although there are many similarities between the types of coverage insurers offer under group and individual health insurance policies, there are also some important differences between these coverages. Significant differences between group and individual health insurance policies exist regarding (1)the pre-existing conditions exclusion, (2)mandated maternity coverage, (3) major medical coverage, and (4) disability income coverage. We will discuss these differences separately.

Pre-existing conditions exclusion

Group health insurance policies either modify or omit the pre-existing conditions exclusion generally found in individual health insurance policies. The exclusion often is not included in a group insurance policy in cases in which the group was previously covered by a group health insurance policy issued by another insurer. If it is included in a group health insurance policy, the pre-existing conditions exclusion usually states that benefits will not be paid for conditions caused by such pre-existing conditions until the insured has been covered under the policy for *three months*. Contrast this three-month period to the two-year period usually found in individual health insurance policies.

Mandated maternity coverage

In 1978, United States federal legislation was enacted which requires that group health insurance policies issued to certain employer-employee groups provide coverage for pregnancy, childbirth, and related medical conditions in the same manner that any other sickness or injury is covered. This legislation affects group health insurance policies which cover at least 15 members *and* which are issued to employers who are engaged in interstate commerce. If such an employer purchases health insurance coverage for its employees, this coverage must provide maternity benefits. As a result of this legislation, both the pregnancy exclusion and the separate maternity benefits provision which often are included in individual health insurance policies are not included in group health insurance policies covering groups to whom the legislation applies.

Major medical coverage

Insurers offer two types of group major medical coverage: (1) supplemental, or superimposed, major medical, and (2) comprehensive major medical. A **supplemental major medical** policy is issued in conjunction with group hospital-surgical expense coverage, and functions in much the same manner as an individual major medical policy. A **comprehensive major medical** policy provides complete and substantial medical expense coverage under one policy, and these comprehensive major medical policies provide benefits to cover most of the medical expenses an insured may incur.

As noted in chapter 14, individual major medical policies usually include certain expense participation features such as large deductible amounts and coinsurance. In contrast, group comprehensive major medical policies usually specify smaller deductibles than individual major medical policies. Commonly, group comprehensive major medical policies specify a deductible of $200 or a smaller amount.

Both comprehensive and supplemental group major medical coverages usually include a coinsurance feature similar to that included in individual major medical policies, which states that the insured must pay a portion of the eligible medical expenses incurred. However, both types of group major medical policies often include a "stop-loss" provision which states that the coinsurance feature will not apply after the insured has incurred a specified amount of out-of-pocket expense, such as $1,000, at which point the insurer will pay 100 percent of the insured's further eligible medical expenses for the remainder of the calendar year.

Disability income coverage

The lengths of the benefit periods and elimination periods included in short-term and long-term group disability income policies differ from those in individual disability income policies.

In short-term group disability income policies there is usually no elimination period for disabilities caused by accidents, and there is usually an elimination period of one week for disabilities caused by sickness. These elimination periods are considerably shorter than those usually included in individual short-term disability income policies. With respect to maximum benefit periods, short-term group disability income policies specify maximum periods of from 13 to 52 weeks, while individual short-term disability income policies specify two- to five-year maximum benefit periods.

Most long-term group disability income policies specify an elimination period of from three to six months, a period which is the same as the elimination period often included in individual disability income policies. As noted in chapter 14, in order for an individual disability income policy to be classified as "long-term," the maximum benefit period usually must be at least 10 years. However, in order for a group disability income policy to be classified as "long-term," the maximum benefit period need only be two years. The period may be longer in these group policies and, in fact, often extends to the insured's normal retirement age or to age 70.

Variations of group health insurance coverage

While the preceding description of the types of coverage available through group health insurance policies applies to most such policies, a "typical" group health insurance policy is impossible to describe because of the many variations of group health insurance coverage found in today's marketplace. As noted earlier, group health insurance policies are usually tailored to meet the needs of the policyholders and, therefore, there is no "typical" policy. This discussion has, therefore, only described the types of coverage most commonly included in group health insurance policies.

BLUE CROSS AND BLUE SHIELD

One of the largest providers of health care protection in the United States is the group of non-profit organizations known collectively as Blue Cross and Blue Shield. These organizations are usually affiliated with medical care providers and are subject to regulations which differ from the regulations which apply to private insurance companies.

The national Blue Cross and Blue Shield Association coordinates the various regional Blue Cross and Blue Shield plans. These regional plans, which are referred to as *member plans*, operate autonomously in specified geographic areas and offer individual and group medical expense coverage to residents of those areas. Persons and organizations who purchase Blue Cross and/or Blue Shield plans are referred to as "subscribers" to the plans.

Nearly half of the non-government medical expense coverage in force in the United States is provided through Blue Cross and Blue Shield plans. *Blue Cross plans* provide hospital care benefits; *Blue Shield plans* provide benefits for surgical and medical services performed by a physician. Disability income coverage is not available through either Blue Cross or Blue Shield.

Blue Cross Plans

Blue Cross plans provide hospital care benefits to their subscribers essentially on a "service-type" basis. Each plan specifies for the insured the services which will be covered rather than the maximum benefit amounts payable for each specified service. In most cases, Blue Cross plans cover hospital services, including the expenses of room and board as well as the cost of using the hospital's other facilities.

Most of the hospitals within a Blue Cross plan's region have contracts with the Blue Cross unit, in which the hospitals agree to accept predetermined payment amounts from Blue Cross in return for the hospital's services. These payments are based on actual costs incurred by the hospital, rather than on the hospital's usual scale of charges to non-Blue Cross patients. The Blue Cross plan pays participating health care providers directly. If the hospital or other health care facility providing the service is not a participating Blue Cross member, Blue Cross will pay only a specified percentage of that nonmember facility's fees, and the subscriber must pay the difference. Participating hospitals and physicians usually are involved in both the direction and the formal administration of the Blue Cross plan with which they are affiliated, often through representation on the plan's Board of Directors or on the plan's Board of Trustees.

Individual Blue Cross subscribers who move into an area serviced by a different Blue Cross plan are permitted to transfer to a Blue Cross plan in the new area. The plan in the new area cannot exclude benefits for the subscriber's pre-existing conditions, unless those conditions were excluded from coverage in the subscriber's original Blue Cross plan.

Blue Cross group insurance plans include a conversion provision which states that a participant in a Blue Cross group plan who leaves the group has the right to subscribe to an individual Blue Cross plan without submitting proof of insurability. The provision further states that the individual plan cannot exclude from coverage pre-existing conditions which were not excluded under the group plan. The cost for an individual Blue Cross plan, however, usually is considerably higher than the cost to an individual for membership in the group plan.

Blue Shield Plans

Blue Shield plans provide medical and surgical expense benefits to their subscribers. As in Blue Cross plans, Blue Shield plans are available on both a group and an individual basis, and conversion privileges are provided.

There are two different types of Blue Shield plans commonly available. Under the terms of one type of plan, the subscriber chooses any physician (or surgeon) he or she wishes to use for a medical service. The Blue Shield plan pays the physician's fee based on a schedule prescribed in the plan; the subscriber pays the difference between the scheduled fee and the amount charged by the physician. Under the terms of the other type of Blue Shield plan, the subscriber is required to use a physician who is a participating member of the plan in order for the plan to cover the full fee for the physician's service. If the subscriber uses a nonparticipating physician, the subscriber must pay the difference between that physician's charge and the Blue Shield payment amount.

Blue Cross and Blue Shield Major Medical Plans

In many localities, Blue Cross and Blue Shield organizations also offer major medical plans both to group and to individual subscribers. These major medical plans usually offer extended coverage to subscribers who are already covered by basic Blue Cross and Blue Shield plans. The coverage provided under these major medical plans includes benefits for ambulance service, prescription drugs, home health care, nursing home care, and other services and supplies not covered under the basic Blue Cross and Blue Shield plans, as well as physicians' fees that are higher than those covered in the basic plans.

These major medical plans usually require that the subscriber satisfy a deductible before any benefits are payable, and they often include a coinsurance feature.

HEALTH MAINTENANCE ORGANIZATIONS

Health maintenance organizations (HMOs) are a relatively new form of health care delivery. An HMO provides a form of prepaid health care to subscribing members of the plan. Individuals and groups who subscribe to the HMO by paying dues are entitled to use the medical services and facilities of the HMO's participating physicians and hospitals. In many HMOs, the subscribing member is charged a nominal amount, such as $3 or $5, to use the services of the HMO facility or a participating physician. In other HMOs, the subscribing member pays no charge for these services other than the membership dues. Subscribing members of the HMO also receive hospital care, usually at no charge, in participating hospitals.

Each HMO is operated independently in a specific region, and benefits vary among the various HMOs. However, all HMOs encourage members to practice preventive health care. Hence, HMO benefits always include regular physical examinations and other preventive care as well as treatment for mild ailments, such as colds and flu. In contrast, most private insurance companies and most Blue Cross and Blue Shield plans usually exclude physical examinations and preventive care from coverage under both their individual and group plans.

Organization

Health Maintenance Organizations can be organized and operated in various ways. The two most common are the Group Practice Model (GPM) and the Individual Practice Association (IPA). Under the **Group Practice Model** organization, physicians in the HMO share the use of a central HMO facility, including the equipment and support personnel of the facility. Subscribing members of the HMO visit this central facility to receive care. The physicians in this facility may be full-time employees, part-time employees, or owner-employees of the HMO.

Under the **Individual Practice Association** organization, the participating physicians maintain their own separate private offices and participate in the HMO on a part-time basis. Subscribing members of the HMO receive a list of the participating physicians and choose a physician from that list. The subscribing member then receives care in the physician's office, and the physician receives a predetermined amount from the HMO each time the physician treats an HMO subscriber.

Health Maintenance Organization (HMO) Act of 1973

The HMO Act of 1973 was passed by the United States federal government to encourage the development of HMOs as an alternative to traditional health insurance. Three of the most important features of this act were that (1) it provided federal loan guarantees to groups who establish new HMOs, (2) it nullified any existing state legislation which would prevent the establishment of HMOs, and (3) it required certain categories of employers to offer an HMO option to their employees as an alternative to an existing group health insurance plan.

GOVERNMENT HEALTH INSURANCE

Various government programs in both the United States and Canada also provide certain types of health insurance coverage, although the specific programs vary considerably between the two countries. We will first discuss government health insurance programs in the United States and then examine the health insurance programs in Canada.

United States

Almost 40 percent of expenditures for personal health care in the United States are made on behalf of individuals by government medical expense programs (see Figure 15-2). The federal and state governments in the United States provide medical expense as well as disability income insurance through several different programs. In this section, we will describe only briefly the four programs which affect the greatest number of United States citizens: (1) Workers' Compensation, (2) Social Security Disability Income, (3) Medicare, and (4) Medicaid. Workers' Compensation and Medicaid are provided through state programs. Medicare and Social Security Disability Income are provided through the federal government under the Old Age, Survivors, Disability and Health Insurance (OASDHI) program, popularly known as Social Security.

Workers' Compensation

All states have enacted legislation that requires most employers to provide Workers' Compensation coverage to their employees. This coverage

FIGURE 15-2

Distribution of expenditures for personal health care in the United States

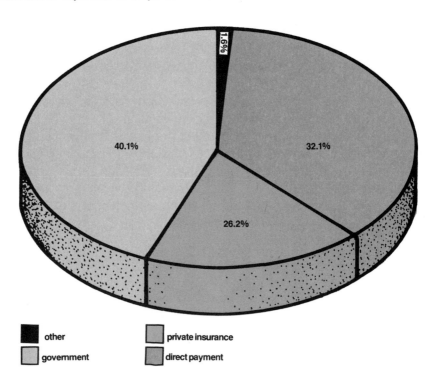

Source: *Source Book of Health Insurance Data: 1982–83* (Health Insurance Association of America)

provides benefits to employees and their dependents if the employees suffer job-related injury, disease, or death. Workers' Compensation benefits include medical care and disability income, as well as a lump-sum death benefit. The specific amounts of the disability income benefit payments vary from state to state, but in all cases benefits are based on the employee's earnings.

Social Security Disability Income

Workers who are under age 65 and who have paid a specified amount of Social Security tax for a prescribed number of quarter-year periods are eligible to receive Social Security Disability Income (SSDI) payments if they become disabled. Social Security defines disability as a person's inability to work because of a physical or mental disability; this disability must have lasted or be expected to last for at least one year, or the disability must be expected to lead to death.

A disabled worker who meets the above Social Security requirements will receive a monthly benefit equal to the monthly benefit which would normally have become payable when the worker retired. Benefit payments will not be made until the insured has been disabled for at least five months and, hence, begin approximately six months after the onset of the disability. The benefit payments continue until either two months after the disability ends or until the insured reaches age 65, the age at which regular Social Security retirement benefits become payable. The spouse and dependent children of a disabled worker may also receive an income benefit while the worker is disabled; their income benefit is equal to a percentage of the amount received by the disabled insured, subject to an overall family maximum benefit amount.

Medicare

Medicare is a program which provides medical expense coverage to certain classes of persons as specified by Congress. In order to be eligible for benefits under Medicare, a person must be

- age 65 or over and eligible for Social Security retirement benefits; or
- entitled to receive Social Security disability income benefits; or
- entitled to receive retirement benefits under the Railroad Retirement Act; or
- afflicted with, or be the dependent of a person afflicted with, kidney disease which requires either dialysis or a transplant.

The Medicare program consists of two parts: Part A, which provides hospital expense coverage, and Part B, which provides supplementary medical-surgical coverage. Coverage under Part A is automatically extended to all eligible persons. Part B of the Medicare program is voluntary and requires that the insured pay a premium for the coverage.

Part A (hospital insurance coverage). Benefits under Part A of Medicare cover the costs of the insured's (1) hospitalization, (2) confinement in an extended-care facility after hospitalization, and (3) home health care services after hospitalization. Part A includes both a deductible and a coinsurance provision. If the insured is hospitalized and/or confined in an extended-care facility, coverage is limited to a specified number of days of confinement. If the insured requires home health care, coverage is limited to a maximum number of home visits by a health care professional.

Part B (supplementary medical coverage). Those who elect coverage under Part B of Medicare may choose to have the premium for the coverage deducted from their Social Security checks. Part B provides benefits for physicians' professional services, whether these services are performed in a hospital, the physician's office, an extended-care facility, a nursing home, or the insured's home. The amount of benefit which will be paid for a physician's service is the "reasonable charge" for the service. This **reasonable charge** is defined as the amount charged by the physician, subject to a maximum based on the physician's customary charge for that service and the charges made by other physicians in that geographic area in the recent past. Part B benefits are also payable for ambulance service, medical supplies, drugs administered by a physician, diagnostic tests, and other services necessary for the diagnosis or treatment of an insured's illness.

Benefits are not payable for medical services unless those services are required for the treatment or the diagnosis of a sickness or injury. For example, benefits are not payable for routine physical examinations. Benefits under Part B are subject both to a deductible and to a coinsurance provision.

Administration of benefits. The federal government uses third parties called *intermediaries* to administer benefit payments under Medicare Part A. The most commonly used intermediaries are the local Blue Cross and Blue Shield organizations. These intermediaries or other third-party administrators pay the benefits directly to the providers of the service. In the Medicare Part B program, the third party administrators are called *carriers*. Carriers pay benefits directly to the insured persons or to the physician or other providers at the insured person's request. Both intermediaries and carriers are reimbursed by the federal government for the benefits paid and for administrative expenses incurred.

Medicaid

The Medicaid program provides for the payment of hospital and medical care expenses incurred by persons who earn less than a specified amount. Funding for the program is shared by the federal government and local governments, but the administration is handled by local governments. Since each administering body sets its own rules regarding eligibility, covered expenses, and benefit amounts payable, the benefit programs under Medicaid vary considerably from location to location.

Canada

The health insurance coverage provided through various government programs in Canada extends to nearly all Canadian residents. Workers' Compensation, medical expense coverage, and disability income coverage are each provided through separate programs to specified residents.

Workers' Compensation

The benefits provided by the Workers' Compensation program in Canada are similar to the benefits provided through the Workers' Compensation program in the United States. However, in Canada the program is sponsored and administered by the federal government, and, hence, the benefits provided through this program in Canada are uniform throughout the country and do not vary by province.

Medical expense coverage

Each provincial government administers separate programs under which people who reside in that province receive hospital care coverage and medical care coverage. The *hospital care* benefits program provides payment for all hospital charges during an insured's stay in a hospital ward. Benefits are provided for both inpatient and outpatient hospital charges, and hospital benefits are not limited to any maximum number of days. The federal government shares the costs of the program with each province.

The *medical care* benefits program, though administered by the provinces, is funded completely by the federal government. The medical care benefits cover most medical care costs not covered by the hospital care program, including physicians' and surgeons' fees and diagnostic costs, both on an inpatient and on an outpatient basis. Some provinces also provide benefits for special services such as psychiatric, chiropractic, or podiatric treatment. Most of these provincial plans exclude from coverage benefits for occupation-related sicknesses and injuries. Some also exclude from coverage benefits for dental care, vision care, hearing aids, prescription drugs, and private nurses.

Since government health insurance programs in Canada provide comprehensive medical expense coverage, the need for private insurers to provide medical expense coverage is less pressing in Canada than in the United States. Hence, the medical expense coverage provided by health insurance companies in Canada usually is limited to social insurance supplement plans. This coverage is available both to individuals and to groups.

Disability income coverage

Both short-term and long-term disability income coverage in Canada are provided through separate government programs.

The short-term disability income program provides benefits to certain persons who are unable to work because of sickness or injury. In order to be eligible for these benefits, an employee must have worked for at least 20 weeks during the year preceding the disability. Benefit payments begin 2 weeks after the onset of the employee's disability, and are equal to two-thirds of the employee's pre-disability earnings, subject to a specified maximum. These payments continue for up to 15 weeks during the disability. The short-term disability income program is funded by the federal

Unemployment Insurance Commission which, in turn, is supported by funds contributed by employers and employees. An employer has the option of not participating in this government program if the employer provides private short-term disability income coverage for employees which is at least as favorable as the coverage provided by the government program. Employers who provide such private insurance coverage receive a refund of an appropriate portion of their contribution to the Unemployment Insurance Commission.

The long-term disability income program in Canada is similiar to the Social Security Disability Income program in the United States. The long-term disability income benefits are provided through the Canada Pension Plan (CPP) for residents of provinces other than Quebec and through the Quebec Pension Plan (QPP) for residents of Quebec. In order to qualify for disability benefits under either plan, a worker must (1) have made contributions to the CPP or the QPP for at least a specified number of years, (2) be under the age of 65, and (3) be afflicted with a severe *and* prolonged disability. A **severe disability** is defined as a disability which prevents the worker from engaging in any substantially gainful occupation. A **prolonged disability** is defined as a disability which is expected to be of infinite duration or which is likely to result in death.

A disabled worker who meets the above requirements will receive a monthly benefit which is based on the worker's pre-disability earnings and the amount he or she has contributed to the Plan. Benefit payments begin approximately four months after the onset of the disability and continue until the person is no longer disabled or until the person reaches age 65, at which age the normal retirement benefit provided through the CPP or the QPP will become payable. Children of disabled workers are also eligible to receive an income benefit under both plans.

COST CONTAINMENT

The rapidly rising costs of health care are of concern both to the health insurance industry and to the persons who need medical care. Figure 15–3 shows the rise in the cost of medical treatment in the United States since 1960. These increased medical care costs and the resulting increased claim payments have necessitated frequent increases in health insurance premium rates. The health insurance industry is attempting to contain these costs by (1) influencing insureds to assist in holding down the size of claims, and (2) inducing health care providers to find less expensive means of supplying adequate care.

By involving the insured in cost containment measures, insurers attempt to obtain the insured's assistance in preventing unnecessary or wasteful health care practices. For example, an insured is encouraged to protest against prolonged hospitalization when he or she could be adequately

FIGURE 15-3

Health care expenditures in the United States

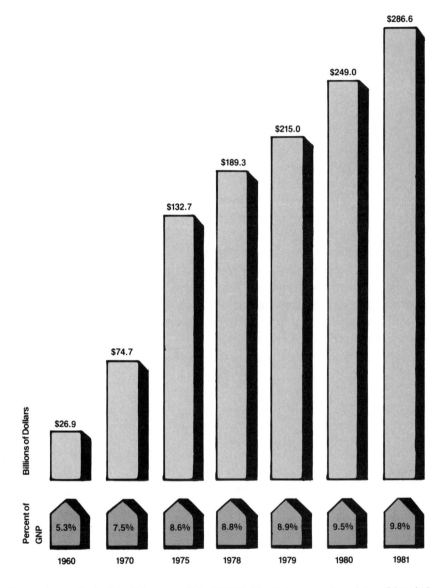

Source: *Source Book of Health Insurance Data: 1982-83* (Health Insurance Association of America).

cared for in a less expensive facility or at home. An insured can also help by protesting duplicate testing and examination procedures and calling the insurer's attention to inaccurate bills.

There are two methods insurers use to induce this cooperation from the insured. The first and most effective method is requiring the insured to share in the costs of medical care through coinsurance. This method is commonly used in both individual and group health plans. The second method is the education of insureds through frequent reminders that unless health care costs are contained, premiums will certainly rise.

The health insurance industry also attempts to contain medical costs by identifying inflated medical care costs and by working closely with health care suppliers to develop money-saving procedures. Insurers review claims to determine whether the treatment administered was proper and was fairly priced. If questionable practices or fees are uncovered, the insurer can refer the disputed bill to local professional physicians' groups. These groups, called **peer review groups**, can be useful both in serving as third-party reviewers to solve disputes and in promoting fair and ethical practices to prevent such situations from arising again.

Health insurers also work closely with hospitals and other health care facilities to find ways of keeping costs down when medically feasible, such as by promoting the development and use of low-cost facilities and out-patient clinics. Hospitals are also encouraged to check patients prior to admission in order to be sure that hospitalization is necessary. In addition, hospitals are urged to continue to monitor patients' progress to assure that continued hospitalization is necessary. Health care facilities also monitor the use of laboratory testing and X-rays in an attempt to eliminate duplication of work and unnecessary expenses.

16
Annuities and Retirement Plans

The majority of this text has been devoted to a discussion of those insurance products which are designed primarily to provide benefits in the event that some misfortune should befall the insured. Such products provide benefits if the insured dies, or becomes sick or injured, or becomes disabled.

In this chapter, we will discuss various funding instruments an individual may use to provide for retirement income. These funding instruments include *annuities*, *individual retirement plans*, and *pension plans*. Most people use a combination of these funding instruments to provide for an income during their retirement years.

ANNUITIES

Technically, the term "annuity" refers to any series of payments, especially yearly or annual payments; however, in insurance terminology, the term "annuity" has come to mean the *contract* which provides for *any* series of periodic payments. An **annuity period** is the time span between the payments in the series. Thus, an annuity which provides for a series of annual payments has an annuity period of one year and is referred to as an annual annuity. An annuity which provides payments each month has an annuity period of one month and is referred to as a monthly annuity. The person who receives the benefit payments is known as the **annuitant**.

Most large life insurance companies sell annuities both on an individual basis and on a group basis. Life insurance companies account for the vast majority of annuity sales, although some other organizations provide annuities. In this chapter, we will discuss only those annuities which are sold by life insurance companies.

Annuities are distinguished from one another according to (1) when benefit payments begin, (2) how the annuity is purchased, (3) how long the benefit payments continue, (4) whether the annuity is payable to more than one person, and (5) whether the benefit payment amounts are fixed or variable. Our discussion of annuities will focus on each of these distinguishing characteristics.

When Benefit Payments Begin

An annuity contract is classified as either an *immediate annuity* or a *deferred annuity*, depending on when the payment of the annuity's periodic benefits is scheduled to begin.

Immediate annuities

Under the terms of an **immediate annuity**, payments begin one period after the annuity is purchased. If the annuity period is one year (the annuity benefits are scheduled to be paid to the annuitant annually) and if the annuity is an immediate annuity, then the first benefit payment will be made to the annuitant one year after the annuity is purchased. If an immediate annuity has an annuity period of one month (the annuity benefits are scheduled to be paid to the annuitant monthly), then benefit payments will start one month after the annuity is purchased. For example, suppose Carl Reed purchases an immediate annuity on February 1, and benefit payments are scheduled to be made to him monthly. He will receive the first benefit payment one month later, on March 1.

Deferred annuities

Deferred annuities are those annuities under which the annuity payment period is scheduled to begin at some future date. This future date must fall more than one annuity period after the purchase date. Deferred annuities are often purchased during a person's working years in anticipation of the need for retirement income; in such cases, benefit payments are usually scheduled to begin on the anticipated retirement date of the prospective annuitant. If the prospective annuitant dies before the annuity payments begin, the amount paid for the annuity, plus interest, will be paid to a beneficiary designated by the purchaser of the annuity.

The purchaser of a deferred annuity is usually permitted to alter the specific date on which the annuity payments are scheduled to begin; the annuity contract specifies the conditions which must be met to make such a change. Changes in the scheduled date may also change the amount of each benefit payment the annuitant will receive.

How Annuities Are Purchased

Annuities, like life insurance policies, are purchased with premium payments. The amount of the annuity benefit which can be purchased for a specified premium amount depends on the length of the guaranteed benefit payment period, the interest the company can earn on the premium money it invests, and the expenses the insurer will incur in administering the annuity. The purchaser of the annuity makes premium payments in one of three ways: (1) once, as a single premium; (2) periodically, with level premium amounts; or (3) periodically, with flexible premium amounts.

Single premiums

An annuity, like a life insurance policy, may be purchased with a single premium payment. Such annuities are called single-premium annuities. Both immediate and deferred annuities may be purchased with a single-premium payment. Retirees often purchase single-premium *immediate* annuities with funds received from an employee profit-sharing plan, a savings account, a matured endowment policy, the cash value of a life insurance policy, or the sale of a home.

Persons who have a large sum of money and who anticipate a need for regular income payments in the future may purchase a single-premium *deferred* annuity. A single-premium deferred annuity will provide larger annuity payments than a single-premium immediate annuity purchased with the same single premium amount, because the amount paid for the deferred annuity will earn interest during the entire deferred period.

Periodic level premiums

Under a periodic level premium annuity, the purchaser of the annuity pays equal premium amounts for the annuity at regular intervals, such as monthly or annually, until the date the benefit payments are scheduled to begin. The period during which premiums are payable is called the **accumulation period**. The periodic level premium annuity is always a deferred annuity because its benefit payments always begin at a specified future date. If the prospective annuitant should die before benefit payments begin, then the premiums paid for the annuity, plus interest, will be refunded to the designated beneficiary.

Periodic flexible premiums

Under the flexible premium annuity, premiums are paid over a period of time, and the flexible premium annuity is always a deferred annuity. Thus.

the flexible premium annuity resembles the periodic level premium annuity in these two respects. However, the purchaser of a flexible premium annuity has the option to vary the premium amount he or she pays between a set minimum and maximum amount. For example, the purchaser might be permitted to pay any premium amount between $250 and $10,000 each year. The premium amount the purchaser actually pays need not remain the same in succeeding years, as long as the amount paid is within the range between the minimum and maximum specified in that contract.

A flexible premium deferred annuity is often purchased by people such as authors and artists, whose incomes may be subject to considerable variation from year to year. The amounts that such people could guarantee they would be able to pay into an annuity each year might be too low to provide the benefits needed for their retirement. However, by paying more in high-income years and less in low-income years, these people could pay enough in premiums over the years to fund an annuity sufficient to meet their retirement needs. One drawback to funding an annuity through flexible premium payments is that the actual amount of the annuity benefit cannot be determined in advance because the premium amounts which will be paid each year are not known in advance. The purchaser of such an annuity must wait until the end of the premium payment period to find out the amount of the annuity benefit he or she will receive. However, at any point during the accumulation period, the purchaser can determine the amount of the annuity benefit purchased as of that date.

How Long the Benefit Payments Continue

Annuitants may elect to receive the series of annuity payments either for a specified period of time or for life. An annuity which is payable for a specified period of time regardless of whether the annuitant lives or dies is called an **annuity certain**. An annuity which is payable at least until the death of the annuitant is called a **life annuity**. An annuity which is payable until either the death of the annuitant or the end of a specified period, whichever occurs *first*, is called a **temporary life annuity**.

Annuity certain

The annuity certain provides for a specified number of benefit payments of a set amount. The specified period over which benefit payments are made is called the **period certain**. At the end of the period certain, the annuity payments will cease, even if the annuitant is still alive. If the annuitant dies before the end of the period certain, the unpaid annuity benefits will be paid to a beneficiary named in the contract by the annuitant. The annuity certain is similar to the fixed period settlement option available in most life insurance policies.

The annuity certain is useful when a person needs an income for a specified period of time. For example, a four-year annuity certain can be used to provide a yearly income to pay college expenses. An annuity certain may also be purchased to provide income during a specified period until some other source of income, such as a pension, becomes payable. Since the benefit payments stop at the end of the specified period regardless of whether the annuitant is still alive, an annuity certain is usually not suitable as the sole source of a person's retirement income.

Life annuities

Since a life annuity guarantees that benefits will be payable at least until the annuitant dies, a company issuing life annuities must consider the life expectancy of the annuitant when the company calculates the amount of the annuity benefit it can provide for a specified premium amount. In most cases, only life insurance companies are authorized to issue contracts which take life expectancies into account.

Determining life annuity rates. Insurers consult special annuity mortality tables to determine premium rates for life annuities. Annuity mortality tables list the projected mortality rates for persons purchasing annuities. These annuity mortality tables are *not* identical to the mortality tables used to determine life insurance premium rates because there is a significant difference between the mortality rates experienced by persons purchasing life insurance and the mortality rates experienced by persons purchasing annuities. In general, these mortality tables show that annuitants as a group live longer than persons purchasing life insurance. For a comparison of annuity mortality rates and life insurance mortality rates, see Figure 16–1.

This longer life span experienced by annuitants as a group is partially the result of the fact that those people who are in good health and who anticipate a long life will be *more* interested in purchasing life income annuities than those people in poor health. This form of antiselection is the opposite of the form of antiselection found in life insurance, where those people who are in poor health or have some other reason to expect a shorter-than-normal life span are *more* interested in purchasing life insurance than those people in good health. Since *life annuity* premium rates *decrease* as mortality rates *increase*, the use of life insurance mortality tables to calculate annuity premium rates would result in annuity premium rates which would be inadequate to provide the lifetime benefits promised.

Annuity mortality statistics, like life insurance mortality statistics, show that females as a group may anticipate living significantly longer than males as a group. Because females as a group live longer than males, insurers generally must pay life annuity benefits to females as a group for a longer period of time than they pay life annuity benefits to males as a

FIGURE 16-1

Comparison of annuity mortality rates and life insurance mortality rates*

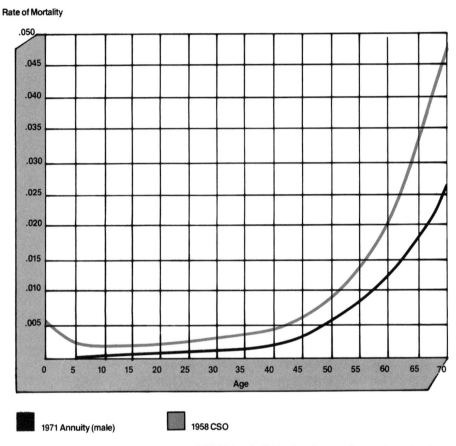

Rate of Mortality

1971 Annuity (male)   1958 CSO

*Life insurance mortality rates based on the 1958 CSO Mortality Table. Annuity mortality rates based on the 1971 Individual Annuity Mortality Table (male).

group. Hence, annuity premium rates are generally *higher* for females than for males of the same age. In other words, insurers compensate for a female annuitant's *lower* mortality rate by charging a *higher* annuity premium rate. Although some insurers have established separate, higher premium rates for females, most insurers simply charge females the premium rates for males four to five years younger. However, in recent years there has been public pressure on insurers to charge the same premium rates for both females and males. The courts are examining the use of sex-based premium rates, and some jurisdictions have enacted laws requiring that the same premium rates be used for both sexes. Hence, some companies are constructing unisex tables and charging both females and males the same premium rates for life annuities.

There are three variations of the life annuity which insurers commonly offer: the *straight life annuity*, the *life income annuity with period certain*, and the *life income with refund annuity*.

Straight life annuity. The straight life annuity provides periodic payments to the annuitant for as long as the annuitant lives. Once the annuitant dies, the contract is fulfilled and no more payments are made. Since the straight life annuity does not provide for any payments to be made after the annuitant's death, this type of annuity requires a lower premium rate for a specified amount of annuity benefit than do other types of life income annuities. If an annuitant died shortly after the straight life annuity payments began, the total amount the annuitant would have received in benefits could be lower than the amount paid for the annuity. Straight life annuities are most often purchased by those persons who require a large amount of retirement income and who do not have any dependents.

Life income annuity with period certain. The life income annuity with period certain guarantees that annuity benefits will be paid until the annuitant dies and also guarantees that the payments will be made for at least a certain period, even if the annuitant dies before the end of that period. The annuitant selects the guaranteed period, which is often five years or ten years, and names a beneficiary. If the annuitant dies before the specified period has expired, then the benefit payments will continue to be made to the beneficiary for the remainder of that period. If the annuitant is still alive at the end of the guaranteed period, payments will continue for the rest of the annuitant's life. Since the insurer must make at least a stipulated number of payments, premium rates for a life income annuity with period certain are higher than those for a straight life annuity.

Let us look at an example of how the life income annuity with period certain operates. Assume John Clarke purchased a single premium immediate annuity to provide a benefit of $6,000 per year. The annuity he purchased is a life income annuity, with a 10-year period certain, and John has named his wife, Marian, as beneficiary. If John dies 7 years after purchasing the annuity, the insurer will continue to pay the annuity benefit to Marian until the end of the guaranteed 10-year period – that is, the insurer will make payments to Marian for 3 years after John's death. If, however, John should live longer than 10 years after the annuity benefits begin, benefits will continue to be paid to him for the rest of his lifetime; upon John's death, the insurer will have met its contractual obligations, since lifetime benefits will have been paid to John for a period longer than the 10-year certain period. Therefore, no payments would be made to Marian after John's death.

Life income with refund annuity. The life income with refund annuity, also known as a *refund annuity*, provides benefits for the lifetime of the annuitant and guarantees that at least the purchase price of the annuity will be paid out in benefits. Under this annuity, benefit payments are made for the life of the annuitant. If the annuitant dies before the total of the payments made under the contract equals the purchase price, a refund will be made to a beneficiary designated by the annuitant. The amount of this refund will be equal to the difference between the amount which has been paid out in annuity benefits and the purchase price of the annuity.

For example, assume that John Clarke purchased a refund annuity which provides benefit payments of $5,000 per year and that this annuity is an immediate annuity purchased with a single premium of $60,000. If John dies seven years after buying the annuity, the total amount of annuity benefits he would have received would equal $35,000 (seven years times $5,000 per year). The amount of the refund paid to his wife, as his designated beneficiary, would be $25,000, which is the purchase price of $60,000 minus the benefits paid of $35,000.

The refund annuity is available in two forms: the **cash refund annuity**, under which the refund is payable in a lump sum to the beneficiary, and the **installment refund annuity**, under which the refund is made in the form of a series of payments to the beneficiary. If in the example above John Clarke had purchased a cash refund annuity, at his death Marian Clarke would receive the $25,000 refund in a lump sum. If John had purchased an installment refund annuity, Marian would receive the $25,000 in five equal annual installments of $5,000.

Since the life income with refund annuity guarantees that at least a certain amount of benefits will be paid, premium rates for a refund annuity are higher than for either a straight life annuity or a life income annuity with period certain.

Temporary life annuity

A temporary life annuity provides that payments will be made until the end of a specified number of years or until the death of the annuitant, whichever occurs *first*. Once the period expires *or* the annuitant dies, the annuity benefits cease. Hence, the annuitant need not designate a beneficiary.

For example, suppose that in John Clarke's case he had purchased a 10-year temporary life annuity. If he were to die 7 years after the annuity benefits began, the insurer, having made the payments during John's lifetime, would have fulfilled its obligations under the contract, and no further payments would be due. Assume, however, John lives past the 10-year period. At the end of the 10-year period, the benefits would stop and no payments would be made after that time.

Although the temporary life annuity is not sold very often, it is sometimes purchased to fill a gap between the end of an earning period and the time some other anticipated income, such as a pension, will begin.

Since the period specified is the maximum length of time for which benefits may be payable, premiums for a temporary life annuity are generally lower than premiums for any other type of annuity.

Joint and Survivor Annuities

Under **joint and survivor annuities**, which are also called **joint and last survivorship annuities**, a series of payments is made to two or more annuitants, and the annuity payments continue until both or all of the annuitants have died. Joint and survivor annuities are often purchased by married couples, so that when one spouse dies, the remaining spouse will continue to receive the annuity benefits for the rest of his or her life.

The majority of joint and survivor annuities specify that the size of each annuity payment will remain the same throughout the benefit payment period, although some such annuities specify that the annuity payments will be reduced after the death of the first annuitant. For example, the annuity benefit payable to the survivor might be reduced by one-third after the death of the first annuitant. Premiums for an annuity contract which calls for reduced payments after the first annuitant's death are lower than those for an equivalent contract under which the annuity benefits remain the same throughout the benefit payment period.

Premiums for joint and survivor annuities are higher than those for life income annuities issued to one person, since the likelihood of a long annuity payment period is greater when more than one life is covered. Joint and survivor annuities may be issued as straight life annuities, life income with period certain annuities, or life income with refund annuities.

Suppose, for example, that John Clarke and his wife Marian purchased a $6,000 per year straight life joint and survivor annuity. They specified that the annuity benefit would be reduced by one-third at the time the first of them dies. Hence, while both John and Marian live, the full annuity benefit amount of $6,000 per year will be payable. If John were to die at the end of seven years, the amount of the annuity benefit would be reduced by one-third, and Marian would receive an annuity benefit of $4,000 per year for the rest of her life. When Marian dies, the annuity benefit payments will cease.

Variable Annuities

Thus far, the annuities we have been discussing provide a specified, guaranteed amount of annuity benefit for a specified premium. Under such annuities, the annuitant receives this guaranteed amount for the length of time specified in the contract. Another type of annuity, called the *variable annuity*, does not provide these payment amount guarantees. Instead, **variable annuities** provide annuity payments that vary according to the investment earnings of a special fund, called a separate account. Separate account funds are usually placed by the insurer in investments which have varying returns, such as stocks and other equity (ownership) investments.

Organizations which sell variable annuity policies have developed a system which helps them to maintain accurate records on the changing values of each annuity's portion of the separate account fund. As shown in Figure 16–2, the value of the money paid in as premiums by a variable

FIGURE 16-2
Illustration of the relationship between accumulation units and annuity units for a variable annuity

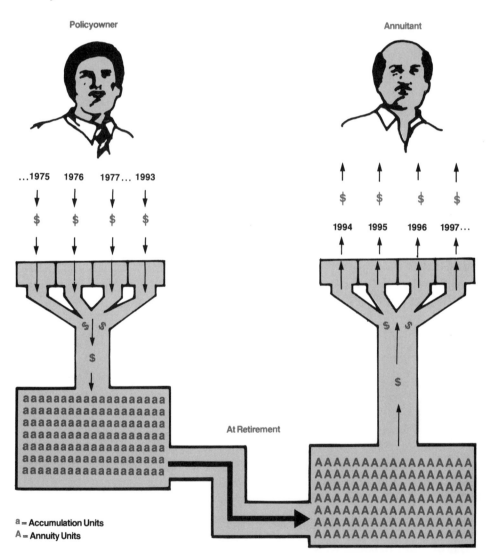

annuity purchaser is expressed in the form of *accumulation units*; the value of the money available to be paid as benefits to the annuitant is expressed in the form of *annuity units*. **Accumulation units** represent ownership shares in the total separate account fund. The number of accumulation units which can be purchased for a given premium amount depends upon the current value of the separate account fund. When the value of the investments held in a separate account fund is low, the value of each accumulation unit will also be low, and, therefore, more units can be purchased for a given amount of premium than when the investment value of this fund is high.

When the annuity benefit becomes payable, the accumulation units are applied to purchase **annuity units**. Each annuity unit provides a specified amount of annuity benefits; hence, the size of the annuity payments the annuitant will receive depends upon the number of annuity units owned by the annuitant and the value of each unit. These annuity units are revalued periodically, usually annually, based on the value of the investments in the separate account fund. Thus, even after the annuity benefit payments begin, the amount of each periodic payment may change yearly in response to each reevaluation.

The purpose of the variable annuity is to provide annuity benefit payments that will vary along with investment earnings. Theoretically, as the cost of living increases, so will the value of the fund from which the annuity payments will be drawn; as the cost of living drops, earnings will drop. Unfortunately, this theory has not always held true. In recent years, the annual increase in the cost of living has often been greater than the increase in the value of the typical fund; therefore, amounts payable to annuitants under these variable annuity contracts have not always kept pace with the cost of living.

INDIVIDUAL RETIREMENT PLANS

Both the United States and Canadian governments have recognized the importance of assisting people in saving money for retirement. As a result, each government has enacted legislation which provides federal income tax advantages to those individuals who deposit funds in government-qualified retirement savings plans. For federal income tax purposes, the amounts deposited into qualified accounts are deductible from a participant's gross income in the year deposited. Neither the amounts deposited, nor any of the plan's investment earnings, are subject to federal income tax *until* the money is withdrawn from the account. The income tax advantage to this deferred taxation derives from the fact that income tax *rates* increase as income increases. Deposits into these qualified accounts are made during a participant's working years, when income is high, and withdrawals are made during a participant's retirement years, when income is lower. Thus, these withdrawals will presumably be taxed at a lower *rate* than the rate at which the contributions would have been taxed had they been taxed as income in the year they were earned.

We will first examine the legislation which has been enacted in the United States to provide these tax advantages; we will then look at Canadian legislation on this subject.

United States

Both the Self-employed Individual Tax Retirement Act of 1962 – known as the Keogh Act – and the laws which are administered under the Employee Retirement Income Security Act of 1974 (ERISA) relating to Individual Retirement Accounts (IRAs) are designed to encourage individuals in the United States to establish savings plans for retirement.

Keogh Act

The legislation known as the Keogh Act applies only to self-employed persons and owner-employees of unincorporated businesses. According to the Keogh Act, *self-employed persons* are those whose personal services earn income, for example, doctors, writers, and other professionals; *owner-employees* are those persons who own either all of an unincorporated trade or business or who own more than 10 percent of a partnership. Both self-employed persons and owner-employees may establish *Keogh plans*, which are also called H.R. 10 plans, to save money for retirement. Although the Tax Equity and Fiscal Responsibility Act of 1982 (TEFRA) eliminated many of the distinctions between Keogh plans and qualified group retirement plans, Keogh plans are still useful retirement planning tools for the self-employed.

Under a Keogh plan, an eligible person deposits money in a government-approved account. These accounts are set up by sponsoring financial organizations such as insurance companies, banks, and investment houses. The sponsoring organization arranges for approval of the plan by the Internal Revenue Service (IRS) and manages the administration and investment of the deposited funds. Keogh plans may specialize in any of several special types of investments, such as stocks, bonds, or real estate. In addition, most banks will set up savings accounts which qualify as Keogh plans.

A Keogh plan participant may deposit a specified percentage of yearly income – up to a legislatively defined maximum amount – into an approved account each year. Once a participant has deposited money into a Keogh plan account, several conditions must be met before the sponsoring organization may distribute money from such an account. If these conditions are not met at the time of distribution, the IRS will assess an income tax penalty against the plan participant.

The accumulated funds in a Keogh plan may be used to purchase an annuity, or the plan itself may be established by depositing funds into a qualified deferred annuity. However, Keogh plans are only intended to assist individuals to save money for retirement; Keogh plans do not, by themselves, necessarily provide annuities at retirement, and a plan participant is not required to use the funds accumulated in a Keogh plan account to purchase an annuity.

Individual Retirement Accounts

In 1974, the United States federal government enacted legislation which permitted individuals to set up accounts called Individual Retirement Accounts (IRAs) which are similar to those established under Keogh plans. Individual Retirement Accounts were originally intended for use by individuals who were not covered by employer or union retirement plans and who were not eligible to set up Keogh plan accounts. In 1980, the rules were relaxed to permit anyone who receives earned income to establish an IRA. Since deposits into these IRAs are eligible for income tax advantages, an extremely large number of new accounts were established in the early 1980s (see Figure 16–3).

As in the case of Keogh plans, IRAs must be established through a financial institution, and the plans must be approved by the IRS in order for the deposits to an IRA to be deductible from a participant's current income. Each year an unmarried individual may deduct from current income IRA deposits of up to $2,000* provided the individual earns at least that amount. A married couple may deduct deposits of up to $4,000 each year if each spouse earns at least $2,000; if only one spouse earns income, the deduction is limited to $2,250 per year. An IRA participant may make withdrawals from the IRA account, but in most such situations a penalty is assessed if these withdrawals are made before the individual is age 59½. By age 70½ the participant must start withdrawing at least a specified percentage of the account each year or monetary penalties are assessed by the IRS against the account.

Like Keogh plan accounts, IRAs do not themselves provide annuities; the individual is permitted, but not required, to purchase an annuity at retirement with the money which has accumulated in the IRA.

---

*These figures and other figures in the discussion of United States and Canadian government plans in this chapter are correct as of the editing of this text. They are subject to legislative change at any time.

FIGURE 16-3
Numbers of persons covered by IRAs established with life insurance companies (000 omitted)

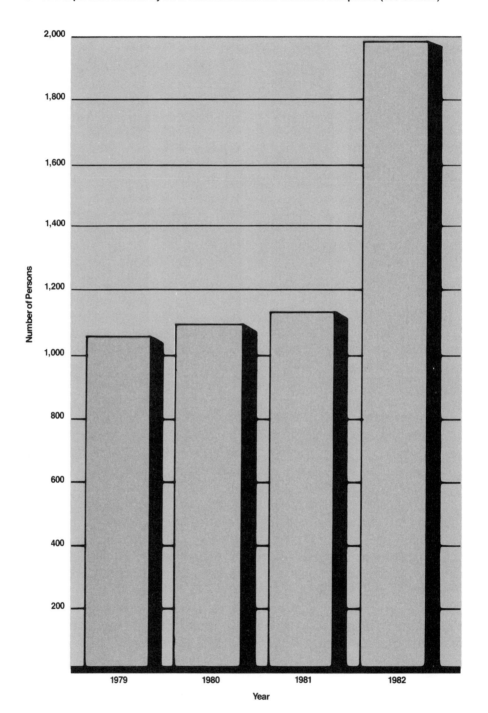

Canada

The Canadian government has also enacted legislation designed to encourage individuals to establish accounts to accumulate money for their retirement. The Canadian equivalent to Keogh plans and IRAs is the Registered Retirement Savings Plan (RRSP).

Registered Retirement Savings Plans

An RRSP may be established by any gainfully-employed individual, including a person who is self-employed. Contributions, within certain limits, to any pension plan (including RRSPs) are deductible from earnings for Canadian federal income tax purposes in the year in which the contributions to the plan are made. A self-employed individual or a person who is not a member of any other pension plan may deposit 20 percent of his or her annual earned income, subject to a maximum of $5,500 per year, into an RRSP; a person covered under a pension plan provided through his or her employer may contribute up to $3,500 per year into an RRSP, as long as the total of that person's pension plan contributions does not exceed 20 percent of earned income.

An RRSP is, in essence, a deferred annuity. According to Canadian law, RRSPs cannot provide a lump-sum payment to the individual at the time of retirement. (United States law pertaining to Keogh plans and IRAs permits this practice.) The RRSP funds must be used to provide a life income, and only a life income, for the retiree or for the retiree and his or her spouse. The annuity payments must begin no later than the time the retiree reaches age 71.

The federal government authorizes only Government Annuities Offices in Alberta and life insurance companies to issue annuities under RRSPs. Trust companies and companies licensed to issue investment contracts may establish savings plans to accumulate funds for the retirement annuity; however, trust companies and investment companies are not legally permitted to issue life income annuities. Hence, at the time of an individual's retirement, such organizations must use the funds which have been accumulated in these savings plans to purchase an annuity for that individual from a life insurance company or a Government Annuity Office. In addition, under Canadian law, the individual may *never* borrow money from the RRSP prior to retirement. Borrowing from Keogh plan accounts and IRAs is permitted in the United States, although the borrower may be subject to substantial monetary penalties.

PENSION PLANS

While individual annuities provide retirement income to a large number of people, most retirement income is received in the form of pensions. Pension plans may be established by governments, employers, and unions. We will first examine the government pension plans provided in Canada and the United States, and then we will discuss the pension plans available to groups, such as employer-employee groups and unions.

Canada

Pensions are provided to Canadian retirees through three separate government plans: the Old Age Security Act (OAS), which is in effect throughout Canada; the Canada Pension Plan (CPP), which operates in all Canadian provinces except Quebec; and the Quebec Pension Plan (QPP), which operates only in Quebec.

Old Age Security Act

The Old Age Security Act (OAS) provides a pension to virtually all Canadian citizens who are age 65 or older. The money to fund the pension is taken from general government accounts, rather than from a special fund. The right to receive a pension under the OAS is *not* dependent on a person's preretirement wages, current employment, or marital status; each person who has attained age 65 receives the same amount of pension. This pension amount is tied to the Canadian Consumer Price Index and rises along with the increases in that index.

Canada Pension Plan and Quebec Pension Plan

The Canada Pension Plan (CPP) provides an additional retirement pension in all provinces except Quebec for wage earners who have contributed money into the plan during their working years. The Quebec Pension Plan (QPP) functions in the same manner as the CPP except that the QPP applies only to wage earners in Quebec. The long-term disability income benefits described in the previous chapter, as well as survivorship benefits, lump-sum death benefits, and benefits for orphans are also provided under these plans.

The amount each individual contributes to the plan is a set percentage of that individual's earned income, subject to a specified maximum annual amount. An individual's employer contributes to the plan a percentage equal to that contributed by the employee. Because a self-employed participant's contributions are not matched by any employer, a self-employed participant must contribute to the plan a percentage which is twice as high as the percentage contributed by an employee.

The amount of the benefit paid at retirement is tied to the amount the individual contributes. This amount is adjusted each year to reflect any cost of living increases.

United States

In the United States, government pensions are provided under the Civil Service Retirement Act, the Railroad Retirement Act, and the Old Age, Survivors, Disability and Health Insurance Act (OASDHI), or, as it is better known, Social Security. Nearly all people employed in the United States are covered under Social Security, including those employed by the armed forces. The only sizeable groups not covered are those federal civil service workers who are covered by the Civil Service Retirement Act, railroad workers who are covered by the Railroad Retirement Act, and some state and municipal civil service workers. Participation in the Social Security system is not mandatory for state civil service workers at this time, and several states provide their own retirement pension program for their civil service workers. Other states, however, have voluntarily joined the Social Security system, and their civil service employees are covered by the Social Security program.

Since Social Security covers far more people than the other government pension plans, we will limit our discussion to the pension plan provided through Social Security.

Social Security

Social Security provides a retirement income to people who have contributed to the system during their income-earning years. Hence, the Social Security retirement plan more closely resembles the Canada Pension Plan and the Quebec Pension Plan than the Old Age Security Act in Canada.

Social Security retirement benefits are available to covered persons who are age 62 or older, though those retiring before age 65 receive a lesser monthly benefit amount than they would receive if they retired at age 65 or older. Social Security benefits may also be paid to spouses and dependent children of covered retirees. The federal government administers the Social Security system and makes frequent changes in the system's funding and benefits.

In order for an individual to be eligible to receive retirement income under Social Security, he or she must have contributed to the system for a specified amount of time. The amount of benefit he or she receives depends on the wages earned during that period, subject to a maximum amount per year. The amount of retirement benefit is adjusted to reflect increases in the cost of living, as measured by the Consumer Price Index (CPI) in the United States. The amount each individual contributes for these Social Security benefits is a set percentage of the individual's earned income, up to a specified maximum yearly contribution amount. The amount each individual receives monthly is also limited to a specified maximum amount.

An individual's employer contributes to Social Security an amount equal to that contributed by the employee. The employer is also responsible for collecting the individual's contributions, usually through payroll deductions, on behalf of the government. A *self-employed* participant must contribute to Social Security an amount which is 50 percent higher than the amount an *employee* with the same earned income would pay. This higher amount partially compensates for the fact that a self-employed person's contributions are not matched by any employer's contributions.

Group Retirement Plans

Almost all major employers and unions sponsor retirement programs for their employees or their members, and many small employers sponsor retirement programs for their employees. **Plan sponsors** are the employers and unions which establish retirement programs; **plan participants** are the employees and union members who are covered under these plans.

While retirement plans are designed to fit a wide variety of needs, all such plans must meet certain government requirements. In the United States, the majority of pension plan legislation is provided by the Employee Retirement Income Security Act of 1974 (ERISA). ERISA establishes standards relating to rights of the plan participants, investment standards for plan assets, and the disclosure and reporting of plan provisions and funding. Further, ERISA provided for the establishment of the Pension Benefit Guaranty Corporation (PBGC), which insures benefits for participants in certain types of pension plans against the possibility that their retirement plan might become insolvent. In Canada, the provincial governments have established regulations which address the same concerns as ERISA.

An employer-sponsored retirement plan consists of three components:

- **the plan document**, which is the plan sponsor's agreement with plan participants regarding the benefits the participants are to receive and the requirements they must meet to become entitled to these benefits
- **plan administration**, which may be handled by an actuary or an administrator, who determines the level of contributions necessary to fund benefits and/or how these funds are to be distributed among participants
- **the funding vehicle**, which is the means for investing the plan's assets as they are accumulated. This funding vehicle may be provided by a bank, an insurance company, and/or an investment committee.

There is often confusion concerning the "plan" and the "funding vehicle." It is important to note that the plan is an agreement between the plan sponsor and the plan participants, while the funding vehicle is the means chosen to invest the plan's assets. We will discuss each of these components of an employer-sponsored retirement plan separately.

The plan

The plan sponsor determines the actual features of the retirement plan. These features are described in the plan document, which is an agreement between the plan sponsor and the plan participants. In this document, a plan sponsor is allowed to specify *eligibility requirements* which a person must meet in order to be allowed to be included in the pension plan. The plan sponsor also specifies the amount of time which must pass before a plan participant is partially or fully *vested*. A participant is vested when he or she is entitled to receive partial or full benefits under the plan even if the participant terminates employment prior to retirement. The plan sponsor must also specify in the document a *normal retirement date*, a point at which, if a plan participant retires, he or she can expect to receive full pension benefits. Provisions for early and late retirement are usually also included in the plan. Finally, the plan sponsor chooses the formulas which will be used to determine the *benefits* which plan participants will receive. The most commonly used formulas will be discussed later in this chapter.

The federal governments of both the United States and Canada provide certain tax incentives to encourage employers to establish pension plans. In both the United States and Canada, the contributions made by most corporations to a tax-qualified plan are considered a business expense and are deductible from the business's taxable income. Moreover, neither the plan sponsor's contributions to the plan nor the investment earnings on those contributions are considered taxable income to the plan participants until those funds are actually received by the participants.

In order for a group pension plan to qualify for tax-favored status, the plan must be designed to meet certain criteria. In general, these criteria are as follows:

- The plan must be intended to be *permanent*; that is, the plan must be established to provide benefits for all current and future employees.
- The plan must be *written* and *published* so that all plan participants are aware of its features.
- The retirement benefit must be *automatically determined* using a formula specified in the plan.
- The plan must be established on a *nondiscriminatory* basis; that is, the plan cannot unfairly single out any employee or class of employees for extra benefits.
- The plan must be deemed to *benefit the plan participants* in general. The plan must be primarily for the benefit of plan participants; a plan

sponsor cannot benefit from a tax-qualified pension plan at the expense of the plan participants.

Since benefits are the primary ingredient of any retirement program, we will focus on the benefit formulas which are commonly used to provide benefits under employer-sponsored pension plans. These benefit formulas can be divided into two general categories: *defined benefit* formulas and *defined contribution* formulas.

Defined benefit formulas. Defined benefit formulas define the *benefit* that a participant will receive at retirement. The plan sponsor guarantees that when the participant has met the other requirements of the plan, he or she will be entitled to this specific benefit. The retirement benefit is usually described in terms of a monthly annuity, and it is the plan sponsor's obligation to deposit enough assets into the funding vehicle to provide the promised benefits.

Defined contribution formulas. Defined contribution, or *money purchase*, formulas describe the contribution which will be deposited into the plan on behalf of each plan participant, rather than the specific amount of each plan participant's retirement benefit. Thus, funds are accumulated on behalf of each plan participant until the participant's retirement date. When a plan participant retires, the amount accumulated for that person is available in either a lump sum or in the form of a monthly annuity. The amount of the annuity benefit that each retiree receives is dependent upon the size of the fund which has been accumulated.

Supplemental benefit plans. Many employers also establish profit-sharing plans, or any of numerous other types of plans, to supplement benefits provided under basic retirement plans. The employer's contributions to profit-sharing plans are based on corporate profits. Other plans used to supplement basic retirement benefits include thrift plans, savings plans, and salary reduction plans.

Plan administration

In order to maintain records on the pension plan and to determine the amount of money the plan sponsor needs to accumulate in order to fund a pension plan, the plan sponsor relies on either an actuary or an administrator, or both.

An actuary must be consulted to determine the amount of contributions required to fund a *defined benefit* plan. The actuary determines the amount of contributions needed to fund the plan by making estimates of employee mortality, employee turnover, plan administration expenses, employees' future salaries, and plan investment earnings. Using these estimates, the actuary can determine the amount of funding required to pay the benefits promised. An administrator is needed to maintain records, pay benefits, and, in the case of *defined contribution* plans, assure that funds are credited correctly to individual accounts. Thus, an actuary has a more limited role in defined contribution plans.

Like group life and health insurance plans, group retirement plans may be funded on a contributory or noncontributory basis. Most defined benefit plans are noncontributory, and most defined contribution plans are contributory. Contributions to the pension fund, however, are not usually referred to as "premiums," because an annuity is rarely purchased until after a plan participant retires. In most cases, contributions to the pension fund are placed in a funding vehicle until a plan participant retires.

Contributory plans are much more common in Canada than they are in the United States, because in Canada the contributions made by a plan participant are generally deductible from the plan participant's income for tax purposes. In the United States, a plan participant's contributions are usually not tax-deductible.

Funding vehicles

Once the plan sponsor has determined the appropriate type of plan and has been advised as to the amount of contributions necessary to provide the promised benefits, the question of how to invest the funds which will accumulate becomes important. The plan sponsor is legally required to adhere to certain standards of prudence in handling and investing plan funds. While the plan sponsor is permitted to directly invest the funds, the plan sponsor generally seeks investment services elsewhere.

Today, most pension plans are "trusteed" plans. In a trusteed plan, the trustee chosen by the plan sponsor is responsible for investing plan assets or for choosing who will invest the assets. The trustee's duties are spelled out in the trust agreement, a contract between the plan sponsor and the trustee. Any or all of the following may act as trustees of a retirement plan: (1) individuals selected by the plan sponsor, (2) a bank trust department, (3) an investment house, and/or (4) a life insurance company.

The plan sponsor or the trustee will choose the institution which will invest plan assets. Institutions used to invest plan assets include life insurance companies, banks, and investment brokerage houses. Each offers various funding vehicles to appeal to the varying needs of plan sponsors. Funding vehicles offered by life insurance companies can provide guarantees against certain financial and mortality risks and are therefore attractive to many plan sponsors and trustees. The funding vehicles more commonly available from a life insurance company include group deferred annuities, deposit administration contracts, immediate participation guarantee contracts (IPGs), separate account contracts, and guaranteed interest contracts (GICs).

Group deferred annuities. A group deferred annuity operates much like a group insurance plan. A master policy is issued by the life insurance company to the plan sponsor, and certificates are issued to each individual plan participant. Each year, the contributions for each plan participant are used to purchase a single-premium deferred annuity for that plan participant. When this person retires, benefit payments from these deferred annuities will provide the scheduled retirement benefit. Thus, since contributions are used to purchase annuities in the years prior to a plan participant's retirement, group deferred annuities require premium payments and are called *fully insured* products. Recently, other funding vehicles have supplanted the group deferred annuity's place in the market.

Deposit administration contracts. Under a deposit administration contract, the plan assets are placed in the insurance company's general investment account. When a plan participant retires, sufficient funds are withdrawn to purchase an immediate annuity for the plan participant. The insurance company usually provides the plan sponsor with guarantees against investment loss, as well as guarantees regarding minimum investment returns. Further, the price of the immediate annuity to be purchased at a plan participant's retirement is usually guaranteed in advance. When the immediate annuity is purchased, the insurance company guarantees the benefit amount which will be paid to the plan participant.

Immediate participation guarantee (IPG) contracts. Plan assets placed in immediate participation guarantee (IPG) contracts are also invested by the life insurance company in an account on behalf of the plan sponsor. However, IPG contracts do not provide the *full* guarantees against investment loss or the guarantees regarding the minimum investment returns which are provided through deposit administration contracts. Instead, IPG contracts are designed to allow the plan sponsor to share in the gains or losses experienced by the life insurance company as it invests and pays benefits from the account. Many IPG contracts, however, provide a guarantee that the plan sponsor will not share in losses greater than a stated amount. When a plan participant retires, funds may be withdrawn to purchase an immediate annuity for that retiree, or the retirement benefit may be paid directly from the account each month.

Separate account contracts. Under a separate account contract, the insurance company invests plan assets in common stocks, short-term markets, bond funds, real estate, and/or other specialized areas of investments. The plan sponsor chooses the account or accounts in which the plan contributions are to be placed. Separate account contracts usually do not make any guarantees regarding investment performance.

Guaranteed interest contracts (GICs). Under a basic guaranteed interest contract (GIC), the insurer accepts a single deposit from the plan sponsor for a specified period of time, such as five years. During that period, interest on the deposit is either accumulated until the period expires, or it can be paid out annually. At the end of the period, the account balance, including any accumulated interest, is returned to the plan sponsor. Numerous variations of this basic guaranteed interest contract have been developed which (1) allow the plan sponsor to make monthly contributions, rather than the single deposit, and (2) provide that the principal and interest can be paid out in installments to make benefit payments to plan participants. A GIC may also be called a guaranteed investment contract or a guaranteed income contract.

Under the terms of both separate account contracts and GICs, the plan sponsor is permitted to purchase an immediate annuity from the insurer at the time of a plan participant's retirement, although the plan sponsor is not required to purchase such an annuity.

The pension funding environment

The demands of plan sponsors for competitive returns, flexibility of investment strategy, and balanced portfolios — combined with frequent legislative changes — have caused vast changes in the pension marketplace. Products common 10 years ago are rarely sold today as the life insurance industry adapts to these changes, and the next decade will bring further changes in the industry's marketing and design of group pension funding vehicles.

Appendix

This appendix contains a sample participating whole life insurance policy, including both an accidental death benefit rider and a waiver of premium for disability benefit rider. The appendix also includes a sample Part I application.

The sample forms included in the body of this text and in this appendix have been designed to fit the space requirements of the book. Hence, each form does not always have the format and appearance of the actual document. However, the language and provisions used in all of the sample forms are indicative of the language and provisions found in the actual forms. As you refer to the forms in the appendix, remember that there are no "standard" policies and applications, and, hence, each insurer's forms will be different.

ABC LIFE

POLICY NUMBER	00 000 000 **POLICY DATE** July 1, 1982 **AGE** 35 Male
ON LIFE OF	John Doe (The Insured)
OWNER	The Insured
PLAN	Whole Life with Accidental Death Benefit (ADB) and Disability Waiver of Premium (WP)

AMOUNT	Face Amount $25,000
	Accidental Death Benefit $25,000
	  (ADB, when payable, is in addition to any other insurance
	  benefit)

BENEFICIARY subject to change	First—Mary Doe, Wife of Insured Second—John Doe, Jr., Son of Insured
PREMIUM SCHEDULE	Premiums Payable At annual intervals, as follows

10 DAY FREE EXAMINATION PERIOD. Please examine your policy. Within 10 days after delivery, you can return it to the Company or to the agent through whom it was purchased, with a written request for a full refund of premium. Upon such a request, the policy will be void from the start.

Beginning as of Mo. Day Year	Premium	Premium includes the following amounts for any supplementary benefits	
		ADB	WP
7-1-1982	$509.75	$20.00	$12.25
7-1-2012	$497.50	$20.00	—
7-1-2017	$477.50 Payable for remainder of insured's life.**		

**Premium paying period may be shortened by using dividend values to make policy fully paid-up.

The pages which follow are also part of this policy.

This policy is executed as of July 1, 1982

which is its DATE OF ISSUE.

ABC LIFE

Robert A. Jones
PRESIDENT

Teresa R. Hippe
SECRETARY

Specimen Copy
COUNTERSIGNATURE

Life Policy.
Proceeds payable at Insured's death.
Premiums payable during Insured's lifetime,
  as shown in premium schedule.
Policy is eligible for dividends.

WE & YOU   In this policy, the words "we", "our"   When you write to us, please
or "us" refer to ABC Life Insurance   include the policy number,
Company, and the words "you"   the Insured's full name,
or "your" refer to the owner of   and your current address.
this policy.

CONTENTS

LIFE INSURANCE BENEFIT	Payment at the Insured's death
POLICY OWNERSHIP	Rights of the owner; Successor owner; Change of ownership
BENEFICIARY	How to name or change beneficiaries; Death of beneficiary
PREMIUMS	Payment of premiums; What happens if a premium is not paid; Reinstatement of a lapsed policy
CASH VALUE AND LOANS	Cash and loan values available and how these can be used; Automatic loan to pay a premium
DIVIDENDS	When dividends are payable and how they can be used; How the policy may be made fully paid-up
PAYMENT OF POLICY PROCEEDS	Ways in which life insurance or surrender proceeds may be paid
GENERAL PROVISIONS	Entire Contract; Application; Incontestability; Suicide Exclusion; Dates; Age and Sex; Policy Changes; Assignment; Protection Against Creditors; Payments to Company; Basis of Computation; Conformity with Law; Voting Rights
RIDERS OR ENDORSEMENTS (IF ANY)	Attached to the policy
TABLE OF GUARANTEED VALUES	A table showing cash values of this policy, amounts of paid-up insurance, and term periods of any extended insurance
APPLICATION	Attached to the policy.

LIFE INSURANCE BENEFIT

Life Insurance Benefit We will pay the life insurance proceeds to the beneficiary promptly when we have proof of the Insured's death, if premiums have been paid as called for in the Premiums section. These proceeds will include the face amount and any other benefits from riders or dividends which are payable because of the Insured's death, all as stated in the policy. When we determine these proceeds, there may be an adjustment for the last premium. We will deduct any unpaid loan.

Please read this policy for full details.

POLICY OWNERSHIP

Owner In this policy, the words "you" and "your" refer to the owner of the policy. As the owner, you have all rights of ownership in this policy while the Insured is living. To exercise these rights, you do not need the consent of any successor owner or beneficiary.

Successor Owner A successor owner can be named in the application, or in a notice you sign which gives us the facts that we need. The successor owner will become the new owner when you die, if you die before the Insured. If no successor owner survives you and you die before the Insured, your estate becomes the new owner.

Change of Ownership You can change the owner of this policy, from yourself to a new owner, in a notice you sign which gives us the facts that we need. When this change takes effect, all rights of ownership in this policy will pass to the new owner.

When we record a change of owner or successor owner, these changes will take effect as of the date you signed the notice, subject to any payment we made or action we took before recording these changes. We may require that these changes be endorsed in the policy. Changing the owner or naming a new successor owner cancels any prior choice of successor owner, but does not change the beneficiary.

BENEFICIARY

Naming of Beneficiary One or more beneficiaries for any life insurance proceeds can be named in the application, or in a notice you sign which gives us the facts that we need. If more than one beneficiary is named, they can be classed as first, second, and so on. If 2 or more are named in a class, their shares in the proceeds can be stated.

The stated shares of the proceeds will be paid to any first beneficiaries who survive the Insured. If no first beneficiaries survive, payment will be made to any surviving in the second class, and so on. Those who survive in the same class have an equal share in the proceeds, unless the shares are stated otherwise.

Change of Beneficiary   While the Insured is living, you can change a beneficiary in a notice you sign which gives us the facts that we need. When we record a change, it will take effect as of the date you signed the notice, subject to any payment we made or action we took before recording the change.

Death of Beneficiary   If no beneficiary for the life insurance proceeds, or for a stated share, survives the Insured, the right to these proceeds or this share will pass to you. If you are the Insured, this right will pass to your estate. If any beneficiary dies at the same time as the Insured, or within 15 days after the Insured but before we receive proof of the Insured's death, we will pay the proceeds as though that beneficiary died first.

PREMIUMS

Payment of Premiums   Each premium is payable, while the Insured is living, on or before its due date as shown in the Premium Schedule. Premiums are payable at our Home Office or at one of our service offices.

   The premium for this policy can be paid every 3 months or 6 months, or once each year. The premium rate for each of these intervals is the rate that was in effect as of the policy date. The interval can be changed by paying the correct premium for the new interval. Premiums can be paid by any other method we make available.

Grace Period   We allow 31 days from the due date for payment of a premium. All insurance continues during this grace period.

Nonpayment of Premium   If a premium is not paid by the end of the grace period, this policy will lapse. All insurance will end at the time of lapse, if the policy has no cash value and no dividend values. If the policy has cash value or dividend values, insurance can be continued only as stated in options 1 or 2 on this page, but any insurance or benefits from riders or dividends will end at the time of lapse.

Options upon Lapse   If the policy has cash value or dividend values at the time of lapse, it will continue as extended term insurance, if available. When extended insurance is not available, it is because this policy has an extra premium payable which is larger than the limit we set. If the Table on the back page shows that extended insurance is not available, or if the amount of this insurance would be less than or equal to the amount of paid-up insurance available, the policy will continue under the Paid-up Insurance option instead.

   Instead of extended insurance, paid-up insurance can be elected or you can surrender the policy for cash. The paid-up insurance can be elected in the application or in your signed notice. We must receive this notice no later than 3 months after the due date of the overdue premium.

   1. Extended Insurance   Extended insurance is term insurance for which no more premiums are due. It is payable to the beneficiary when we have proof that the Insured died after the end of the grace period and before the end of the term period. The amount of this insurance will be the face amount of this policy, plus the amount of any paid-up additions and dividend accumulations, less any loan. No insurance or benefits from riders or dividends will be provided after the end of the grace period.

We calculate the term period as of the due date of the overdue premium. We do this by applying the sum of the cash value and dividend values, less any loan, at the net single premium rate for the Insured's age on that date. The term period is measured from that due date.

This insurance can be surrendered at any time for its cash value, but it has no loan value and is not eligible for dividends.

2. Paid-up Insurance   Paid-up life insurance begins as of the date we record your notice electing it, or begins at the end of the grace period if later. No more premiums are due for this insurance. It is payable to the beneficiary when we have proof that the Insured died while this option was in effect.

We calculate the amount of paid-up insurance as of the due date of the overdue premium. We do this by applying the sum of the cash value and dividend values, less any loan, at the net single premium rate for the Insured's age on that date. In most cases, this amount will be less than the face amount of this policy. No insurance or benefits from riders will be provided.

This insurance can be surrendered at any time. It has cash value and loan value, and is eligible for dividends.

3. Surrender for Cash   Instead of options 1 or 2, you can surrender this policy for its cash value and dividend values, less any loan, as stated in the Cash Value provision.

Reinstatement   Within 5 years after lapse, you may apply to reinstate the policy if you have not surrendered it. We must have evidence of insurability that is acceptable to us. All overdue premiums must be paid, with interest at 6% per year from each of their due dates. Any unpaid loan, and any loan deducted when we determined the extended or paid-up insurance, must also be repaid. Interest on the loan will be compounded once each year and will be based on the interest rate or rates that were in effect since the time of lapse. All or part of these payments can be charged as a new unpaid loan if there is enough loan value.

We do not need evidence of insurability if we receive the required payment within 31 days after the end of the grace period, but the Insured must be living when we receive it.

Premium Adjustment at Death   We will increase the proceeds by any part of a premium paid for the period after the policy month in which the Insured dies.

If the Insured dies during a grace period, we will reduce the proceeds by an amount equal to the premium for one policy month.

CASH VALUE AND LOANS

Cash Value   Cash values for this policy at the end of selected policy years are as shown in the Table on the back page, if premiums have been paid as called for in the Premiums section. These values do not include dividend values, and they do not reflect an unpaid loan. Cash values at other times depend on the date to which premiums have been paid, and on how much time has passed since the last anniversary. When you ask us, we will tell you how much cash value there is.

The cash value on the due date of an unpaid premium will not decrease during the 3 months after that date. Also, the cash value of any extended or paid-up insurance on an anniversary will not decrease during the next 31 days after that.

At any time after the policy has cash value or dividend values, you can surrender it for the sum of these values, less any unpaid loan. All insurance will end when you send us your signed request for these surrender proceeds.

We may defer paying these proceeds for up to 6 months after the date of surrender. Interest will be paid on any amount deferred for 30 days or more. We set the interest rate each year. This rate will be at least 3½% per year.

Loan Value   You can borrow any amount up to the loan value, using this policy as sole security. On a policy anniversary, on a premium due date, or during the grace period, the loan value is the cash value, plus any dividend values, less any unpaid loan and accrued interest. At any other time, the loan value is the amount which, with interest, will equal the loan value on the next anniversary or on the next premium due date, if earlier. Extended insurance has no loan value.

We may require that you sign a loan agreement. We may defer a loan, except to pay a premium due us, for as long as 6 months after we receive your loan request.

Loan Interest   Loan interest accrues each day. Interest is due on each anniversary, or on the date of death, surrender, a lapse, a loan increase or loan repayment, or on any other date we specify. Interest not paid when due becomes part of the loan and will also bear interest.

Loan Interest Rate   The loan interest rate of this policy may go up or down. However, this rate will never be less than 5½% a year, and will never be greater than that permitted by law. We can change this rate as often as once every 3 months. On any date when we determine how much interest is due on an unpaid loan, we will take into account, to the extent required, the loan interest rate or rates that have been in effect since the prior anniversary.

Each time you borrow against this policy, we will tell you what the loan interest rate is at that time. When a premium is paid by an automatic loan (APL), we will tell you, just as soon as we can, what that rate was at the time of payment.

If there is an unpaid loan, and an increase in the loan interest rate is to take effect, we will tell you the facts about that just as soon ahead of time as we can.

Automatic Premium Loan (APL)   If elected, APL provides an automatic loan which pays an overdue premium at the end of the grace period, subject to 2 conditions. First, the loan value must be enough to pay that premium. Second, if premiums have been paid by APL for 2 years in a row, the next premium will not be paid by APL. After a premium is paid other than by APL, before the end of the grace period, premiums can again be paid by APL.

APL can be elected in the application. You can also elect APL in your signed notice which we must receive before the end of the grace period. You can cancel this election for future premiums by telling us in your signed notice.

Loan Repayment   All or part of an unpaid loan and accrued interest can be repaid before the Insured's death or before you surrender the policy. We will deduct an unpaid loan when policy proceeds are payable.

If the policy is being continued as extended or paid-up insurance, any loan which we deducted in determining that insurance may be repaid only if the policy is reinstated. If that loan is not repaid, we will not deduct it again when policy proceeds are payable.

When Unpaid Loan Exceeds Loan Value   In a given policy year it may happen that, based on the loan interest rate in effect when that year began, an unpaid loan and accrued interest will exceed the sum of the cash value and any dividend values. If so, we will mail a notice to you at your last known address, and a copy to any assignee on our records. All insurance will end 31 days after the date on which we mail that notice.

DIVIDENDS

Annual Dividend   While this policy is in force, except as extended insurance, it is eligible to share in our divisible surplus. Each year we determine the policy's share, if any. This share is payable as a dividend on the policy anniversary, if all premiums due before then have been paid. We do not expect a dividend to be payable before the second anniversary.

Dividend Options   Each dividend can be applied under one of the 4 options listed below. An option can be elected in the application. You can also elect or change the option for future dividends if you tell us in your signed notice.

1. Paid-up Addition   Applied to provide paid-up life insurance at the single premium rate for the Insured's age at that time. No more premiums are due for this insurance. It has cash value and is eligible for dividends. Before the Insured's death, you can surrender paid-up additions for their cash value that has not been borrowed against. The amount of this insurance in force at the Insured's death will be part of the proceeds.

2. Dividend Accumulation   Left with us to accumulate at interest. On each anniversary, we credit interest at the rate we set each year. This rate will be at least 3½% per year. Before the Insured's death, you can withdraw accumulations that have not been borrowed against, with interest to the date of withdrawal. Any accumulations which we still have at the Insured's death will be part of the proceeds.

3. Premium Payment   Applied toward payment of a premium, provided any balance of that premium is also paid when due. Any part of the dividend not needed to pay the premium will be used to pay any loan interest due, unless you have asked to have that part paid in cash. Any part of the dividend not used to pay a premium or loan interest will be paid in cash.

4. Cash   Paid in cash.

Automatic Dividend Option   If no other option is in effect when a dividend becomes payable, we will apply it as a paid-up addition. If we pay a dividend in cash, and the dividend check is not cashed within one year after that dividend became payable, we will apply the dividend as a paid-up addition instead.

Dividend Values   Dividend values are any dividend accumulations plus the cash value of any paid-up additions.

Fully Paid-up Policy   You may shorten the premium paying period for this policy by having it made fully paid-up with no more premiums due. This may be done on any premium due date, if the sum of the cash value and dividend values equals the total single premium for the policy and any riders, based on the Insured's age on that date. We must receive your signed notice within 31 days of that date.

Dividend at Death   The part of any annual dividend payable from the last anniversary to the end of the policy month in which the Insured dies will be part of the proceeds.

PAYMENT OF POLICY PROCEEDS

Payment   We will pay the policy proceeds in one sum or, if elected, all or part of these proceeds may be placed under one or more of the options described in this section. If we agree, the proceeds may be placed under some other method of payment instead.

Any life insurance proceeds paid in one sum will bear interest compounded each year from the insured's death to the date of payment. We set the interest rate each year. This rate will be at least 3½% per year.

Election of Optional Method of Payment While the Insured is living, you can elect or change an option. You can also name or change one or more beneficiaries who will be the payee or payees under that option. After the Insured dies, any person who is to receive proceeds in one sum (other than an assignee) can elect an option and name payees.

The person who elects an option can also name one or more successor payees to receive any unpaid amount we have at the death of a payee. Naming these payees cancels any prior choice of successor payee.

A payee who did not elect the option does not have the right to advance or assign payments, take the payments in one sum, or make any other change. However, the payee may be given the right to do one or more of these things if the person who elects the option tells us in writing and we agree.

Change of Option If we agree, a payee who elects Option 1A, 1B, 2A, or 2B may later elect to have any unpaid amount we still have, or the present value of any elected payments, placed under some other option described in this section.

Payees Only individuals who are to receive payments in their own behalf may be named as payees or successor payees, unless we agree to some other payee. We may require proof of the age or the survival of a payee.

It may happen that when the last surviving payee dies, we still have an unpaid amount, or there are some payments which remain to be made. If so, we will pay the unpaid amount with interest to the date of payment, or pay the present value of the remaining payments, to that payee's estate in one sum. The present value of any remaining payments is based on the interest rate used to compute them, and is always less than their sum.

Minimum Payment When any payment under an option would be less than $20, we may pay any unpaid amount or present value in one sum.

Options 1A and 1B. Proceeds at Interest

The policy proceeds may be left with us at interest. We set the interest rate each year. This rate will be at least 3½% per year.

1A. Interest Accumulation

We credit interest each year on the amount we still have. This amount can be withdrawn at any time in sums of $100 or more. We pay interest to the date of withdrawal on sums withdrawn.

1B. Interest Payment

We pay interest once each month, every 3 months or 6 months, or once each year, as chosen, based on the amount we still have.

Options 2A and 2B. Elected Income

We make equal payments once each month, every 3 months or 6 months, or once each year, as chosen, for an elected period of years or for an elected amount. We set the interest rate for these options each year. This rate will be at least 3½% per year.

2A. Income for Elected Period

We make the payments for the number of years elected. Monthly payments based on 3½% interest are shown in the Option 2A Table. If the rate is more than 3½%, we will increase each payment to reflect this.

OPTION 2A TABLE

Minimum Monthly Payment per $1,000 of Proceeds

Years		Years		Years		Years	
1	$84.65	5	$18.12	9	$10.75	15	$7.10
2	43.05	6	15.35	10	9.83	20	5.75
3	29.19	7	13.38	11	9.09	25	4.96
4	22.27	8	11.90	12	8.46	30	4.45

When asked, we will state in writing what each payment would be, if made every 3 months or 6 months, or once each year.

2B. Income of Elected Amount

We make payments of the elected amount until all proceeds and interest have been paid. The total payments made each year must be at least 5% of the proceeds placed under this option. Each year we credit interest of at least 3½% on the amount we still have.

Options 3A, 3B, and 3C. Life Income

We make equal payments each month during the lifetime of the named payee or payees. We determine the amount of the monthly payment by applying the policy proceeds to purchase a corresponding single premium life annuity policy which we are issuing when the first payment is due. Payments are based on the appropriately adjusted annuity premium rate in effect at that time, but will not be less than the corresponding minimum amount based on the tables for Options 3A, 3B, and 3C in this policy.

When asked, we will state in writing what the minimum amount of each monthly payment would be under these options. It is based on the sex and the adjusted age of the payee or payees. To find the adjusted age in the year the first payment is due, we increase or decrease the payee's age at that time, as follows:

1985 & earlier	1986–95	1996–2010	2011–25	2026 & later
+2	+1	0	–1	–2

3A. Life Income—Guaranteed Period

We make a payment each month during the lifetime of the payee. Payments do not change, and are guaranteed for 5, 10, 15, or 20 years, as chosen, even if that payee dies sooner.

OPTION 3A TABLE

Minimum Monthly Payment per $1,000 of Proceeds

Payee's Adjusted Age	MALE Guaranteed Period				FEMALE Guaranteed Period			
	5 Yrs	10 Yrs	15 Yrs	20 Yrs	5 Yrs	10 Yrs	15 Yrs	20 Yrs
60	$5.66	$5.56	$5.38	$5.16	$5.21	$5.16	$5.07	$4.95
61	5.79	5.67	5.48	5.23	5.32	5.26	5.16	5.02
62	5.93	5.79	5.57	5.29	5.43	5.37	5.26	5.09
63	6.08	5.92	5.67	5.36	5.55	5.48	5.35	5.16
64	6.24	6.06	5.78	5.42	5.69	5.60	5.46	5.24
65	6.41	6.20	5.88	5.48	5.83	5.73	5.55	5.31
66	6.59	6.35	5.98	5.54	5.99	5.87	5.67	5.38
67	6.78	6.50	6.09	5.60	6.16	6.02	5.79	5.45
68	6.99	6.67	6.19	5.66	6.34	6.18	5.90	5.52
69	7.21	6.83	6.30	5.71	6.54	6.35	6.02	5.58
70	7.44	7.01	6.40	5.75	6.75	6.52	6.13	5.64
71	7.69	7.19	6.50	5.80	6.98	6.70	6.25	5.69
72	7.96	7.37	6.60	5.84	7.23	6.89	6.36	5.74
73	8.24	7.56	6.69	5.87	7.49	7.09	6.47	5.79
74	8.55	7.75	6.78	5.90	7.78	7.29	6.58	5.82
75	8.86	7.94	6.86	5.92	8.08	7.50	6.68	5.86
80	10.71	8.86	7.18	5.99	9.92	8.52	7.06	5.96
85 & over	12.98	9.58	7.31	6.00	12.16	9.30	7.24	5.99

3B. Life Income—Guaranteed Total Amount

We make a payment each month during the lifetime of the payee. Payments do not change, and are guaranteed until the total paid equals the amount placed under this option, even if that payee dies sooner.

OPTION 3B TABLE

Minimum Monthly Payment per $1,000 of Proceeds

Payee's Adjusted Age	Male	Female	Payee's Adjusted Age	Male	Female
60	$5.36	$5.04	69	$6.56	$6.12
61	5.47	5.13	70	6.73	6.28
62	5.58	5.23	71	6.92	6.46
63	5.69	5.33	72	7.11	6.64
64	5.82	5.45	73	7.32	6.84
65	5.95	5.56	74	7.55	7.05
66	6.09	5.69	75	7.78	7.27
67	6.24	5.82	80	9.22	8.61
68	6.39	5.97	85 & over	11.25	10.37

3C. Life Income—Joint and Survivor

We make a payment each month while both or one of the two payees are living. Payments do not change, and are guaranteed for 10 years, even if both payees die sooner.

OPTION 3C TABLE
10 YEAR GUARANTEED PERIOD

Minimum Monthly Payment per $1,000 of Proceeds

Male Payee's Adjusted Age	Female Payee's Adjusted Age				
	60	65	70	75	80
60	$4.72	$4.96	$5.17	$5.34	$5.45
65	4.87	5.20	5.52	5.80	6.00
70	4.99	5.41	5.86	6.30	6.65
75	5.09	5.56	6.15	6.78	7.31
80	5.18	5.68	6.36	7.15	7.89

GENERAL PROVISIONS

Entire Contract   The entire contract consists of this policy and the attached copy of the application. Only our Chairman, President, Secretary, or one of our Vice Presidents can change the contract, and then only in writing. No change will be made in the contract unless you agree to it in writing.

Application   In issuing this policy, we have relied on the statements in the application. All such statements will be considered as representations and not as warranties. We assume these statements are true and complete to the best of the knowledge and belief of those who made them.

No statement made in connection with the application will be used by us to void the policy unless that statement is a material misrepresentation and is part of the application.

Incontestability   We will not contest this policy after it has been in force during the lifetime of the Insured for 2 years from the date of issue.

Please refer to the Incontestability of Rider provision that may be in any rider or riders attached to this policy.

Suicide Exclusion   Suicide of the Insured, while sane or insane, within two years of the date of issue, is not covered by this policy. In that event, this policy will end and the only amount payable will be the premiums paid to us, less any loan.

Dates   Policy years, months, and anniversaries are measured from the policy date.

Age and Sex   In this policy when we refer to a person's age on any date, we mean his or her age on the birthday which is the nearest that date. If a date in the Premium Schedule is based on an age that is not correct, we may change the date to reflect the correct age.

If the age or sex of an insured person is not correct as stated, any amount payable under this policy will be what the premiums paid would have purchased at the correct age and sex.

Policy Changes If we agree, you may have riders added to this policy, or have it changed to another plan or to a smaller amount of insurance.

Assignment While the Insured is living, you can assign this policy or any interest in it. If you do this, your interest, and anyone else's is subject to that of the assignee. As owner, you still have the rights of ownership that have not been assigned.

An assignee may not change the owner or the beneficiary, and may not elect or change an optional method of payment. Any policy proceeds payable to the assignee will be paid in one sum.

We must have a copy of any assignment. We will not be responsible for the validity of an assignment. It will be subject to any payment we make or other action we take before we record it.

Protection Against Creditors Except as stated in the Assignment provision, payments we make under this policy are, to the extent the law permits, exempt from the claims, attachments, or levies of any creditors.

Payments to Company Any payment made to us by check or money order must be payable to ABC Life. When asked, we will give a receipt, signed by our President or Secretary, for any premium paid to us.

Basis of Computation All cash values and single premium rates referred to in this policy (except those for extended insurance) are based on the 1958 CSO Table of Mortality if the Insured is a male. They are based on the 1958 CSO Female Table of Mortality if the Insured is a female. All extended insurance rates and cash values are based on the corresponding 1958 CET Insurance Tables. Continuous functions are used. Interest is compounded each year at $4\frac{1}{2}\%$.

At the end of each policy year not shown in the Table on the back page, the cash value is the reserve based on the Commissioners Reserve Valuation Method. At any time, the cash value of any extended or paid-up insurance or paid-up additions is the reserve on each of these.

We have filed a statement with the insurance official in the state or district in which this policy is delivered. It describes, in detail, the method we use to compute these cash values. Each value is at least as much as the law requires.

Conformity with Law This policy is subject to all laws which apply.

Voting Rights Each year there is an election of persons to our Board of Directors. You have the right to vote in person or by mail if your policy is in force, and has been in force for at least one year after the date of issue. To find out more about this, write to the Secretary at our Home Office, 100 Ordinary Avenue, New York, New York 00000.

RIDER

ACCIDENTAL DEATH BENEFIT (ADB)

Benefit We will pay this benefit to the beneficiary when we have proof that the Insured's death was caused directly, and apart from any other cause, by accidental bodily injury, and that death occurred within one year after that injury and while this rider was in effect.

When Benefit Not Payable We will not pay this benefit if death is caused or is contributed to by any of these items.

1. Disease or infirmity of mind or body.
2. Suicide, while sane or insane.
3. Travel in or descent from an aircraft, if the Insured at any time during the aircraft's flight acted in any role other than as a passenger.
4. Any kind of war, declared or not, or by any act incident to a war or to an armed conflict involving the armed forces of one or more countries.

We will not pay this benefit if the Insured dies prior to his or her first birthday, or dies after the anniversary on which he or she is age 70.

Values This rider does not have cash or loan values.

Contract This rider, when paid for, is made a part of the policy, based on the application for the rider.

Incontestability of Rider We will not contest this rider after it has been in force during the lifetime of the Insured for 2 years from its date of issue.

Dates and Amounts When this rider is issued at the same time as the policy, we show the amount of ADB and the rider premium amount on the front page of the policy. The rider and the policy have the same date of issue.

When this rider is added to a policy which is already in force, we also put in an add-on rider. The add-on rider shows the date of issue and the amount of ADB. The rider premium amount is shown in a new Premium Schedule for the policy.

When Rider Ends You can cancel this rider as of the due date of a premium. To do this, you must send the policy and your signed notice to us within 31 days of that date. If this rider is still in effect on the anniversary on which the Insured is age 70, it will end on that date.

This rider ends if the policy ends or is surrendered. Also, this rider will not be in effect if the policy lapses or is in force as extended or paid-up insurance.

When this rider is part of an endowment policy, the rider will end on the day just before the endowment date, and will not be in effect if that date is deferred.

ABC LIFE INSURANCE COMPANY

By _____
Robert A. Jones
President

_____
Teresa R. Heppe
Secretary

RIDER

DISABILITY WAIVER OF PREMIUM (WP)

Waiver of Premiums   We will start to waive the premiums for this policy when proof is furnished that the Insured's total disability, as defined in this rider, has gone on for at least 6 months in a row.

If a total disability starts on or prior to the anniversary on which the Insured is age 60, we will waive all of the premiums which fall due during that total disability. If it goes on until the anniversary on which the Insured is age 65, we will make the policy fully paid-up as of that date, with no more premiums due.

If a total disability starts after the anniversary on which the Insured is age 60, we will waive only those premiums which fall due during that total disability, and prior to the anniversary on which the Insured is age 65.

Premiums are waived at the interval of payment in effect when the total disability started. While we waive premiums, all insurance goes on as if they had been paid. We will not deduct a waived premium from the policy proceeds.

Definition of Total Disability   "Total Disability" means that, because of disease or bodily injury, the Insured cannot do any of the essential acts and duties of his or her job, or of any other job for which he or she is suited based on schooling, training, or experience. If the Insured can do some but not all of these acts and duties, disability is not total and premiums will not be waived. If the Insured is a minor and is required by law to go to school, "Total Disability" means that, because of disease or bodily injury, he or she is not able to go to school.

"Total Disability" also means the Insured's total loss, starting while this rider is in effect, of the sight of both eyes or the use of both hands, both feet, or one hand and one foot.

Total Disabilities for Which Premiums Not Waived   We will not waive premiums in connection with any of these total disabilities.

1. Those that start prior to the fifth birthday of the Insured, or start at a time when this rider is not in effect.
2. Those that are caused by an injury that is self-inflicted on purpose.
3. Those that are caused by any kind of war, declared or not, or by any act incident to a war or to an armed conflict involving the armed forces of one or more countries while the Insured is a member of those armed forces.

Proof of Total Disability   Written notice and proof of this condition must be given to us, while the Insured is living and totally disabled, or as soon as it can reasonably be done. As long as we waive premiums, we may require proof from time to time. After we have waived premiums for 2 years in a row, we will not need to have this proof more than once each year. As part of the proof, we may have the Insured examined by doctors we approve.

Payment of Premiums   Premiums must be paid when due, until we approve a claim under this rider. If a total disability starts during a grace period, the overdue premium must be paid before we will approve any claim.

Refund of Premiums   If a total disability starts after a premium has been paid, and if it goes on for at least 6 months in a row, we will refund the part of that premium paid for the period after the policy month when that disability started. Any other premium paid and then waived will be refunded in full.

Values   This rider does not have cash or loan values.

Contract   This rider, when paid for, is made a part of the policy, based on the application for the rider.

Incontestability of Rider   We have no right to contest this rider after it has been in force during the lifetime of the Insured for 2 years from its date of issue, unless the Insured is totally disabled at some time within 2 years of the date of issue.

Dates and Amounts   When this rider is issued at the same time as the policy, we show the rider premium amount on the front page of the policy. The rider and the policy have the same date of issue.

When this rider is added to a policy which is already in force, we also put in an add-on rider. The add-on rider shows the date of issue. The rider premium amount is shown in a new Premium Schedule for the policy.

When Rider Ends   You can cancel this rider as of the due date of a premium. To do this, you must send the policy and your signed notice to us within 31 days of that date. If this rider is still in effect on the anniversary on which the Insured is age 65, it will end on that date.

This rider ends if the policy ends or is surrendered. Also, this rider will not be in effect if the policy lapses or is in force as extended or paid-up insurance.

ABC LIFE INSURANCE COMPANY

By _____

President

_____

Secretary

ABC Life Insurance Company   **100 Ordinary Avenue, New York, N.Y. 00000**

A Mutual Company

Life Policy.
Proceeds payable at insured's death.
Premiums payable during insured's lifetime,
as shown in premium schedule.
Policy is eligible for dividends.

TABLE OF GUARANTEED VALUES
(These values do not include dividend values nor reflect an unpaid loan)

End of Policy Year	CASH VALUE	ALTERNATIVES TO CASH VALUE			End of Policy Year
		REDUCED PAID-UP INSURANCE or	EXTENDED TERM INSURANCE		
			Years	Days	
1	.....	...	..	...	1
2	.....	...	..	...	2
3	$300.00	$1,150	3	13	3
4	625.00	2,325	5	211	4
5	975.00	3,475	7	264	5
6	1,325.00	4,550	9	135	6
7	1,675.00	5,550	10	233	7
8	2,050.00	6,575	11	268	8
9	2,425.00	7,500	12	211	9
10	2,825.00	8,450	13	117	10
11	3,225.00	9,325	13	323	11
12	3,625.00	10,150	14	108	12
13	4,050.00	10.975	14	242	13
14	4,450.00	11,675	14	309	14
15	4,900.00	12,450	15	29	15
16	5,325.00	13,100	15	58	16
17	5,775.00	13,775	15	84	17
18	6,225.00	14,400	15	85	18
19	6,675.00	14,975	15	65	19
20	7,125.00	15,525	15	26	20
Age 60	9,400.00	17,825	14	41	Age 60
Age 65	11,725.00	19,625	12	319	Age 65

LIFE INSURANCE APPLICATION (PART I)

ABC LIFE INSURANCE COMPANY 100 Ordinary Ave., New York, N.Y. 00000

Application for New Policy □

If not Application for New Policy:

Change Policy No. . . . . (Give Details)

Amend Application Dated . . . . 19 . . . . . .

Exercise Guaranteed Insurability Option □, or

Conversion Privilege □, in Pol. No. . . . .

Reinstate Policy No. . . . .

1. (a) PROPOSED INSURED? . . . . (b) Soc. Sec. or Soc. Ins. No.? . . . . (c) Sex? M □ F □

   (d) Birth Date? Mo. . . . . . . Day . . . . . . Yr. . . . . . . (e) State (Prov.) & Country of Birth? . . . .

   (f) ADDRESS? (Complete address, including any apartment number, and Zip or Postal Code.)

   (i) Residence . . . . (v) Time at Residence

   . . . . Yrs. . . . . Mos.

   (ii) Business . . . . (vi) Time with Employer

   (incl. Employer's Name) . . . . Yrs. . . . . Mos.

   (iii) Previous Res. (within 2 yrs.) . . . . (vii) Mail Address

   (iv) Previous Bus. (within 2 yrs.) . . . . Res. □ Bus. □

   (g) OCCUPATION(S) (i) Present . . . .

   AND DUTIES? (ii) Previous (within 2 yrs.) . . . .

   (h) TELEPHONE NUMBER? (. . .). . . .-. . . . . Best time to call, 8 a.m.–5 p.m. (EST)? . . . a.m. . . . p.m.

2. (a) PLAN? (APL□) . . . .

   (b) FACE AMOUNT? $ . . . ., AND/OR scheduled . . . . (mode) premiums of $ . . . .

   (c) RIDERS? ADB $. . . . . WP □ $. . . . . . . GI □ $. . . . . . . FAMILY{SCI □, CI □} . . . .

   Units (See Q. 9) . . . . CPB □ (See Q. 13) OCI □ (See Q. 13) Other . . . .

   (d) DIV. OPTION? Pd.up Addn. □, Accum. □, Prem. □, Cash □, 1 Yr. Term □

   (e) Other Life Insurance on Prop. Insured? (If none, enter "0".) In Force $ . . . . Pending $ . . . .

   (f) "Non-Transferable" □ (g) Automatic Option at Lapse is Reduced Paid-up Insurance □

3. PREMIUM MODE? Ann □ Semi □ Qrtly □ PAC □ Other . . . .

4. POLICY DATE? If no "other date" is shown, policy date is: (a) later date of Part I and any required Part II, if cash paid with Part I; (b) the policy's date of issue, if cash not paid; or (c) the option date, if insurability option being exercised. Other Date: . . . . 19 . . . . .

5. REPLACEMENT? Is the policy applied for intended to replace, in whole or in part, any existing insurance or annuity? Yes □ No □

   If "Yes", (a) Company? . . . . (b) Policy number, if known? . . . .

   (c) Plan? . . . . (d) Amount replaced? . . . . (e) Termination date? . . . .

6. BENEFICIARY? (Subject to change. Complete (a), (b), or (c), as applicable.)

   (a) 1st: . . . ., Spouse (b) For SCI or CI: Standard □; CI Special
   2nd: Children born of Insured's marriage to spouse Standard □ (give spouse's full name)
   named above. . . . .

   (c) Give Full Name and Relationship to Proposed Insured. . . . .

   . . . .

7. CURRENT HEALTH? Answer, so far as known, for all persons proposed for coverage in Questions 1, 9 and 13. If "Yes" to Ques. 7(a) or 7(b), cash cannot be paid with application.

	Yes	No
(a) Has any such person been in a hospital or other medical facility for more than a total of 5 days within the last 2 years?	□	□
(b) Is any such person consulting with, or intending to consult with, a physician for any illness, or for symptoms of undiagnosed origin? (Do not include colds, minor virus infections, minor injuries, or normal pregnancy.)	□	□

8. (a) Answer if cash intended to be paid with this application. Is it agreed that cash will be received subject to the terms of the attached receipt, that any coverage will be provided only as stated in the attached receipt and only if all conditions to coverage are met, and that any such coverage will be temporary and limited in amount? .... □   □
If "No", or if Questions 7(b) or 7(c) are answered "Yes", cash cannot be paid.

(b) CASH PAID? $ .... (If amending application, cash previously paid: $ ....)

9. ANSWER IF APPLYING FOR FAMILY INSURANCE COVERAGE (SCI or CI) ON SPOUSE OR CHILDREN (also answer Question 12).

(a) Spouse, Unmarried Dependent Children Residing with Prop. Insured?	(b) Relationship to Prop. Insured?	(c) Born Mo., Day, Yr.?
....	....	....
....	....	....
....	....	....

10. ANSWER FOR ANY PROPOSED OR OTHER COVERED INSURED UNDER 14 YRS. 6 MOS. (explain any "No")   Yes   No

(a) Is Applicant a parent or legal guardian of Proposed Insured or other Covered Insured (attach proof of guardianship)? .... □   □

(b) Is Applicant employed and providing Proposed Insured's or Other Covered Insured's main support? .... □   □

(c) Is all life insurance in force and pending on Applicant and Spouse at least 2 times that on Proposed or Other Insured? .... □   □

(d) Are all other children in family insured or to be insured for an amount at least equal to that on Prop. or Other Insured? .... □   □

11. ANSWER IF ISSUE AGE OF PROPOSED OR OTHER COVERED INSURED (SEE QUES. 13) WOULD BE 20 OR OVER ON POLICY DATE.

Has Prop. Insured or Other Covered Insured smoked in last 12 months? Prop. Insured: Yes □, No □; Other Covered Insured: Yes □, No □

					Last Smoked Cigarettes	Never Smoked Cigarettes
If "Yes", indicate:	Pipe	Cigars	Cigarettes	If "No", indicate:		
For Proposed Insured	□	□	.... packs per	For Proposed Insured	Mo. .... Yr.	□
For Other Insured	□	□	.... packs per	For Other Insured	Mo. .... Yr.	□

12. ANSWER, SO FAR AS KNOWN, FOR ALL PERSONS PROPOSED FOR COVERAGE IN QUESTIONS 1, 9 AND 13.
Within last 2 years, has any such person: Yes   No

(a) piloted an aircraft, driven a motorcycle or snowmobile, engaged in motorized racing, scuba or sky diving, hang-gliding, ballooning, ultralight flying, mountaineering, or rodeo riding, or does any such person intend to do so? .... □   □
If "Yes", submit Form 0123 and give name if not Prop. Insured: ....

(b) been arrested (not counting dismissed charges) or had his or her driver's license suspended or revoked? .... □   □
If "Yes", submit Confidential Form 56789 and give name if not Prop. Insured: ....

(c) been declined for issue, reinstatement, or renewal of any type of Life or Health Insurance? □   □
If "Yes", give name, company, and reason, if known: ....

13. APPLICANT (IF NOT PROPOSED INSURED), CPB APPLICANT OR OTHER COVERED INSURED?

(a) Full Name & Relationship to Prop. Insured: ....

(b) Address: Same as–Ques. 1 Res. □, Ques. 1 Bus. □, Other (incl. Zip/Postal Code & Name of Employer)   Mail Address

Residence ....   Res. □

Business ....   Bus. □

(c) ANSWER IF PERSON NAMED IN QUES. 13(a) IS CPB APPLICANT OR OTHER COVERED INSURED.

Note: CPB Applicant or Other Covered Insured is a "person proposed for coverage." Answer Ques. 11-12, as applicable, for that person.

(i) Birth Date? Mo. ..... Day ..... Year ....   (ii) Sex? M □, F □
(iii) Soc. Sec. (Ins.) No.? .... (iv) State (Prov.) & Country of Birth ? ....
(v) Occupation(s) Present ....
       and Duties? Previous (within 2 yrs.) ....
(vi) Amount of Insurance applied for if Other Covered Insured? $ ....
(vii) Other Life Insurance on Other Covered Insured? (if none, enter "0".) In Force $ .. Pending $ ..

14. OWNER NOT THE PROPOSED INSURED (if a corporation, give place and year incorporated).
    (a) OWNER? [Prop. Insured will be the Owner unless otherwise indicated.] Applicant ☐
    Other (Full Name & Relationship to Prop. Insured) ....

    (b) Mail Address? As indicated in Ques. 1 ☐, 13(b) ☐, Other ....

    (c) Soc. Sec. (Ins.) or Tax No.? ....

    (d) SUCCESSOR OWNER? Prop. Insured ☐, Other ....

15. AMENDING APPLICATION PREVIOUSLY SUBMITTED.
    Since the date the application for the policy (including any Part II) has been completed, has any person proposed for coverage:

    (a) been admitted to a hospital, sanitarium, or other medical facility ? Yes ☐   No ☐   If "Yes" to (a), submit a new application Part II.

    (b) had any illness, or consulted any physician or practitioner for any reason? Yes ☐   No ☐   If "Yes" to (b), give full details.

16. EXERCISING A GUARANTEED INSURABILITY OPTION.

    (a) Option Date? ...., 19 ....   (b) Scheduled Option Date ☐; Alternate Option Date ☐
    (c) If Alternate Option Date: date of marriage ☐, birth ☐, adoption☐? Mo. .... Day .... Year ....

17. EXERCISING CONVERSION PRIVILEGE FROM INDIVIDUAL COVERAGE TO PERMANENT INSURANCE.

    The Insurer is requested to:

    (a) ISSUE the policy applied for on (check one): Attained Age Basis ☐, Original Age Basis ☐ and

    (b) TERMINATE OR MODIFY the following, when the policy applied for takes effect, in the policy(ies) listed on page 1 of application:
        (i) All coverage on: term policy ☐; term rider ☐; 1 Yr. Term Dividend Option ☐;
        life of covered family member ☐

        (ii) Part of the insurance on: term policy (with pro rata reduction of any ADB) ☐; term rider ☐; and reduce the amount of insurance on the term policy or rider to $ ....

    Answer only if the coverage to be converted includes Waiver of Premium Benefit: Does the Insured have any disability which prevents him or her from being actively at work or attending school? Yes ☐ No ☐ If "Yes", give dates and details.

THOSE PERSONS WHO SIGN BELOW AGREE THAT:

1. All of the statements which are part of the application are correctly recorded, and are complete and true to the best of the knowledge and belief of those persons who made them.

2. No agent or medical examiner has any right to accept risks, make or change contracts, or give up any of ABC's rights or requirements.

3. "Cash Paid" with the application, with respect to a new policy or additional benefit, provides a limited amount of temporary coverage for up to 60 days, if the terms and conditions of the receipt are met. Temporary coverage is not provided if a policy or benefit is applied for under the terms of a conversion privilege or a guaranteed insurability option, or if reinstatement is applied for.

4. To put a policy or benefit issued in response to this application in force, the policy or written evidence of the benefit must be delivered to the Applicant and the full first premium paid while all persons to be covered are living. If temporary coverage, with respect to a policy or benefit, is not in effect at time of delivery, there must not have been any material change in the insurability of those persons, as described by the statements in the application; this means that these statements must still be complete and true if made at that time.

However, if the policy or benefit is being applied for under the terms of a conversion privilege or guaranteed insurability option, and ABC's approval is not required to put it in force, the policy or benefit will take effect as soon as the requirements of that privilege or option have been met.

Dated at _____

on _____, 19 ___
I certify I have truly and accurately recorded all answers given to me.

Witness _____
                                    Agent

_____
Countersigned by Licensed resident agent (if required)

_____
                        Signature of Applicant

_____
     Signature of Proposed Insured if other than Applicant

_____
Spouse, Other Covered Insured or Other Required Signature

Glossary

ABA. American Bankers Association.

absolute assignment. In life insurance, the type of assignment that transfers complete ownership of the policy permanently.

accidental death and dismemberment (AD&D) rider. Rider (or endorsement) that adds to a policy both an accidental death benefit and a benefit for dismemberment.

accidental death benefit (ADB) rider. A supplementary benefit rider which provides for an amount of money in addition to the face amount of a life insurance policy. This additional amount is payable only if the insured dies as the result of an accident.

accumulation period. The period during which premiums are payable on a deferred annuity.

accumulation units. The term used to express ownership shares in a variable annuity's separate-account fund. The premiums paid by the purchaser of a variable annuity are credited to the purchaser's account in the form of accumulation units. The value of these accumulation units is tied to the market value of the separate-account investments of variable annuity funds held by the insurance company.

actuary. A technical expert in life insurance, particularly in mathematics. The actuary applies the theory of probability to the business of insurance and is responsible for the calculation of premiums, policy reserves, and other values.

ADB. Accidental death benefit.

adjustable life insurance policy. A life insurance contract designed specifically to allow policyowners to adjust the amount of their coverage and the amount of their premium as their needs change.

adverse selection. *See* **antiselection**.

agency relationship. In law, the relationship between two parties by which one party (the agent) is authorized to perform certain acts for the other party (the principal).

agent. In insurance, a salesperson who represents a life insurance company for the purpose of soliciting applications, collecting initial premiums, and servicing insurance contracts. (Also known as a **life underwriter, field underwriter, insurance agent, soliciting agent,** and **sales representative**.) *See also* **agency relationship** and **home service agent**.

age of majority. The age at which a person has the legal capacity to enter into a contract.

aleatory contract. A contract under which one party provides something of value to another party in exchange for a conditional promise – that is, a promise that the other party will perform a stated act *if* a specified, uncertain event occurs.

American Bankers Association (ABA) Assignment Form #10. A standard collateral assignment form available for use by a policyowner and a lender/creditor to assign a life insurance policy as collateral for a loan.

annually renewable term (ART). *See* **yearly renewable term**.

annuitant. The person who receives annuity benefit payments.

annuity. Any series of payments made or received at regular intervals *or* a contract that provides for a series of periodic payments.

annuity certain. An annuity which provides a benefit amount payable for a specified period of time regardless of whether the annuitant lives or dies.

annuity period. The time span between the benefit payments made under an annuity contract.

annuity units. The term used to express the annuitant's share of the funds in a variable annuity account after the accumulation period has ended. When a variable annuity's benefit payments are scheduled to begin, annuity units are purchased with accumulation units.

antiselection. The tendency of persons who possess a greater likelihood of loss to apply for or continue insurance to a greater extent than others. These persons are also more inclined to take advantage of favorable options such as renewal and conversion of term life insurance policies. (Also referred to as **adverse selection** and **selection against the insurer**.)

applicant. The party applying for an insurance policy.

application. A form which must be completed by an individual or other party who applies for insurance to provide the insurance company with information relevant to its decision to accept or reject the risk.

APS. Attending Physician's Statement.

ART. Annually renewable term.

assessment method. An early method of funding life insurance under which members of the plan were charged in advance the amount estimated to be required to pay each year's claims. (Also referred to as **pre-death assessment method**.)

assets. All of the things of value which are owned by a company or person.

assignee. The party to whom all or certain rights are transferred under an absolute or collateral assignment.

assignment. The legal transfer of ownership rights under a life insurance policy or other contract from one party to another; also the document effecting the transfer.

assignor. The person or party who executes an assignment.

Association of Superintendents of Insurance. Organization of Canadian provincial-level regulators equivalent to the United States National Association of Insurance Commissioners.

attained age conversion. Conversion of insurance from one form to another (such as from term life insurance to whole life insurance) at a premium rate that is based on the age the insured person has reached at the time the conversion takes place.

Attending Physician's Statement (APS). A form filled out by a medical doctor who has treated an insured or a proposed insured for an illness or injury. The form provides the insurance company with information relevant to underwriting the risk or settling a claim.

automatic premium loan (APL). A policy loan authorized in advance by the policyowner to be used only to pay a premium which remains unpaid at the end of a grace period.

aviation exclusion. A life insurance policy provision stating that the policy proceeds will not be paid if the insured's death results from aviation-related activities.

back-date. To make the effective date of an insurance policy earlier than the date of the application. (Also referred to as **dateback**.)

bargaining contract. A contract under which both (or all) parties, as equals, set the terms and conditions of the contract.

beneficiary. The person, persons, or other party designated to receive policy proceeds.

beneficiary for value. Under early Canadian legislation, a beneficiary who was named as beneficiary in return for providing consideration to the person whose life is insured.

bilateral contract. A contract under which both parties can be compelled under law to perform what they have promised.

binding receipt. In insurance, a premium receipt which immediately binds the insurance company to a temporary contract of insurance.

Blue Cross plan. A regionally operated hospital expense plan which generally provides benefits on a "service-type" basis. Each regional Blue Cross plan is affiliated with the National Blue Cross and Blue Shield Association.

Blue Shield plan. A regionally operated physician's expense plan. Each regional Blue Shield plan is affiliated with the National Blue Cross and Blue Shield Association.

bond. A certificate which promises to repay a lender a specified sum at a given date in the future.

Buyer's Guide. A publication given as a consumer's guide to persons contemplating purchasing an insurance policy.

Buy-sell agreement. An arrangement whereby partners in a business or stockholders in a small corporation agree that, on the death or withdrawal of one partner or stockholder from the business, his or her portion of the business will be sold to the remaining partners or stockholders, and those remaining will be obligated to purchase the portion of the business left by the withdrawing or deceased partner or stockholder. It is usually accompanied by life insurance on each partner or stockholder.

calendar year deductible. A deductible that applies to any eligible medical expenses incurred by the insured during any one calendar year.

Canada Pension Plan (CPP). A plan which primarily provides retirement income and long-term disability income benefits to residents of Canadian provinces other than Quebec.

cancellable. An individual health insurance policy that can be cancelled by the insurer at any time.

cash surrender value. *See* **cash value.**

cash value. The amount of money which the policyowner will receive as a refund if the policyowner cancels the coverage and surrenders the policy to the company. (Also referred to as **surrender value,** and **cash surrender value.**)

certificate holder. An insured member of a group insurance plan.

certificate of insurance. A document which is given to insured members of a group insurance plan and which outlines the plan's coverage and the member's rights.

change-of-occupation provision. An individual health insurance policy provision that grants the insurer the right to adjust a policy's premium or benefits when the insured changes occupations.

***chose* in action.** Intangible property that provides or represents evidence of value or desirability.

***chose* in possession.** Tangible property which has value in and of itself.

claim. A request for payment under the terms of a policy.

claimant. Person or party making a formal request for payment of benefits due under the terms of an insurance contract.

claims examiner. Insurance company employee who has responsibility for conducting a claim examination.

class designation. A beneficiary designation which identifies a certain group of persons, rather than naming each person.

class of policies. A class consisting of all policies of a particular type or all policies issued to a particular group of insureds.

clean-up fund. In life insurance, a lump-sum life insurance death benefit designed to pay outstanding debts and final expenses.

collateral assignment. The type of assignment that transfers only some ownership rights under a contract, generally for a temporary period.

coinsurance. A method of expense participation which requires that the insured pay a specified percentage of all the eligible medical expenses (in excess of the deductible) which he or she incurs as the result of a sickness or injury. (Also referred to as **percentage participation.**)

common disaster clause. Insurance policy wording which states that the primary beneficiary must survive the insured by a specified period, such as 15 or 60 days, in order to receive the policy proceeds.

community property states. States in which each spouse is legally entitled to an equal share of the income earned and, under some circumstances, property acquired by the other during the period of marriage.

commutative contracts. A legal agreement under which each party specifies in advance the values which will be exchanged; each party generally exchanges items of equal value.

compound interest. Interest earned on interest. The amount of interest earned by investing money that has been earned as interest.

comprehensive health insurance policy. A health insurance policy that combines the features and benefits of a hospital-surgical expense policy and the features and benefits of a major-medical policy, thus providing complete health insurance protection.

comprehensive major medical. A form of health insurance coverage which provides complete and substantial medical expense coverage under one policy. Comprehensive major medical coverage is usually issued under a group health insurance plan.

conditionally renewable. A health insurance policy that grants an insurer a limited right to refuse to renew a policy at the end of a premium payment period.

conditional receipt. A premium receipt given to an applicant which makes the insurance effective only if or when a specified condition is met. Conditional receipts may be of the insurability type or of the approval type.

consideration. Something of value, tangible or intangible, exchanged by the parties to a contract.

Consumer Price Index (CPI). A statistical measure of the change in the cost of goods and services purchased by typical consumers. This measure is expressed as a percentage of the cost of these goods and services at a certain time. (Also referred to as a **cost-of-living index.**)

contestable period. The period of time during which an insurer may contest (dispute or deny) the validity of a policy in a court of law. The length of the period is specified in the incontestability provision of a life insurance policy.

contingency reserve. A reserve against unusual, unexpected conditions that may occur.

contingent beneficiary. The party designated to receive policy proceeds if the primary beneficiary should predecease the person whose life is insured. (Also referred to as a **secondary beneficiary** or **successor beneficiary.**)

contingent payee. The party who will receive any policy proceeds that are still payable under a settlement option at the time of the primary payee's death.

contract. A legally binding agreement between two or more parties.

contract of adhesion. A contract which is prepared by one party and which must be accepted or rejected as a whole by the other party, without any bargaining between the parties to the contract.

contract of indemnity. A contract in which the amount of the benefit is based on the actual amount of financial loss as determined at the time of loss.

contributory plan. A group insurance (life, health, or pension) plan which calls for participants to pay a portion of the cost.

conversion privilege. The right to change (convert) insurance coverage from one policy to another. For example, the right to change from an individual term insurance policy to an individual whole life insurance policy or the right to change from a group policy to an individual policy when group insurance coverage terminates.

corporate stock. A document that represents ownership (equity) in a corporation. A share of stock is a share of ownership in an incorporated organization.

corridor deductible. An expense participation feature found in major medical policies that supplement hospital-surgical expense policies. A flat amount which the insured must pay above the amount paid by his or her hospital-surgical expense policy before any benefits are payable under the major medical policy.

CPI. Consumer Price Index.

CPP. Canada Pension Plan.

credit life insurance. A type of decreasing term life insurance designed to pay the balance due on a loan should the borrower-insured die.

creditor group. *See* **group creditor life.**

date back. *See* **back-date.**

death certificate. A document that lists the cause of a person's death; it is signed by a physician, issued by a local coroner or other government official, and usually has some type of government seal.

debit agent. *See* **home service agent.**

debit insurance. *See* **industrial insurance.**

deductible. A flat amount which the insured must pay before the insurance company will make any benefit payments under a policy.

deferred annuity. Those annuities under which the annuity payment period is scheduled to begin at some future date.

deferred compensation plan. A plan established by an employer to provide benefits to an employee at a later date, such as after retirement.

direct response marketing. A method of selling insurance products directly to the consumer without the aid of a salesperson. Direct mail, advertising in print and broadcast media, and telephone solicitation are commonly used methods.

disability income coverage. Health insurance under which benefits are payable in regular installments designed to replace some of the insured's income when he or she is totally disabled as defined in the policy.

dividend. *See* **policy dividend** and **experience refund.**

dividend addition. An amount of paid-up insurance purchased using policy dividends. (Also referred to as **paid-up addition.**)

dividend option. One of several choices available to the owner of a participating policy concerning the disposition of policy dividends.

divisible surplus. The portion of an insurance company's surplus which is available for distribution to the owners of the company's participating policies.

double indemnity. *See* **accidental death benefit.**

dread disease policy. *See* **limited coverage policy.**

eligibility period. In contributory group insurance plans, the period of time, usually 31 days in length, during which a new employee may apply for group insurance coverage.

eligibility requirements. The conditions a person must meet in order to be a participant in a group life insurance, health insurance, or retirement plan.

eligible expenses. Medical expenses for which a health insurance policy will provide benefits.

elimination period. A specific period of time, beginning at the onset of a disability, which must pass before any policy benefits will be paid. (Also referred to as a **waiting period.**)

Employee Retirement Income Security Act of 1974 (ERISA). A congressional act that established (1) standards relating to rights of pension plan participants, investment standards for pension plan assets, and the disclosure and reporting of plan provisions and funding, and (2) the Pension Benefit Guaranty Corporation (PBGC), in order to insure participants in certain types of pension plans against loss if their retirement plan becomes insolvent.

endorsement. *See* **rider.**

endorsement method. The method of changing a policy's beneficiary or owner which requires that the policy itself be returned to the insurer so that the change can be recorded directly onto the policy.

endowment insurance. An insurance contract that provides a benefit amount equivalent to the face amount of the policy regardless of whether the insured lives to the end of the policy's term *or* dies during the policy's term.

entire contract provision. Life insurance policy provision which states that the policy itself, along with a copy of the application for insurance, if attached, will constitute the entire contract.

ERISA. Employee Retirement Income Security Act of 1974.

estate taxes. Taxes on the money and property left by someone who has died.

expense participation. The means used by insurance companies to require an insured to pay some portion of the eligible medical expenses he or she incurs. Both deductibles and coinsurance are expense participation features.

experience rating. The method used by insurers to adjust a group's premium to reflect the group's actual claims experience.

experience refund. The portion of a group insurance premium which is refunded to a group policyholder whose claims experience is better than that which was expected when the premium was calculated. (Also called a **dividend.**)

extended term insurance. A nonforfeiture benefit under which the net cash value of the policy is used to purchase term insurance for the amount of coverage available under the original policy.

face amount. The amount stated in the policy as payable at the death of the insured or at the maturity of the contract. The amount is generally shown on the first (face) page of a policy. (Also referred to as **face value.**)

facility-of-payment clause. The policy wording which permits the insurance company to make payment of all or part of the proceeds of a life insurance policy to either a blood relative of the insured or to anyone who has a valid claim to those proceeds.

family income policy. A policy which combines whole life insurance with decreasing term insurance. The decreasing term insurance portion of the policy provides an income benefit which helps support a family for a specified, limited period of time.

family insurance policy. A life insurance policy that covers all the members of a family under one contract.

field underwriter. *See* **agent.**

first beneficiary. *See* **primary beneficiary.**

fixed amount option. A settlement option under which the insurance company uses the policy proceeds plus interest to pay a preselected sum in a series of annual or more frequent installments for as long as the proceeds (plus interest) last.

fixed period option. A settlement option under which the company pays the proceeds and interest in a series of annual or more frequent installments for a preselected period.

flexible premium annuity. A deferred annuity which gives the purchaser the right to vary the amount of each premium paid to the insurer during the accumulation period.

formal contract. A contract that is legally binding because of its form; a formal contract must be written and/or endorsed in a specific way, or issued with a legal seal attached.

fraudulent statement. A misstatement that was made with the intent to deceive and do harm to another party.

free examination period. The period of time after delivery of an insurance policy during which the policyowner may examine the policy and return it to the company for a full refund of the initial premium. (Also called **10-day free look**.)

funding vehicle. The means chosen to invest a pension plan's assets as they are accumulated.

grace period. The length of time (usually 31 days) after a premium is due and unpaid during which the policy, including all riders, remains in force. If a premium is paid during the grace period, the premium is considered to have been paid "on time."

gross premium. The total premium for a life insurance policy. The gross premium is composed of the net premium plus a loading for expenses.

group creditor life. Group insurance coverage wherein a master policy is issued to a creditor to cover the lives of current and future debtors of that creditor.

group insurance. The type of insurance which provides coverage for a group of people under one contract, called a master contract. The master contract is issued to the group policyholder, and the insured group members are not parties to the group contract.

guaranteed insurability (GI) rider. A rider that gives the policyowner the right to purchase additional insurance of the same type as the original policy on specified dates for specified amounts without supplying additional evidence of insurability.

guaranteed renewable. A health insurance policy that specifies that the insurer will renew the policy until the insured reaches a specified age, if premium payments are made when due. (Premium rates are not guaranteed.)

health insurance. Insurance that pays specified benefits if the person who is insured becomes sick or is injured. Health insurance coverage includes both medical expense coverages and disability income coverages.

health maintenance organization (HMO). An insurance-like plan for providing health care on a prepaid basis to subscribing members of the organization.

home service agent. A life insurance sales agent who is assigned by his or her company to a specific geographic territory; the home service agent is responsible for all new sales of home service products and for policyowner service to all owners of the company's home service products within the territory, whether or not that agent originally sold the policy.

home service system. A method of marketing insurance products which relies on agents both to sell specified products and to provide premium collection and other policyowner service functions within a geographically defined area.

hospital confinement policy. A health insurance policy which provides a predetermined flat benefit amount for each day an insured is hospitalized; the amount does not vary according to the amount of medical expenses the insured incurs. (Also called **hospital indemnity policy.**)

hospital indemnity policy. *See* **hospital confinement policy.**

hospital-surgical expense policy. A health insurance policy which provides benefits related directly to hospitalization costs and associated medical expenses incurred by an insured for treatment of a sickness or injury.

immediate annuity. An annuity under which income payments begin one annuity period (e.g., one month or one year) after the annuity is purchased.

income protection insurance policy. A disability income policy which specifies that an insured is disabled if that person suffers an income loss caused by a disability.

incontestability provision. Life insurance policy wording that provides a time limit on the insurer's right to contest a policy's validity based on misstatements in the application.

indexed life insurance. A whole life plan of insurance that provides for the face amount of the policy and, correspondingly, the premium rate to automatically increase every year based on an increase in the Consumer Price Index.

Individual Retirement Account (IRA). A retirement savings plan which allows most United States citizens to make contributions to an approved account on a tax-sheltered basis. The contributions are taxable as income only when paid out after retirement.

industrial insurance. The type of individual life insurance which is available for face amounts less than a specified maximum, such as $2,000 or $3,000. Industrial insurance is marketed through the home service system, and premiums may be paid as frequently as weekly. (Also referred to as *debit insurance*.)

in-force. In effect; an insurance policy that is in force will provide a benefit if the insured loss occurs.

informal contract. A contract whose enforceability does not depend on the form in which it is written, but rather on whether it meets certain prerequisites which give rise to an enforceable contract.

inspection receipt. A receipt stating that the policy has not been "delivered" even though it has been placed in the hands of the policyowner. Insurance protection is not in effect during the inspection period.

inspection report. A report made by an investigating agency which provides the results of an investigation of such underwriting factors as the applicant's lifestyle, activities, occupation, and economic standing.

institutional advertising. Advertising which promotes an idea or "institution," without attempting to promote the immediate sale of a specific product.

insurable interest. A person's or party's interest – financial or emotional – in the continuing life of an individual; a person or party must have an insurable interest in the life of a proposed insured in order to purchase an insurance policy on the proposed insured's life.

insurance. A means of providing or purchasing protection against some of the economic consequences of loss.

insured. The person whose life is insured under the policy. Under the Uniform Life Insurance Act of Canada, the insured is defined as the person who applies for the insurance and may therefore be someone other than the person whose life is insured.

insurer. The party in an insurance contract that promises to pay a benefit if a specified loss occurs.

interest. Money paid for the use of money; the amount of money earned when an insurance company invests the premium dollars that have been paid for insurance policies.

interest option. The settlement option under which the proceeds are temporarily left on deposit with the insurance company and the interest earned on those proceeds is paid out annually, semiannually, quarterly, or monthly to the beneficiary-payee.

interpleader. A method or procedure for settling a claim under which the insurance company pays the policy proceeds to a court, stating that the company cannot determine the correct party to whom the proceeds should be paid, and asks the court to decide the proper recipient. The court examines the evidence, determines the proper party to receive the proceeds, and awards the money.

IRA. Individual Retirement Account.

irrevocable beneficiary. A named beneficiary whose rights to life insurance policy proceeds are vested and whose rights cannot be revoked (cancelled) by the policyowner, unless the beneficiary consents.

joint and survivor annuity. An annuity under which the series of payments is made to two or more annuitants. The annuity payments continue until both or all of the annuitants have died. (Also referred to as **joint and last survivorship annuity.**)

joint and survivorship option. A life income settlement option under which payments will be made to two or more payees. These payments will continue until both or all the named payees are deceased.

joint life insurance policy. An insurance policy that covers two lives and which generally provides for payment of the proceeds on the death of the first insured to die.

juvenile insurance policy. An insurance policy which is issued on the life of a child but which is owned by an adult.

Keogh Act. Unofficial name for the Self-employed Individuals Tax Retirement Act of 1962.

key-person insurance. Life insurance purchased by a business on the life of a person (usually an employee) whose continued participation in the business is necessary to the firm's success and whose death or disability would cause financial loss to the company.

lapse. Termination of a policy due to non-payment of renewal premiums. If the policy has cash value, then the policy's insurance coverage may remain effective as extended term or reduced paid-up insurance through the use of a nonforfeiture option.

law of large numbers. The theory of probability which specifies that the larger the number of observations made of a particular event, the more likely it will be that the observed results produce an estimate of the "true" probability of the event's occurring.

legal actions provision. An individual health insurance policy provision which (1) limits the time period during which a claimant who is in disagreement with a settlement offered by an insurer may sue the insurance company to collect the amount the claimant believes is owed to him or her and (2) specifies that no suit may be brought against the insurer until 60 days have passed since a claim was submitted.

legal capacity. The ability, under law, to make a legal contract. An insurer acquires its legal capacity to make a contract by being licensed or authorized to do business by the proper regulating authorities; an individual usually has the legal capacity to enter into a contract as long as he or she is of legal age and mentally competent.

legal reserves. *See* **policy reserves**.

legal reserve system. The pricing system now in use by most life insurance companies.

level premium system. A pricing system whereby the purchaser (policyowner) pays the same premium rate each year of a policy's term.

liability insurance. A kind of insurance which provides a benefit payable on behalf of a covered party who is held legally responsible (liable) for harming others or their property.

life annuity. An annuity under which benefit payments are made by the insurer at least until the death of the annuitant.

life contingency. Refers to a risk undertaken by an insurer that involves uncertainty because of estimating the duration of human life.

life income option. A settlement option under which the company uses the proceeds and interest to pay a series of annual or more frequent installments over the entire lifetime of the person designated to receive the policy benefit.

life income with period certain annuity. A life annuity which both guarantees that annuity benefits will be paid until the annuitant dies *and* guarantees that the annuity payments will be made for at least a certain period, even if the annuitant dies before the end of that period.

life income with period certain option. A life insurance policy settlement option which functions in the same manner as a life income with a period certain annuity.

life income with refund annuity. *See* **refund annuity**.

life insurance. A type of insurance which provides a sum of money if the person who is insured dies while the policy is in effect.

limited coverage (dread disease) policy. A type of medical expense policy that is designed to cover only those medical expenses incurred by an insured who has contracted a specified disease, such as cancer, which is named in the policy.

loading. The total amount which is added to the net premium in consideration of all of the insurer's costs of doing business.

loss rate. The number and timing of losses that will occur in a given group of insureds while the coverage is in force.

major medical policy. A medical expense policy which provides broad coverage both for hospital expenses and outpatient expenses. Major medical policies have few limitations and high maximum benefit amounts.

manifestation of assent. The appearance, to any reasonable person, that there was agreement between the parties involved in a particular contract.

marketing. The complete function of determining consumer needs, designing products and services to meet those needs, and establishing methods of promoting and distributing those products and services to the public.

master contract. A life insurance policy that insures a number of people under a single insurance contract; a contract between an insurance company and a group policyholder in which the individuals insured are not parties to the contract.

material misrepresentation. In insurance, a misrepresentation that is relevant to the company's acceptance of the risk because, if the truth had been known, the insurance company would not have issued the policy or would have issued the policy only on a different basis, such as for a higher premium or for a lower benefit amount.

matured endowment. An endowment insurance policy that has reached the end of its term during the lifetime of the insured, and therefore its face amount is payable.

MDO. Monthly debit ordinary.

Medicaid. A government-sponsored health insurance program in the United States which provides payment for medical expenses and hospital care for the poor.

medical application. An insurance application which includes a section which must be filled out by a physician following an examination of the proposed insured.

medical expense coverage. A form of health insurance which provides benefits for the treatment of sickness or injury.

Medicare. A United States government program that provides medical expense coverage to persons over age 65 and to certain other classes of persons, as specified by Congress.

member plans. Autonomous, regional plans (organizations) of the national Blue Cross and Blue Shield.

minor. A person who has not attained the legal age to make a contract.

misstatement of age provision. Individual life insurance policy wording which specifies that if the age of the insured is misstated, and this misstatement has resulted in an incorrect premium amount for the amount of insurance purchased, then the face amount of the policy will be adjusted to the amount the premium actually paid would have purchased had the insured's age been stated correctly.

mode of premium payment. The frequency with which premiums are paid, e.g., annually, quarterly, monthly.

model bill. A sample bill developed by the National Association of Insurance Commissioners. States may adopt the model bill into law exactly as written or use the model bill as the basis for developing their own legislation. Also referred to as **model act** and **model law.**

monthly debit ordinary (MDO). Monthly-premium ordinary life insurance sold and serviced by home service agents.

morbidity rate. The relative incidence of sickness and injury occurring among a given group of people.

morbidity table. A chart that shows the rate of sickness and injury occurring among given groups of people categorized by age.

mortality. Death; the relative incidence of death.

mortality charge. The cost of the insurance protection element of a universal life insurance policy. This mortality charge is based on the net amount at risk under the policy, the insured's risk classification at the time the policy was originally purchased, and the insured's current age.

mortality experience. Actual number of deaths occurring in a given group of people.

mortality table. A chart which displays the rate of mortality by age among a given group of people.

mortgage redemption policy. A form of decreasing term insurance which covers the life of a person who takes out a mortgage so that if death occurs during the term of insurance, the policy proceeds will approximate the remaining amount of the mortgage loan.

mutual assent. Agreement to the terms of the contract by the parties to the contract.

mutual benefit method. An early method of funding life insurance formerly used by mutual benefit societies (e.g., fraternal orders or guilds) under which the promised death benefit was provided by charging participating members an equal amount after the death of an insured member. (Also known as the **post-death assessment method.**)

mutual company. A life insurance company owned by policyowners rather than stockholders.

National Association of Insurance Commissioners (NAIC). A voluntary organization composed of United States state insurance commissioners who exchange information and promote standardization of insurance legislation and regulation.

necessaries. Items needed to sustain well-being, such as food, housing, and clothing; necessities of life.

net amount at risk. The difference between the face amount of a policy – the death benefit – and the policy's reserve at the end of a policy year.

net cash value. The amount the policyowner will actually receive when surrendering a policy for its cash value. The net cash value is the cash value, minus such items as policy loans, and plus such items as accumulated dividends.

net premium. A premium rate which is based only on mortality rates and interest; a premium rate which has been calculated without allowance for the insurer's projected expenses.

noncancellable policy. A health insurance policy for which the premium cannot be changed (raised) by the insurer and which is guaranteed renewable.

noncontributory plan. A group insurance plan for which the insured members are not required to pay any portion of the cost of the plan.

nonforfeiture benefits. Cash or insurance benefits available to the owner of a policy which has a cash value.

nonforfeiture options. The choices available to a policyowner concerning the methods under which the owner can apply the policy's cash value when the policy lapses.

non-guaranteed premium life insurance policy. A whole life policy which specifies both a maximum potential premium rate and the premium rate which will actually be paid by the policyowner for a specified period of time after the policy is purchased. The premium rate may be changed by the insurer, after the specified period expires, but the new premium cannot exceed the maximum specified. (Also sometimes called a **flexible-premium policy** or **variable-premium policy.**)

nonmedical application. An application form for life or health insurance that does not include a section which must be filled out by a physician or a paramedical service employee.

nonparticipating policy. A life insurance policy which does not grant the policyowner the right to policyowner dividends.

Old Age Security Act (OAS). Canadian legislation that provides a pension to virtually all citizens who are age 65 or older.

Old Age, Survivors, Disability and Health Insurance Act (OASDHI). United States legislation which provides primarily long-term disability income coverage and a pension to nearly all people employed in the United States. Commonly referred to as **Social Security**.

optionally renewable policy. An individual health insurance policy which is renewable on a policy anniversary only at the option of the insurer.

optional modes of settlement. Choices given the policyowner or the beneficiary with respect to the method by which the insurer will pay policy proceeds.

ordinary life insurance. The type of individual life insurance which is available in relatively unrestricted maximum amounts, though generally the face amount must be at least a specified minimum amount. Premiums for ordinary life insurance may be paid monthly, or less frequently.

original age conversion. Converting a term policy to a whole life policy at a premium rate based on the age of the insured at the time the term policy was purchased.

overinsurance provision. A health insurance policy provision which specifies that the benefits payable under the policy will be reduced in cases in which the insured is overinsured.

paid-up policy. An in-force policy for which no further premium payments are required.

paid-up addition. *See* **dividend addition.**

paramedical examination. A physical examination conducted by a medical technician, physician's assistant (P.A.) nurse, etc., rather than by a medical doctor.

participating policy. A policy under which policy dividends may be paid to the owner of the policy.

partnership. A business owned and run by two or more people.

payee. The person to whom benefits are payable under a supplementary contract.

payroll deduction. A premium payment method under which an individual policyowner's employer deducts insurance premiums directly from the employee's paycheck and sends the premium to the insurer.

peer review groups. Third-party reviewers comprised of local physicians who help solve claim disputes and promote fair and ethical practices in the health-care industry.

pension. A life income payable to a person who has retired from employment or service in the armed forces.

per cause deductible. A deductible that applies to all eligible medical expenses caused by a single illness or injury.

percentage participation. *See* **coinsurance.**

period certain. The specified period during which the insurer unconditionally guarantees that benefit payments will be made to someone.

periodic level premium annuity. A deferred annuity under which the purchaser of the annuity pays equal premium amounts for the annuity at regular intervals, such as monthly or annually, until the date the benefit payments are scheduled to begin.

physical examination provision. A health insurance policy provision that grants the insurer the right to have an insured who has submitted a claim examined by a doctor of the insurer's choice at the insurer's expense.

plan administration. Performing the various administrative tasks necessary to maintain a pension or other group insurance plan.

plan document. A retirement plan sponsor's agreement with plan participants regarding the benefits the participants are to receive and the requirements they must meet to become entitled to these benefits.

plan participants. Employees, union members, or other participants in a group insurance or pension program sponsored by an employer, union, or other organization.

plan sponsors. Employers, unions, and other organizations that establish retirement programs.

policy. The contract between the insurance company and the policyowner under which the insurance company agrees to pay the policy benefit when specific losses occur, provided the insurer receives the required premiums.

policy anniversary. The yearly anniversary of the date on which a policy was issued.

policy dividend. The share of divisible surplus that is payable to the owner of an individual participating policy. In group insurance, an **experience refund.**

policyholder. The employer or other party that applies for and is issued a group insurance contract. The owner of any insurance policy.

policy loan. A monetary advance made by a life insurance company to a policyowner which is secured by the cash value of the policy.

policyowner. The person or party who owns an individual insurance policy; often, the policyowner is also the person whose life is insured.

policy reserve. In life insurance, a liability account which measures the money which the insurance company has promised to pay in future claims. The term "policy reserve" is also often used to refer to the assets offsetting this liability account.

policy summary. A document, often in the form of a computer printout, which contains certain legally required data regarding the specific policy being considered by an applicant.

preauthorized check (PAC) method. A method of paying premiums under which the policyowner authorizes the insurance company to generate checks against the policyowner's account. The insurer then sends these checks directly to the policyowner's bank for payment when premiums are due.

pre-existing condition. An injury which occurred or a sickness which first appeared or manifested itself before the policy was issued and, generally, which was not disclosed on the application.

pre-existing conditions provision. A health insurance policy provision which states that until the insured has been covered under the policy for a certain period, the insurer will not pay benefits for any health conditions which were present before the policy was issued and, generally, which were not disclosed on the application.

preference beneficiary clause. Insurance policy wording which states that, if no specific beneficiary is named, the company will pay the policy proceeds in a stated order of preference according to a list which is included in the policy.

preferred beneficiary. A member of the class of beneficiaries provided for in early Canadian insurance legislation and which consisted of the husband, wife, children, parents, and grandchildren of the insured.

preferred risk. A person classified as an above-average risk because the person's physical condition, health history, occupation, and/or lifestyle indicate the probability of a lower-than-usual mortality rate. (Also called **superstandard risk.**)

premium. The payment, or one of a series of payments, required by the insurer to put an insurance policy in force and to keep it in force.

presumptive disability. A condition (e.g., total and permanent blindness, loss of two limbs, etc.) which, if present, automatically causes an insured to be considered totally disabled.

primary beneficiary. The party or parties who have first rights to receive policy proceeds when the proceeds become payable.

principal. In agency law, the party to a contract who authorizes an agent to act on its behalf; in finances, an amount loaned, the sum that earns interest.

probability. The likelihood that a given event will occur.

probationary period. A period of time which must pass after a new employee is hired before the new employee is eligible to enroll in the company's group insurance plan. (Also referred to as a **waiting period.**)

property insurance. A type of insurance which provides a financial benefit should covered property be damaged or lost because of fire, theft, accident, or other cause described in the policy.

pure endowment. A contract that pays a benefit only to those persons who survive a certain period of time; those who do not survive that period of time receive nothing.

Quebec Pension Plan (QPP). A plan which primarily provides retirement income and long-term disability income benefits to residents of Quebec.

rated policy. A policy issued to cover a person classified as a substandard risk. The policy's premium rate is higher than the rate for a standard policy, or the policy is issued with special limitations or exclusions or both.

real estate. Real property. Land and whatever is affixed to, erected on, or growing upon the land.

reasonable and customary charge. The prevailing charge made by surgeons of similar expertise for a similar procedure in a particular geographic area.

recording method. The way of changing a beneficiary designation which requires only that the policyowner notify the company in writing of the change in beneficiary in order for the change to be effective.

reduced paid-up insurance. A nonforfeiture option under which the net cash value of the policy is used as a net single premium to purchase paid-up life insurance of the same plan as the original policy.

refund annuity. An annuity which (1) provides benefits for the lifetime of the annuitant and (2) guarantees that at least the purchase price of the annuity will be paid out in benefits.

refund life income option. A settlement option which guarantees that the company will pay out at least the amount of the original policy proceeds; payments are made for the lifetime of the payee, but if the payee dies before the total amount the company has paid in installments equals the amount of the original policy proceeds payable, then the company pays the difference to the contingent payee.

Registered Retirement Savings Plan (RRSP). A plan enabling Canadian citizens to establish accounts to accumulate money toward retirement on a tax-sheltered basis.

reinstatement. The process by which a life insurance company puts back in force a policy which had lapsed because of nonpayment of renewal premiums.

reinsure. To transfer the risk of potential loss from one insurer to another insurer.

renewal premiums. Premiums payable after the initial (first) premium.

renewal provision. An individual life insurance policy provision that gives the policyowner the right to renew the insurance coverage at the end of the specified term without submitting evidence of continued insurability.

representation. A statement made by a person or party which is substantially true (as opposed to a **warranty**, which must be literally true).

residual disability. A disability which prevents an insured either from engaging in some of the duties of his or her usual occupation or from engaging in his or her occupation on a full-time basis.

revocable beneficiary. A named beneficiary whose right to life insurance policy proceeds is not vested during the insured's lifetime and whose designation as beneficiary can be revoked (cancelled) by the policyowner at any time prior to the insured's death.

rider. An addition to an insurance policy that becomes a part of the contract and which expands or limits the benefits otherwise payable. Examples are the accidental death benefit and the waiver of premium for disability benefit riders. (Also called an **endorsement**.)

risk appraisal. *See* **underwriting**.

RRSP. Registered Retirement Savings Plan.

savings bank life insurance (SBLI). Life insurance sold by authorized savings banks. SBLI is available only in three states and only to persons residing in or employed in the state in which the savings bank is located.

secondary beneficiary. *See* **contingent beneficiary**.

selection against the insurer. *See* **antiselection**.

selection of risks. *See* **underwriting**.

separate account. A special fund (account) established by a life insurance company for the investment of money received from policyowners under insurance contracts in which the policyowner bears some or all of the investment risk.

settlement agreement. The agreement formed between an insurer and policyowner when the policyowner selects an optional mode of settlement for the beneficiary.

settlement options. *See* **optional modes of settlement**.

single premium annuity. An annuity purchased with a single premium payment.

social insurance supplement policy. A medical expense policy which provides benefits to supplement the benefits available from a specified government health insurance program. Such a policy is available exclusively to those persons eligible for benefits under a particular government program.

Social Security. *See* **Old Age, Survivors, Disability and Health Insurance Act**.

Social Security Disability Income (SSDI). A long-term disability income program which provides benefits to disabled workers who are under age 65 and who have paid a specified amount of Social Security tax for a prescribed number of quarter-year periods.

sole proprietorship. A business owned and operated by one person.

solvent. Able to pay financial obligations when they are due.

special class risk. *See* **substandard risk**.

spendthrift trust clause. Policy wording that protects (under certain conditions) policy proceeds held by the insurer from being seized by a beneficiary's creditors.

standard premium rate. The premium rate charged for a person classified as a standard risk.

standard risk. Average risk; a person possessing an average or less-than-average likelihood of loss.

stock company. In life insurance, a company initially funded by the sale of ownership shares (stock) in a corporation.

stop-loss provision. A health insurance policy provision which specifies that the insurer will pay 100 percent of the insured's eligible medical expenses after the insured has incurred a specified amount of out-of-pocket expenses – such as $1,000 – under the coinsurance feature.

straight life annuity. An annuity which provides periodic payments to the annuitant for as long as the annuitant lives and which provides for no benefit payments after the annuitant's death.

straight life income option. A life insurance policy settlement option under which payments to the beneficiary-payee will continue until the payee's death, after which no further payments are made.

subscribers. Persons or organizations who purchase Blue Cross and/or Blue Shield plans.

substandard premium rate. The premium rate charged for a substandard (special class) risk. This premium rate is higher than a standard premium rate.

substandard risk. Below-average risk. A person possessing a greater-than-average likelihood of loss.

succession beneficiary clause. *See* **preference beneficiary clause**.

successor beneficiary. *See* **contingent beneficiary**.

successor payee. *See* **contingent payee**.

suicide clause. Life insurance policy wording which specifies that the proceeds of the policy will not be paid if the insured commits suicide within a specified period of time (such as two years) after the policy's date of issue.

superimposed major medical. *See* **supplemental major medical**.

superstandard risk. *See* **preferred risk**.

supplemental major medical. A group major medical policy issued in conjunction with (to supplement) group hospital-surgical expense coverage. (Also referred to as **superimposed major medical**.)

supplementary benefit rider. A rider (endorsement) that is added to an insurance policy to provide additional benefits.

supplementary contract. A contract between the insurer and the beneficiary which is formed when policy proceeds are applied under a settlement option.

surgical schedule. That part of a health insurance policy that describes the maximum benefit amounts payable for specified surgical services.

surplus. The accumulation of earnings (profits) resulting from a company's operations.

surrender value. The amount available to a policyowner in cash upon surrender of a life insurance policy.

tabular mortality. The rate of mortality, at any given age, as shown in the mortality table that is used when calculating premium rates.

temporary life annuity. An annuity which provides that payments will be made until the end of a specified number of years or until the death of the annuitant, whichever occurs *first*.

term insurance. Life insurance under which the benefit is payable only if the insured dies during a specified period of time. No benefit is payable if the insured survives to the end of the term.

testamentary disposition. Using a will to indicate the person or party to whom the proceeds of a life insurance policy should be distributed.

third-party application. An application for insurance which is submitted by a person or party other than the proposed insured.

third-party endorsement. A method of marketing insurance policies whereby the life insurance company works through various organizations, such as clubs and associations, to sell insurance to members of those organizations.

third-party policy. A policy which is owned by a person or party other than the insured.

travel accident benefit. An accidental death benefit often included in group insurance policies issued to employer-employee groups which provides coverage only for accidents occurring while an employee is traveling for the employer.

trustee. A person or an organization designated to control or manage another party's property.

underwriter. An employee of a life insurance company who is responsible for evaluating and classifying the potential degree of risk represented by a proposed insured.

underwriting. The process of identifying and classifying the potential degree of risk represented by a proposed insured. (Also called **selection of risks.**)

unilateral contract. A contract under which only one of the parties to the contract can be compelled by law to perform what that party has promised to do.

usual and customary charge. *See* **reasonable and customary charge**.

valid contract. A contract that is enforceable at law.

valued contract. A contract under which the amount of the benefit is set in advance.

variable annuity. A form of annuity policy under which the amount of each annuity payment is not guaranteed and specified in the policy, but which instead varies according to the earnings of a separate account fund.

variable life insurance policy. A form of whole life insurance under which the face amount and the cash value of the policy vary according to the investment performance of a separate account fund.

vested interest. An interest that a person or party cannot be deprived of without giving his or her consent.

void. A term used in law to describe something, such as a contract, which never had validity. The full term used is *void ab initio*, which means *void from the start*.

voidable contract. A contract that can be legally rejected (avoided) by a party to the contract.

waiting period. *See* **probationary period** and **elimination period**.

waive. To voluntarily give up a right.

waiver of premium for disability benefit. A rider or a policy provision under which the insurer promises to waive its right to collect the policy's premium if the insured becomes disabled, as defined in the policy.

waiver of premium for payor benefit. A rider or policy provision often included in juvenile insurance policies which provides that the insurer will waive payment of the policy's premiums if the adult policyowner, not the insured child, dies or becomes disabled.

war exclusion. A provision which states that the policy benefit will not be paid if the insured's death is connected with war.

warranty. A statement made by a party or person which is literally true (as opposed to a **representation**, which only need be substantially true).

whole life insurance. Life insurance under which coverage remains in force during the insured's entire lifetime, provided premiums are paid as specified in the policy.

Workers' Compensation. Government-mandated insurance that provides benefits to employees and their dependents if the employees suffer job-related injury, disease, or death; known as Workmen's Compensation until the 1970s.

yearly renewable term (YRT). One-year term life insurance. (Also known as **annually renewable term (ART)**.)

Index

PRINCIPLES OF LIFE AND HEALTH INSURANCE

Text type for this book is Century Light II, set 11 on 13
on a Compugraphic MCS42/8400 by
Fishergate Publishing Company, Inc., Annapolis, Maryland

Type for all figures is Helvetica, set on a
Compugraphic 8600 Printer by 23 Skidoo, Atlanta, Georgia

Printing, binding, and laminating was done by
George Banta Company, Menasha, Wisconsin.

Paper for the text is Landmark Opaque smooth offset, 60 lb.

Cover paper is Kivar 6 Chrome with ½ mil film lamination.